Embossed Series

Edition 1 - 7

A special acknowledgment to Ali Rahim, my partner at Contemporary Architecture Practice. At the University of Pennsylvania Weitzman School of Design I would like to thank Dean Fritz Steiner, Chris Cataldo, Winka Dubbeldam and the Urban Housing Studio Team-Scott Erdy, Brian Phillips, Kutan Ayata, Ben Krone, Jonas Coersmeier and Gisela Baurmann for their invaluable support and encouragement. David Goldblatt, Katie McBride, Madison Green, Patrick Monte, Leon Yi-Liang Ko and Caleb White for their valuable contributions in making this book possible. The team at Routledge at Taylor & Francis, particularly Fran Ford, Sean Speers, Veronica Morgan and Kathryn Schell for their wise counsel. And for Ayla—who makes both the journey and destination worthwhile.

UNDER PRESSURE

First published in 2022 by Routledge
605 Third Avenue, New York, NY 10158

and by Routledge
2 Park Square, Milton Park, Abingdon, Oxon, OX14 4RN

Routledge is an imprint of the Taylor & Francis Group, an informa business

Library of Congress Cataloging-in-Publication Data
Under pressure : essays on urban housing / edited by Hina Jamelle.
1 Edition. | New York : Routledge, 2021. | Includes bibliographical references and index.
Identifiers: LCCN 2021011975 (print) | LCCN 2021011976 (ebook)
Subjects: LCSH: Housing. | Housing policy. | Housing–Finance. | Architectural design.
LCC HD7287 .U353 2021 (print) | LCC HD7287 (ebook) | DDC 363.5–dc23
LC record available at https://lccn.loc.gov/2021011975
LC ebook record available at https://lccn.loc.gov/2021011976

ISBN 9780367481711 (hbk)
ISBN 9780367465032 (pbk)
ISBN 9781003038375 (ebk)

DOI: 10.4324/9781003038375

Typeset in Helvetica
by Madison Green

Assistant Editor: Leon Yi-Liang Ko
Assistant Editor: Katie McBride
Book and Cover Designer: Madison Green

Publisher's Note
This book has been prepared from camera-ready copy provided by the editor

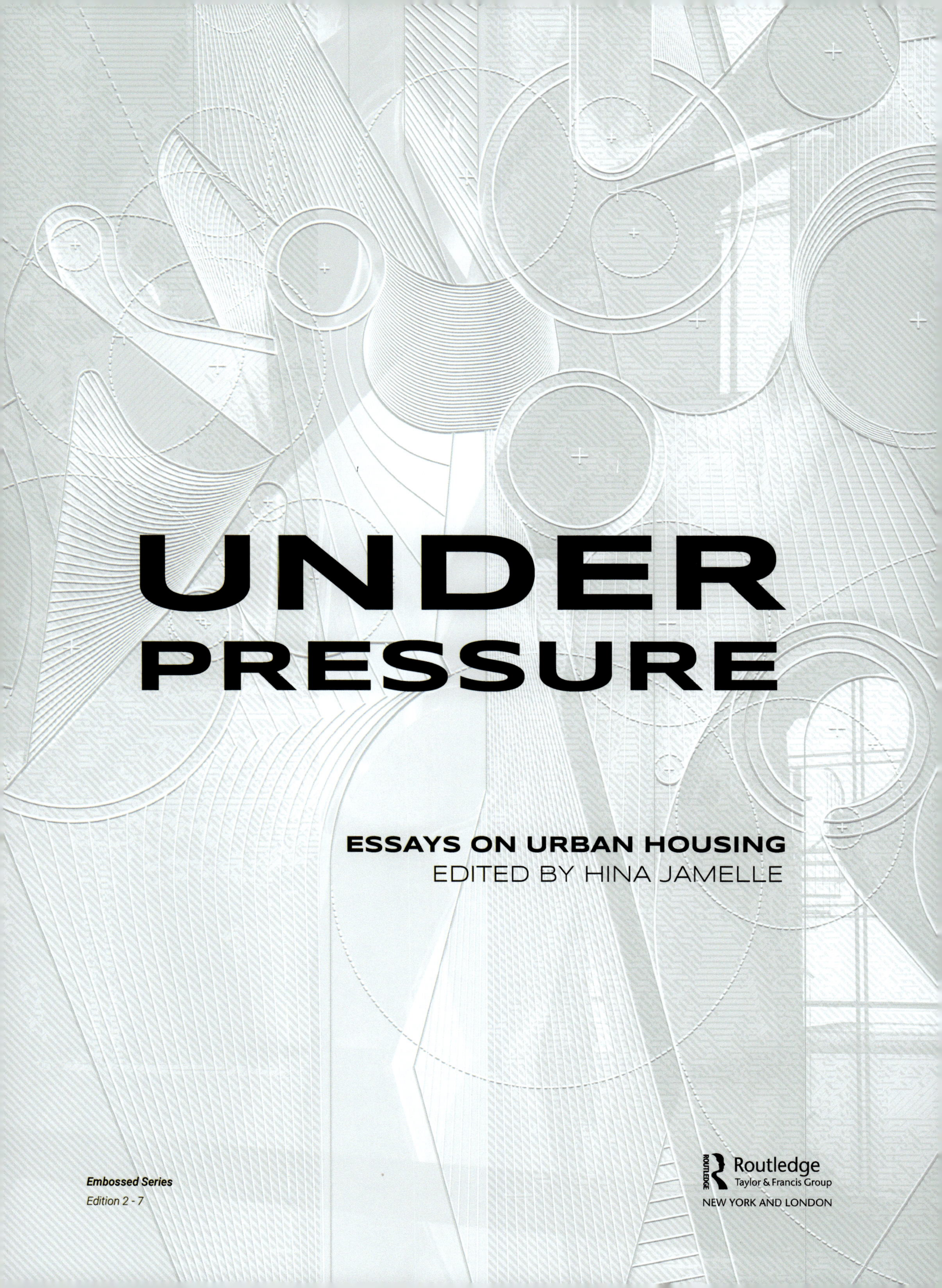

UNDER PRESSURE

ESSAYS ON URBAN HOUSING

EDITED BY HINA JAMELLE

Embossed Series

Edition 2 - 7

Routledge
Taylor & Francis Group
NEW YORK AND LONDON

Embossed Series
Edition 3 - 7

INTRODUCTION

PART 1: LEARNING FROM HISTORY

Embossed Series

Edition 4 - 7

PART 2: CHANGING DOMESTICITIES

PART 3: HOUSING FINANCE AND POLICY

Embossed Series

Edition 5 - 7

PART 4: DESIGN AND MATERIAL INNOVATION

CREDITS

URBAN HOUSING UNDER PRESSURE

Hina Jamelle

Pressure brings one face to face with urgency. It exposes the limits and stability of a structure, whether material, societal, or individual in nature. In addition, it instigates a call to action and a need for resolution. Reactions that emerge under pressure can take the form of breakdowns, recombinations, or resilience—all of which have creative and transformative potential. Urbanization has brought pressure to bear on housing and the home in new and profound ways. And, Architecture is under pressure to respond when change forces material transformation.

Urbanization is occurring at unprecedented speeds and scales. The UN reports that urban population growth combined with the overall growth of the world's population could add another 2.5 billion people to urban populations by 2050 or 1.4 million people per week.[1] The number of "megacities"—cities with more than 10 million inhabitants—nearly tripled between 1990 and 2020, a trend that is expected to continue and increase.[2] These rapid expansions are placing increased demands on resources and services in urban centers as well as the rural areas that support them.[3] Energy systems, infrastructure, transportation, as well as employment, education, health care, and housing all face urgent short- and long-term challenges.[4] These challenges are marked by shifting relations and dynamics in the global economy and within cities themselves. In the United States, for instance, cities are undergoing paradigm shifts in terms of both demographics and economic activity. On the one hand, cities are growing racially and ethnically more diverse, immigration is rising, and the number of older adults comprising urban populations is increasing.[5] On the other hand, cities have by and large shifted from manufacturing economies to economies driven by technology, service, and finance. Such shifts underscore that while cities are expanding, their needs and the way they function at both local and global levels are simultaneously changing. This dual process requires not just policy to guide it, but also creativity and vision. Cities that rely on policy alone to navigate these changes will fracture under the pressures of urbanization; they require imaginative ways of reconfiguring existing systems and inaugurating new ones.

Left

Kerry Hohenstein
Shifting Hybrids: Adaptive Reuse of the Sunshine Theater, Lower East Side, New York City

Hina Jamelle Urban Housing Studio with Caleb Ehly

University of Pennsylvania
Weitzman School of Design, 2019

Apartment corner detail.

The COVID-19 pandemic and its turbulent social and economic impacts in cities across the globe may cause one to second guess these trends. Massive crises, however, tend to accelerate changes already taking place. In the aftermath of 9/11, for instance, the idea of living in high-rise residential towers in centralized districts of Manhattan seemed preposterous because of the atmosphere of fear around those tragic events. And yet since 2001, Manhattan has experienced its most prolific period of high-rise residential development to date, including the emergence of an entirely new super-high typology known as "the pencil tower."[6] On a more global scale, it is extremely difficult to imagine a scenario where fast-paced developing countries across sub-Saharan Africa, the Middle East, Asia, and South America decouple their strategies for growth and prosperity from urbanization. Countries may press pause for a few months or instantiate specific containment strategies for a few years, but urbanization is with us for the long haul over the coming decades and requires constant thought and inquiry.

Housing, as both an urban infrastructure and a fulcrum of daily life, is one of the most critical areas of interest in negotiating urbanization and shifting urban dynamics. Urban housing is a bellwether for economic, social, and political change. It varies widely in quality, typology, and audience and lies between formal and informal systems. Housing's complexity and modularity offers unique and exciting opportunities to architects. Its entwinement with private equity and public authority presents important challenges amplified by urbanization. Yet, for too long, there has been a distance between policy makers, designers, economists, and developers on the topic of housing. Multifaceted examinations of urban housing are required to understand both the city and its context as well as current and future ways of living in contemporary society.

Under Pressure is about instigation and design in urban housing. In looking at a broad spectrum of urban housing, this book raises a series of questions and strategies that are focused on design opportunities. The work gathered here contextualizes current conversations about urban housing unfolding today across architecture. Its authors represent a broad spectrum of thought leaders from fields including architecture, material design, economics, finance, and real estate. Collectively, the perspectives here maintain that urban housing should be viewed as a confluence of pressures from multiple agents. Pressures are emphasized as sites of agency and effectivity for architects projecting toward the future of urban life, and they are shown to work at different scales ranging from the global economy to cities, industry, buildings, and individuals themselves.

Cities occupy multiple strata as engines of economic growth, centers of commerce, icons of culture, and homes—whole ways of life—to millions upon millions of people. While the issue of housing can be theoretical and abstract, it is always grounded in the everyday. It is localized in expanding cities that often struggle to provide quality housing to diverse markets which complements neighborhoods and workplaces by meeting the needs of real people at the heart of the matter. For instance, affordability

Right

NYC Skyline Post 9/11.

Since 2001, Manhattan has experienced its most prolific period of high-rise residential development to date, including the emergence of a new typology known as "the pencil tower."

has emerged in cities across the United States due to a variety of economic conditions. Changes in both policy and industry practice have lagged behind population growth in addressing housing prices, further compounding these issues. Moreover, they often repeat past mistakes and patterns by assuming that simply increasing the number of homes will solve the problem. In "Living Off the Land," Scott Erdy outlines a proposal to resolve housing affordability, food insecurity, and unstable employment by creating a new type of self-sustaining architecture. Erdy revisits an unbuilt proposal by Le Corbusier that sought a symbiotic relationship between buildings and the land to address problems of housing and overcrowding in cities, and he proposes a new model for urban housing as an economic engine. The concept of self-sustenance is reflected as larger development processes in Mark A. Willis and Benjamin Heller's contribution "Confronting Affordable Housing Challenges: The Local Role." They argue that cities and towns need to be proactive in developing and implementing well-tailored local housing strategies, taking advantage of the knowledge and expertise of groups who understand local housing needs and market conditions. Using New York City and Singapore as case studies, they show that near opposite policy structures and financial mechanisms can address affordability issues effectively when grounded in a local approach.

The pressure to densify and create new affordable housing stocks has often led to conventional strategies seeking maximal square footage and minimal cost while conforming to legal and social codes. This approach has led in many cases to homogeneous aesthetics at odds with the very uniqueness that makes cities so attractive. Local solutions to affordability are not only effective but also productive and can spur great creativity. In "The Value of a Home: A Critical Approach to Local Practice," Brian Phillips argues that the design of urban housing should be embedded in the local information of a city. Phillips outlines a methodology that mines a city's historical, physical, and socio-economic past to leverage a project's context and site constraints to deliver authentic, locally specific urban housing designs. This method emphasizes that authenticity is an important aspect of how cities project identity and foster culture, both locally and globally, and that housing has an important role to play in this regard. Taking issues of identity a step further, Neil Denari, in "Tectonics and Urban Identity," explores ambitious architectural projects, most notably driven by housing programs in New York City. He argues that, although cities contain stable monuments such as memorial plazas, parks, and cultural institutions, residential buildings shape the global and the local images of a city. Using his project HL23 as a case study, he describes how a housing project, particularly via the façade, can create a public persona regardless of its private program.

When initiating new design approaches, architects are often faced with not only code constraints but also industry limitations. The construction industry is confronted with high demand and will continue to be under pressure to deliver, yet it is also consistently slow to change. The construction sector is well behind other fields in innovation spending. Construction industry research and development runs less than 1% of revenue, compared with 3.5% in the automotive industry and 4.5% in the aerospace industry.[7] The construction industry has also lagged behind others in going digital. Thin margins and the volatility of returns are partly to blame, as is reluctance among builders to adopt new technologies without guaranteed savings or profits. Only recently is the industry looking toward digitization to eliminate delays and cost overruns. With pressure to create housing that can adapt to contemporary and future needs, architects can leverage their position, savvy, and craft despite a variety of constraints. New manufacturing processes and material advancements offer designers toolsets for transforming housing design and construction in the process. Prefabrication, as highlighted in my own contribution to this volume, "(Re)configuring Typology," can yield results that address a range of housing concerns. These include increased affordability through streamlined and efficient manufacturing processes, improved construction logistics through optimized production, transportation, storage, and assembly workflows, and greater programmatic and performance flexibility through mass customization. These issues are all raised in the context of mass housing design in Seoul, South Korea, where prefabrication is shown to be both an urgent necessity and a form for counteracting drawbacks of top-down large-scale development.

On a more fine-grain scale, housing materials used today such as glass, metal, ceramics, and concrete use enormous amounts of energy during extraction, processing, and recycling. There is concerning use in regions with fast-growing populations where housing is a primary demand. Substituting only a few unsustainable building materials with biopolymers, reverse-engineered proteins, or bio-composites could alleviate waste, energy, and health problems derived from the construction of typical building envelopes. In "Material Speculation: A Science and Craft," Laia Mogas-Soldevila looks at important developments for future architectures that can regenerate, self-heal, respond to, and sense their surroundings. She outlines how new partnership possibilities between material science, biomedical engineering,

Right

Construction fabrication and assembly facilities.

The construction industry is confronted with high demand and will continue to be under pressure to deliver, yet it is also consistently slow to change. The construction sector is well behind other fields in innovation spending. Construction industry research and development runs less than 1% of revenue, compared with 3.5% in the automotive industry and 4.5% in the aerospace industry.

and experimental design can make responsive materials economically viable. By focusing on often overlooked areas of housing design, Mogas-Soldevila shows how working between the code can yield radical results in banal contexts. Further emphasis on dynamism and responsive performance can be raised at the building scale through flexible program configurations that incorporate the possibility for change over time while meeting local needs. Architects can use their agency in the development of housing projects to substantiate meaningful change. Nader Tehrani, in "Speculating with Constraints," draws from one case study, the Macallen Building by NADAAA. As Tehrani shows, the architect serving as both a figurehead and mediator between various interests can be effective in achieving new programmatic housing types. Bolstering this point, Martha Kelley shows that architects can leverage their ability to add both design and economic value in "Urban Housing and the Value of the Architect." Using Herzog & de Meuron's luxury condominium project at 56 Leonard Street in Manhattan's TriBeCa neighborhood as an example, she provides an overview of how real estate investors think about risk and return in the context of residential real estate. Further, in "The Architect's Agency in a Developers' Market," Patrik Schumacher considers the possibilities that emerge from positioning the architect as an entrepreneurial partner. Chronicling housing projects from Zaha Hadid Architects, he argues that architects can discover or create new markets when allowed to enter the design process earlier. How architecture figures in to the economy and finance is elaborated by Michael Bell and Eunjeong Seong in "Ten Points on a Projective Economy and Architecture." They argue that housing is becoming a form of spatial arbitrage and advocate for new forms of architectural investment in renewable energy. They propose that architects have skills that can instigate new architectures without being subservient to economics.

Shifts in the global economy and communication as well as the nature of work have challenged longstanding office and residential building typologies. These have put new far-reaching pressures on both the individual and housing. Virtual work practices that were recently limited to tech savvy firms are now commonplace across a broad spectrum that includes everything from software companies to public schools. The effects of such changes are asymmetrical. In some cases, they unlock vast new economic opportunities with higher incomes, new jobs, time flexibility, and access to social networks and better health. In other cases, the individual is working ever more hours plugged in from home, work, and in between. There are ever greater pressures on individuals to navigate this terrain, and likewise, pressures on housing units to accommodate it. These pressures are differentiated and multi-scalar. The needs of significant portions of the workforce who work as independent contractors simply do not line up with traditional office and residential typologies, creating vacuums and excess pressures in both. The results of macro shifts in spatial routines can be disturbing, as for example when increased time spent at home by individuals during the height of the pandemic brought surges in domestic violence.[8] All of this signals a paradigm shift in domesticity, which requires thoughtful inquiry, urgent action, and a forward-looking disposition to allow new ideas to come to the forefront and be realized faster.

SPONSOR
TIMES SQUARE 2014
TOSHIBA
TDK
CHILL IN THE AIR
ameless
Budweiser
PALACE
DECEMBER
RIGHT LANE ENDS

In, "New Domesticities, New Realities," Clifford Pearson outlines how the rising numbers of "non-traditional" constituencies including singles, unrelated people living together, and the elderly in urban housing have spurred designers to explore new models of residential architecture. New building typologies and living arrangements such as micro-housing, live/work entrepreneurship, social housing, and hybrid co-living configurations are emerging in relation to new social arrangements, work dynamics, and lifestyles. With new models of living have come new ways of launching and financing them, often from technology-driven companies whose methods and values may diverge from those of typical real estate and development firms. Pearson looks at how new funding streams for several projects in Asia have enabled new, blurred relationships between manufacturing and construction as well as life and work. By 2028, "solopreneurs," independent contractors, and freelancers will account for 53% of the US workforce, most of whom will seek out either co-working spaces or home-offices. At the same time, large enterprises are using the trend of remote and smart work to save costs and provide their employees with increased flexibility. Simone Tarantino looks at the fall of WeWork in "Empowering Entrepreneurship," and then provides an overview of a new co-living model called "Startup Home," initiated in London as a service offering lodging to startups accepted in a local accelerator. Notably, the company creates entrepreneurial hubs for underrepresented entrepreneurs and minorities in secondary and tertiary cities. Such efforts and their focus on a structured process to alleviate pressures on individuals highlight inventive ways of retooling spatial assets to accommodate new live/work situations. Other more generalizable strategies focus on typology. Mimi Hoang and Zachary Weimer, for instance, take up the concept of micro-living in "Micro–Macro Living." By decreasing the unit size from 400 to 300 square feet, they test the ability of prefabricated units to shift program from private toward communal spaces while serving as a new form of urban development.

Other works in this volume as well as its featured projects highlight formal, material, and aesthetic strategies that can operate and relieve pressures at multiple scales. In "Voids and Other Invisible Objects," Marcelo Spina speculates on opportunities to create unexpected urban silhouettes, new program, and leisure spaces by creating voids which disrupt the flatness of urban façades and the fixity of city grids in rapidly densifying urban cores. In "Future Histories," Kutan Ayata contemplates lessons from 20th-century modernist mega-blocks, many of which became spatial vacuums and did not work as planned. Ayata suggests designing new "micro-narrative" buildings that can be inserted into mega-blocks with a focus on individuality of expression.

The issues and works outlined above are organized as a series of four frameworks for analyzing and acting upon the pressures affecting urban housing: *Learning from History*, *Changing Domesticities*, *Housing Finance and Policy*, and *Design and Material Innovation*. Learning from History takes a fresh look at architectural examples from the near and distant past for both their recognized and latent potential in shaping housing design visions. Changing Domesticities recognizes that people's living patterns are out of sync with past housing design precedents and examines pressures on the

Left

Urban density, New York.

The UN reports that urban population growth combined with the overall growth of the world's population could add another 2.5 billion people to urban populations by 2050, or 1.4 million people per week.

housing unit and the individual onset by paradigm shifts in domesticity. Housing Finance and Policy provides an overview of current and future challenges cities face in meeting housing demand as it relates to economic pressure, with an emphasis on locating domains of greatest agency, influence, and effectiveness for architects and designers. And Design and Material Innovation highlights architects who are developing innovative housing designs by experimenting and speculating with new materials, housing unit configurations, fabrication and construction methods, and building concepts that respond to a variety of pressures upon housing at the scale of architecture itself. The essays in this book are complemented by urban housing design studies created in the graduate architecture department of the University of Pennsylvania's Weitzman School of Design which serve to contextualize and highlight the most relevant and provocative issues in each project. The studies provide focused responses to concepts raised in and across the book's distinct parts as well as visual and hypothetical roadmaps for how specific concepts can be realized. The studies suggest new formal identities for housing design, elevating the typology's status through careful, highly articulated designs. They present new modes of conceiving the housing unit, design, urban conditions, and material systems. They also explore the potential for mixed-use programming to function as a design and planning tool that can redistribute services and empower constituents. University of Pennsylvania students were rigorous in their research and employed quantitative information in their design developments. Together, the essays and studies offer a multidisciplinary amalgam of thought, research, and design intelligence gleaned from urban housing at every scale and a unique rethinking of the condition of contemporary urban housing *Under Pressure.*

Right

Urban density, Tokyo.

The number of "megacities"—cities with more than 10 million inhabitants—nearly tripled between 1990 and 2020, a trend that is expected to continue and increase.

References

1. https://population.un.org/wup/Publications/
2. Ibid.
3. Ibid.
4. Ibid.
5. https://www.pewsocialtrends.org/2018/05/22/demographic-and-economic-trends-in-urban-suburban-and-rural-communities/
6. See for instance Oliver Wainwright, "Super-Tall, Super-Skinny, Super-Expensive: The 'Pencil Towers' of New York's Super Rich," *The Guardian*, February 05, 2019. https://www.theguardian.com/cities/2019/feb/05/super-tall-super-skinny-super-expensive-the-pencil-towers-of-new-yorks-super-rich
7. https://www.wsj.com/articles/the-construction-business-goes-digital-1474250580
8. https://www.nytimes.com/2020/04/06/world/coronavirus-domestic-violence.html

Shadow Series
Edition 1 - 4

01

LEARNING FROM HISTORY

FUTURE HISTORIES

Kutan Ayata | Young & Ayata

Architecture often oscillates between relevance and irrelevance, effectiveness and ineffectiveness, as it so desperately tries to respond to socio-political pressures of the day to set a course for a better tomorrow. Shifting politics, unstable markets, uneven distribution of wealth, growing geopolitical conflicts, worsening ecological realities, racial inequalities, mass migration, housing shortage, pandemics, combined together with our ease of accessing the most up-to-date information regarding their status, continuously redefine our reality, as well as our context of intervention. Sometimes the rate of emerging and evolving conditions in our world are so rapid, rhetoric to tackle every issue continuously outpaces thoughtful inquiry, development of strong discourse and innovation. The reality is that architecture is always left behind by the evolving conditions that it is trying to frame.

The clumsy nature of physical manifestation of architecture always seems to be too late as a reaction to the changing world events. The crawling pace of its materialization, the inanimate nature of its posture, the indirectness of its medium, the indeterminate nature of its consumed messages, combined with all the immaterial qualities, makes Architecture an insufficient tool to shape and counter the transformations of our world. Take the "sharing" paradigm of the last decade for instance. WeWork flourished, we became co-workers. We made new vocabulary, as we "Ubered" or "Lyfted." New economies and communities developed around Airbnb. Remember all the buzz about "co-living" from the last few years? The macro-unit, which pushed all redundancy out of the unit under the disguise of shared amenities, consolidated all repetitive infrastructure, so more units could be placed in buildings, yielding more transactions. Ironically, this resulted in an architectural typology, at least within the organization of the plan, something that began to resemble layouts of communist housing from the early 20th century, where all else other than bedrooms were communal. In this instance, it is almost surreal to see when pressures of capitalism, pushed to an extreme, yield architectural consequences which mirror models generated through ambitions of communism. Is Architecture capable of embodying any specific ideology?

Left

Aerial view of Hong Kong City, Hong Kong

A typical "new town" residential district in Hong Kong consisting of stand-alone towers situated in mega-blocks.

Countless speculations were produced in academic spheres, which examined the potentials of the "shared-living" paradigm. We all imagined potentials of co-living in so many creative ways through specific architectural outcomes, where we speculated on sharing the materials, resources, programs, time, and infrastructure around living conditions. Then came COVID-19. All our habitual behaviors within the collective of our mass existence, urban or suburban, were shocked to the core by the responsible necessity of face covering, social distancing, self-quarantine, online working, online learning and more altered usual customs. Could you imagine anything shared through these days of the pandemic? It feels like the reconsideration and plausibility of all the speculative work of the recent past regarding the "sharing paradigm" became nothing but useless, just like that into the thin air. While it is unclear whether a vaccine or a potentially effective treatment protocol would reorient us back to the old normal, for now the new normal of working from home seems to be the predictable future.

Our community is agile though, as architectural discipline adjusts to new pressures and contexts rather rapidly. Almost instantaneously a number of design competitions were implemented to speculate on this "new normal," projections emerged around the "comeback of the cubicle," 1960s discourse about inflatables found renewed relevance, live/work discussions and future of the de-densification of dense urban centers towards rural settings deemed inevitable, public space planning for socially distanced realm redefined the rules of engagement of bodies. Architectural rhetoric rapidly adjusted to this new condition on the ground. But then, another paradigm shift: Even before the submission deadline of the aforementioned competitions arrived, we witnessed the horrific police brutality around the death of George Floyd and the rapid galvanization of masses around Black Lives Matter movement. Just like that, literally overnight, many of us found ourselves on the streets, shoulder to shoulder in solidarity with thousands of others from all walks of life, to protest racism, racial injustice, and police brutality. Suddenly, the new normal we just began to adjust to in terms of social distancing, morphed into a new condition of proximity and unity, where we took health risks for ourselves and for others in order to ensure the plausibility of a more just future. Sure enough, spatial speculations are underway to take on this new reality as well.

The world around us is unpredictable and in constant flux at an accelerating rate. It seems futile to rely on a medium like architecture and its capacity of convoluted mediation, either through its spatial organization or its image to bear responsibility of transforming the behaviors of the populace. It is somewhat strange to expect positive results in the ability of lifeless material in static form to convey messages to overcome socio-political problems where even spoken words fail so often to elevate the norms of common human decency and move the needle within our divided political and cultural paradigms. Maybe architecture operates differently, maybe its cultural impact, valuation, appreciation occur independent of the zeitgeist pressures, at a different timescale. Maybe the optimism and power some architects place in architecture in terms of its ability to improve the world is a noble but nevertheless a misplaced ambition. Maybe architect as citizen can be more effective and influential

Right

Minoru Yamasaki
Pruitt -Igoe Housing Complex
Completed 1955, demolished 1972

Demolition of Pruitt–Igoe, an image that in many ways symbolizes the end of "modern architecture."

through other means like policymaking or direct activism. Can we as a collective dare to accept the possibility that architecture is perhaps not highly influential and important to enable immediate cultural, political, and social change? Can we as a collective deem architecture, well, somewhat unimportant? Can we consider it just as a background condition to the unfolding of reality? Can we be that modest?

Historically, we had no such claim. Architects always believed in culture making by projecting the conditions of near-future reality. New paradigms of technological innovation, socio-political transformations brought with themselves opportunities to redefine how we live as a collective. Architects always claimed a front seat in driving these efforts, as their ability to imagine, represent, and visualize scenarios made them important key players as visionaries. Responding to changes in culture at large, technology and urbanization, they framed arguments and created visions as how to define living in a modernizing world. After 150 years of technological advancement through industrial revolution, with the advent of mass production at a large scale, with an ability to process materials at a radically increased pace and with the ability to access and disseminate information rapidly, along with the increase in world population, the 20th century has witnessed the most radical urbanization period of human history. How we imagine these new urban conditions, how we imagine new visions to house the modernizing populace, has been at the center of our disciplinary inquiry for much of the last century.

The discipline of architecture, especially through modernism, relentlessly speculated on the future of the city with comprehensive concepts of urban housing. Architects, sometimes working collectively in structures like CIAM, imagined and at times implemented large-scale projects centered around new housing visions to define the growth and development of the modern city. Proposals by figures like Le Corbusier, Frank Lloyd Wright, Mies van der Rohe, Ludwig Hilberseimer or the mass housing models of the socialist states or the projects by the members of Team-X in the post-war period welfare economies or the projects of metabolist architects in Japan are all too familiar examples of urban visions which secured significant status (for better or worse) within the canon of our discipline. These projects were all speculations on the growth and transformation of vast amounts of urban land by imagining a different urban experience than the dense structure of the historical city where the binary of building and nature projected a different balance. Le Corbusier's Plan Voisin for Paris, perhaps the most well-known example of this genre, imagined a simultaneous experience of architectural and natural authenticity as part of modern urban life. All these visions imagined new social and spatial structures for the city with the principal of individual dwelling at the core of their concepts. The DNA of all these proposals in various permutations has been part of many large-scale housing developments in the cities around the world. Even to this day, this approach continues to be a strategy for mass-housing efforts in a number of Asian countries which confront massive population shifts from rural areas to urban centers as they continue their modernizations. Though there are few well-matured examples of these large-scale housing projects, the modernist notion of city building with social housing as the driving engine of urbanity is currently a rather rare practice, especially in the ongoing development of the American City.

Charles Jencks's very broadly published declaration of the "death of modern architecture," following the all-too-familiar event of the Pruitt–Igoe's demolition in 1972, more or less marks a definitive moment for the discipline with regards to its efforts to produce comprehensive housing schemes articulated with the ambitions and aesthetics of modernism. Though the social program of these visions continued to be dressed in aesthetics of postmodernism, the scale, scope, and ambition of these projects gradually began to shrink. Internationale Bauausstellung or IBA 1987 Berlin Research and Design program perhaps marks the last moment of a collective and rigorous housing speculation by few celebrated figures of the discipline. The projects realized by IBA 1987 also mark a definite change in attitude from conceiving large-scale urban housing fields towards implementations of singular architectural entities. Though there are rare exemptions to the following claim, the public stake as a civic, cultural and monetary investment in the development of urban housing seems to have vanished by the end of the 1980s. The shift to market economy and the spread of neoliberal economic policies fully relocated the efforts of the architect away from the comprehensive housing schemes at urban scale down to the scale of a building, or at best a set of buildings. The broad commodification of housing as an investment asset could be said to have marginalized the architect to serve private interests which naturally privilege profitability.

One of the most significant impacts of 20th-century modernist urbanism in dense urban environments was the implementation of mega-blocks for large-scale public housing projects. They can be described as exceptionally large urban blocks comprising a number of typical blocks to enable large-scale interventions for social housing within densifying urban areas. They are also known as "towers in the park," where concentrated density for housing is organized without street infrastructure in an

Right T–B

Zaha Hadid
IBA Housing
Berlin, 1986–1993

Rem Koolhaas
Checkpoint Charlie Apartments
Berlin, 1980–1990

Peter Eisenman
IBA Housing
Berlin, 1981–1985

Images of public housing projects by Zaha Hadid, OMA, and Peter Eisenman, Berlin, initiated by Internationale Bauausstellung (IBA).

open field, resulting in stand-alone buildings and open space throughout. This open ground, which usually allowed up to 80% building-free territory, was billed as "living with nature in city." The city never came, nature was reduced to grass and trees, mostly unmaintained and underused. Origins of these projects can be traced back to Le Corbusier's Plan Voisin for Paris. As modernist visions of new utopias for the city ambitiously attempted to redefine the city by replacing its small-scale fabric with large interventions in the name of "new living," their less finessed and realized versions, in most cases regardless of their location in the world, created mostly undesirable consequences such as segregation, lack of density, urban discontinuity, increased crime, lack of urban character, and homogeneity. The majority of these realized projects became black holes in the city, sucking out all potential urban life in and around them, defining abruptions in the flow of the city's physical flux. They are too big to fail, they are deeply rooted and most likely here to stay. They are products of our own discipline, occupying a significant territory in the discourse of architecture and urbanism. They have been imagined with noble intentions and realized with endless optimism; things just did not go according to the plans. What do we do as a discipline to deal with our own garbage? Paradigms eventually shift, but architectural residue remains in place. It would be a tremendous material waste to contemplate their faith with tabula rasa, just like they were initially implemented. A face-lift or interior retrofit seems too timid, given their history and perhaps their untapped potential. Maybe there exists another transformative trajectory in terms of imagining the future of these massive housing complexes, one that breaks their mold, one that begins to alter their homogeneous definitions of spatial and material qualities, one that begins to dilute the overarching ideological narratives defining their aura, one that attempts to overcome their stigma.

What is more central for the argument here is the nature of speculation on the future social context surrounding these interventions, given transformations at these scales would take fairly significant time to implement. Instead of casting a large net which would define a singular narrative and prediction about the potential future reality of our social structure, a mishap perhaps committed by the modernists, one could imagine multiple micro-narratives to define a collection of plausible trajectories for the future society. It is crucial to step out of the present and all its pressures to contemplate how our visions and the conditions which frame them might play out into the future. By imaging the future histories of these projections as realistically as possible, by seeing how they age and weather as literally as possible, by visually constructing the consequences of our usually naïve and simplistic assumptions regarding cultural evolutions, by contemplating multiple scenarios of social transformations, by playing out both positive and potentially negative outcomes, we might just re-calibrate our positions in the present and alter the way we speculate on the future of these public housing projects.

"*Public*" though is a word we must unpack here. It is one of the most commonly and casually used words in architecture. After all, we are in the discipline of curating qualities of public and private life to varying degrees. But what kind of *public* are we referring to? What is the make of the *public*? Is *public* a word of inclusion for every spectrum of us or is it a blanket word identifying us all as an equal but generic human mass? It is bothersome to contemplate these questions while we try to be inclusive of all with positive intentions. We just might be oversimplifying the diversity we are surrounded with. How can we then reconsider the word "*public*" more specifically? Since we, as architects, do not get to pick the make of the public we design for, we must, without any exceptions, embrace its potential diversity and instability. The reality is that we are becoming more and more diverse. We are all part of various micro constituencies and constellations with differing backgrounds, politics, interests, motivations, aspirations, and aesthetics. We must embrace far more divergent and inclusive future narratives around race, gender, age, and citizenship. Totalizing assumptions regarding diverse living and lifestyle realities cannot be bracketed in an overarching and singular vision of society and its architecture, which historically always resulted in inadequate architectural manifestations of mono-isms with shorter than envisioned life spans.

In the absence of a common unifying ideology, with the lack of a political binding agency, with only singular interventions to undertake and offer, the architect is pressured into a peculiar position currently as architecture attempts to define the nature of the city through instances ... As a response to such pressure, we can yield and basically provide just services, follow from behind and at best try to represent politics of established agendas, be stylistically relevant to continue to serve and profit more/help others profit more, we can always resist and withdraw to paper space, we can represent alternative visions outside of the realities of the world we operate in, more fantasies ... or we can embrace this position and explore the potentials of the architectural object with a newfound rigor, as we contemplate the future reality of our environment. How we think about the future from the vantage point of the present with the historical knowledge we inhabit, is what defines architectural speculation. We have witnessed so many heroic predictions of the future fall prey to fizzled fantasies, we have witnessed so many utopias never materialize. Perhaps speculation about the future plausibility can steer clear from idealism of novelty and contemplate the subversion of the familiar through the transformation of what is already present.

Right

Ricardo Boffill
Les Espaces d'Abraxas
Noisy-le-Grand, 1982

Image of "Les Espaces d'Abraxas" by Ricardo Boffill, completed in 1982, is one of the landmark buildings of Marne-la Vallée, a new town built near Paris.

CONSTRAINED TRANSFORMATIONS

Kutan Ayata

There are a significant number of large-scale modernist housing complexes constructed all through the 20th century, all over the world. Their deficiencies are crystal clear, yet still to this date they sustain lives and provide housing for large masses. Their shortcomings in terms of their architecture and urbanism are well documented. The end of their previous glory as modernist utopias has been verified many times over. Yet, they are still here as things in the world, functioning to some extent. In the current state of environmental pressures, to imagine their demise through tabula rasa seems wasteful, both in terms of already deposed materials and the potential they might hold for alternative futures. Mega-Block Redux explores the transformation of these constructed historic visions to cultivate new possibilities of collective living through near-future scenarios.

The specific site we engaged for this project was in Moscow, Russia. While examples of this type of public housing project are widespread across the world, no other place has seen more of this typology implemented than Soviet Russia throughout the communist regime. The study seen here is the collective work of the studio to transform the current condition of two "Round House" buildings in Moscow, both almost identical nine-story mega-structures containing 956 apartments in a circular planimetric arrangement with a courtyard in the center. Built originally for the 1980 Moscow Olympics, symbolizing one of the rings in the Olympics logo. Two of the five rings were built in time for the event, the other three never materialized. These two Round Houses have been fully occupied since their completion.

Left

Studio Collective
Mega-Block Redux-Roundhouse
Moscow

Kutan Ayata Urban Housing Studio
with Ryan Henriksen

University of Pennsylvania
Weitzman School of Design, 2019

Collective mid-level plan of Circle 2.

The buildings were built according to centrally governed prefabrication regulations and are in fact an assembly of multiple parts of the same repeated module. Though the buildings look singular and monolithic in their appearance in the form of a complete circle, they have been conceived as multiple buildings with parti-walls, severing a potential connection between segments. The configuration students faced was a set of nine-story tall joined but isolated towers in a circular configuration. In many ways, the buildings act like an urban wall towards themselves and define a fortress-like

Jingyi Zhou
Mega-Block Redux-Roundhouse, Moscow

View towards the blank wall of the multi-generational living residences at Circle-2.

condition in their context. The courtyards are densely populated with trees which were planted after the construction. Now fully grown, they define a lush common space and a rather dense canopy experienced both from below or above depending on one's position inside or outside of the buildings. One peculiar condition that was originally implemented was to allow cars to drive into the center of the buildings and utilize their inner edge as parking.

The task to manipulate the condition of the Round House as a collective design intervention required multiple students to develop projects growing off the same building. This is a radically different scenario than asking students to intervene in separate buildings towards defining a collective of individual projects. In the latter scenario, the degree of difference in design language from one student's intervention to the next would not really matter, in fact would positively contribute to the diversity of overall configuration as amplified articulations towards increased heterogeneity. In the case of Round House, the adjacency of different interventions required significantly more calibrated design coordination amongst the students to verify the cohesive outcome of the transformed building. While the overall ambition remained focused on challenging the homogeneous characteristics of the original spatial and material definitions of Round House, it was clear from the beginning that this had to be a tailored exercise to negotiate the differences between multiple design authors. In some way the design language and intensity of expression had to be constrained for clear and precise articulations in the formal, material, and programmatic alterations of the original building. A formal exuberance would seem unproductive as an expression, perhaps too intense and radically different. A far more measured and surgical precision which engaged the existing physical constraints of the "context" was embraced.

The two circles of the Round Houses were divided into pie-like shapes and assigned to students as site. Students collectively developed additions that dealt with the strong figure of the circle as well as the ground in the courtyard. We fully embraced the permanence of the physical condition of the host building as context and accepted all that it has as a three-dimensional site to operate on. Dimensions of the structural modules, aperture, balconies, material articulations were all embraced as cues and constraints to advance and grow new definitions. What is there remained there to initiate the next stage of its evolution. We added, subtracted, intersected, fused, gutted, grew, connected, disconnected, reconfigured, refigured to produce new characteristics to alter the monotonous spatial and aesthetic definitions of these otherwise very mundane structures. Their overly simplistic, singularly centric spatial conditions were altered to define multiple centers through multiple appendages. The circumference was elongated and reconfigured to define new points of entry and inclusion in the circles. The hope was to still maintain a cohesive formal definition to the buildings but also to establish a much wider range of qualities and specific local variation of spaces within their bounds. How do you maintain coherence, how do you let subjective expressions remain in place without breaking the whole, how do you maintain formal continuity, how do you manage discontinuity, which developing formal

Left Top

Paul McCoy
Mega-Block Redux-Roundhouse, Moscow

View of Live/Work artist residences addition to the Circle-2, seen from outside of the original building.

Left Bottom

Peik Shelton
Mega-Block Redux-Roundhouse, Moscow

View looking up towards the cantilevering tower of the assisted living residences at Circle-1.

Above

Studio Collective

Collective model photograph, Circle-2.

qualities work better next to another, how does material change from one intervention to the next, does it change? ... These are questions students constantly debated as they collectively redefined the formal and material characteristics of the host building.

Alongside the physical developments of the projects, a parallel effort in trying to speculate on the future social context was underway. The transformation of a structure this scale takes a long time. To only speculate through the pressures and conditions of the present time would either limit or misplace the potentials of other plausible futures. We considered new lifestyle, demographic, political, economic, and social realities for the near future, usually through a 20-year leap. Instead of casting a large net which would define a singular narrative about the potential direction of future reality, the studio developed multiple micro-narratives to define a collection of plausible future trajectories. This exercise asks students to highlight a current issue which is pressuring the social make of the current metropolis and consider its potential future outcome and how it might impact our assumptions in housing configurations. A building this size cannot sustain a viable collective without the inclusion of various ancillary programs but also without diversity of living conditions which allows the make of the building's populace to include a wider spectrum of society.

Right

Peik Shelton
Mega-Block Redux-Roundhouse, Moscow

Partial elevational view of the aperture and balcony articulation of the assisted living residences at Circle-1.

LIVING OFF THE LAND

Scott Erdy | Erdy McHenry Architecture

"The Engineer, inspired by the law of economy and governed by mathematical calculation, puts us in accord with universal law. He achieves harmony."[1]

At its most basic level, Architecture is the art of making shelter—it must keep us warm, dry and safe from the dangers of our surroundings. The larger vision for architecture, however, is to nurture—to allow a community to live, grow and prosper in ways that address the greater needs of society. We have the opportunity to solve some of our greatest problems—lack of affordable housing, food insecurity and an underlying unstable employment economy—by creating a new type of architecture, one that is self-sufficient, one that provides employment opportunities, and one that allows us to reduce our physical and ecological footprint by living off the land. The new type of architecture lives off the land, grows its own food, provides housing and employment, and ultimately allows for a rewilding of an exhausted landscape now freed from the necessity of food production.

The unavailability of affordable housing is one of the biggest contributors to homelessness. In 2017, 6.7 million households spent more than 50% of their income on rent. This lack of affordability intersects with poverty to exacerbate the crisis. A lack of employment opportunities, combined with a decline in public assistance leaves low-income families just an illness or accident away from being put out on the street. According to the National Alliance to End Homelessness census, on a single night in 2018, roughly 553,000 people were experiencing homelessness in the United States.[2] This crisis will only worsen over the next two decades without a radical reimagining of American housing. Over the next 50 years, the human population of 7.6 billion is expected to rise to at least 9.3 billion. By 2050, 70% of this population is expected to live in cities, increasing the strain on food, energy and water systems at an unsustainable rate.[3]

Left

Library of Congress, Prints and Photographs Division, John C.H. Grabill Collection, 1891 [reproduction number LC-USZ62-90145].

This young Oglala girl sitting in front of her tipi, with a puppy beside her, probably on or near Pine Ridge Reservation (1891) exemplifies the traditional notion of living off the land, utilizing the resources that the environment offers. Her minimal shelter is constructed from renewable resources and materials that are direct byproducts of the tribe's food supply.

To feed our current world population requires a land area approximately the size of South America, not including land areas and resources used for animal grazing.[4] The expected population rise to 9.3 billion over the next 50 years will require an additional 10^9 hectares (an area roughly the size of Brazil) to feed humanity using current technologies. The increased demand for arable land could result in further deforestation, reducing the amount of potential hardwood carbon sequestration.[5]

New typologies are needed to answer the questions of how we can best house the homeless. How do we create housing for people who are in need and who have been marginalized in society? What lessons can be learned from history? How can architecture provide a self-sustaining physical, cultural and economic model for cities?

The Contemporary Hunter-Gatherer

Traditional forms of subsidized and affordable housing are based on government-sponsored economic assistance aimed towards helping people with low to moderate incomes. This aid includes rent supplements, non-profit housing, public housing and subsidized cooperative and private sector housing. These programs have not been effective in stemming the current homeless crisis nor do they offer solutions for the future because they do not provide long-term benefit to the residents nor are they self-sustaining. Additionally, the current system fails to adequately address food scarcity or joblessness. Giving the impoverished more control over their lives will lead to better long-term outcomes.

Prior to the National Housing Act of 1937, which began subsidized housing, the private housing market was responsible for housing those of modest means. Before implementation of the Act, the National Housing Association's policy was to focus on the essentials of housing—building straightforward, highly functional housing types such as the Brooklyn Brownstone. The National Housing Act was a turning point—increased regulations complicated the straightforward mandate to create simple, affordable housing. Under current building codes and zoning laws, much of the distinctive lower-cost housing that has shaped the architectural identity of America's cities—such as Brooklyn's brownstones—could not be built.[6] Aspects of this well-intended oversight have limited innovation and forced many homeless to take matters into their own hands, creating their own new forms of living on the margins.

Above

NASA/Eugene Cernan
Gemini 9 and Earth Limb, 1966

The Gemini 9 spacecraft, taken by Eugene Cernan during his Extravehicular Activity (EVA) in 1966 represents the minimum shelter required to sustain life in a hostile environment, bringing into focus its performative nature.

Many who have been left out of the country's economic boom have gravitated towards communal living, like historical hunter-gatherers. This is by no means an ideal situation, but it reminds us that self-sufficiency often breeds invention. As a response to the unsheltered epidemic, many homeless across the country have resorted to living in "Tent Cities." In these self-organizing settlements, sometimes described as "urban camping," the homeless have formed supportive communities where they are able to sleep in modest shelters, maintain minimal levels of security and share limited resources to combat hunger. Similar to the "Hoovervilles" of the Great Depression, most of these settlements operate outside of all building and zoning codes and are an organic response to essential and basic needs for housing. These tent cities have developed their own governance, bylaws and policing. Self-organizing and organic, the tent city is an important example of the inextricable link between food gathering/consumption and questions of housing and domesticity.

There are many examples of encampments that have become safe and useful short-term solutions for homelessness. One such example settlement, "Nickelsville" in Seattle, provided a safe, self-governing solution to the chronic homelessness that was ignored by local government.[7] While tent cities are not a long-term solution to the housing crisis, they can be a valuable stopgap response to the immediate needs of the unsheltered. These settlements bring their inhabitants into the proximity of supportive services necessary to break the cycle of homelessness. Many cities such as Portland, Seattle, Sacramento and Fresno are now allowing these encampments to exist legally and are sponsoring social programs to support the residents.[8]

Above T–B

Tent City
SF Weekly, *2016*

View of the homeless encampments along Central Avenue in Downtown Los Angeles, California. Where the homeless are left to their own means, fashioning shelter from found objects.

Displaced by economic and event-based gentrification these homeless encampments along Central Avenue in Downtown Los Angeles exemplify another mode of "living off the land." Here, the homeless are left to their own means, forcing them to fashion shelter from found objects.

Throughout history, humans have engineered more and more efficient ways to satisfy their housing needs. For example, the nomadic Sioux tribe of the American West devised an ingenious system of housing that met their need for portability. As a hunting people, the Sioux used the hides from their kills as well as other found objects to build their homes. A lightweight and sustainably built home provided shelter that was adapted to the nomadic nature of their tribe. This "mobile home" was hauled from place to place along with their means of sustenance; the homes were so well conceived that the tribe could disassemble their camps and continue on their journey in less than an hour.

Today's homeless act in much the same way. Those left behind by a politics of abandonment create makeshift housing from readily available materials. They look to their environment and make the most of what is available—whether it be a discarded tent, lost tarps or "borrowed" milk crates. But what does this say about our culture? Although basic human needs are the same, the Sioux tents represent the careful manipulation of the built environment by an advanced civilization, while the homeless encampment is an acute symptom of a failed society.

History of Practical Domesticity

Le Corbusier's famous example of the Certosa di Firenze is a case in which domesticity and productive labor intertwine. Each resident maintains their own garden to provide sustenance for himself, supplemented by food grown by the novitiates who tend the fields that surround the monastery. This combination of private and communal gardens creates a symbiotic utopia where shared labor results in shared benefit while each inhabitant is invested at a personal level in their own production and consumption. Each unit of the monastery contains a sleeping area, modest kitchen, loggia and a courtyard containing a vegetable and herb garden that provides much of the inhabitant's sustenance. There is also a root cellar for long-term crop storage, designed to forestall the normal shortages that occur throughout the year in a temperate climate. This self-contained unit provides space for domestic, labor and production activities and models a holistic approach to living. Similar units are assembled as modules into a larger community, which accommodates shared social functions and agricultural production. Key to this model is the social aspect of the community, working together for a common goal. The tacit underlying principle of this model is the intrinsic link between humans and the Earth.

The Certosa di Firenze is a sustainable housing model that addresses many contemporary concerns about ecology, consumerism and the harmful effects of the current agricultural industry. The symbiotic relationship between housing and food production has a long history but has not been manifested in contemporary architecture. This model demands to be revisited, applying today's available technologies in order to address both food scarcity and the housing crisis.

The Current Agricultural Complex

Farming is not an instinctual human activity; it was invented over 11,000 years ago. In the US, agriculture is by far the largest consumer of natural resources, requiring 70% of available fresh water[9] and accounts for 20% of the consumption of fossil fuels.

We have created an agriculture that requires the use of herbicides, fossil fuels, fertilizers and pesticides. While this has allowed the productivity to increase at the rate of demand, the outcome is a deadly, uncontrolled and mostly unregulated agricultural runoff that is poisoning our waterways, estuaries and oceans.[10] The ever-increasing need for food results in over farming, damaging mono-cultures, nutrient depletion and rampant consumption of energy.

As agribusiness becomes more centralized and industrial, the scale of farms increases, as does their distance from the city; the idea of the farming community has been lost. Also, the nature of centralized organization requires that principles are applied generally across different regions and landscapes, diluting cultural and ecological regionalism.

These concerns were raised at the 5th CIAM Conference (1937) in Paris, in a debate between the "Bureaucratic Collectivists" and the "Syndicalists," who were in favor of locally controlled cooperative organizations.[11] In the proceedings Norbert Bézard advocated for small-scale organizations and community over complete rationalization because of the overwhelming benefit of autonomous, local control over crop selection and management.

After meeting Bézard, Le Corbusier took a more focused interest in agriculture, and together they developed an idealized farm. By consulting with the Syndicalists they were able to establish a functional kit of parts that could be adapted for multiple

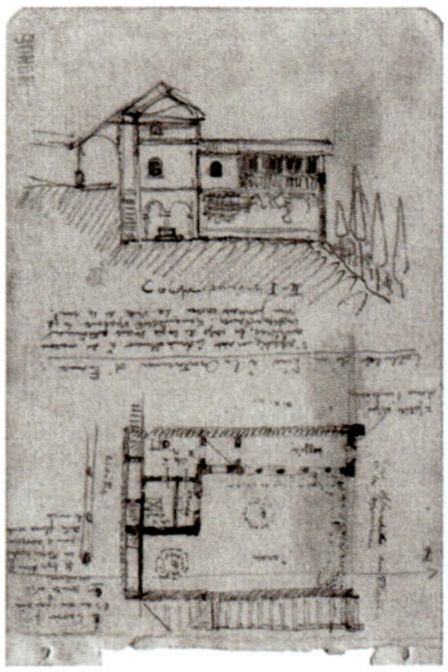

Above

Le Corbusier
Sketch of the Certosa di Firenze, cell plan and section, 1907

This seminal sketch of the Certosa di Firenze documents a historical approach to housing that integrates multiple functions for efficiency, comfort and sustainability. Its orientation toward the functional aspects of domesticity became a model for much of Le Corbusier's later research in housing.

Right

Le Corbusier
Village Radieux, model, 1937

As an idealized farming community, Village Radieux included communal, cultural and educational aspects that were generally limited urban areas. Its axial organization was based on efficiency and iconographic potential and the grain storage bins, which acted as the gateway to the complex.

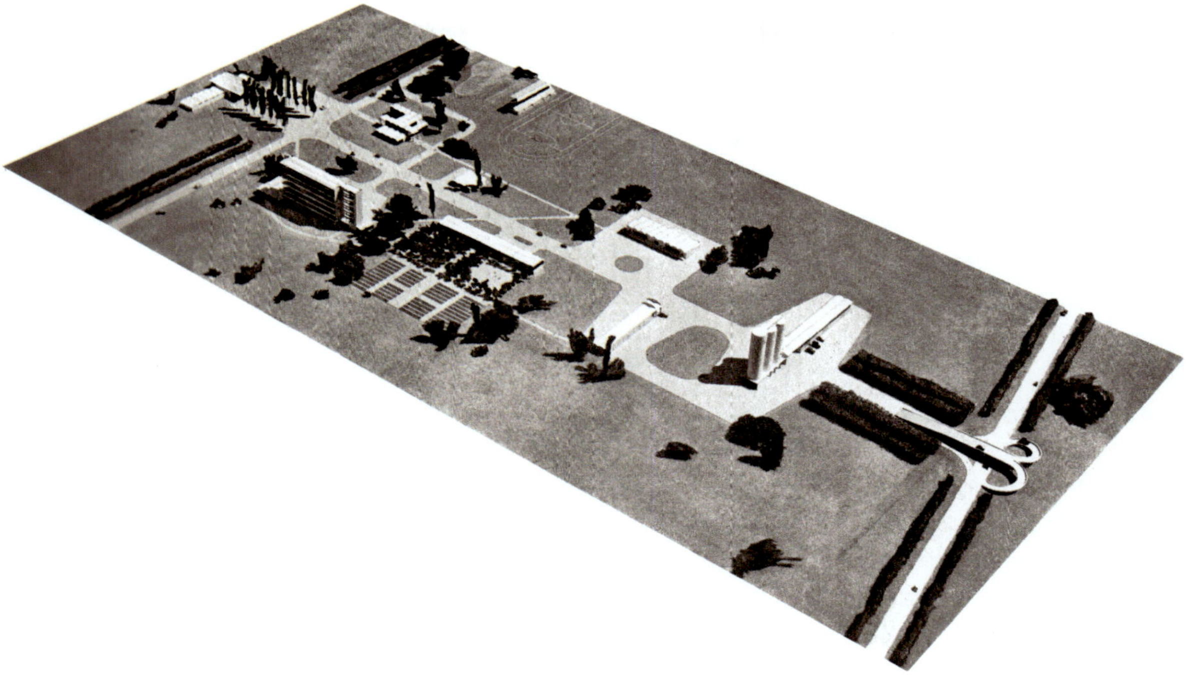

regions and site configurations. Much of their work was rooted in Le Corbusier's earlier urban planning proposals that organized buildings and open space in ways that extended their utility. The collaboration between Bézard and Le Corbusier as well as their cooperation with the surrounding community resulted in the design of Ferme Radieuse, his first purpose designed farm.

This was later expanded to Village Radieux, which included a school, post office, market, machinery and repair shops and an 11-story apartment building for the farm workers. The scheme employed an axial organization, beginning with a propylaea-like gateway, comprising three large grain elevators, and terminating in the Center for Regional Culture.

Rewilding the Land

Urban growth and suburban sprawl push farmland further from urban centers, which requires a vast network of transportation and distribution, further increasing the needed resources and carbon footprint of food production. Increasingly, the low-density development of sprawl, spiraling outward from urban centers, has led to habitat fragmentation, water and air pollution, increased infrastructure costs, inequality and social homogeneity.[12]

In *Feral: Rewilding the Land, the Sea, and Human Life* (2013), George Monbiot examines how the Earth, if left to its own devices, can quickly return to its pre-human intervention condition.[13] This inspires the hope that increased density in cities will free land from development, allowing it to become reforested—"rewilding" the land.

So far rewilding has only occurred on a large scale as the inadvertent result of a political or environmental disaster. The aftermath of the Chernobyl nuclear disaster in 1986 demonstrates nature's ability to recover. Although high levels of radiation remain, plant and animal wildlife has flourished. The Korean Demilitarized Zone (DMZ) is another example of nature's ability to heal once left alone, and it is now recognized as one of the best-preserved areas of temperate habitat in the world.[14]

Reforestation could begin if suburban sprawl and farmland were abandoned and depopulated—leaving the land to its natural processes, allowing it to heal, sequester carbon and provide breathable air to the planet.

A Contemporary Machine for Living

Le Corbusier's sustained interest in productive domesticity inspired an architecture in which aesthetic decisions were in large measure based on utility. He developed several communal housing types, including the "honeycomb housing" for workers in the garden city of Ville Contemporaine in 1922, which were based on his visit to the Certosa di Firenze in 1907.[15] In that model, he developed individual terraced gardens as extensions of the interior living space. Stacking this module allowed for greater residential density, supporting his argument that greater density could be achieved in conjunction with more open space.

While the terraced gardens were small and largely ornamental in nature, the open space at grade was an amalgamation of allotment gardens and perimeter orchards that allowed residents of the community to grow their own food. The design anticipated that a professional farmer would be employed to assist and advise the residents. The rational geometric layout of the gardens facilitated both the movement of large machinery and the installation of an automatic irrigation system.[16] The separation of the allotment gardens from the apartment buildings was likely due to the shading caused by the stacked modules and his commitment to an urban vision that incorporated open green space, light and air. Today, an alternative path to his model of integrated living and gardening is made possible by technological advances in hydroponic and controlled environment agriculture.

Le Corbusier's interest in the development of a "machine for living" spurred further research, which culminated in a full-scale prototype and masterplan for the city of Paris: the Pavillon de L'Esprit Nouveau and the Plan Voisin. These experiments challenged long-accepted comforts in order to focus on the capacity of design to reshape human life. The Pavillon de L'Esprit Nouveau was a temporary building created in 1925 for the International Exposition of Decorative Arts in Paris. The pavilion was a model dwelling unit, with an integral garden, which was designed to function either as a free-standing house or as an apartment in a multistory residential building. An attached exhibition gallery housed dioramas and drawings of his grand urban projects: the Contemporary City of 3 Million Inhabitants (1922) and the Plan Voisin (1925). The Pavillon de L'Esprit Nouveau provided a tangible, full-scale mock-up of living in these visions of the future.

There is more than a passing connection between Plan Voisin and Le Corbusier's interests in agriculture and ecology. A foe of the Schreber movement, which categorized gardening as a leisure hobby, he took great interest in a form of communal urban living that included agriculture. This was in large part due to his negative reaction to Soviet Dis-Urbanist theories that were put forward in response to the Soviet Green City competition, where theorists M. Okhitovich and M. Ginzburg exhibited their ideas that sought to dissolve the division between town and country by proposing that settlement be dispersed evenly across the Soviet Union in its entirety.[17]

Right Top

Le Corbusier
Garden City Honeycomb Housing
1925

The Garden City Honeycomb Housing reinforces the modern notion of continuous space, where both the ground and the upper terraces flow seamlessly with the interior spaces, and nature is integrated into the architecture.

Right Bottom

Le Corbusier
Cellular Housing System, 1925

The exterior gardens that are created by the Cellular Housing System provide each apartment equal access to nature, light and air, regardless of location within the building and represents a much denser and compact model of the "garden apartment."

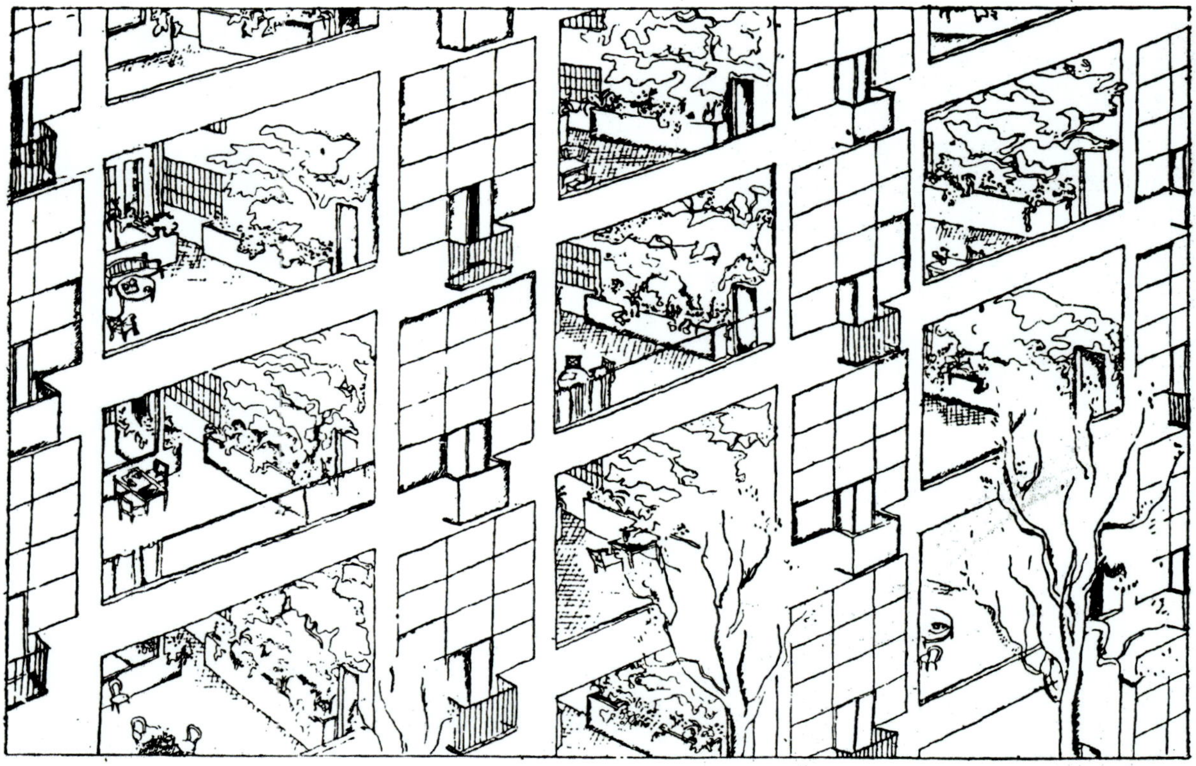

Plan Voisin built off the ideas developed in the Ville Contemporaine as Le Corbusier further developed the connection between agriculture and architecture. The masterplan consolidated most of the housing into central towers, while the periphery became a patchwork of parks and allotment gardens. Le Corbusier's scheme maximized vertical density in order to provide open space that could be used for food production or expansive parkland. He opposed movements where gardening became merely a leisure hobby (such as the Schreber movement) as well as centralized, state-run reorganization of the urban environment and agriculture (as seen in the Soviet Green City competition). Le Corbusier's Plan Voisin saw agriculture as a modern industrial production under the control of the local community: rationalized, standardized and employing economies of scale.[18] Le Corbusier's urban planning of the 1920s responded to the urban ills of density, pollution and overcrowding. By promoting vertical density, light and air were protected and land was made available for recreation—all for the benefit of the residents. What is remarkable about Le Corbusier's urban proposals from nearly a century ago is the "rewilding" the land that they entailed, dramatically increasing the potential amount of carbon sequestration. Ville Contemporaine and Plan Voisin are both architectural models for "living off the land" and a logical step in the development of a model building that feeds its residents.

Living off the Land—A Self Sustaining Proposal

We live in a land of great wealth. But still, a large swath of the population is impoverished in part due to a lack of affordable housing and food insecurity. Unsustainable techniques for food production, unchecked growth in land use and the depletion of natural resources have us living beyond our means. This is only possible because we have mortgaged the future by consuming far more than our share and causing tremendous harm to our earth. As our population continues to grow the built environment needs to be reconsidered. We need to develop bold strategies that solve homelessness and hunger simultaneously.

"Living off the land" is an architecture invested in self-sustaining food production that provides a viable alternative to over farming and the development of land that could otherwise be used for carbon sequestration. Bringing productive farming into population centers would mean fresher food and less pollution-emitting transportation.[19] Concentrating population density and food production in cities allows the rewilding of the surrounding landscape. At the same time, this new paradigm is an opportunity to reinvent the goals of social housing—a model that incorporates food security *and* shelter. The agricultural component of the program focuses on food production utilizing Controlled Environment Agriculture (CEA) techniques. This new housing typology could go beyond environmental net-zero standards and lead to the true, multi-factor sustainability of neighborhoods. Providing food and housing in a symbiotic system would provide relief to broad swaths of the impoverished population, and would contribute to the economic and social stability of a neighborhood.

Left Top

Le Corbusier and Pierre Jeanneret Pavillon de L'Esprit Nouveau at the International Exhibition of Modern Decorative and Industrial Arts Paris, 1925

The unarticulated surfaces of the Pavillon de L'Esprit Nouveau allow it to frame nature and express its symbiotic relationship to the architecture.

Left Bottom

As a prototype for a new way of living, the Pavillon de L'Esprit Nouveau integrates nature, light and air into the program of living. It rejects decorative ornamentation detail in favor of articulation born purely of function.

Components of this hybrid building typology can be calibrated in response to regional climate, housing needs, energy consumption and urban context. In most cities, areas of unemployment, homelessness, poverty and malnutrition persist, and building in these areas can utilize the embodied energy of people and place. Transforming an abandoned building or vacant lot into productive agricultural-based housing could be the first step toward providing food and shelter to large at-risk populations. This approach also frees the land outside of the city, allowing it to "rewild," i.e., return to its natural state.

The premise of Modernism was heroic. It was a project that sought to use modern technology and rational analysis to solve modern problems and that adopted abstraction as its language. Le Corbusier applied these principles to create a symbiotic relationship between buildings and the land that sought to address problems of housing, overcrowding in cities, access to light and air, and to ultimately celebrate a clean, humane environment. Le Corbusier's visions of the 1920s can serve as the starting point for imagining a city of self-sufficient housing.

Right Top

Le Corbusier
Ville Contemporaine, 1922

Ville Contemporaine densifies housing in order to free up the ground plane for other uses, including the opportunity for a rewilding of the land.

Right Bottom

Le Corbusier
Housing Scheme with Honeycomb Principle, 1925

The plan layout of the Honeycomb Housing Principle provides large expanses of integrated crop fields and smaller areas for orchards. The density of the housing minimizes shadow and the perforated nature of the building envelope provides wind breaks for the fields.

References

1. Le Corbusier, "The Engineers Aesthetic and Architecture." In *Towards a New Architecture*. London: John Rodker, 1931, pp. 7–16.
2. Move for Hunger. "About Hunger and Homelessness: Move for Hunger." Move for Hunger: Everyone Can Fight Hunger. https://moveforhunger.org/hunger-and-homelessness
3. UN DESA Department of Economic and Social Affairs. "World Population Projected to Reach 9.7 Billion by 2050." United Nations. www.un.org/en/development/desa/news/population/2015-report.html
4. Dickson D. Despommier, *The Vertical Farm: Feeding the World in the 21st Century*. New York: Picador, 2011.
5. According to the UN, the Amazon alone absorbs 2 billion tons of carbon dioxide a year (or 5% of annual emissions), which makes it a vital part of preventing climate change. These factors, however, are under debate as absorption has slowed.
6. Howard Husock, Max Eden, and Christopher F. Rufo, "We Don't Need Subsidized Housing," *City Journal*, June 18, 2019. https://www.city-journal.org/html/we-don't-need-subsidized-housing-11954.html
7. Aimee Curl, "Welcome to Nickelsville," *Seattle Weekly*, August 19, 2008. https://www.seattleweekly.com/news/welcome-to-nickelsville/
8. National Coalition for the Homeless, "Tent Cities in America," March 2010, p. 10. http://nationalhomeless.org/publications/TentCitiesReport FINAL03-4-10.pdf
9. Centers for Disease Control and Prevention, "Agricultural Water," October 11, 2016. https://www.cdc.gov/healthywater/other/agricultural/index.html
10. EPA, "The Issue," February 04, 2019. https://www.epa.gov/nutrientpollution/issue
11. Mary McLeod, "The Country Is the Other City of Tomorrow." In *Food and the City Histories of Culture and Cultivation,* edited by Dorothée Imbert. Washington, DC: Dumbarton Oaks Research Library and Collection, 2015.
12. Samuel Brody, "The Characteristics, Causes, and Consequences of Sprawling Development Patterns in the United States," *Nature News*, 2013.
13. George Monbiot, *Feral: Rewilding the Land, the Sea, and Human Life*. Chicago, IL: The University of Chicago Press, 2015.
14. Nick Easen, "Korea's DMZ: The Thin Green Line," *CNN*, August 25, 2003. https://edition.cnn.com/2003/WORLD/asiapcf/east/08/22/korea.bio.dmz/
15. Cartusialover, "Le Corbusier e La Certosa," Cartusialover's blog, March 27, 2018. https://cartusialover.wordpress.com/2018/06/29/le-corbusier-e-la-certosa/
16. Le Corbusier, 'The City of To-morrow and its Planning.' Translated from the 8th French Edition of *Urbanisme*. Translated by Frederick Etchells. London: John Rodker, 1929.
17. Jean-Louis Cohen, *Le Corbusier and the Mystique of the USSR: Theories and Projects for Moscow, 1928–1936.* Princeton, NJ: Princeton University Press, 1992.
18. Mary McLeod, "The Country Is the Other City of Tomorrow."
19. Dickson D. Despommier, *The Vertical Farm: Feeding the World in the 21st Century.*

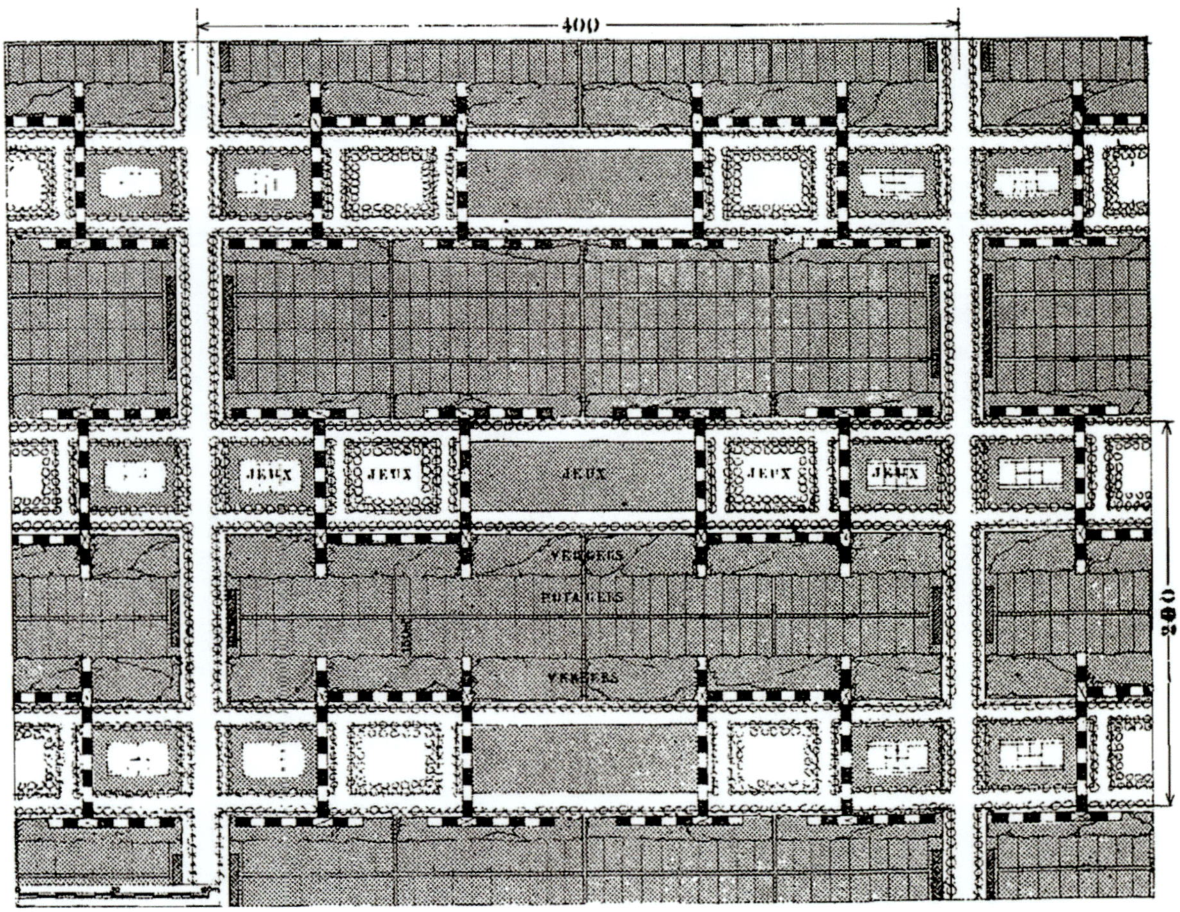
400
JEUX
JEUX
JEUX
JEUX
JEUX
VERGERS
POTAGERS
VERGERS
280

PHILADELPHIA FARMHOUSE

Scott Erdy

Center City Philadelphia is both vibrant and bleak, and like most cities it is constantly vacillating between progress and regression. The site for Ian Pangburn's proposal for The Philadelphia Farmhouse sits amid a plethora of public services: The Family Court to the west and the Municipal Services Building to the south, meals served daily on Thomas Paine Plaza, shelters within walking distance and multiple adult education and job training programs within the shadow of City Hall. But still, signs of hunger, homelessness and unemployment remain. Project Home, a local non-profit, has even opened the "Hub of Hope," a below ground safe place in the subway concourse that offers a warm cup of coffee, shower and laundry facilities, and the opportunity to speak to peers or case managers to begin the process of finding permanent housing. Basic needs of food, shelter and employment are currently not being provided by a robust economy that far too often bypasses those most in need.

Pangburn's Philadelphia Farmhouse is designed for immigrant, migrant and transitory residents, giving them the opportunity to live in a supportive communal environment that grows and harvests crops from the vertical fields within a new city infrastructure. The residents can tackle the needs of the growing city while also generating the financial stability for themselves and their families.

Agriculture is an essential practice for humans to sustain life. Conventional farming, far from cities, requires large areas of land cleared of its indigenous vegetation and extensive amounts of water to grow the vast quantities of the food we need. This has led to the deforestation of 40% of our woodland and the consumption of 70% of our freshwater reserves. Our current supply chain requires products in the United States to travel an average of 1,400 miles to market shelves. Currently, agriculture is responsible for one third of the world's greenhouse gas emissions and is projected to rise to 80% by 2050 as food production increases. Reducing the distance between where our food is consumed and where it is grown will lessen our impact on the environment and make our food fresher, our cities healthier and more self-sufficient.

Left

Ian Pangburn
Living off the Land

Scott Erdy Urban Housing Studio with Graham Nelson

University of Pennsylvania Weitzman School of Design, 2017

Detailed assembly model illustrating the greenhouse with its rotational growing system, the wood building structure and the Controlled Environment Agriculture growth chambers.

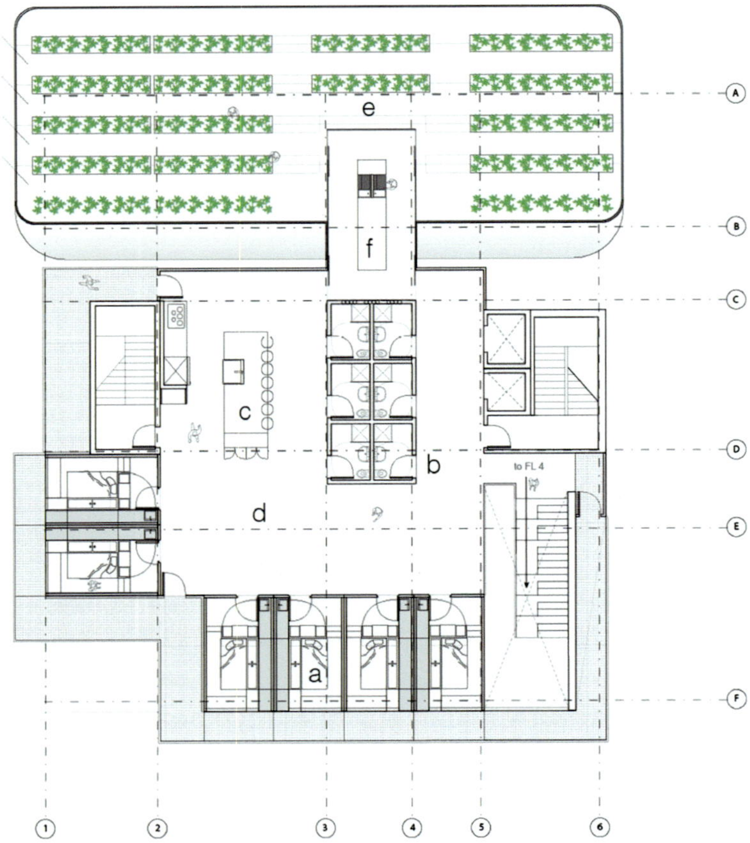

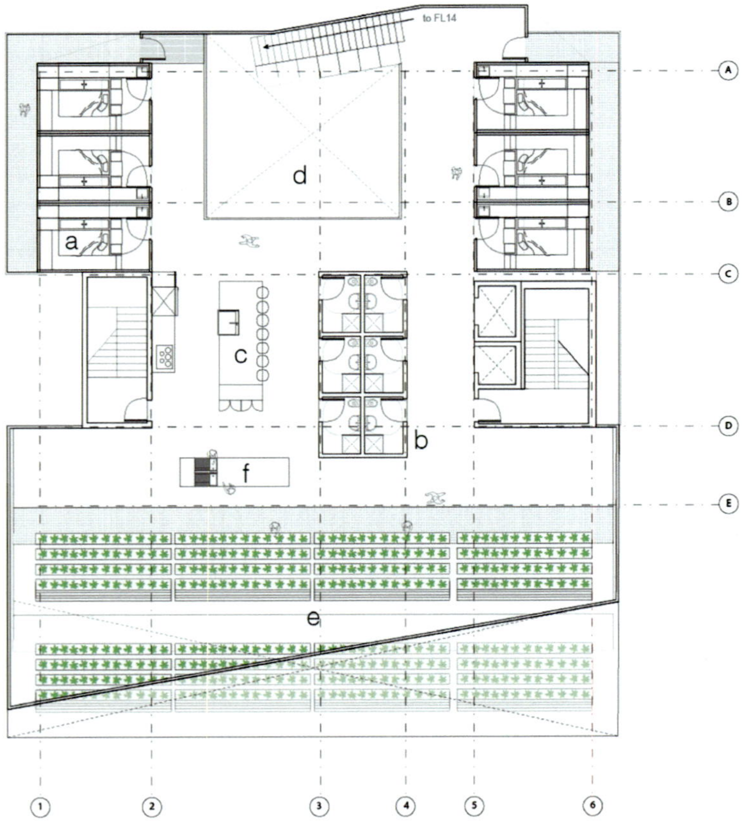

Legend

a. Sleeping Rooms
b. Circulation Space
c. Kitchen and Communal Dining
d. Collaborative Space
e. Growth Chamber
f. Plant Processing

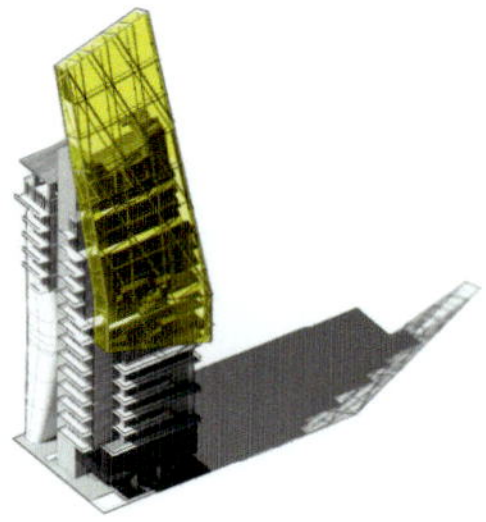

Greenhouse Agriculture

Garden Terraces

Controlled Environment Agriculture

Housing Units

Left

The building section and plans illustrate the causal relationship between the building form and the program.

Above

The form of each component, optimized to its interior function is then modified by external forces of the site context and solar orientation.

Pangburn's proposal imagines an alternate model for self-sufficient urban living that combines food production and housing in a way that addresses both homelessness and the undeniable need for a new system of delivering fresh produce to our cities.

The Farmhouse inserts food production directly into the center of Philadelphia. The tower wraps three methods of intensive agricultural production around a core of dwelling units and communal spaces. The living units are positioned around large central kitchens and prep areas where residents break bread together. The kitchens are bound on two sides by "vertical fields" where produce is harvested.

Life within the tower is communal at its core. Planting, growing, harvesting, cooking and eating are all communal acts positioned in close proximity without boundaries, allowing functions to blend throughout the day. In contrast, the sleeping rooms are designed to be personal and secluded. They provide reconfigurable personal space that includes a small seating area and a bed which can be stored to clear the floorspace. The outside wall hosts a built-in writing table facing towards a terrace and the city beyond. The sleeping rooms are intentionally small to allow the communal spaces to remain large and open. The shared areas include the essentials for meditation, cooking, bathing and socialization.

The entire building is structured using mass timber that sequesters more than 11,000 tons of carbon making it more sustainable compared to the use of conventional concrete or steel systems. The floors, walls and columns are all fire resistant due to their large cross section. During a fire the outer surface chars, protecting the structural integrity of each member. The timber, left exposed, gives the interior a warm, rich character, eliminating the need for additional building materials for finishing.

The food production program is intensive. Through the use of hydroponic and aquaponic growing systems the building can produce up to 1 million calories through all four seasons while using 70% less water than traditional farming. The south façade is a hydroponic greenhouse raised above the street and tilted vertically to capture daylight within the dense urban context. The hydroponic beds are supported on a rotating frame based on the Singapore 'Sky Greens' system that ensures each plant gets adequate light throughout the day. Nutrient-rich water cycles through each bed and acts as a natural weight allowing the frame to rotate using gravity rather than electricity. The inner corner of the tower, which receives no direct sunlight, utilizes Controlled Environment Agriculture (CEA) techniques that regulate for optimal lighting, humidity, water and essential plant nutrients. The aquaponic system produces fish as well as plants in a symbiotic cycle where the plants benefit from the fish waste and in turn purify the water for the fish.

Pangburn's Philadelphia Farmhouse (2017) presents a holistic approach to housing that incorporates living and growing into a single structure. It incorporates traditional greenhouse growing techniques as well as Controlled Environment Agriculture.

His infrastructure addresses a lack of available fresh produce within the city coupled with increasing concerns about CO_2 emissions, and the clearing of forests for farmland. The Farm produces more than twice as many calories per year than would be consumed by its inhabitants, allowing the excess to be sold to the community at the market on the ground floor.

Designed to address homelessness and food insecurity, the Philadelphia Farmhouse reveals a new city infrastructure. One acre of a vertical farm can produce as much food as ten acres that is farmed using conventional farming techniques. The building's form optimizes solar gain of the traditional greenhouses while the lower portions are used for Controlled Environment Agriculture production. Vertical farms provide a more efficient and productive generator of vegetables, allowing what was once farmland in the countryside to heal itself and reestablish hardwood biomass which sequesters carbon as it "rewilds," returning to its indigenous state.

The Philadelphia Farmhouse creates a new type of architecture that addresses some of our greatest problems—lack of affordable housing, food insecurity and the underlying unstable employment economy. An architecture that grows its own food, provides housing and employment, and ultimately allows for a rewilding of an exhausted landscape now freed from the necessity of food production, is self-sufficient, provides employment opportunities and allows us to reduce our physical and ecological footprint.

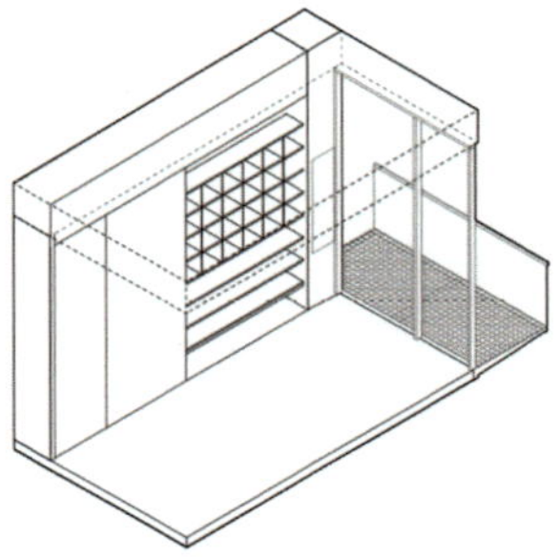

Packed Away

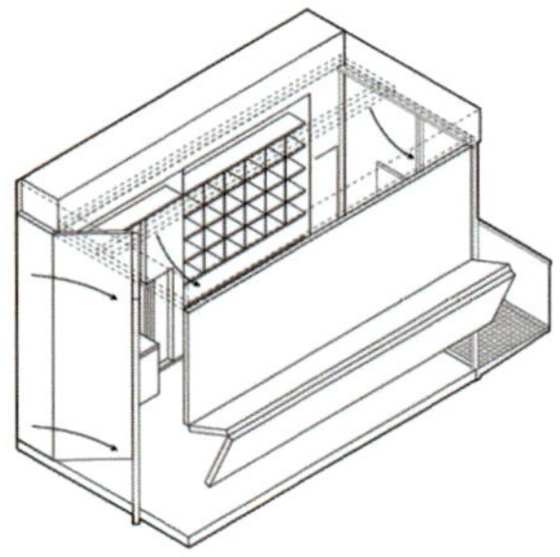

Unpack Walls

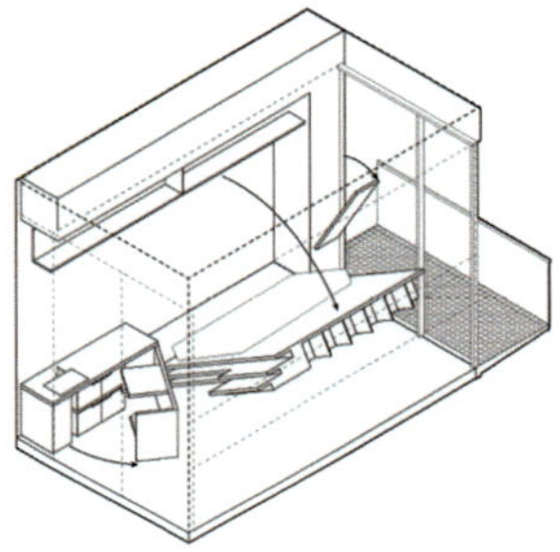

Unpack Furniture

Above

The sleeping rooms are made from CLT (Cross Laminated Timber) panels and feature a configurable interior. Natural light is filtered through the greenhouses as it comes into the private sleeping spaces.

Right

The building structure is made from CLT. Because of its fire-resistive qualities it can be fully exposed. The collaborative work areas (top) show the contrast between the low biomass plants grown in the greenhouse and the carbon-sequestering structure. The private sleeping areas (center) feature a multi-functioning interior, while versatility of the food processing areas (bottom) is shown by the sliding panels that allow for spaces to expand or contract based on need.

THE VALUE OF A HOME: A Critical Approach to Local Practice

Brian Phillips | ISA

Housing has been at the theoretical and spiritual heart of urbanism for the last century. Fetishized by architects, delivered dispassionately by governments and traded as commodity by private developers—the spaces we call home represent the most intimate boundary between the public and the personal experience of the built environment. Housing also forms an infrastructure for cities, occupying the majority of their land area. From Budapest with its Hapsburg-era courtyard blocks, to Beijing with its single-story Hutong mazes, to Philadelphia with its tightly packed and gridded rowhouses, the highly specific forms of a city's residential urban fabric can be relied upon to tell the many stories of its past. These typologies reflect a history of politics, economics, climate and cultural conditions concretized around the needs of urban dwelling to produce environments which in turn shape the future of cities.

More than other kinds of architecture, housing is influenced by invisible forces extending beyond the architect's control. Politicians, neighbors, planning boards, developers, real estate agents, contractors and banks all have a hand in influencing the design of urban housing, requiring the design team to curate and manage an especially wide range of stakeholders. However, this group of influencers rarely includes the people who will eventually live in the homes themselves. Although housing is ultimately called upon to represent the personal identity of its residents, it first serves as an embodiment of a society's deep economic and regulatory structures, reflecting and reinforcing the culture and history of its particular time and place.

Left

Aerial views
Kensington area of Northeast Philadelphia, 1951

Aerial view of typical lower North Philadelphia urban fabric showing rowhouse density and block structure organized by the street grid. Factories and churches are intermixed with housing creating an organic and opportunistic distribution of scale and functionality.

City as Lab

As a unitized and repetitive architectural program, housing typically fits within a highly organized spatial pattern. In early, unplanned cities, these patterns were informally improvised; in later, planned cities, architects and urban planners set forth deliberate structures serving as templates for housing development. Philadelphia is considered one of the earliest planned grid cities, initially laid out in 1682 by William Penn.

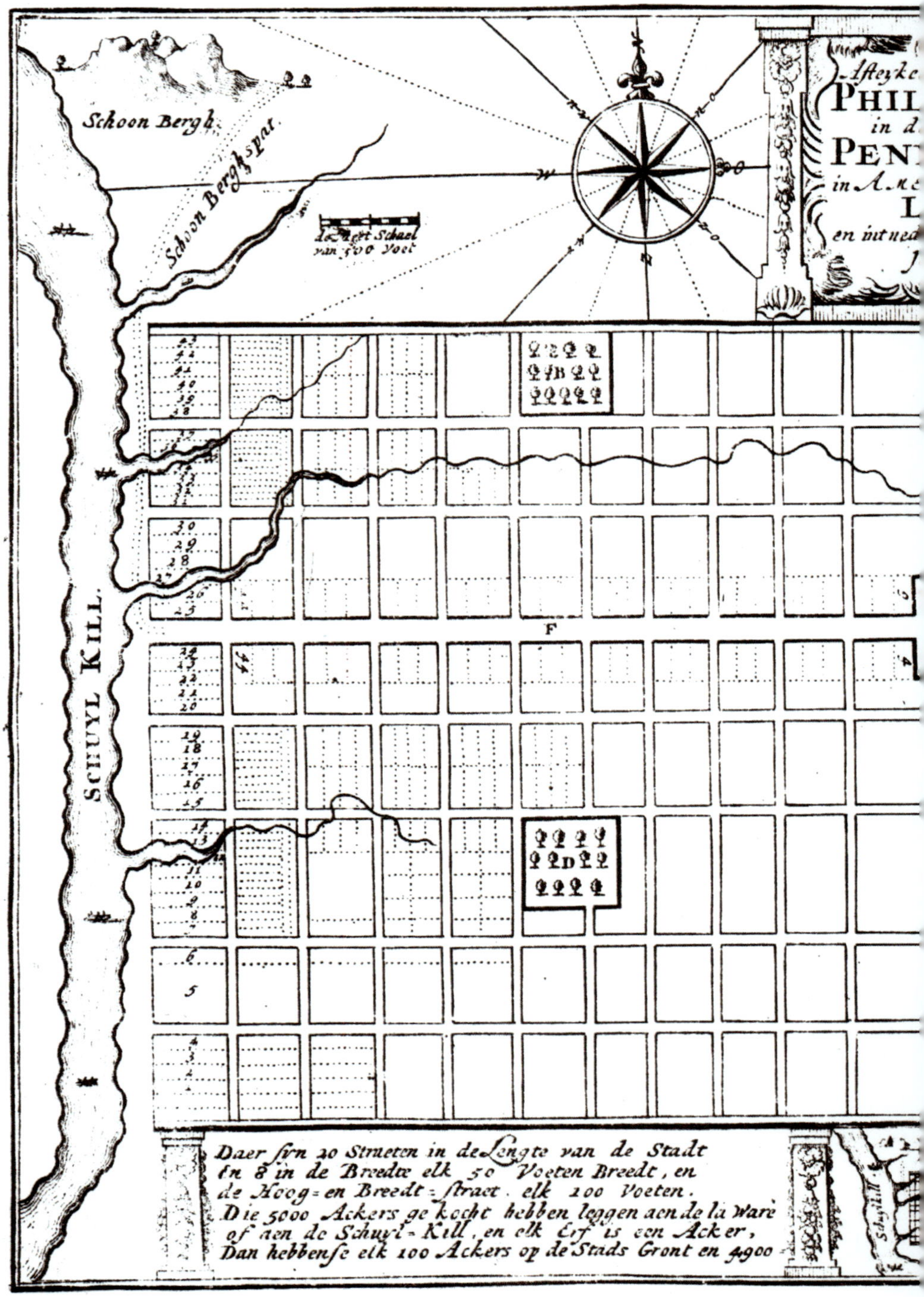

Thomas Holme
A Portraiture of the City of Philadelphia
Philadelphia, 1683

William Penn commissioned surveyor Thomas Holme to create a plan for Philadelphia in the late 1600s, laying out the city into a grid of one-acre square parcels sized to provide space for detached houses and gardens in contrast with London's congestion. Due to the city's rapid growth in the decades following, these lots were quickly subdivided to house Philadelphia's growing population in attached homes lined up along avenues, streets and alleys in rows. Typically 14 to 20 feet wide, there are more than 400,000 rowhouses in the city today.

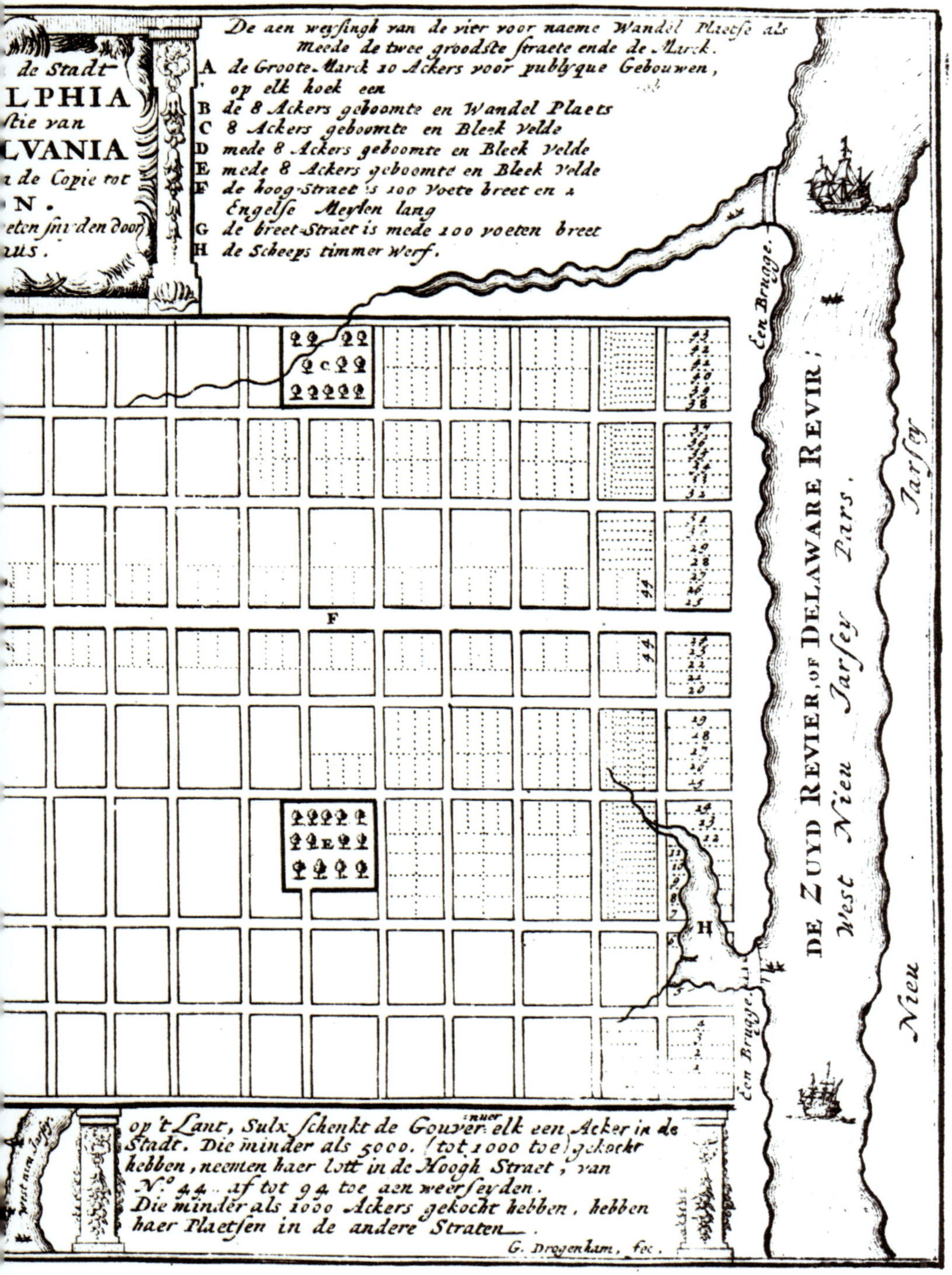
de Stadt
LPHIA
ltie van
LVANIA
de Copie tot
N.
eten snyden door
us.
De aen weysingh van de vier voor naeme Wandel Plaetse als
meede de twee groodste straete ende de Marck.
A de Groote Marck 10 Ackers voor publyque Gebouwen,
op elk hoek een
B de 8 Ackers geboomte en Wandel Plaets
C 8 Ackers geboomte en Bleek Velde
D mede 8 Ackers geboomte en Bleek Velde
E mede 8 Ackers geboomte en Bleek Velde
F de hoog-Straet is 100 Voete breet en 2
Engelse Meylen lang
G de breet-Straet is mede 100 voeten breet
H de Scheeps timmer Werf.
Een Brugge.
Een Brugge
F
H
DE ZUYD REVIER, OF DELAWARE REVIR;
West Nieu Jarsey Pars.
Nieu Jarsey
op 't Lant, Sulx schenkt de Gouverneur elk een Acker in de
Stadt. Die minder als 5000. (tot 1000 toe) gekocht
hebben, neemen haer lott in de Hoogh Straet, van
N.° 44. af tot 94 toe aen weerseyden.
Die minder als 1000 Ackers gekocht hebben, hebben
haer Plaetsen in de andere Straten.
G. Drogenham, fec.

Promoted as a kind of gameboard of opportunity marketed to European investors, its neat one-acre square parcels were designed for freestanding houses and large gardens in contrast to the congestion of London.[1] Although conceived as a rigid Cartesian structure, the power of Philadelphia's grid has been its ability to evolve and adapt to unexpected opportunities. By 1700, the city's population had grown substantially, and its original large lots were subdivided and sold off to accommodate newcomers within a much denser fabric of small lots.[2] These parcels were scaled to accommodate attached single-family homes with narrow street-facing frontages and rear yards, lined up along blocks in rows. Philadelphia's blocks were parceled out in unevenly scaled, opportunistic ways, with larger homes facing the wider original streets and more modest housing for working families facing narrow mid-block alleys. The resulting rowhouse fabric formed unusually economically and socially diverse communities at the scale of the neighborhood, with shops, factories, taverns and places of worship interspersed across the city to serve local communities.

As an infrastructure, housing in Philadelphia provides an unusually equitable and adaptable social structure for its neighborhoods. The Fishtown section, built originally as modest homes for workers employed in the riverfront fishing and shipbuilding industries, now serves as entry-level housing for the millennial creative class. The same small, tight-packed rowhomes a short commute away from the city center have provided a jumping off point for generations of residents to start a career, a business or a family. Its housing stock provides a consistent layer of domestic infrastructure that facilitates proximity to the jobs, experiences and artistic production of urban life, connecting generations of city dwellers across time.

Small Batch Infill

Philadelphia's housing fabric was developed as an accumulated community, an extraordinary canvas for experiments in small batch housing design. Much of the city's housing development was speculative, created unit-by-unit or in small chunks by opportunistic developers without buyers or tenants in mind. The city is the ultimate example of bottom-up infill, with many small pieces adding to an unpredictable whole, as opposed to the masterplanned, zoned living environments favored by 20th-century rationalist planners. As the Philadelphia grid transitioned from Penn's initial low-density vision of the green country town to a more densely packed organization of rowhouses, the city became known around the world as a city of homes.[3] Philadelphia's most memorable contribution to Chicago's Columbian Exhibition of 1876—an exhibit called "The Workingman's Home"—focused on the city's housing stock, including a full-scale rowhouse on display for visitors to experience. Described in a real estate publication from the era, "the two-story dwellings of this city are, beyond all question, the best, as a system, not only owing to the single-family idea they represent, but because their cost is within the reach of all who desire to own their homes ... They are what make Philadelphia a city of homes, and command the attention of visitors from every quarter of the globe."[4]

Right

ISA
100K House
Side elevation with screenprinting
Philadelphia, 2007

Stripping the classic Philly rowhouse to its essentials, 100K House updated the rowhouse typology for contemporary lifestyles. An open interior, super insulated walls and flat, integral materials contributed to the homes' energy performance while also appealing to buyers interested in customizing their home to fit their needs. The fiber cement panels on the façade of the home pictured were silkscreened by a local artist.

If the rowhouse is the quintessential Philadelphia housing typology—with more than 400,000 rowhomes spread across nearly every neighborhood of the city—it is a primary animator of the city's street. Occupying narrow lots, typically 16 feet wide, but varying from 12 to 20 feet, rowhouses plug into the city grid with individually personalized façades opening directly out to sidewalks. Doors and windows are often ajar, and neighbors sit on stoops, creating an intimacy between home and street, private and public life. Though compact, they provide each owner a front stoop or porch, a roof—more recently often featuring a deck—and a small rear garden. It is in many ways the densest version of the classic American Dream of sovereign domestic space.

Unlike non-urban developer-driven housing, where designers and builders often cater to the whims of buyers seeking particular interior finishes, period styling or bedroom count, urban housing in Philadelphia is typically constrained by pragmatic considerations—parcel size, zoning regulations, building code and financing. In this context, the designer acts as a problem solver, working from the outside in rather than the inside out, solving for constraints while tuning the design solution to its local context. The often impossibly tight spatial parameters lead to a process of hacking the system as the architect looks for opportunities to generate new possibilities for program, form, social connectedness and flexibility.

Curating the Local

Our firm rooted in the local context of Philadelphia, has mined and reflected upon the city's physical and socio-economic past to propose new ways of living in the city. Using information and research to create an attitude about context critically shapes the architectural and urban qualities of the work which includes built projects, conversations and exhibitions. The practice is immersed in the extreme localisms of the Philadelphia context—its aging bureaucracy, outdated codes, high construction costs, soft consumer market and surprisingly extreme climate (hot, humid summers and cold, dry winters). These challenges by necessity developed into a methodology for leveraging constraints into dynamic drivers of program, form and urbanism. As the city's population grew, its zoning code was updated, and its market supported a wider array of development possibilities—creating a whole new framework of possibilities and constraints. Even as the projects have grown in scale and variety they still look to Philadelphia urban context for keys to unlock each new project's potential. Engaging with the right clients, the key concerns of neighborhoods, the supply chain for materials, the realtors that influence development decision-makers, the lawyers and investors that understand the value of design—along with on-the-ground understanding of site and place—provide the information necessary to execute a locally critical urban housing practice model.

Our urban housing practice is engaged in a process of curation of local context. Data collection is never perfect or comprehensive—yet its fragmentary or incomplete form can still enhance the ability for a project to embed itself in its local context. A curatorial approach allows us to critically filter a wide array of contextual information to develop

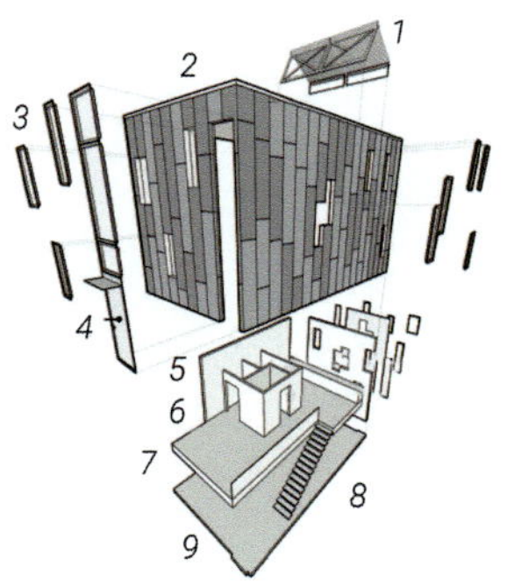

1. Solar Hot Water Panel
2. SIP Panels (R24 Walls, R40 Roof)
3. Energy Star Windows
4. Insulated Steel Door
5. ERV Recovery Ventilator
6. Dual Flush Toilet (Low Flow)
7. EnergyStar Appliances
8. Low VOC Coating
9. Radiant Floor

Above

ISA
100K House
Philadelphia, 2007

The 100K House design approach broke down the components of the rowhouse in a process akin to that of industrial design. The result was a minimal home with a thickened, high performance envelope, an open floor plan, few windows and a single interior door on the bathroom. The homes achieved LEED Platinum ratings on a tight budget, while also creating flexible living environments tuned to contemporary lifestyles.

Right

The 100K House was a contemporary take on the classic Philadelphia rowhouse model, developed in response to a wave of young people newly interested in living affordably and sustainably at the city's developing edges. The project underbuilt allowable zoning envelopes with two-story, 1,000 sqft homes that cost $100,000 to build and achieved LEED Platinum ratings.

a project direction tailored to make an impact on local experience. Playing equal parts journalist and detective, we immerse ourselves in each project's context through images, stories, interactions with existing neighbors and future residents, economic data and regulatory codes. Information is uncovered and edited into a series of cues, constraints and inspirations that produce vocabularies for engagement with stakeholders and rationales for particular design directions. This editorial, information-driven approach asks the designer to listen more than speak, and to use our agency as curators more than makers.

Like many simple, repetitive systems, the tight spatial parameters of the rowhouse make it flexible and adaptable. Although our work has grown in scale, geography and typology, we continue to design within the small lot format as a recipe for creating high density, socially connected urban housing at a reasonable cost. Across cities as diverse as Philadelphia, Boston and Chicago, we have produced designs for infill housing that are subsidized, affordable, work-force, market-rate and luxury. Included below are a series of vignettes highlighting some of our rowhouse-inspired projects and their relationship to their local context. The examples were selected to demonstrate a range of inspirations and reactions—from form, to program, to social impact.

100K House (2007)

The client for our 100K House project challenged us to design a rowhouse infill prototype that would appeal to the wave of young, environmentally conscious, first-time homebuyers resettling Philly's long-disinvested neighborhoods in the early 2000s. This context forced a reappraisal of the value of urban housing, where consumers often knew more about their sneakers, bikes and smartphones than their homes. In solving for the seemingly impossible parameters of 1,000 square feet, $100,000 construction cost and a LEED Platinum rating, we stripped the typical Philly rowhouse to its minimum.

Exterior Stair To Roof

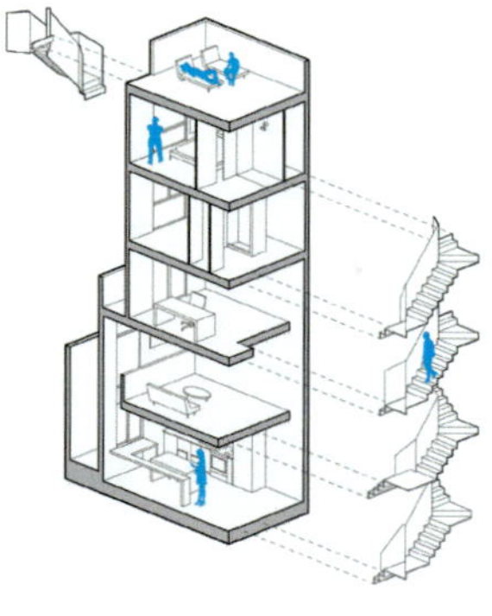

Folder Plate Steel Stair

Treating the house more like an industrial design product, we not only pursued a high level of performance on sustainability metrics—we asked questions about how homebuyers research, shop for and ultimately decide to purchase a house. If typical market-rate housing was optioned on statistics (square feet and number of beds/baths), social context (neighborhood safety and school district) and product selections (hardwood floors and granite countertops)—the 100K House needed to deliver on performance, but with a new set of embedded values. We underbuilt the zoning envelope with a two-story open loft, flat, integral finishes, a single interior door (for the one bathroom) and a super thick and well-sealed envelope. Buyers were able to customize their homes through a website that allowed them to understand the costs and benefits of the baseline 100K model versus upgrades like a solar PV array. The 100K House brand became so strong that we still receive inquiries over a decade later, though the local labor and market conditions that made it possible in the first place are a challenge to replicate in most cities today, including Philadelphia.

100K House inspired new projects in Philadelphia, led our practice to other cities and provoked other designers and developers to produce variants on the idea. In the neighborhood around the original case study house, the project catalyzed a renewed interest in one of the city's historically disinvested neighborhoods, with real estate listings including the phrase "near 100K House." This intentionally modest case study house applied positive pressure to its neighborhood market, opening the door to housing that both fit within its context and with the needs of contemporary urban dwellers.

Tiny Tower (2018)

In revitalizing neighborhoods, early waves of redevelopment tend to take advantage of sites with standard dimensions, leaving behind the odd-shaped or extra small parcels facing alley streets. Unlocking the development potential of these tiny sites is critical as Philadelphia looks to increase its supply of low-cost housing for a diverse range of lifestyles. A decade after 100K House was completed, a client came to us with one such parcel—a vacant lot measuring just 12 by 29 feet—wondering what could be done with it. Adjacent properties were being used as parking spaces for the homes facing the larger street on the next block, but the zoning code allowed an as-of-right single-family house with no associated parking on the lot. In fact, a row of classic trinities—tiny rowhouses typically less than 1,000 square feet in which single rooms stack vertically in three stories linked by a steep winding stair—had been torn down on the block prior to the sale of the parcel.

Inspired by the trinity typology, but looking to expand the traditionally tiny square footage to a more livable 1,250 square feet, the Tiny Tower project used a carefully designed vertical circulation strategy to link six levels (including basement and roofdeck) within the zoning envelope. While trinities typically buried winder stairs deep in the middle of the house to preserve full front and back windows, Tiny Tower seized the extra-shallow parcel dimension as an opportunity to place a feature stair

Left

ISA
Tiny Tower
Philadelphia, 2018

Tiny Tower was built on a lot measuring just 12 x 29 feet in Philadelphia's Brewerytown neighborhood. Inspired by the classic trinity typology, the home's stair was pushed to the front façade, connecting six living levels (including basement and roof deck) within a 38-foot-tall envelope.

Above

Folded plate metal construction minimizes the footprint of Tiny Tower's front-facing stair, making best use of the building's extra small footprint. Connecting flexible program spaces for eating, cooking, living and sleeping on each level, the stair unlocks the tiny lot for development.

constructed out of folded plate steel at the front of the house. Since the house is so vertical, the stair itself operates as a room—a light-filled procession with oblique views up to the sky and down to the sidewalk. A large window strip defines the front façade, allowing ample light in through the perforated metal stair guardrail, acting like a privacy blind for the rooms within.

The design promotes vertical living, occupying the entire footprint of the site in the required setbacks with a lower level window garden, a second level walk out terrace, and a roof deck. With a kitchen at the lower level and tucked away bathrooms on upper ones, each floor is free to define live, work and play in multiple configurations. The experience of going up and down the stair is integral to the daily life of the building, adding a sense of adventure for the occupants. Tiny Tower demonstrates how—for urban dwellers willing to trade quantity of space for quality—small in scale can feel large in amenity and experience.

XS House (2019)

As Philadelphia's market has matured, with its population rising again after decades of depopulation, its small lot structure continues to feel additional pressure to add residents, pushing housing developers and designers to increasingly consider formerly overlooked non-standard lots as well as multifamily configurations for added density. The site for XS House was a sliver of land left behind after a 1960s-era sunken thruway was constructed through the center of Philadelphia's downtown business district. The 11 by 90 foot development parcel lies between Philadelphia's Chinatown district to the south and a pair of surface arterial streets flanking the 100-foot wide Vine Street Expressway cut to the north. At the outset of the project, the site was nearly invisible as a developable lot—surfaced in asphalt, it was being used informally by the adjacent property owner as tandem surface parking for two cars. XS House packed seven units onto the site in a dramatically narrow envelope, adding urban density while preserving the street life and walkable lifestyles of typical Philadelphia fabric.

Though the XS House parcel had no height limitation, a typical high-rise building would have required an elevator and two egress stairs, which in the narrow footprint would have left very little area for units. We instead proposed a single-stair, stick-frame building which utilized mezzanine levels and projecting bays to maximize the four-story building code limit for a wood-frame structure while providing dramatic double-height interior spaces overlooking the highway. Despite being a four-story building, the 63-foot-tall section connects seven levels of occupied space within its very small footprint. Utilizing the mezzanine portion of the building code expanded four of the seven units by nearly one-third, changing them from very small studio units (380 square feet) into comfortable one-bedrooms (500 square feet) with private sleeping areas in otherwise open layouts. Two micro-lofts and a basement one-bedroom flat (650 square feet) are accessed directly from Vine Street, while the other two micro-loft apartments flank a central stair that also serves upper level two-bedroom bi-levels (850 square feet each). XS House also addresses the needs of residents and

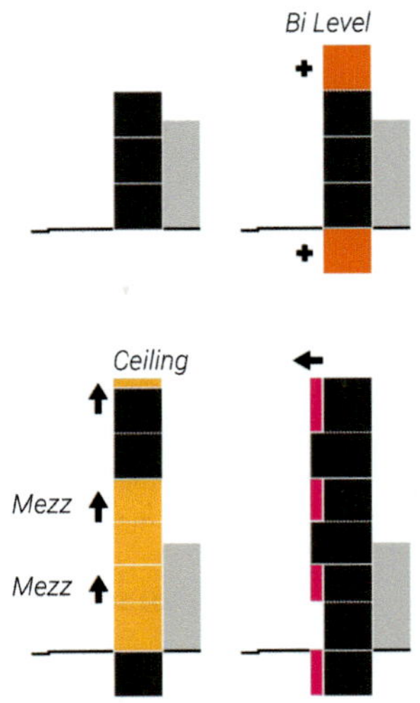

Single Stair Building Envelope

Above

ISA
XS House
Philadelphia, 2019

A single stair layout minimized circulation space allowing for additional unit density at XS House. Adding mezzanine levels to the three stories allowed under the building code transformed units from micro studios to comfortable one- and two-bedrooms flanking the central stair.

Right

The site for XS House was an urban leftover—a sliver of land 11 by 90 feet that was left behind from the construction of Philadelphia's Vine Street Expressway in the 1960s. The building's thin profile captured additional width through cantilevered projections over the sidewalk, placing seven units on a parcel formerly used for tandem parking for two cars.

visitors with mobility challenges within a walk-up building configuration—two of the project's one-bedroom micro-loft units fulfill accessibility requirements with at-grade entry points also serving to activate the street edge along Vine. The project took advantage of the city's interpretation of the parking portion of the zoning code at the time of development, which allowed zero parking spaces for multifamily residential projects with fewer than ten units. By providing no parking for residents on or off site, the building footprint, number of rentable units and interior unit area were maximized, the high cost of developing parking was eliminated and walkable lifestyles were encouraged.

Leftover lot projects often demand extra effort on behalf of both the design team and the developer, as solving them is an intricate puzzle rather than a prototypical, replicable solution. While unique in their deployment, projects like XS House promote naturally occurring market-tempered housing by unlocking the development potential of sites that historically have felt less economic pressure.

Revisiting Regionalism

Urban housing is embedded in the local information of a city—both arising from it and contributing to its ongoing formation. The pursuit of housing as a utopian, universal strategy—or alternatively as the highly individualized expression of the architect—seem equally to miss the mark. In 2007—the same year that 100K House was built—a comprehensive collection of essays on Architectural Regionalism was released, revisiting the writing of Harwell Hamilton Harris, Paul Ricoeur and Kenneth Frampton, among others. As editor Vincent Canizaro put it, the concept of Regionalism forms "a habit of thought ... a theory that supports resistance to various forms of hegemonic, universal, or otherwise standardizing structures that would diminish local differentiation."[5] In a time of renewed interest in cities as generators of authentic, locally specific experience in opposition to globalized corporate aesthetics and universalizing culture, context matters once more.

Designing urban housing with context in mind can uncover, amplify and adjust the social, economic and urban relationships among people, buildings and neighborhoods. Although architects may not control the many forces shaping housing, those sensitive to local context can find the critical pressure points where change is possible. Embracing the small batch bottom-up urbanism that many American cities like Philadelphia have been built upon can provide designers with tools for productive critical engagement. Architectural approaches that utilize existing constraints to produce novel results have the potential to make a positive impact on the social fabric of cities.

Right

ISA
XS House, exterior side view
Philadelphia, 2019

The south façade of XS House displays its narrow footprint and expanded section made possible by three-foot bay projections on floors above. A steel moment frame braces the lower two levels of the wood-frame construction.

References

1. Emily Mann, "Story of Cities #7: Philadelphia Grid Marks Birth of America's Urban Dream," *The Guardian*, March 22, 2016. https://www.theguardian.com/cities/2016/mar/22/story-of-cities-7-philadelphia-grid-pennsylvania-william-penn-america-urban-dream
2. Donna J. Rilling, *Making Houses Crafting Capitalism.* Philadelphia, PA: University of Pennsylvania Press, 2001, p. 3.
3. Philadelphia Chamber of Commerce, *The City of Philadelphia as it Appears in the Year 1894.* Philadelphia, PA: Palala Press, 2015, p. 74.
4. Ibid.
5. Vincent B. Canizaro, ed., *Architectural Regionalism: Collected Writings on Place, Identity, Modernity, and Tradition.* Hudson, NY: Princeton Architectural Press, 2007, p. 20.

Site Research: Change in New Housing Units per Year
Data Sources: Social Explorer

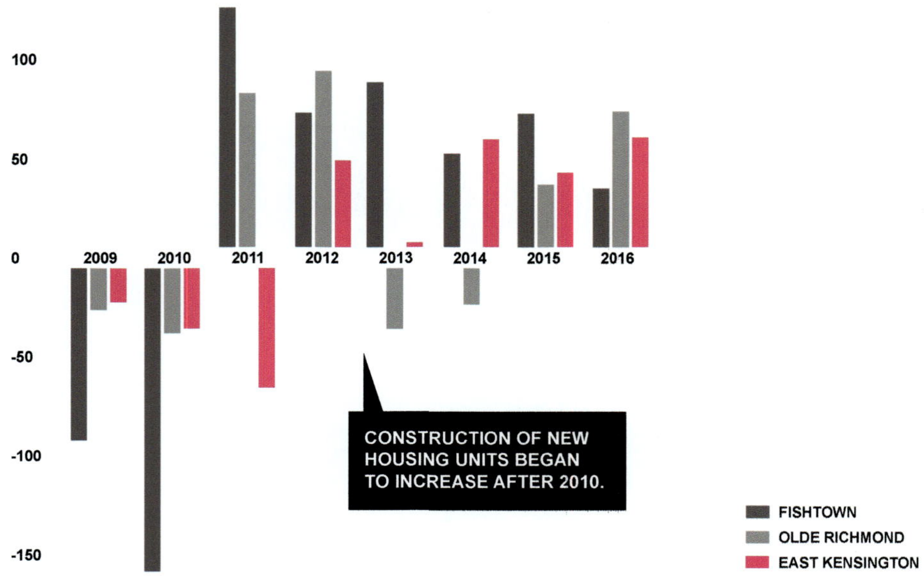

Site Research: Change in Family Income per Year
Data Sources: Social Explorer

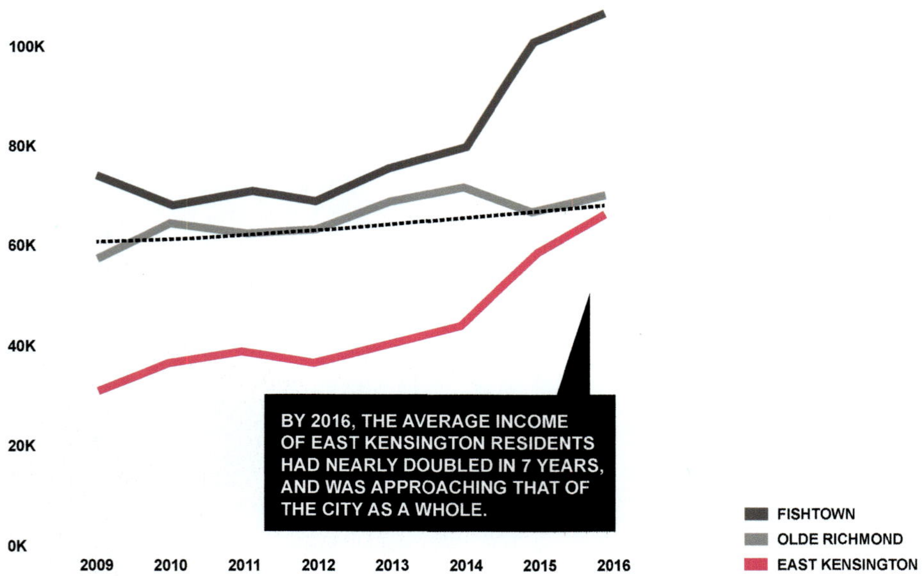

ADAPTIVE MISUSE

Brian Phillips

During the early 20th century, Philadelphia was known as the Workshop to the World, with an industrial might of epic proportions. At its height, the city's Kensington neighborhood produced more textiles than any other city in the world. The scale of this production made its mark on the city, with millions of square feet of factory buildings constructed throughout North Philadelphia. Many of these larger centers of production became organizers of urban fabric as housing, taverns, churches and shops clustered around them, forming neighborhoods. As mid-century globalization displaced industry and suburbanization displaced people, Philadelphia's urban precincts became plagued by vacancy and economic and social distress. The urban fabric that had worked hand-in-hand with the city's industrial prowess became a source of challenges, with many large-scale buildings falling into disrepair and the surrounding residential blocks following suit.

Today, Philadelphia has an extraordinary volume of underutilized formerly industrial structures. These buildings, once dedicated to the manufacture of hats, textiles, and locomotives are now providing fascinating opportunities for adaptation. The design act of adaptation is potent as it stores cultural identity and character while also creating a canvas for old and new to negotiate fresh relationships among program, form and material. The Adaptive Misuse studio values existing structures for how they can be relevant to the present and future and create novel hybrids.

The dramatic cycle of economic and social fortunes has created a visual and experiential environment of contradictions and collisions in the city. Vacant overgrown land can be found adjacent to well-tended gardens. Brand new ground-up construction is juxtaposed against empty, dilapidated structures. Curious and bizarre material, formal and programmatic conditions abound. Students began the studio by building a catalog of local curiosities that capture the textured and dynamic conditions found in the context. Catalog relationships were mined for project inspirations.

Left

Siyi Wang
Adaptive Misuse

Brian Phillips Urban Housing Studio
with Ariel Cooke-Zamora

University of Pennsylvania
Weitzman School of Design, 2018

Infographics charting changes
in real estate values and income
through time.

Context Oddities

BLANKFACE

INFILLED WINDOWS
KEEP OUT LIGHT, AIR, VIEWS
DEACTIVATE STREETSCAPE

ODDITIES

OFF BALANCE

UNEVEN DISTRIBUTION OF WINDOWS
LIMITED ACCESS TO LIGHT
DEACTIVATED STREETSCAPE

ODDITIES

ROOFTOP UNIT

NEW INSERTION ON EXISTING BUILDING
CREATES INTERSECTING FACADE

ODDITIES

FLAMINGO

VENTING PIPES REACH OUT OF
BUILDING FACADE LIKE HEADS OF
FLAMINGOS ARRANGED IN AN ARRAY
WEIRD BUT ATTRACTIVE

ODDITIES

DRAIN FACE

ANGLED DRAINAGE CREATES
FACADE WATER PATH AS GEOMETRY
GENERATOR

ODDITIES

MAILBOX MANIFESTO

PLASTIC MAILBOX STANDS OUT FROM
TYPICAL METAL MODELS ON BLOCK
SUBURBAN IN URBAN
PLAYFUL AND PRACTICAL

ODDITIES

Above

Catalog excerpt of oddities identified in and around the project context as a generator of new vernaculars.

Right

Excerpt of context research showing examples of key findings across six themes of inquiry.

Context Research

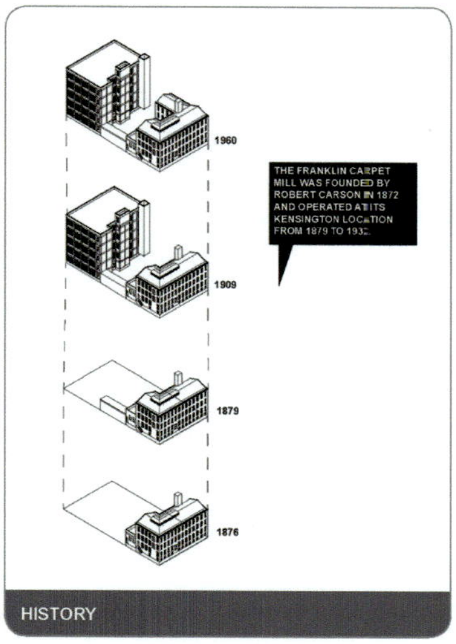

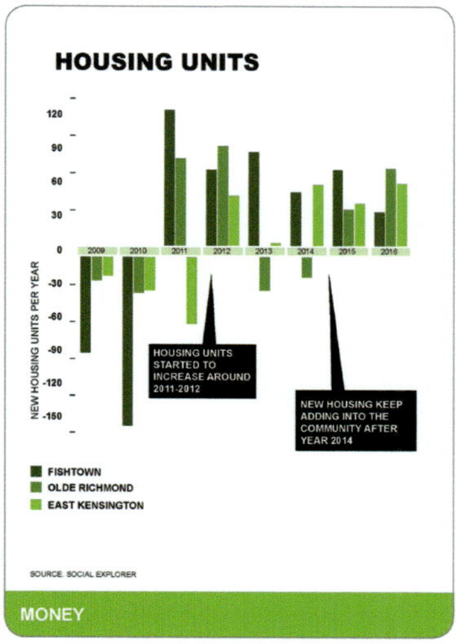

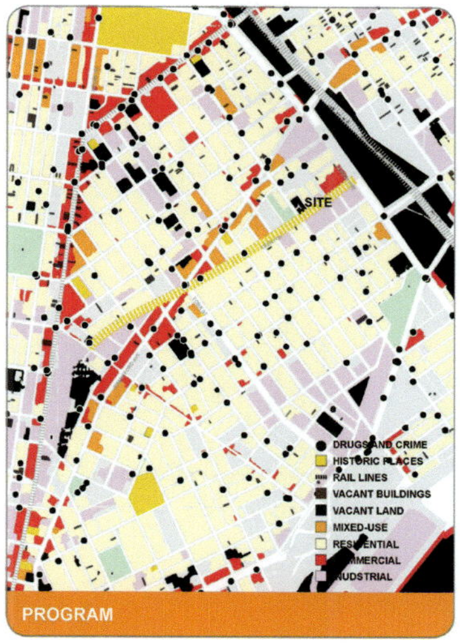

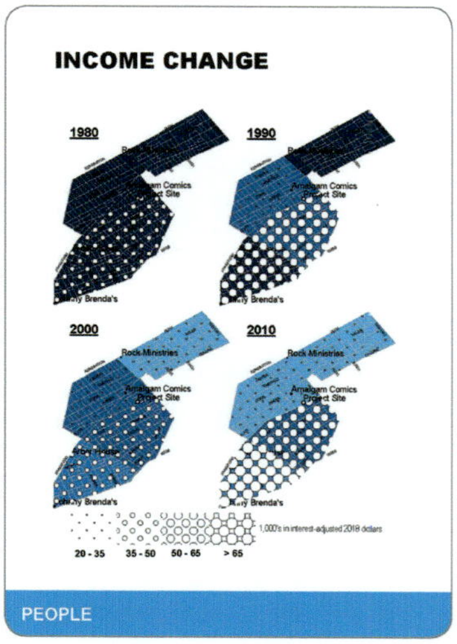

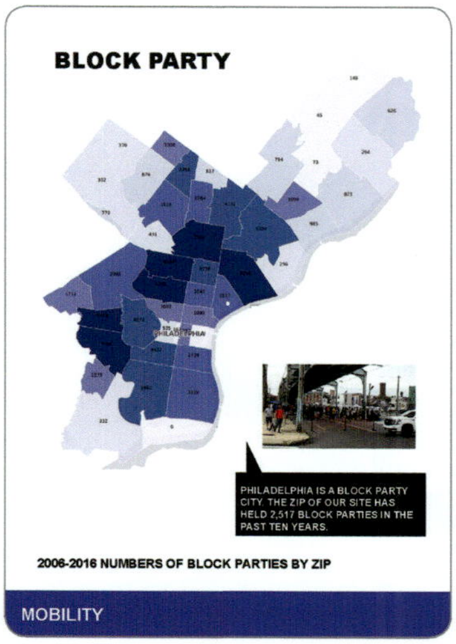

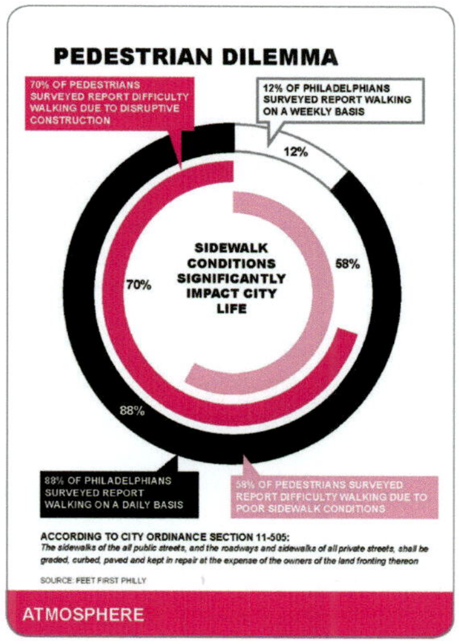

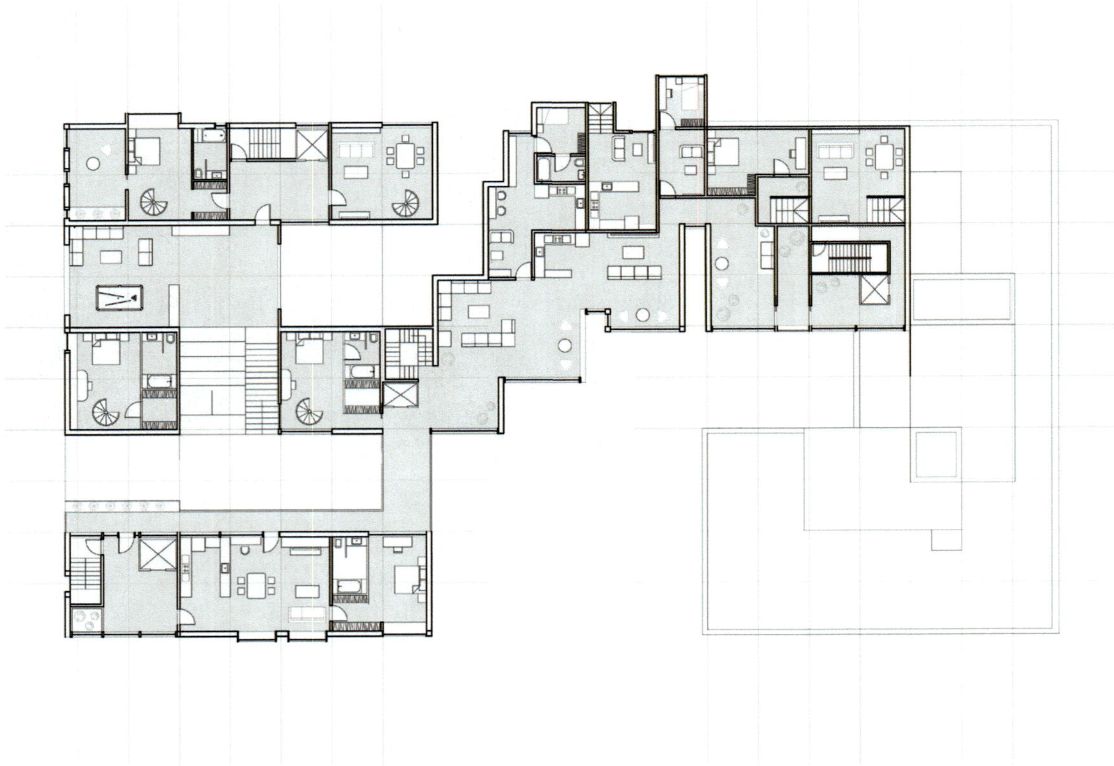

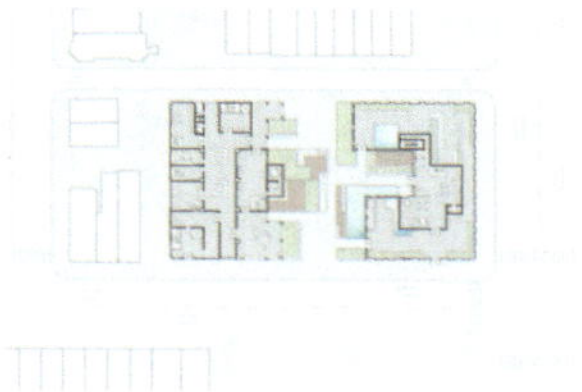

Studio projects looked to connect with deep aspects of existing conditions and elevate them as defining characteristics. Rather than simply promoting good, polite reuse, which tends to emphasize the superficial value of historical features, students were encouraged to make proposals for novel, relevant and expressive buildings that enhance the authentic urban atmosphere of their local neighborhood.

OVER THE TOP / Siyi Wang Studio Project

The Adaptive Misuse studio site was situated on the developing edge of the Fishtown–Kensington neighborhood, one of the most popular destinations in Philadelphia for nightlife and young, creative class renters. It includes two existing warehouse buildings—a larger concrete structure and a smaller heavy timber structure. OVER THE TOP was interested in literally bridging the gap between these two buildings—both physically and metaphorically.

The project took the idea of "overbuild" as a point of departure for a radical look at how urban multifamily buildings often comprise contrasting tops and bottoms (apartments over commercial uses). Above the concrete structure to the west, several floors of construction were added to take advantage of the stout concrete frame's capacity, while the heavy timber structure to the east was more carefully occupied with renovated and excavated areas. The massing and program create a gradient of higher-density overbuild focused on apartment living to the west, and a hotel and other amenities to the east—with these two programmatic zones meeting at the bridge element in the middle. The bridge affords a clear through-block connection that gives the small residential block to the north better access to primary streets, the new courtyard proposed by the project, as well as a direct link to a nearby skatepark and playground.

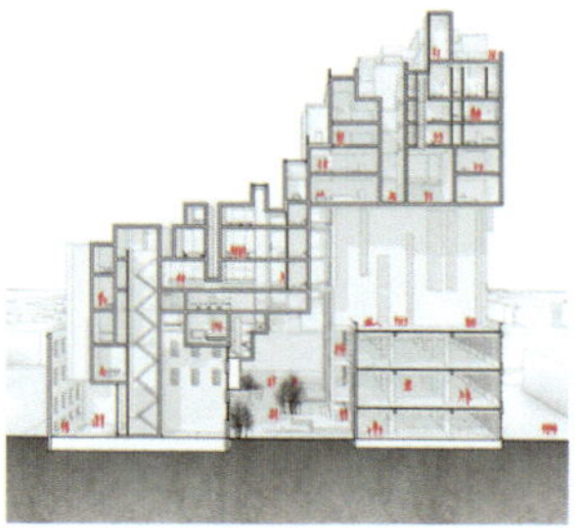

The overbuild portion takes the form of attenuated mini-towers that at times merge together, elsewhere revealing gaps and pockets that draw light deeper into the mass and create opportunities for outdoor spaces. Larger units occupy the lower floors, while smaller units are situated toward the top where the floor plates are more perforated. As the massing bridges over to the timber building—which has far less structural capacity—the existing structure is hollowed out, making way for the new construction to land on the ground within the mask of the preserved existing perimeter walls. This zone features a more eroded architectural character with gardens, open frame structures and smaller building chunks that all feel more connected to ground and invite short-stay guests.

Left

Typical residential level floor plan at middle level bridging between the two existing structures. Typical residential level floor plan at upper level.

Above

Site plan of proposal within the context of existing structures as well as the surrounding urban fabric.

Section perspective showing massing of new construction on top of and within the existing buildings.

Façades and fenestration look to draw from and expand the language of the existing buildings into something curious and novel. The plan grid and façade bays are direct extensions from the existing structural grid toward the bottom, while deviations and anomalies become more common toward the top. Windows are both punched and expansive depending on the program and relationship to light access.

OVER THE TOP takes an unapologetic view of putting old buildings back into service in aggressive and productive ways. Industrial buildings were originally constructed to carry out work—and this project looks to make good on that promise for generations to come.

1. Horizontal and Vertical Access

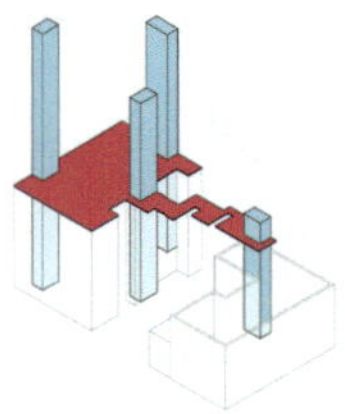

2. Housing

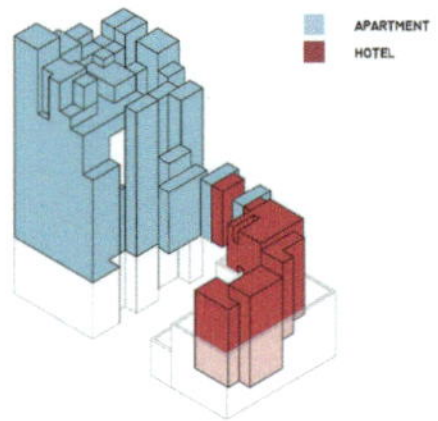

3. Existing vs New Condition

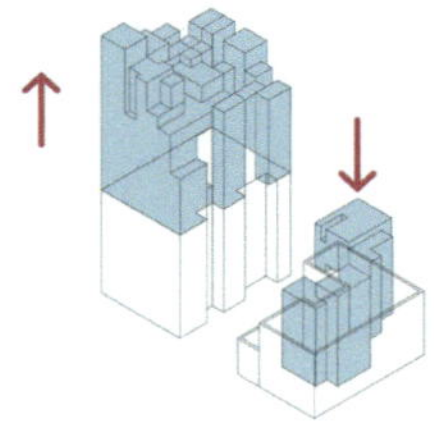

4. Unit Calibration

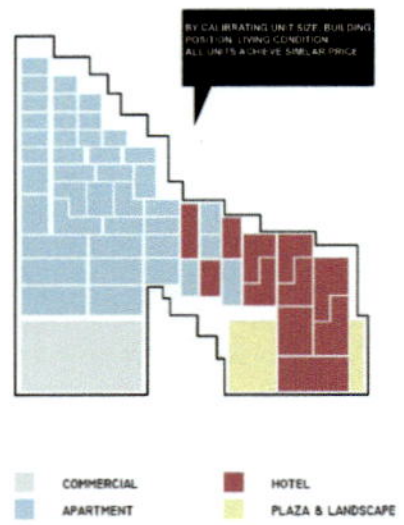

Above

Diagram concepts detailing program and massing strategies across the two contrasting existing building types.

Right Above

Rendering of new construction on top of and within the existing buildings.

Right Below

Rendering from courtyard showing new construction spanning between the two flanking existing buildings.

TECTONICS AND URBAN IDENTITY

Neil Denari | Neil M. Denari Architects

New York History

In the roughly two decades before 9/11, New York could have been described as a desultory accumulation of attempts to enliven a city whose architectural identity was bound up and defined by the inimitable skyline of Manhattan, a profile of ambition and power unrivaled anywhere in the world. New York could never be reduced to a postcard rendition of itself, yet the highly articulated world of Manhattan had, for better or for worse, always represented the entirety of the city's immense pride in its people and their civic actions. At the end of the 1970s, the city was in the final stages of chiseling its physical features, Rushmore-like, onto the face of still the newest, greatest urban agglomeration, joining the pantheon of (old) world cities such as London, Rome, and Paris. Of course, New York had come of age long before that, but in spite of the challenges during the 1970s, architecture still had the power to symbolize resilience and pride. Hugh Stubbins's chamfered icon, the Citicorp Tower, completed in 1977, was the last tall building of the era. Standing on three cores with cantilevered corners and a tuned mass damper at the top developed by brilliant structural engineer William LeMessurier, it seemed to sum up all the will and nerve on which New York had been built. Citicorp's daring tectonic balancing act was, as it would turn out, the city's penultimate event in skyline transformation.

New York fought through the recession of 1981–82, when unemployment in the city reached nearly 13%. As a guarded optimism emerged around 1984, the final act in the construction of New York's 20th-century identity was, quite possibly, the completion that year of Philip Johnson's (Johnson & Burgee) AT&T tower, a 37-story sarcophagus containing the corpse of Modernism. In its ambition to retroactively critique the apparently soulless mission of architectural abstraction, the AT&T tower was Johnson's erstwhile dagger into the heart of Miesian universality, a crime (of passion?) felt up and down Park Avenue and beyond. The tower's arrival brought new meaning to the idea of progress, ironically in the form of regression, and with it a dispiriting 20

Left

Gordon Bunshaft
SOM
Manhattan House
New York City, 1951

The most well known of the expedient, yet elegant, white brick apartment blocks in New York.

years in which New York architects would only subsist off the paltry offerings from a risk-averse real estate market, while the rolled up entrance carpets of culture signified its disinterest in architectural speculation.

Fallow

A few years went by and while new towers were added, the lion's share of architects in the city were still left to search for commissions outside New York. For most of those who could build in the local milieu, exposed slab edges were the best they could do, an expression not of honest modern construction (à la Louis Kahn) but of hands tied by low budgets. Buildings for a mid- to upper-level market had begun to look even more expedient than the clean brick boxes of the 1950s, a strange sublimation of New York's proud history of architectural ambition. Of course, this wasn't the fault of architects, regardless of their ideologies. It was simply a time period in which New York's reserve of money, power, and ideas were nearing a point of depletion. What city has not experienced this, especially those from whom much is expected?

A New City

After a period of broad-based prosperity under the Clinton Administration, the millennium turned and New York was six years into the Giuliani regime. The city found itself a safer and more economically stable environment, the product of a four-year economic boom—the strongest in four decades. Fueled by Wall Street and an economy that had diversified well beyond the financial sector into other rising markets such as publishing, advertising, and motion pictures, this era sponsored a change that had some wondering what had happened, amongst all the improvements, to urbanism for the masses. Safe streets meant more tourism and higher rents in the city, sending locals to New Jersey and the outer boroughs to find affordable housing, a diaspora loaded with political and social implications. Wages in the city soared in this buoyant climate, an element within a larger set of phenomena that irrevocably changed the identity of Manhattan. As land values increased, it became clear that in the world of anything goes, at least in the realm of real estate speculation, developers would issue demands to architects that foreshadowed the expectations of a new design culture in the city.

Architecture Again

In 1969, Richard Meier transformed a Bell Telephone Laboratory into the Westbeth Artists' Housing just a few blocks north of where, in 1999, he was commissioned to design two new 16-story glass apartment towers. Thirty years had elapsed between serious New York projects for Meier (a Pritzker Prize winner), who, despite this, had been prolific beyond his backyard. Commonly referred to as the project that started the new wave, the Perry Street towers were the direct manifestation of faith not only in the economy and the flow of wealth into the city, but also in architecture as a civic statement, albeit within the apparatus of luxury housing.

Above

Philip Johnson,
Johnson & Burgee
AT&T Headquarters model, 1979

Johnson seized the Post Modern moment by enlarging a Chippendale hutch to epic proportions.

Right

Richard Meier & Partners
173/176 Perry Street and
165 Charles Street
New York City, 2002 and 2004

These projects signaled an awakened interest in architectural design after 9/11.

Neil M. Denari Architects
HL23
New York City, 2012

View looking north above the High Line.

THE HALF KING

Massive Loss

Then, in 2001, the ultimate indignity came: the massive, indescribable, and immeasurable loss of life, the destruction of twin abstract icons at the foot of Manhattan, and economic havoc wreaked on a city with a mission to build up. The stock market closed for four days and, for some time, fear and uncertainty gripped the city while the void left by the towers created nothing but infinite sadness. Forever dismissed as all bulk and no style, the World Trade Center towers had instantly become, in their absence, things of beauty and lost references for New York's position at the top of the global financial and cultural structure. With mourning though came a sense of urgency, even defiance, in the desire to restore not only a sense of urban security and calm but also the economic vitality the city had worked so hard to establish prior to 9/11.

Architecture Again, Again

By 2005, the year HL23 began, the market for condominium design in New York had expanded to epic proportions. This avalanche of design was largely welcomed in a city haunted by the economic aftereffects of 9/11 which had further exacerbated an existing construction dry spell and architectural aridity. But beyond shaping a new urban profile for the city, the public profile of architecture itself underwent dramatic revision. Indeed, it was impossible to avoid the media presence of design-conscious condos as they metastasized across the internet, magazines, and even television. And while celebrated new cultural institutions (the Morgan Library and New Museum for example) were finally constructed in this hot global economy, they were outweighed by their residential counterparts whose mass media and market fervor acquired an unprecedented public presence. In essence, the private domain—both the program of living and the economics of development—had been transposed into the public sphere. Amid this volatility, HL23 landed on a fault line of shifting urban plates. In the heady conditions in New York at the time, precision and talent could deliver value, but hubris could produce a regrettable ending.

Background Becomes Foreground

Although cities contain stable monuments such as memorial plazas, parks, cultural institutions, etc., it is the sustained flux of the masses that makes cities thrive. The inert mass of architecture then, stands as a literal set of brick walls that, like a particle accelerator, contains the energies and flows of bodies and, more virtually, the flows of capital and politics. Moreover, in an urban context, all buildings—at least at the level of the façade—acquire a public persona, especially those buildings that differentiate themselves through form or material. HL23, regardless of its private program, was immediately annexed into public space because of its site—23rd Street at the High Line—catalyzing and contributing to a timely discourse on urban sustainability in New York.

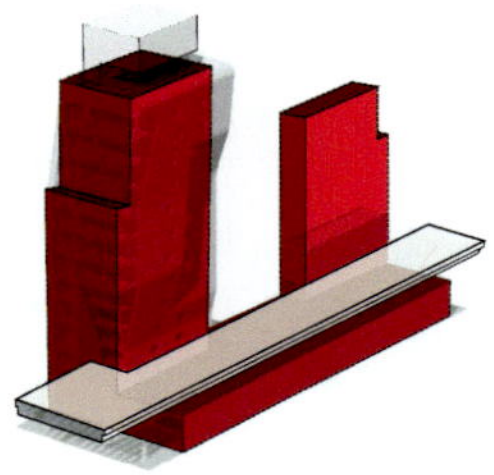

Maximum Building Envelope

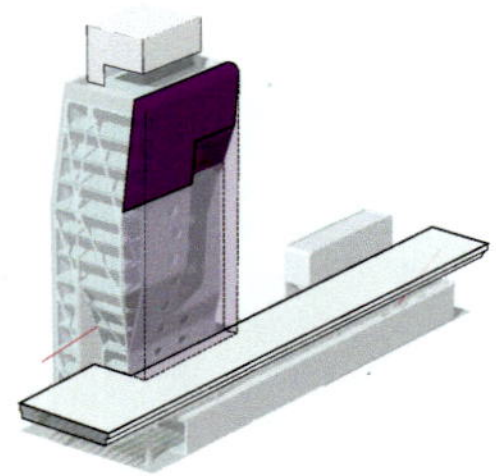

Modifications to Yards and Setbacks

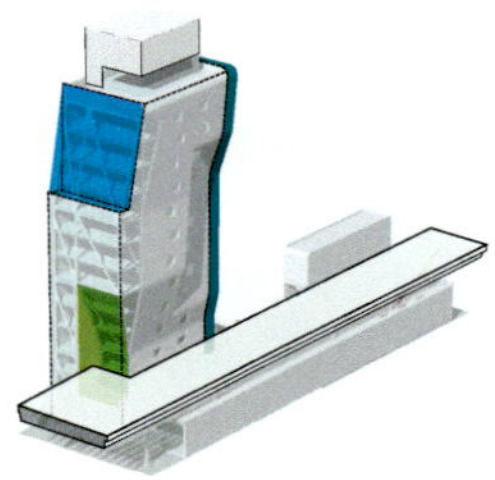

Modifications to Yards and Setbacks

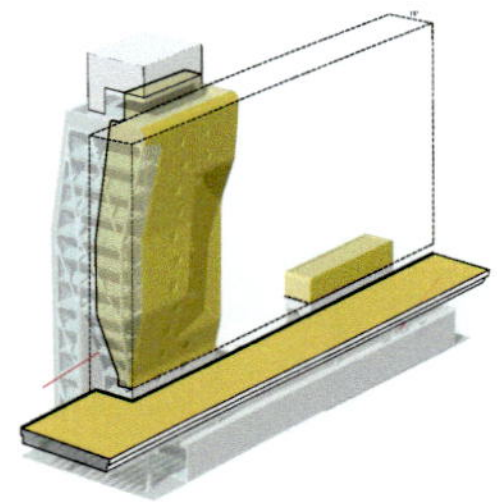

High Line Frontage

Above

Neil M. Denari Architects
HL23
New York City, 2012

Zoning waiver diagrams.

Right

View of north façade as it migrates out over the High Line.

Urban Alchemy

With the High Line, a new urban park appeared in New York. Plans to reclaim the West Side elevated rail tracks caused an unprecedented chorus of political and emotional voices to call for the long-neglected piece of urban flotsam to be converted into a linear garden. For decades a dead-tech hulk, a reminder of New York's stunning growth and subsequent antiquation of much of its infrastructure, the High Line was to become a 20-block-long nature walk, presenting the city around it as a kind of living diorama of architectural specimens. Along with the flora planted in the High Line's elegantly designed concrete plank system, the world just beyond its guardrails showcases a diverse urban genera: 1960s social housing slabs, billboards, car parks, distant river views, and already near-famous buildings.

Over the course of its life, from its commission in March 2005 to its completion in the first quarter of 2012, HL23 maintained a constant presence in the public sphere. The project emerged through careful introspection and debate in the New York City Planning Commission. Seven zoning waivers were granted to developer Alf Naman to construct a project that would challenge the best laid plans of the Special West Chelsea District's sensitive zoning codes. Given a site that was considered unbuildable in previous eras of development—a sliver of land next to an infrastructural relic—HL23 began and eventually ended as a nonconformist project: a building whose restive massing defies zoning because of client demand, not out of premeditated architectural ambition. It was clear, however, that even without the permissive nature of the commission, the pressures of the building's context would force a formally unique solution. 23rd Street provides the midpoint access to the High Line, and serves as a major east–west artery in Manhattan, so HL23's immediate proximity to the horizontal flow of people, cars, and (formerly) goods created the need for its vertical Z-axis expression at Chelsea's most important urban cruciform.

515
HL23

Dictated more by the cultural and urban contingencies of the site than by the zoning envelope given in the Special West Chelsea Plan, HL23's spatial and material logic was imbued with speculation at every turn and by everyone involved.

The building, it seemed, would be charged with monumentality even though it was a relatively small, private program, and thus it would have to negotiate between standing out and fitting in. Although HL23's unconventional site provided a combustible array of restrictions and freedoms, even more straightforward sites in the vicinity had equally eccentric buildings placed on them. In fact, most of the new work that has emerged in West Chelsea and the West Village is often thought to be a collection of monuments: a Roman Forum for art and architecture created not by the hand of a single architect but by an array of offices looking to change the face of civic space through individual buildings. It seemed that if the irrational exuberance of New York's post-9/11 building frenzy were to become opportunity rather than mere opportunism, the work around the High Line would ultimately define the era's practices—not those of architectural offices but rather the customs and rituals of investing and building—and surely the media glare would be most blinding there. In the frenetic pace to develop ideas, it would be necessary to find time to reflect on the urban environment and consider the ways in which design—possibly of a spectacular form—could become something more than an instant monument reliant on nonconformity and aesthetic difference. This would set the critical agenda for the balance of the decade and perhaps the start of the next. No project stood closer to that perilous agenda than HL23.

Beyond Zoning

HL23 architecture is a volatile mix of unstable elements, especially the ones that form the initial conditions under which design takes place. HL23 was a mixture of pressure and opportunity. The problem was how to distinguish between the two. With the demand placed on us to produce a building that would volumetrically push beyond the special West Chelsea Zoning envelope, the questions arose as to how high, how wide, and how deep the project would become. How would we know when a response to the demand would produce diminishing returns, either in terms of acceptability to the city, floor area for our client, and formal properties for us? The physical, social, political, and economic forces operating on the project seemed conceptually clear but they were not defined metrically. Everything would have to be determined in a process of approximation. In a complex game of air-rights transfers and lot rezoning, HL23's as-of-right zoning would not allow maximum FAR to be built on the site, a deal-breaker for most developers. Most intrusive and therefore most instrumental in making the site difficult to build on was at the same time its most powerful asset, its direct proximity to the High Line. Zoning called for a 15-foot setback in building mass starting at 25 feet above grade that equaled a loss of 37.5% of the possible built volume. While this setback, essentially the donation of private land to the public good, would greatly benefit the High Line's environmental impact, it was a challenge for real estate investors seeking to build on New York's newest and most provocative park space.

Left

Neil M. Denari Architects
HL23
New York City, 2012

View of 23rd Street lobby with art installation by Joseph Kosuth.

Conditioned Form

For every moment of constriction in the site, a response was found within one of two methods of design: move the bounding envelope to a point of agreement with zoning or pushback against the limits. All three exposed sides of the building required zoning variances that ultimately allowed the project to avoid the stacked or stepped massing inherent in New York Zoning laws. On the West 23rd Street façade, sloping surfaces define the skyplane setback line on the top four floors while floors two through six have a split profile caused by the intrusion of the High Line spur. The sloping facets of the façade allow for a more crystalline or prismatic building form, a result that produces a higher degree of difference between it and the context. The project then assumes a high level of fitness to the site (the High Line) and a moderate to high level of resistance to the default massing and materiality of its context. Extensive studies were carried out to determine the potential negative effects of added volume (bulk). The site's exposure to daylight as well as its location on the north side of the park mitigated deepened shadow lines.

The Problem of the Façade

Façades are so vulnerable these days. They bear many burdens, not only of thermal enclosure, but also of the type that are meant to disclose political and cultural intent. As architects, they awaken our senses when done beautifully and incite pathos or even anger when poorly designed. Not even a well-detailed, technically resolved façade can escape the scrutiny of expert critics, the public, other architects, and of course, the owners. We all ask not only of our own work, but that of others: Why that material? Why this pattern? Is there anything behind the façade?

Today, it is never enough to simply say that the envelope is now the site of the most extreme forms of experimentation and novelty in construction as a way to legitimize the expenditure of so much energy on one aspect of architecture. Yet that very same claim can gain currency when it's put into the context of the city. All building façades are interfaces at some level—surfaces to be visually, physically, and psychologically navigated. Whether they are designed from the outside in (as may be the case with more generic programs), inside out (specific lighting or vision requirements for instance), or a combination of both, the envelope speaks to a range of logics and freedoms that architects must negotiate in order to find intent. Indeed, façades are caught in a world of ambivalence, necessary devices for both resource management (sustainability) and self-expression, but also instruments of urban identity and development mandates (profitability). HL23 was sponsored by a market that had come to understand the value of an envelope that would produce an image. To design a façade *with intent* in a climate of ambivalence is to accept the labor that it must perform in order to attain value. It must be highly crafted; it must have internal logic; it must say something to the city; it should, when a site calls for it, produce difference; and it must be coherent within its own language.

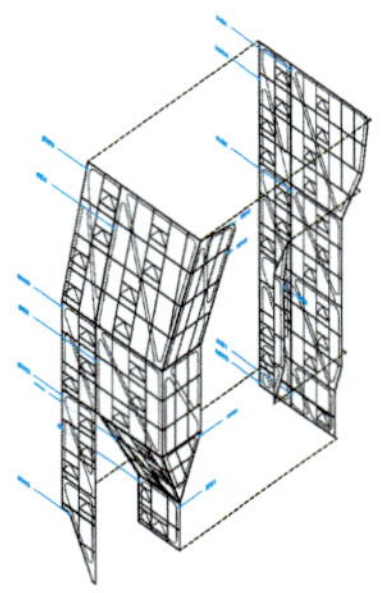

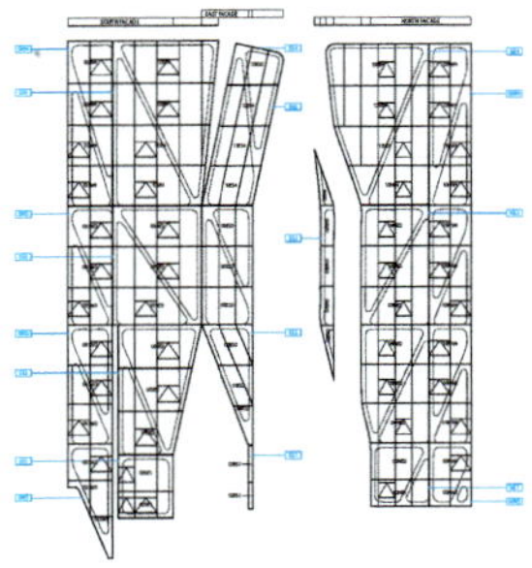

Above

Neil M. Denari Architects
HL23
New York City, 2012

Glazing megapanel atlas.

Right

Detailed wall section at curved terrace parapet.

Section Detail at Roof and East Mega-Panel

01 MC-2 Cover
02 MC-2 Cover Supoort
03 MC-5 Coping Cover
04 Aluminum Coping
05 (2x) 3/4" P.T. Plywood
06 MC-5 75mm Support System
07 Vaporshield Membrane
08 MC 2 System
09 3" Thermafiber Insulation
10 MC-2 Support Vertical Hat Channel
11 Insulated Glass Unit
12 Henry Blue-Skin S.A.
13 2 x 5/8" GlasRoc
14 Waterproof Sheeting
15 Insulation
16 Light System
17 Drain Flashing
18 Electrical Conduit Ø1"
19 Fastened Terminator Bar with Sealant
20 Paver
21 Cont. 6" X 1" X 1/4" Erection Angle
22 Field Framing
23 Aluminum Flashing
24 Bead-Blasted Stainless Steel
25 4" Panel Frame
26 2 X 5/8" GlasRoc
27 Purlin
28 3 1/2" Unfaced Membrane installed with Primer
29 3 1/2" Unfaced CW40 Thermafiber Insulation
30 Henry Blueskin Membrane installed with Primer
31 Flashing Membrane
32 Roof Topping Slope to Drain
33 Smoke Sealant
34 Firestop 4" Mineral Wool
35 3" 18 GA. Composite Metal Deck with 4" Normal Weight Concrete
36 4" LGM Panel Frame TYP. 4"-Stud 16 GA. Stud @ 16 O.C.
37 Primary Structural Steel with Cementitious Fireproofing
38 Hardwood Floow with 2 X 1/2" Layer of Plywood Underlayment and 1/4" Acoustical Insulation
39 3" 18 GA. Composite Metal Deck with 3" Normal Weight Concrete
40 Curtain Wall Mega-Panel Stud-Frame with 4" 16 GA. Stud (16" O.C.) 2 X 5/8" Layer of Exterior Grad Gypsum Board, Non-Permeable Air/Vapor/Rain Barrier Membrane and 3 1/2" Thermal Insulation Held by 4" Aluminum Stick Pin (Five Pins per 24" X 48" Piece of Insulation)
41 Rain Screen System with 12' Long Stamped Stainless Steel Panels, 3" Air Space, Panels Supported on Purlin and Hat Channel
42 Backer Rod and Sealant
43 4 GA. Continous Erection Angle Anchored to Slab
44 Mold-Resistant Drywall with 1 5/8" Steel Stud Framing and Vertical Slip Connection
45 4" Mineral Wool Firestop and Smoke Sealant

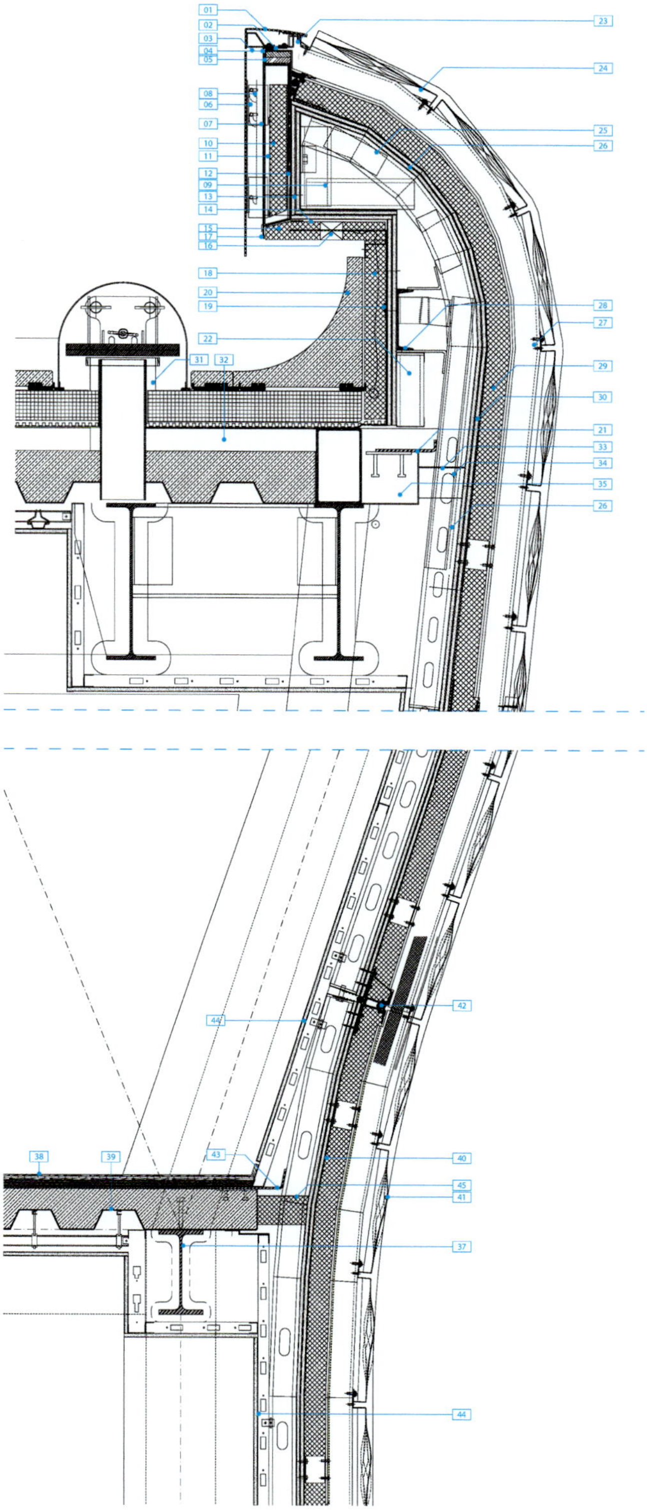

Epilogue 2020

Every building in an urban environment, by the nature of its proximity to the public sphere, is called upon to not only fill in zoning envelopes with approved programs, i.e., to behave based upon collective planning ambitions and guidelines, but also to participate in the discourse of urbanity. The program of housing, in particular, mediates most powerfully between the public and private realms of life and as such plays a unique role in this discourse. As housing fills the spatial matrix of the city, which in turn makes the concept of civitas possible, it produces urban identity, even in its most macroscopic form. Here, for example, we think of Paris, and its continuously extruded six-story grain, punctuated by urban voids and monumental solids. In Manhattan, with its striations and irregularities of development across time so easily read neighborhood by neighborhood, housing has always defined economies as much as it has expressed any architectural ambition. Moreover, housing in America represents most clearly the tense relationship between market logics and whatever largesse exists in the process of helping to build urban environments on the part of real estate speculators. But whether for the inhabitant, for the neighbor, or the passerby, housing should always seek, within the limits and logics of its conditions, to be sublime, indeed regardless of its fit and finish. HL23's aspirations toward that end were largely activated by its unique site, which in addition to its physical context, was loaded with invisible forces such as air-rights transfers, politics, and public opinion. In other words, it was a perfect site and over the course of its brief existence in the consciousness of New Yorkers, it has become a marker, possibly even an icon (but that's for culture to decide), of a city willing to speak sharply and confidently after both 9/11 and the recession of 2008. While the project provides luxury accomodations for its inhabitants, the least it otherwise could do was become a hospitable sort of public object in its site, working with the peculiarities presented.

Above

Neil M. Denari Architects
HL23
New York City, 2012

View of folded south façade from 23rd Street.

Right

View of north and east facades from London Terrace.

SOLAR ENERGY

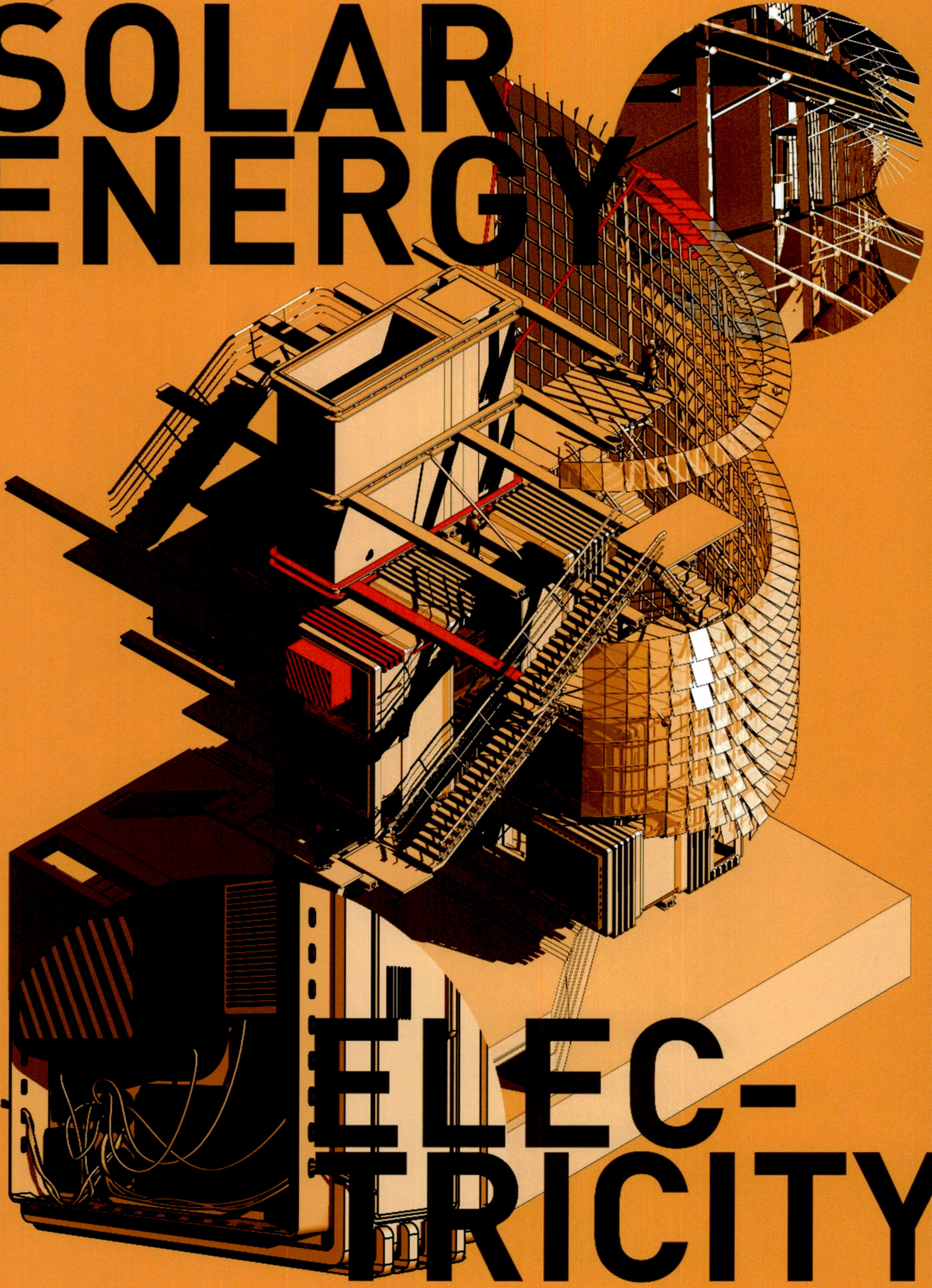

ELEC-TRICITY

TRANS-URBAN DWELLING

Scott Erdy

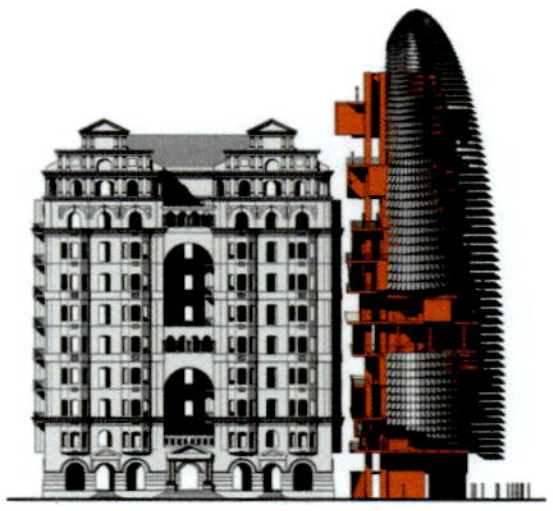

Left

Yuheng Ouyang
Trans-Urban Dwelling

Scott Erdy Urban Housing Studio with Ruo Wang

University of Pennsylvania Weitzman School of Design, 2015

The propaganda poster presents a unique summary that focuses on the project thesis. Here, the transformational aspect of the project—turning sun into electricity—is done through a surface of articulating solar panels.

Above

The new TRANS-URBAN DWELLING (shown on the right) has a highly articulated form based on the expression of equality, ecology, and utility. The historical Divine Lorraine building (left) has a highly articulated surface based on a superficial expression of wealth.

The Divine Lorraine has long been a Philadelphia icon. It represented a city that ebbed and flowed based on the economic fortunes of the country and the neighborhood. Designed by architect Willis G. Hale and constructed between 1892 and 1894, the building originally functioned as luxury apartments, housing some of Philadelphia's most wealthy elite. The Lorraine was one of the most luxurious and best preserved late 19th-century apartment houses in Philadelphia.

Both the location of the building and the architecture reflect the changes that were occurring rapidly in the city of Philadelphia and in the country at the time. North Philadelphia of the 1880s attracted many of the city's nouveau-riche, who became wealthy as a result of the industrial revolution. The Lorraine was a place of luxury, providing apartments with new amenities such as a central kitchen from which meals were delivered to residents, a concierge staff and electricity.

In 1948, the building was sold to Father Divine (Reverend Major Jealous Divine), who was the leader of the International Peace Mission movement and preached a gospel of self-help, abstinence, economic independence and social equality. The Divine Lorraine was the first hotel in the nation to be fully racially integrated and was open to all men and women, regardless of their religion, who were willing to follow the rules of the movement. Believing that all are equal in the sight of God, Father Divine was involved in many social welfare activities as well, and transformed several parts of the building for public use. The 10th-floor auditorium was converted to a place of worship and the ground floor became a public dining room where persons from the community were able to purchase low-cost meals.

The hotel was abandoned in 1999 and deteriorated quickly. It became a preferred spot for the homeless and a canvas for the local graffiti scene. Over the years, ownership changed multiple times and was marked by failed redevelopment attempts and the indiscriminate "quarrying" of its interior finishes and appointments.

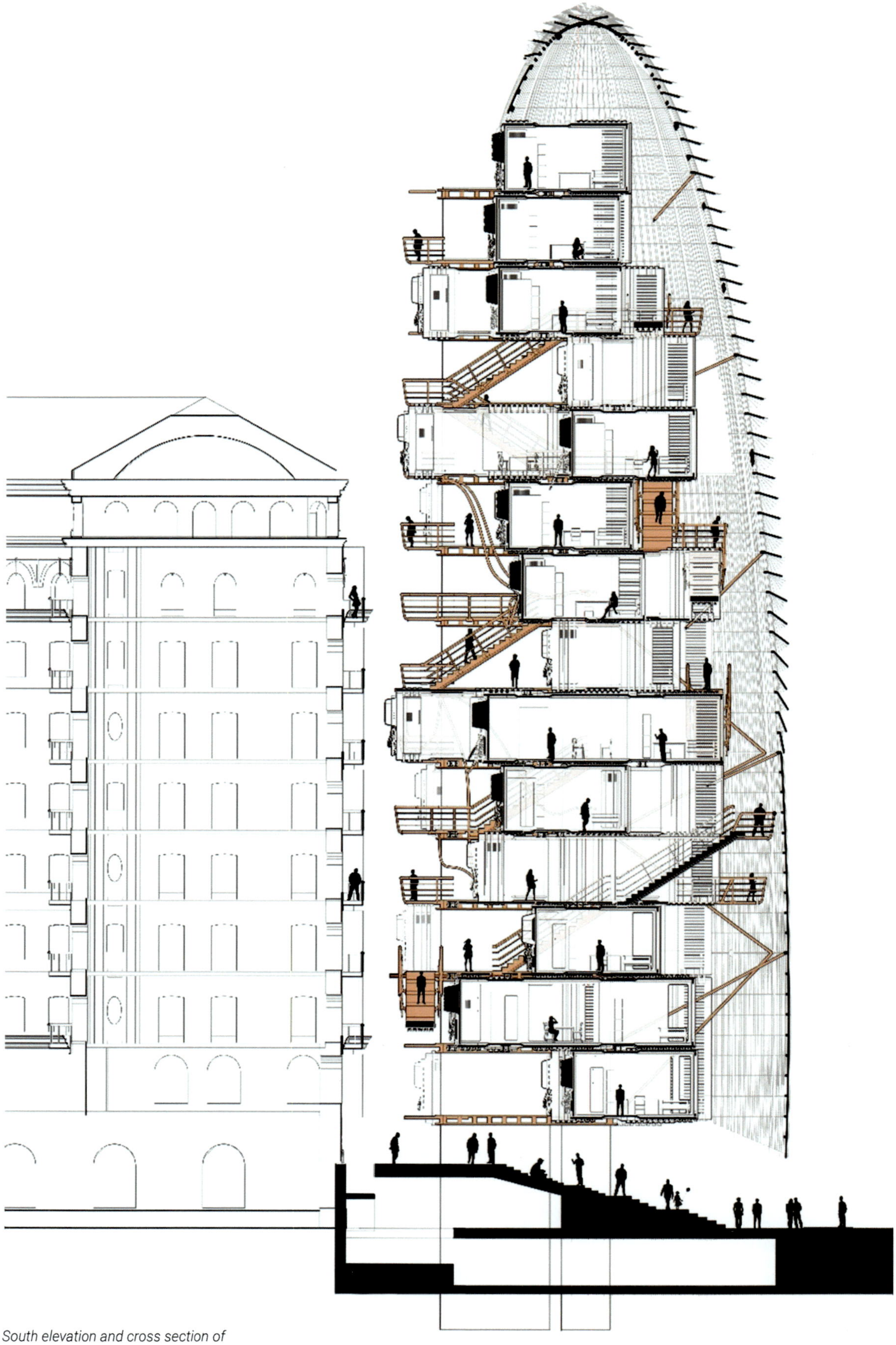

South elevation and cross section of the building illustrates the performative nature of the articulating solar enclosure and the housing. The interstitial space serves the community through various group and collaborative functions.

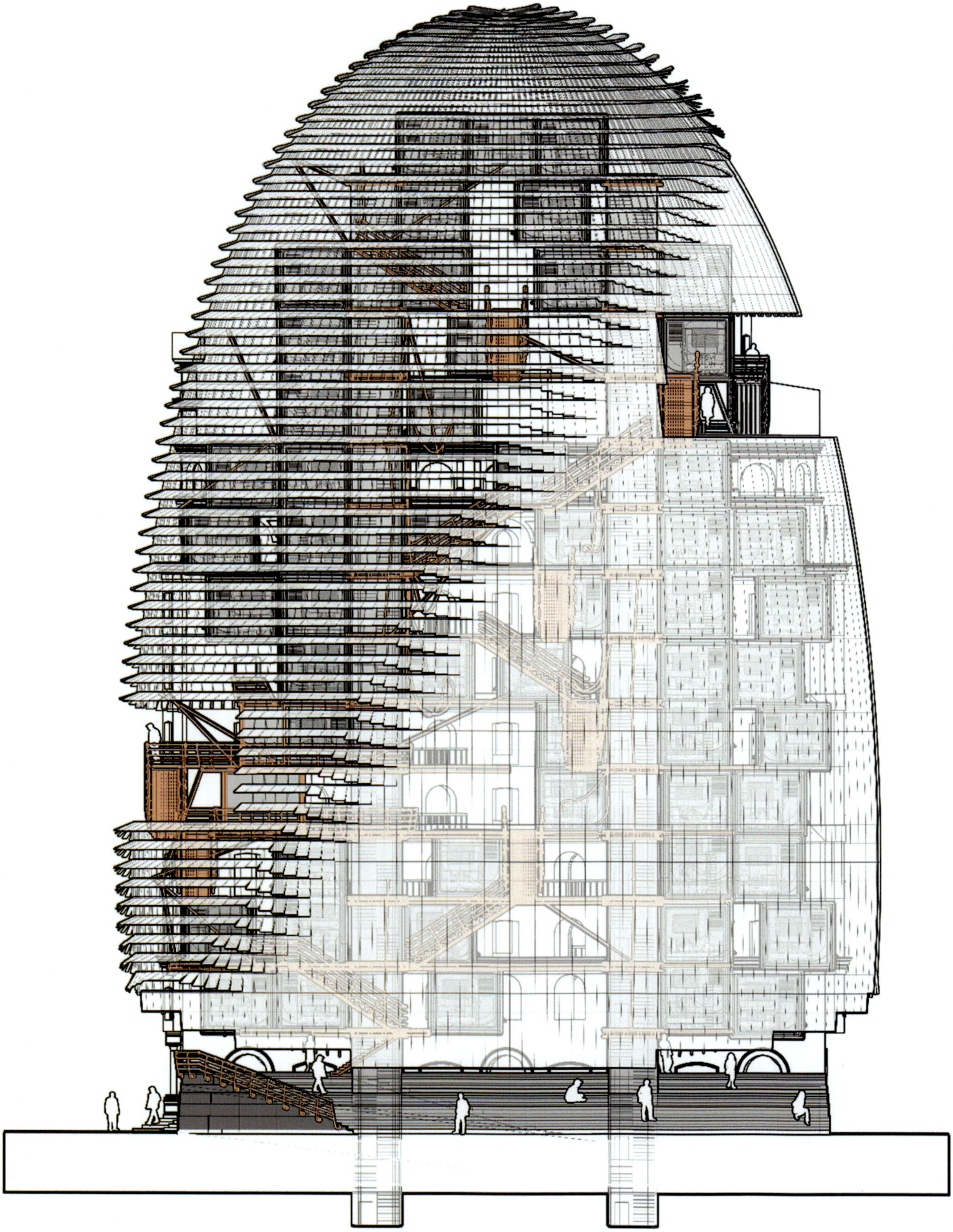

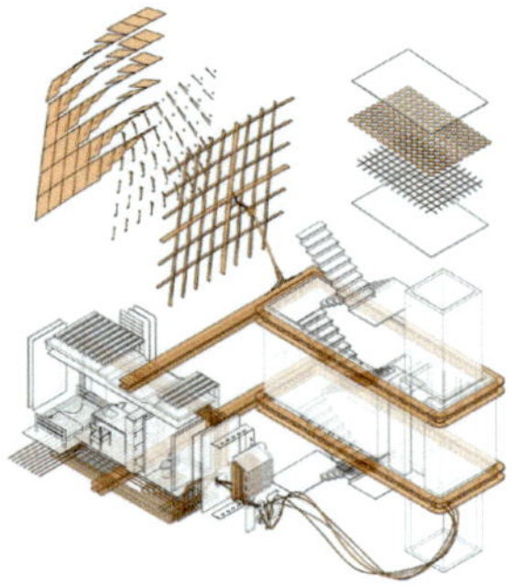

In 2012 self-aware developer Eric Blumenfeld was the only bidder at the city's monthly Sheriff's sale, and he has since renovated the building to again be luxury apartments. The historical significance of the building's architecture and its Civil Rights history required a thoughtful renovation to return it to its original appearance. The iconic rooftop "Divine Lorraine Hotel" neon sign was also stipulated to be restored and was relit in 2016 for the first time in 40 years. The iconic nature of the neon sign is symbolic for the project. The original Victorian building with its highly articulated and backward-looking façade was ironically the most advanced building of its time in Philadelphia. At ten stories and with its modern amenities (including electricity) it well represented its nouveau-riche inhabitants who capitalized on the technological advances of the industrial revolution. The building's throwback façade gave these industrialists instant credibility among Philadelphia's old-money crowd. Stretching to ten stories gave it memorability similar to David Byrne's "large suit," based on Japanese Noh Theater. When Father Divine erected the "Divine Lorraine" hotel sign, he redirected its history in Philadelphia lore. His large illuminated sign announced to all Philadelphians his stand on racial fairness and equality.

Directly south of the Divine Lorraine, the site for the project is able to capitalize on its orientation to maximize solar collection and views to the city. The mission of the *Trans-Urban Dwelling* is to empower persons to break the cycle of homelessness and poverty, to address structural causes of poverty, and to enable individuals to attain their fullest potential as members of the broader society. In the spirit of Father Divine, the program includes neighborhood-based affordable housing, economic development, and environmental enhancement programs, and provides access to employment opportunities, adult and youth education, and health care.

Yuheng's propaganda poster outlines his commitment to sustainable energy, and his focus on electricity is no coincidence. His expressive articulation of both the living units and the solar collection system are a stark contrast to the original building's gilded Victorian façade and the electricity it consumed, created by coal-burning power plants. The static and heavy, decorative façade of the original is contrasted by a new structure with lightweight tectonics that are derived from articulating solar panels configured to maximize their orientation to the sun. This smooth surface is in constant motion throughout the day as each hinged panel in the array tilts up to meet the sun as it arcs across the sky. The ovate form increases the efficiency of the panels' south facing wall from 302,156 kWh/year to 390,719 kWh/year (a 30% increase) and the articulating of the panels brings the yield to 521,610 kWh per year, representing another 33% improvement.

The nouveau-riche industrialists who inhabited the Lorraine Hotel at the end of the 19th century have now been replaced by a "woke" generation of wealth who yearn to atone for their place in history, without sacrificing their material comforts. Yuheng's confrontational positioning of the affordable apartments allow the south-facing elites to enjoy the sunlight and views filtered by the transitional housing units, or simply close their blinds.

Left Top

Views from the individual units are constantly changing based on the position of the solar panels. During summer, the panels are projected more horizontally to optimize their angle to the sun while providing greater ventilation. During winter, when the sun is lower in the sky, the panels are in the downward position and shield the units from the wind.

Left Bottom

The circulation among the residents provides various opportunities for views and interaction. Natural lighting to the interior spaces is solely dependent of the position of the sun.

Above

The LIVING MODEL is supported by a visible electrical armature that collects, stores and distributes energy from the sun. Each component is an overt expression of its function, amplifying its life-giving purpose and giving legibility to its form.

The articulation of the individual building components objectify their function to an extent that borders on contemporary mannerism. Like Hawksmoor's version of Wren, the architecture exaggerates the individual elements of domesticity and warns of a potentially dystopic future if our stewardship of the earth doesn't change. The individual housing modules are staggered in plan and section, allowing them to become a series of terraces where guests can socialize—all within view of the tenants of the Lorraine Hotel.

The transitional units, completely powered by the sun, enjoy a view of the city through a scrim of solar panels that open as the panels orient for maximum efficiency. The interstitial space, bounded to the south by the arc of the array, gives the units a sense of community that makes visible the natural phenomenon of the sun's path throughout the day.

The proximity of Yuheng's proposal relative to the Divine Lorraine Hotel forces an awareness of homelessness, poverty, and sustainability. The industrial revolution represented the pinnacle of the harvest and exploitation of the earth's resources for the benefit of a few. The historical introduction of electricity into the original building and its inherent luxury was fueled by the spoils of young affluent industrialists who gained their wealth through gross exploitation of people and the environment.

The "Divine Lorraine Hotel" sign, later erected by Father Divine, was in stark contrast to the Victorian gilded ornament of the original building, became an icon in Philadelphia and represents a hopeful future of racial and economic equality. The sign remained dark for more than 40 years before it was relit by the developer in the hope that it would again bring attention to the building, filling it with the wealthy elite who can afford the exorbitant rents. Yuheng's building blocks the view of the now mis-appropriated sign, and instead presents an iconic structure that elevates the impoverished into a new luxury that is focused on community, equality, light and air. All without exploitation of the earth's resources.

Above

Renewable wood planking lines the interior of the living units giving them a comfortable, cabin-like domestic environment.

Right

Interior view from the Divine Lorraine detailing the battery packs, charged by the sun, for each of the residential modules. The formerly light-filled southern view of the luxury residences is replaced by a view of the technicities of the self-sufficient impoverished.

07
21
23
02
04

Shadow Series

Edition 2 - 4

02

CHANGING DOMESTICITIES

NEW DOMESTICITIES, NEW REALITIES

Clifford Pearson

The nuclear family isn't dead, but it has a lot of competition these days. Mom, Dad, and 2.3 kids living together under one roof still happens. Indeed, 24 percent of American households were nuclear families in 2000. Just 30 years before, though, this most iconic household type accounted for 40 percent of the US total. During the same time frame, singles rose from 16 percent to 26 percent, while the "other family" category jumped from 10 percent to 15 percent and "other non-family" grew from 1.5 percent to 5 percent. The married-without-children grouping held steady at 28 percent of all households, down just 1 percent from three decades before.[1] You could see the country's demographic twists and turns on TV, from *Leave It To Beaver* (1957–1963) to *Modern Family* (2009–), from *Happy Days* (1974–1984) to *Transparent* (2014–2019). Love it or hate it, popular culture reflects what's happening in society, giving us the chance to chuckle at or choke up about the way we live and whom we live with.

At the same time, we're living longer, so the elderly represent a larger part of our society; 16.9 percent of the US population now is 65 or older, compared to just 10 percent in 1970.[2] Domestic arrangements are changing accordingly, with seniors moving in with their adult children or their siblings or unrelated caregivers. Attitudes are changing too. While homeownership for the population as a whole has held steady at about 65 percent for many decades, only about 33 percent of Millennials owned their own homes in 2017.[3] The figure for Millennials reflects both a dearth of housing they can afford and, perhaps, less desire on their part to own things.

The rise of the sharing economy in the past ten years has disrupted our relationship to cars, apartments, even jobs. What had been rigid in the past, now seems fluid. Grab a Zipcar, drive across the country, find a short-term rental on Airbnb, store your belongings in a space found on Stashbee, and start a new life. Then do it again a few months later. Such changes call for new forms of housing. In the past, it wasn't always easy for a widow to find someone to rent an extra bedroom to or for a group of garden-loving vegans to attract enough cohorts to buy that three-story Victorian with the big backyard. Now it is. Bringing different people together today is just a few clicks

Left

SsD
Songpa Micro Housing
Seoul, 2014

The five-story project connects to its neighborhood with an open ground floor that can be used for community gatherings.

away. Inter-generational, non-family, non-traditional, and multi-cultural are all housing options readily available online. While the COVID-19 pandemic has turned social distancing into a new habit, it's unclear if it will change long-term attitudes to sharing rides, living arrangements, and other such things. Stay tuned.

Some of the builders of non-traditional housing these days are themselves non-traditional players. The car company MINI, for example, has converted an old paint-factory complex in the busy Jing'An district of Shanghai into a co-living compound with small serviced apartments and lots of communal space. Designed by Universal Design Studio, a Japanese firm headed by Satoshi Isono, MINI Living Shanghai opened in autumn 2020 and features dwelling units where residents share spaces for cooking, socializing, and storage. It also includes co-working areas, a restaurant, exhibition space, a magazine shop, and a small cinema. Instead of turning inward to create a sense of exclusivity, it opens much of its ground floor to the public and invites the neighbors to interact with residents. For young professionals, singles, ex-pats, and new arrivals to Shanghai, it offers an attractive way of connecting to each other and the larger community. No longer just an automobile manufacturer, MINI, which is part of BMW, now sees itself as providing "creative use of space" for city living.[4]

Aimed at both Chinese and ex-pats, MINI Living Shanghai offers a hybrid living experience that combines the communal character of traditional hutong and shikumen housing with Western notions of privacy, says Oke Hauser, the creative lead for MINI Living. So each unit has its own bedroom and bathroom, but clusters around a living and cooking space shared by four to ten residents. Other communal areas are scattered around the complex, from galleries on the ground floor and co-working spaces on the third floor to a terrace on the roof. Apartments can be rented for three to 12 months at prices ranging from $1,200 to $1,800. About six guest rooms will be available on a nightly basis, but the project is not a hotel and guest rooms are reserved mostly for friends or relatives of residents.

"We're not targeting a particular demographic or age group," says Hauser. "We want to attract people looking for a flexible way of living, who are happy with a small personal footprint in exchange for lots of social space." Because the apartments are already hooked up to an electronic infrastructure, new residents can move in without the hassle of opening accounts with internet and electricity providers. No one knows how COVID-19 will affect projects like MINI Living Shanghai. Increased concern about infection might make people fearful of sharing living quarters with strangers. But the pandemic might actually make co-living more attractive, says Hauser. "Instead of quarantining alone, you'll be part of a community where you can move around in a protected environment and get help from neighbors, if you need it."

Other new-fangled companies, such as the WeWork spin-off WeLive and Soho House, are also trying to fill this emerging need for co-housing. The British enterprise called The Collective is now expanding beyond its London base to develop properties in New York. In 2019, it opened a project called The Collective Paper Factory in

Left Top

MINI LIVING and Universal Design Studio
MINI Living
Shanghai, 2020

A division of the car company MINI converted five buildings at an old paint factory into a co-housing project that invites the public inside with shops, galleries, a restaurant, and a lounge on the ground floor. The 85,000-sqft project tries to embed itself in the Jing'An neighborhood of Shanghai.

Left Bottom

Apartments are small, but cluster around shared living and cooking spaces. Walls that slide or rotate can open bedrooms to the communal areas.

SsD
Songpa Micro Housing, Seoul, 2014

Architect Jinhee Park of SsD addressed the issue of housing affordability by designing a project in Seoul that provides 14 apartments as small as 120 sqft.

the Long Island City neighborhood and is working on projects in Williamsburg and Bedford-Stuyvesant. The complex in Bed-Stuy is being designed by Sou Fujimoto in conjunction with Ismael Leyva Architects and will have 440 two- and three-bedroom, serviced apartments that can be rented for a day, a month, or a year. Communal kitchens and living areas will offer a sense of community, and shared facilities for exhibiting art, performing, eating, and socializing will be open to the public. As its name implies, The Collective is betting that Millennials and Gen-Xers are willing to trade off private space for shared amenities, to forsake traditional apartments for co-living arrangements.

While smaller apartments without full kitchens are less expensive alternatives to traditional apartments, these co-living complexes are not exactly cheap. At The Collective Paper Factory rents start at $2,300 for a 29-day stay, $1,250 for two weeks, and $135 for one night. As these rates indicate, The Collective falls somewhere between an apartment complex and a hotel. People come and go all the time, which can generate an active vibe, but may also reduce the sense of a stable community where residents know each other. In terms of design sophistication, location, and price, projects run by The Collective, Mini, and WeLive are a long way off from your hippy parents' rural commune in upstate New York or northern California.[5] They're also quite different from the cooperative housing projects that emerged in the early decades of the 20th century, which were often built by labor unions or leftist organizations to provide affordable apartments for their members. Instead of owning individual apartments, residents bought shares in the entire development, which appealed to their socialist leanings, but didn't actually change much in terms of the living arrangements or physical design of these places. Today, many people in cities like New York and Washington, DC, live in co-op apartments, but have no idea of the communal sensibilities that gave rise to these complexes.

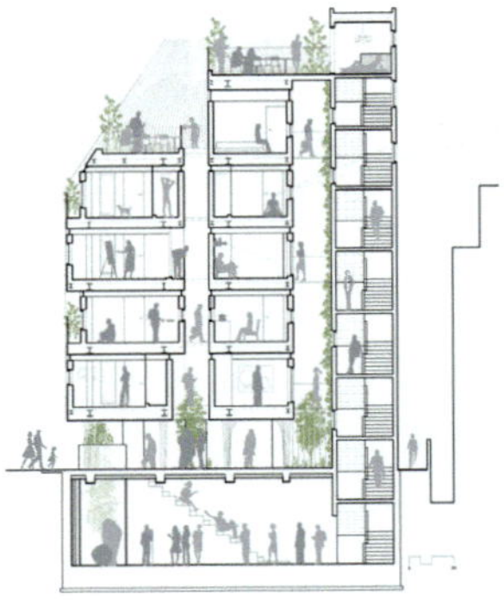

Above

SsD
Songpa Micro Housing
Seoul, 2014

This section shows how the spaces between apartments can be shared by residents to create a vibrant community.

Right

Each apartment has "tapioca" space around it where residents can socialize both indoors and out. Most daylight comes into the units through bands of clerestory windows that maintain privacy for the people inside.

A new generation of architects is beginning to explore more radical models of shared housing. In Seoul, South Korea, for example, the architecture firm SsD created a five-story housing project called Songpa, which opened in 2014 and surrounds each of its 14 micro-units with shared space that can be used for circulation and socializing. Jinhee Park, who founded the firm, likens these semi-public, semi-private areas to the ambiguous gel around tapioca pearls and says they serve as a soft intersection between indoors and out, residential and communal. Together they act as a social fabric for residents. They also provide each apartment with three exposures, which allows cross-ventilation and reduces the need for air-conditioning.[6]

Like cabins on a ship, the apartments at Songpa maximize the use of every square inch by incorporating built-in furniture such as Murphy beds that can be docked in a wall during the day to make room for working and socializing. Units are just 120 square feet, but can be combined to accommodate multiple residents or multiple uses such as exhibiting art and living. Clerestory windows just below the ceiling bring daylight in from three sides, while maintaining the privacy of people inside the apartments. In addition to the tapioca space around the units, the project offers shared amenities—including a covered, open-program area on the ground floor, a

small auditorium and cafe below grade, and an exhibition space on the second floor. Wrapping the entire building is a metal screen that allows air to flow inside, while reducing solar loads and directing drainage. It also blurs the division between indoors and out, much as the tapioca spaces do.

Six years after the project opened, all of the units are rented and there's a waiting list for people who would like to move in. According to Park, the apartments rent for between $700 and $1,200 per month, which is about 20 percent more on a per-square-foot basis than comparable units in the area. In terms of energy performance, the project has earned a 79 on the Energy Star Source Energy Use Intensity rating scale, significantly below a United States average of 98.9. Its success in reducing energy use is due to a number of factors, including radiant flooring, motion-sensing LED lighting, efficient micro-cooling units, and the placement of storage units lining already "super-insulated" walls, states Park. Emphasizing flexibility and sharing, Songpa expresses the values of a generation of young professionals who are willing to give up individual space for a greater sense of community. As their needs change, residents can add an extra unit for a new partner or convert their apartment into a work or exhibition space. Instead of stability, the project embraces change. Instead of single use, it enables multiplicity.

A different set of combinations is the driving force behind Side-by-Side, a prototype for a co-living project that aims to bring together people of various ages and abilities. Designed by the Harlem-based firm Brandt: Haferd for a site in the Cleveland neighborhood of Old Brooklyn, the project places a pair of three-story houses Side-by-Side on adjacent lots and connects them with an over-sized, double-decker elevator. Inspired by the office space that rises and descends through the center of Rem Koolhaas's Maison Bordeaux, the elevator acts as a moveable room as much as a means of vertical circulation. An interstitial zone of communal spaces wraps around this central spine, encouraging residents to socialize and do things together—much as SsD's tapioca space does at Songpa.

A shared kitchen on the lowest level, a roof deck, and a rear garden provide additional opportunities for residents to congregate. The goal is to create a place with five apartments—two for families and three for singles—where alter-abled and able-bodied people can live together.

"We wanted to make architecture accessible in multiple ways—visually, physically, and socially," says K. Brandt Knapp, one of the founding principals of Brandt: Haferd. The firm's scheme won the grand prize in the #ZeroThreshold design competition, run in 2019 by the nonprofit North Coast Community Homes, which operates more than 200 group homes for more than 1,000 developmentally disabled people in northeast Ohio. The Cleveland Foundation is providing $149,000 in funding for the project and North Coast Community Homes is raising more money to build one or more of the winning designs in the mixed-income, ethnically diverse area of Old Brooklyn.

While exploring opportunities to integrate people of various abilities and ages, Brandt: Haferd also examined ways of stitching Side-by-Side to the neighborhood around it. So the firm went beyond the scope of the competition brief and proposed using an adjacent third property as a temporary community garden and park with a bus kiosk at one end and Side-by-Side at the other. "We wanted to use domesticity to deal with urban issues such as the lot," explains Jerome Haferd, the firm's other founding principal. The DNA of the neighborhood—with its mix of incomes and ethnic groups—informed what Haferd and Knapp did as architects. "The concept of territory, of fitting puzzle pieces together helped shape our proposal," adds Haferd.

Occupying an urban edge where the residential part of Old Brooklyn gives way to retail and light-manufacturing, Side-by-Side helps negotiate the shift in scales and uses. Knapp and Haferd say they want their project to act as an "interlocking joint" connecting with its larger urban context. They also try to weave nature into their scheme with green spaces on the roof, in the backyard, and in the community garden in the front. "Our interest in forms of ecology connects with our attempts to create shared territories and territories of care," says Knapp.

In Singapore, an innovative project called Kampung Admiralty combines senior housing with a medical center, shopping, daycare, a large public plaza, and stepped rooftop gardens. Instead of isolating seniors in specialized housing blocks, the project—which opened in 2018—integrates them into the mainstream of urban life. The idea is to create a public amenity that brings together people of different ages and gives them a rich variety of things to do.[7]

Designed by WOHA—the architecture firm founded by Wong Mun Summ and Richard Hassell—Kampung Admiralty forms an architectural sandwich with a spacious community plaza at the base, a medical center in the middle, and a public park with apartments for seniors in the upper portion. The word "kampung" means "village" and the project aims to encourage the kind of inter-generational and diverse relationships found in traditional Southeast Asian communities. The plaza is open to the streets around the development and invites the public to come inside. Wong and Hassell designed the plaza as a welcoming place porous to the larger urban context. Shaded by the medical center above it, the plaza is a great place to relax, shop, or participate in activities such as dancing or tai chi. A hawker center with a range of food stalls occupies a second level and acts as a magnet for all kinds of people in the area.

Inserting a medical center into a residential and retail development is a novel idea that should be considered for other projects and places. It makes healthcare more accessible, especially to a group—such as the elderly—who may have mobility issues. And it makes better use of valuable urban land than building separate facilities in different locations. Consultation and waiting areas in the medical center occupy the perimeter of the building, so they can take advantage of daylighting and views to the community plaza below and the park above. Connecting patients to nature and other people helps promote wellness and reduce healing times.

As it has done with many of its projects, WOHA created a tropical garden on the upper portion of Kampung Admiralty. The multi-level green space serves as a lush oasis in the middle of a dense city and a wonderful retreat for both residents and the public. Two 11-story towers provide 104 apartments for elderly singles and couples. To encourage residents to come out and socialize with others, "buddy benches" are strategically located at shared entrances. A childcare center and an active aging hub sit side by side, so generations can mix and help one another. A community farm and exercise programs offer other opportunities for people of all ages to come together. A post-occupancy evaluation of Kampung Admiralty found that the project had greater bio-diversity in terms of total species, insect species, mammals, amphibians, reptiles, and fish than nearby areas. It also found that the great majority of people living there and visiting appreciated the green aspects of the project.

Left

SsD
Songpa Micro Housing
Seoul, 2014

Apartments can be combined into double-size units for living, working, or exhibiting art.

Above

Park designed the apartments with built-in furniture that can be deployed as needed, such as a bed stored in a wall and a work surface tucked into a cabinet.

As society becomes more fluid in terms of its definitions of "household" and "family," new forms of housing will continue to evolve. Some of these models will focus on particular needs—such as micro-dwellings for young professionals without a lot of money to spend on rent. Others will emphasize flexibility, accommodating a variety of residents—whether they be people of different generations or different abilities. Architects will design these projects to change over time, evolving to serve different kinds of people as markets and populations shift. Responding to various scenarios will allow housing to be socially and economically resilient in the face of evolving needs. Such flexibility might also include the ability to operate in different modes, depending on the need for social distancing. Communal areas, for example, might be designed to allow large planters to slide into place and spread out seating. Much of this new residential work, though, will highlight the connective tissue that brings people together and allows them to interact in meaningful ways. So even as we embrace new kinds of households, the housing we provide for them may promote a traditional sense of community.

Right

WOHA
Kampung Admiralty
Singapore, 2017

A public park occupies multiple levels of this mixed-use project, turning a residential, retail, and medical complex into a green oasis in the center of a big city.

References

1. U.S. Census and Wikipedia. https://en.wikipedia.org/wiki/Nuclear_family
2. U.S. Census and Statista.com. https://www.statista.com/statistics/457822/share-of-old-age-population-in-the-total-us-population/
3. Statista.com and CNBC. https://www.statista.com/statistics/184902/homeownership-rate-in-the-us-since-2003/; https://www.cnbc.com/2019/02/28/63-percent-of-millennial-homebuyers-have-regrets-heres-why.html
4. https://www.mini.com/en_MS/home/living/shanghai/welcometominiliving.html
5. https://www.thecollective.com/locations/paper-factory
6. Clare Jacobson, "Songpa Micro Housing," *Architectural Record*, October 2014.
7. https://www.woha.net/#Kampung-Admiralty

IN RESIDENCY

Ben Krone

Within the shifting landscape of attitudes around living and responses in development, there exist subsets of living types that are centered around the 'work' environment as equally important to our domestic 'home' life. In fact, it can be argued that a big part of the reason that millennials own less and therefore need less space is because work life and home life are no longer considered isolated parts of living. The shift from 'permanent' to 'flexible' working environments in which there is no longer a need for a stationary terminal or desk space gave birth to the idea that fewer tools require ownership. Sharing culture goes beyond just how we work. It also pertains to domestic life where we do everything else. It's not by accident that one of the early adopters of the sharing economy of living WeLive was born from the successes and by the same company WeWork.

What does it mean when these two facets of life come together into a singular place? Where our living environment is shifted outward from being a place where we 'house what we own' to common areas where we 'share what we need'? Where building amenities are no longer focused toward program elements such as gyms and pools but instead flexible spaces for doing business outside of the sleeping unit?

One early example can be identified in the re-zoning of traditionally industrial and manufacturing districts to residential ones. In the 1960s many artists had moved into vacant industrial lofts after manufacturing had moved out of city centers. These buildings lay dormant and were extremely cheap to acquire. In 1982 in New York City loft law was passed which allowed for a hybrid model of the live/work loft. Zoning ordinances rewrote some of the rules and regulations that previously prohibited residences from being converted from older building stock. The stipulation was that the resident had to in some way carry out the practices that may require the use of such spaces. This building type consisted of wide-open spaces and heavy timber or concrete that was required to support large industrial machinery. It was the inherent flexibility of these live/work spaces where the artist loft was born. The artist 'resident' could use what was a generic environment and appropriate it according to their

Left

Xinyu Wang
Co/Habitation–Red Hook

Ben Krone Urban Housing Studio
with Adrian Subagyo

University of Pennsylvania
Weitzman School of Design, 2016

Rear neighborhood facing elevation
with shared primary living spaces.

Pioneer Works facing elevation detail with housing units above and private gallery spaces below.

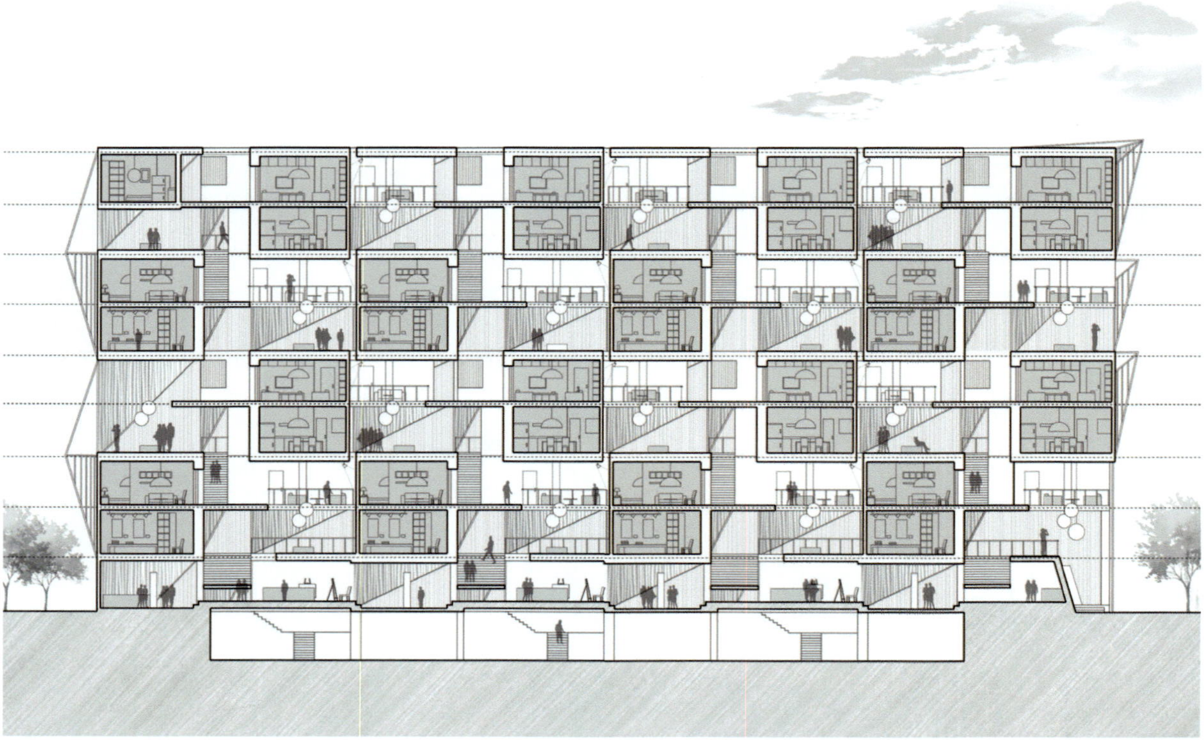

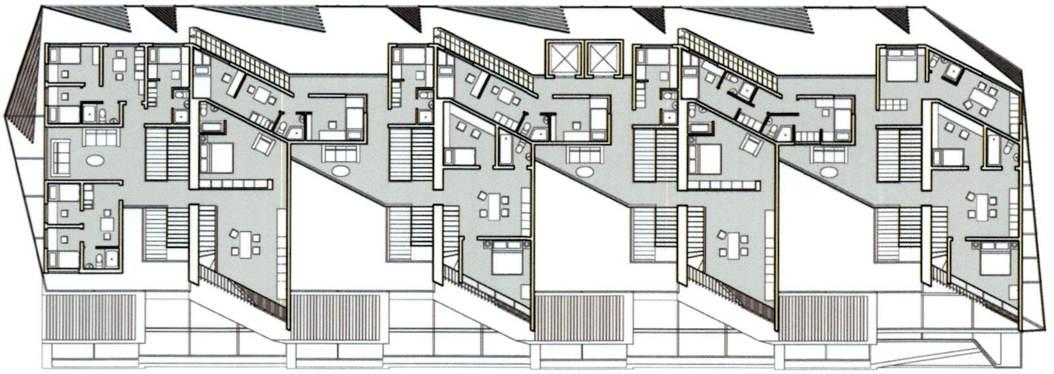

needs. The result was a sort of patchwork environment that was extremely specialized for one individual. It would temporarily solve the problems for both living and working in this context but did neither particularly well given that it truly only worked for its current inhabitant.

New Live/Work Types

As the current pandemic has illustrated, 'live' and 'work' are more intermingled than previously considered. At this moment, the 'office' has transformed unused corners of our homes and appropriated our kitchen tables. There is a new awareness that typical commercial office space may be redundant in many industries. Companies are rethinking strategies for the workplace that are likely to reinforce and perhaps revisit past housing types for combining living and working programs. The question now is whether it's the actual dwelling unit that intends to support this, or if the evolution of common building spaces will sustain the need for a workspace outside of the traditional office. Or perhaps we consider a new housing prototype where we live and work as a singular housing strategy?

My design studio has been using artist's live/work situations as well as nomadic artist residency housing as our laboratories for testing ideas. In a sense 'residency' housing, although highly specific in nature, is the purest form of the live/work scenario and has proven to be fertile testing ground for both programming and physical space experimentation. The basic premise is that artists by nature tend to have a certain degree of integration between their process and how they live. Some more than others, and naturally it also depends on their type of objects (or non-objects) and specific spatial requirements. Similar to the way housing approaches design through private scenarios of sleeping, eating, personal hygiene, etc. and then seeks a universality in spatial implementation, designing working spaces for artists considers specifics such as scale, access, light conditions, materials, hanging and mounting requirements, structural support, and ventilation. Where and how these requirements coincide is the design problem at hand. Grappling with the overlap of the generic requirements of living and the specific requirements of working while remaining flexible and adaptable sets up a unique problem that the traditional artist loft never solved.

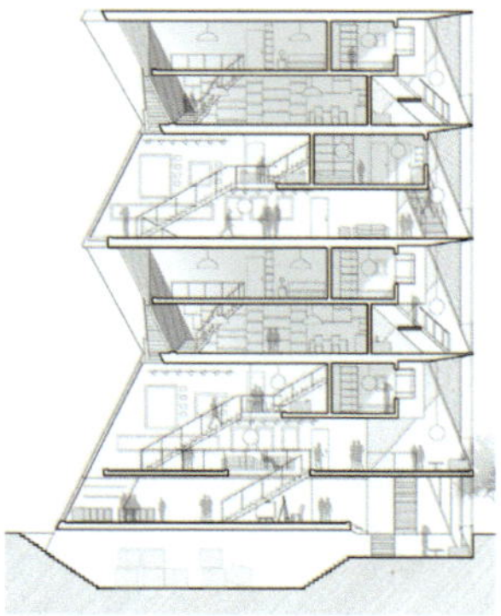

Left Top

East/West section cutting across live/work housing units: urban elevation.

Left Bottom

Plan cut through the dwelling levels overlooking the public gallery spaces below.

Above

North/South section.

One example that came from the research from the studio is illustrated here with this text. The 'Co-Habitation' project by Xinyu Wang asks the question through an extremely important lens. It attempts to allow the artist-in-residence to monetize what is created as part of a residency, where the 'work' is a means for earning a living and the living is earned through such transactions. The building is highly tuned to facilitate both the work and the transactional nature of making art for a living. This includes both public and private spaces which are owned and shared with other residents. The building divides these spaces along each of the two primary façades; one is public facing composed primarily of spaces for exhibiting the resident's work and gracefully facilitating transactional needs, while the other contains private spaces that are specific to the ways in which artists live. Halfway between the domestic and the transactional are the studios where the work itself is created. The public façade is made up of storefronts, galleries (both shared and private), entertaining spaces and public outreach, while the private façade expresses sleeping, eating, and personal use.

It would be an oversimplification of the design to suggest that each live/work space is unitized and inhabited by one individual working with one medium. Instead, the intersections within the studio spaces are interwoven and facilitate interaction between inhabitants. The sharing of ideas and resources creates a working environment that is both collaborative and regulated. The building becomes a machine geared for living, creating, and earning a living.

Old housing types are no longer valid due to a shifting landscape in urban centers, changes in the makeup of the family unit, and ideals of millennial generations toward a shared economy. Of course, these are all fundamental to why housing is starting to see a change in design tactics. The onset of the COVID-19 pandemic has taught us of some additional important lessons about the relationship of working and living: firstly, that large commercial office spaces, combined with individually owned workspaces, may be redundant and wasteful; secondly, that the isolation of home life and work life no longer exists; and finally it is no longer valid for design to separate work and living. These two primary facets of life have become completely intertwined. By accepting this we must then consider new realities of domesticity as a live/work hybrid condition.

Above

Interior views.

Right

Cross section of a physical model of public gallery spaces where the residences display the work created within the housing studio spaces.

Percent of Freelance Workers per Age Group, 2020
Data Source: Freelancers Union

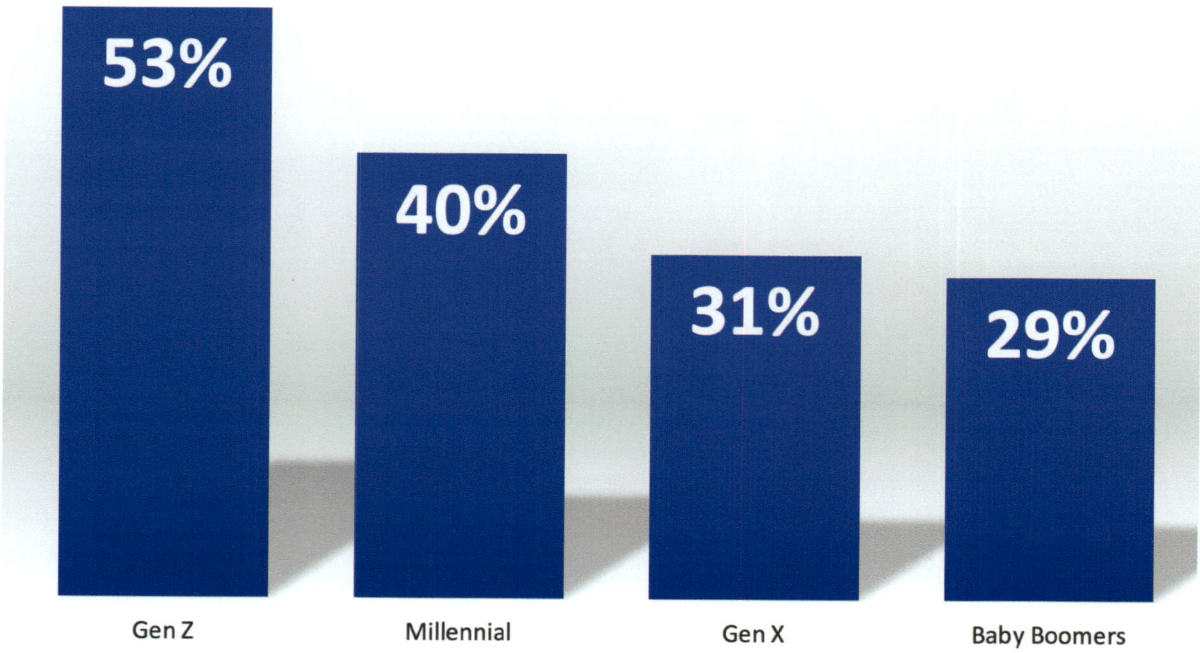

EMPOWERING ENTREPRENEURSHIP

Simone Tarantino | Startup Home

Entrepreneurship Landscape

The way we work today is very different from the way our parents and grandparents worked. The rate of new entrepreneurs in the economy, calculated as the percentage of adults becoming entrepreneurs in a given month, gives us a very detailed picture of this new landscape: in the US alone, the Department of Labor calculates that in 2019 about 6.5 million people started a business, or about 542,000 each month. Even though only a small amount of these companies manage to survive more than five years, the picture is quite clear. A staggering number of those new entrepreneurs, and a substantial percentage of businesses, are moving out from the typical office environment to work from home or in a more communal and shared way.

Only a few years ago, working from home or in a coworking space seemed unfeasible, but with the advancements in technology and the 2020 COVID-19-related acceleration, the changes in the way we do business, the places we do business in, and the way business itself is morphing following new trends, makes working from the comfort of your home or from a shared desk across the street perfectly manageable. According to the Advocacy Office of the SBA (Small Business Administration) statistics, 50% of American small businesses are "home-based," including 60.1% of firms without paid employees.[1]

Just to put the numbers of the coworking phenomenon in perspective, in 2017, there were 542,000 people working in 4,043 coworking spaces in the US (up from only 14 spaces in 2007), and this is forecasted to increase to about 1.08 million in 2022. If you just look at a city like Philadelphia, in 2017 there were 27 active coworking spaces, with a projected square footage of "flexible workspace" surpassing 1.2 million by 2022 (up from just 233,000 square feet dedicated to it in 2014).[2]

Left

Simone Tarantino
Percentage of freelance workers per age group, 2020

Based on 2019 data, younger generations have a higher propensity for freelancing. Gen Z is the newest generation to be named and were born between 1995 and 2015. There are nearly 74 million in the US. Millennials were born between 1980 and 1994 and number about 73 million. Gen X was born between 1965 and 1979 and count 82 million people. Baby boomers were born between 1944 and 1964 and count 76 million people.

More than half of the American workforce will experience self-employment at some point in their careers, and many will cycle back and forth between self-employment and traditional employment in years to come. The importance of looking at this trend lies in the fact that, according to Statista,[3] by 2028 over 53% of the entire US workforce, or about 90 million people (up from 62.2 million in 2019), will be composed of solopreneurs, independent contractors or freelancers, most, if not all of them, looking for ergonomic, comfortable and fitted-out workspace. Architecture and design need to service these people and their evolving work needs.

Coworking Statistics at the Beginning of 2019
Data Source: Statista, GCUC global coworking report

- ***There were nearly 19,000 coworking spaces worldwide***
- ***There were more than 3 million coworkers globally***
- ***With over 80 million square feet of flexible workspace, the US leads the global coworking market in terms of real estate.***
- ***With over 11,000 coworking spaces, the Asia-Pacific region is the world's largest coworking region***
- ***The average number of members per coworking space is 185 (global)***

It's equally important to notice that this change is impacting not just in the startup or entrepreneurial ecosystems: large enterprises are changing the way they work too. Big companies like Microsoft, Cisco are shifting their workforce towards a more collaborative, and flexible environment. Data from the IPO filing shows that a bit less than 40% of WeWork's members belong to companies with more than 500 employees, including IBM, Facebook and Microsoft. The data show that not just tech enterprises are moving to coworking: UBS, the Bank of Canada, Oscar Health and Puma are tenants in various cities.

The biggest acceleration in this already fast trend has been recorded right at the beginning of the 2020 COVID-19 pandemic, with companies like Twitter, Google and Square, among others, announcing new work from home policies.[4]

All this transformation is creating a definite shift in the real estate, finance, architecture and design industry. The core of this shift is a challenging re-thinking of real estate and architecture, supporting the changes in lifestyle, work style, and everything in between. The industry needs a new wave of disruption and innovation to address the new conditions of live/work that are blurring and overlapping the lines between working, living and private space.

Right

Simone Tarantino
Number of freelancers in the US, 2020

This statistic shows the number of freelancers in the United States from 2017 to 2028. It is projected that in 2027, 86.5 million people will be freelancing in the United States and will make up 50.9 percent of the total US workforce.

Lesson Learned: Coliving and Coworking

Today's coliving and coworking landscape, if we base our analysis on five of the main companies in the arena, is that they have a clear and definite focus on major metropolitan areas. For example, WeWork is the largest office tenant in New York City, surpassing J.P. Morgan Chase in 2018, and holds leases for 8.9 million square feet of office space in more than 100 locations in Manhattan alone, and is one of the major tenants in other big cities in the US.[5]

Number of Freelancers in the US, 2020
Data Source: Statista

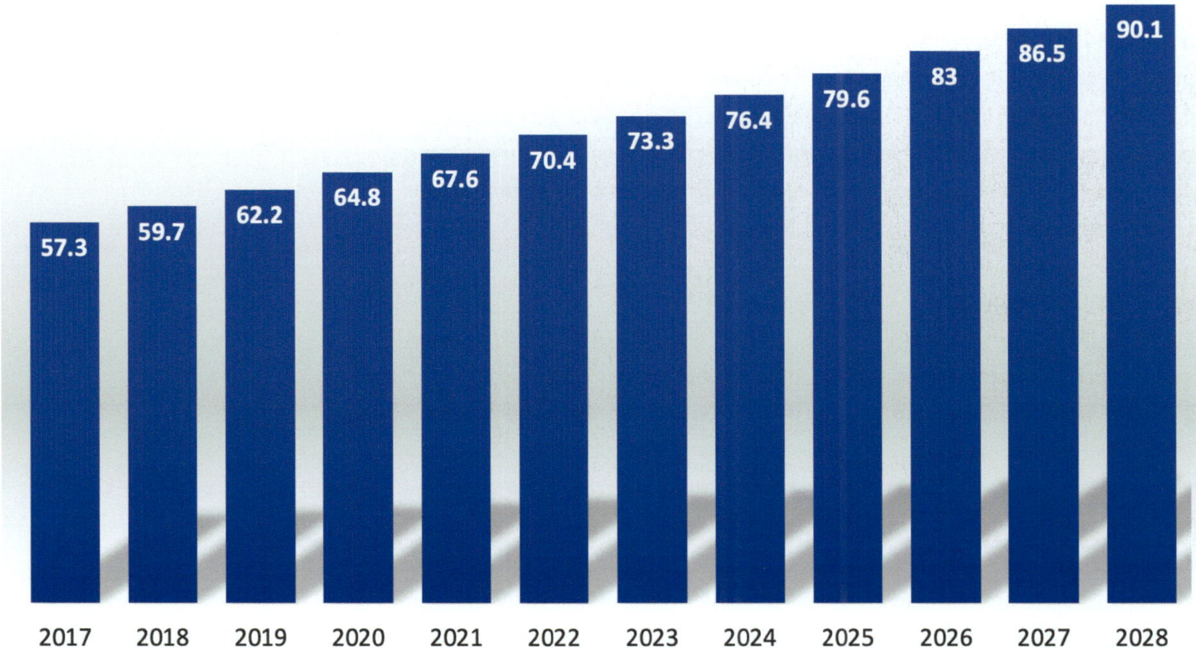

This strategy may seem profitable on paper but will not work in the long term, because focusing on major metro areas, big companies like WeWork are not just missing out on more affordable real estate opportunities in secondary and tertiary cities, but also underserving their own demographic and closing the doors to everyone that does not live in the vicinity of the locations.

If you look at the numbers, the average price for a bed or a desk is far above what a young entrepreneur, a freelancer or a bootstrapping startup company can or want to pay. Simply put, if they spend their cash on rent, they won't have the necessary resources to grow the company.

If we analyze the rise (and fall) of a giant like WeWork, it is easy to spot the basic mistakes they made in their expansion strategy and market approach. The company started in Brooklyn in 2008, serving the startup ecosystem under the GreenDesk name, and offering affordable offices to growing companies and freelancers. With the economic growth of the past six or seven years, and a considerable amount of funding, they saw the opportunity to expand to New York City and by 2010 they spun off WeWork, without accounting for the major difference in real estate prices and turn around. The company then expanded quickly, leasing more spaces across the city, locking in ten-year contracts for entire floors of buildings, adding lots of losses on the balance sheet. This was subsidized by investors that believed the company would, at a certain point, turn the square feet into profits. That never happened: WeWork focused on long-term leases, so was excessively exposed to market volatility, never created a real community and, more importantly, never took the time to listen to what the ecosystem needed—a place where to start and grow their ventures. One blatant example of that was the "experiment" they made with WeLive, some sort of coliving facility in the heart of Wall Street in Manhattan. They leased space at an egregious price, with the result renting to tenants at impossible rates, even by New York standards (according to the WeLive website,[6] rooms go up to $4,000 for a bed in a minuscule studio, or $1,850 per month for a murphy bed in a shared room with three other people). All of that, with no workspace or any sort of arrangement for people working from home.

A New Model—StartupHome

StartupHome had a very different approach since the beginning in London, UK, in 2015. Given the economy at that time and newly released subsidies for startups by the Government, London saw a big influx of people coming from outside the city and from other countries in Europe. Given London's housing situation, an old city with very few inexpensive rentable spaces, it quickly became problematic for entrepreneurs to find affordable lodging for six months to a year. Opportunity became immediately obvious and the partners decided to launch StartupHome. At the time of writing, the company manages three buildings in London and is working on a bigger fourth one outside city limits.

StartupHome is also working on expanding the coliving concept started in the UK in the United States (there are also plans to expand in the rest of Europe, with active projects in Berlin, Rome and other countries). What are the main differentiators that make StartupHome more effective than other coliving spaces? Coworking as we know it typically attracts the full undifferentiated spectrum of independent workers, from graphic designers to lawyers, from game developers to startups, from insurance salespeople to life coach and tech support, whereas StartupHome attracts a vertical subset of startups and entrepreneurs: the ones starting new ventures, or needing help in growing them. The concept is that a growing number of startups and entrepreneurs need structure, programming, support, not just a live/work environment. While a typical coliving company, such as Common (operating in New York City, LA, San Francisco, Chicago, Washington, DC, Seattle), WeLive in Manhattan and DC, Roam

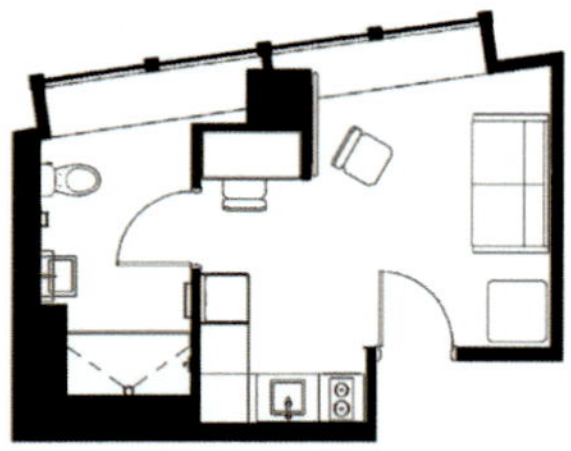

Above

Simone Tarantino
WeLive studio apartment, 2018

Floorplan for a studio apartment with sofa bed in the WeLive coliving building in Wall Street, New York. Other floorplans for studios or one- and two-bedroom spaces have either murphy-beds or bunk beds to maximize space.

(operating in Miami, San Francisco, London, Tokyo, Bali), Quarters (operating in Berlin, New York City, Chicago) or others, offer beds and bedrooms inside a coliving community, with the promise of a fun shared experience, operating mostly in major cities; however, they leave out an important part of the ecosystem, the one that possibly needs more support.

The selection process of the startups that are accepted in the program is similar to that of a typical business accelerator. In the case of StartupHome, the starting point is whether the company is at least 51% owned and managed by minority entrepreneurs. The success of StartupHome is linked to the success of the startups so it is important to try to select ideas that create value, jobs and potentially a social impact. Analyzing the team is also critical, since they need to be able to carry the project forward and possibly scale it, but they must also harmonize with the other teams that will live and work in the same spaces. The company's goal is to apply what was learned from its experience in London, from the mistakes of our competitors, and most importantly deeply analyze what an evolving ecosystem of "work-from-home" entrepreneurs really need. Entrepreneurs need to be in proximity to primary markets, they need access to capital, either venture or angel, and most of all they require support, knowledge-sharing and mentoring. In addition, and possibly most importantly, they need value. Startup founders, bootstrapping entrepreneurs and freelancers are not there for a bed or a desk; they are there for what we call programming. And with programming, they expect all the support an incubation infrastructure can give. If a typical accelerator receives more than a thousand applications for each cohort, typically twice a year, we can expect to be able to analyze hundreds of startups and entrepreneurs, in order to select from 15 to 25 in each location.

StartupHome developed a multifaceted programming which provides its tenants the support they require and need to make the best of the time they spend in the facilities. At the end, this strategy maximizes the chances of success for every venture that stays at StartupHome, with the idea of not working with quantity, but rather, quality. Knowing how slim are the chances for a startup to make it—nearly 40% of businesses with employees close within two years from starting, from the less than 5% of startup businesses that get to have employees by the end of year one—it is imperative to offer much more than just plain accommodation. StartupHome tries to "build" entrepreneurs, offering them a stable infrastructure and supporting them every stage of their life. Couple that with the fact that StartupHome's focus on underrepresented founders—minorities, immigrants or other underserved demographics operating in areas where those demographics are more represented—and you have the full picture of the potential social and economic impact the venture can have, and why it is strategic to be in secondary and tertiary cities.

The StartupHome programming is the combination of different experiences with incubators and accelerators, both local and international. Considering that the program will accept startups at different growth stages, the program, after an initial period aimed at building or solidifying the essential foundations (pitch deck, product-market fit and market sizing/opportunity value) is adapted to offer a path aligned with the needs of each founder. Each startup accepted in the program will go through the initial assessment, where the team defines the best path, adapting it to the company's internship and the skills of the team members. Thanks to this assessment, and the industry vertical where the startup operates, specific mentors are assigned to follow the founders during their growth path.

Global Deal Volume Toward Female-Founded Startups
Data Source: Crunchbase 2020

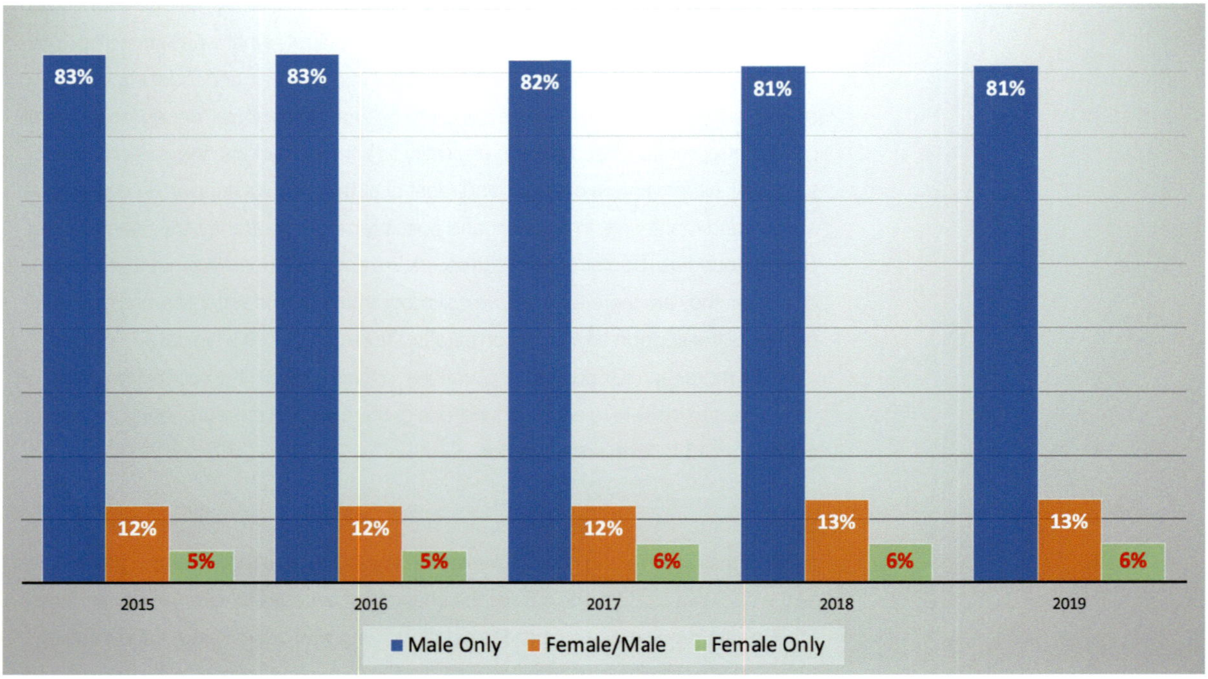

Above

Simone Tarantino
Deal volume for female founders, 2020

The percentage of global deal volume for female founders seems not to be changing over time. In this chart Startups without founders listed on Crunchbase or private equity are excluded.

Towards the end of the six-month incubation cycle, each startup is evaluated to see if and how it has evolved in the context of the program, and if it makes sense to stay for a subsequent six-month cycle or if it must leave the program and make room for another startup.

StartupHome: Women in Startups

Another unique aspect of StartupHome, in addition to the customized programming, is creating vertical industry micro-ecosystems inside the network, aggregating startups and entrepreneurs that operate in the same or adjacent markets and fostering collaboration. In the same way, and with the same strategy of fostering collaboration, the company also created an inclusive female-only environment, operating in London, and called Women in Startups. Women are founding startups and new companies more than ever before. The increase between 1997 and 2014 is a staggering and very promising plus 70%.[7] According to CrunchBase, in 2019 almost 20% of startups had a female founder. They are growing at a faster pace than any other sector, yet there's a gap in the startup industry: the ecosystem itself is not supporting this growth. Again from CrunchBase, the year 2019 closed with only 3% of the total dollar volume going to female-founded and 10% to male/female co-founded companies making up 13% of all seed, venture and corporate venture investments. But the important datapoint is that starting in 2016 the proportion to female only and male/female co-founded has not shifted from that 13% overall (excluding 2018 with Ant Financial, female-funded and owned, that raised $14 billion).[8] Of that number, just slightly more than half a percentage point goes to women of color. On top of that, other minorities are outright excluded from the traditional venture capital funding opportunity.

Looking at the problem in the context of design and architecture, in 2017 StartupHome London opened a coliving specific for women and mother entrepreneurs, hosting 10 to 12 women entrepreneurs per cohort. In the last cohort, two were mothers. What the company had to work with was the notion that London's non-commercial building footprints are quite small, and quite rare to find. We're talking about typical townhouses, usually single-family homes. Once a suitable space was found, it was entirely designed and refitted to fulfill the specific needs. This included a multifunction space that had to double as a nursery for the babies of two of the founders of the cohort, and video room for presentations, on top of an extended play area designed to be children-friendly.

This first experiment proved that collaboration between the entrepreneurs was critical to the success of the startups in the house, as well as the optimization of live/work space.

Post-COVID-19: Following WHO and ESG Standards

Considering the enormous impact that the 2020 pandemic had globally, and how each facility had to adapt to a new way of working and interpreting workspaces, StartupHome decided to adopt the environmental, social and governance (ESG) guidelines of the UN Sustainable Development Goals 2030 Agenda and the World Health Organization (WHO) directives. This choice involves changes in the governance of society, and also how StartupHome can reinterpret the work and coliving spaces. The strategies that will be adopted as a company, in each of the locations that will be opened in the post-pandemic future, involve a combination of approaches to minimize risks for founders who live in close contact with each other and use common workspaces. Technologies such as beams for spatial intelligence and people counting, autonomous cleaning and the adoption of more broad smart building tech and low-touch voice activated appliances will contribute to the security of the people and at the same time advance the overall sustainability of each space.

Conclusion

StartupHome's method to quickly understand if a city is suited for a StartupHome building, and a successful programming, is developed using a specific algorithm, of 18 different variables, including general demographic data, ecosystem data, real estate statistics and some less scientific variables like city support for startups, willingness to invest, general health and affordability among others, it is possible to grade a city and understand the effort needed to open. For the future, Philadelphia emerged as a great candidate, given its proximity to New York, health of the local ecosystem and support from the state, city and venture community, persistence of startups and general demographic. Based on that, in 2020, StartupHome plans to acquire and lease between three and five buildings in different neighborhoods, providing the benchmark and model for other cities in the US.

As a way to give back to the city, StartupHome works with city officials and community leaders to expand the range of possible social impact and generate needed economic development in specific city neighborhoods, interacting with the community as well as fostering the creative ecosystem and adding outreach initiatives. The engagement goes well beyond real estate and includes civic and community engagement, making an active and positive difference in the community.

Architecture and design have today a real opportunity and strong responsibility to serve a growing demographic of workers, with the ultimate goal of empowering entrepreneurship to generate social impact and economic development. This new wave of workers is looking for a different way to interpret accommodation in a space where the confluence of live and work blurs into a single domesticity, but fosters social collaboration and opens to dialogs within communities.

Above

Startup Home London, 2016

Inside of one of the StartupHome buildings in London. Spaces are studied to foster collaboration with a flexible and comfortable layout that allows aggregation and private work at the same time.

Right

Startup Home London, 2017

Rear of one of the StartupHome London buildings.

References

1. Business Employment Dynamics (BED), Bureau of Labor Statistics, US Department of Labor. www.bls.gov/bdm; Business Dynamics Statistics (BDS), US Census Bureau, US Department of Commerce. www.census.gov/ces/dataproducts/bds; International Trade Administration (ITA), US Department of Commerce. www.trade.gov/ NES Nonemployer Statistics; US Census Bureau, US Department of Commerce. www.census.gov/programs-surveys/nonemployer-statistics.html; Survey of Business Owners (SBO), US Census Bureau, US Department of Commerce. www.census.gov/programs-surveys/sbo.html; Statistics of US Businesses (SUSB), US Census Bureau, US Department of Commerce. www.census.gov/programs-surveys/susb.html
2. https://www.statista.com/statistics/797546/number-of-coworking-spaces-us/
3. https://www.statista.com/statistics/921593/gig-economy-number-of-freelancers-us/
4. https://www.forbes.com/sites/danabrownlee/2020/05/18/twitter-square-announce-work-from-home-forever-optionwhat-are-the-risks/
5. https://www.marketwatch.com/story/heres-a-look-at-how-weworks-50-billion-pile-of-office-leases-could-unravel-2019-10-10
6. https://www.welive.com/new-york-city/
7. https://news.crunchbase.com/news/eoy-2019-diversity-report-20-percent-of-newly-funded-startups-in-2019-have-a-female-founder/
8. Funding to Female Founders 2020. http://about.crunchbase.com/wp-content/uploads/2020/03/Funding-To-Female-Founders_Report.pdf

AVE B
ONE WAY
DO NOT
ENTER

CO-WORKING BUBBLE

Kutan Ayata

This project speculates on the future demise of WeWork and WeLive and imagines a scenario where an existing building would programmatically transform twice in the near future: an adaptive reuse of an adaptive reuse; a transformation from housing to a co-working space to a day-care center. The student's scenario scripted a complete WeWork / WeLive takeover of a building she was assigned to on the edge of Stuyvesant Town in Manhattan.

A little bit of background information on the site is necessary to contextualize the studio ambitions. Stuyvesant Town borders East Village in the north and comprises 18 city blocks as a housing complex with roughly 33,000 residents spanning from 1st Avenue to FDR Drive and from 14th Street to 20th Street. This complex was originally conceived in 1947 as public–private joint venture for veterans returning from World War II. It was later converted to market rate housing, was sold twice in 2006 and again 2015, following a default in 2010. Still to this date, these two sales respectively represent the top two single largest private real estate transactions in history at 5.4 and 5.3 billion dollars.

There are absolutely no architectural qualities present: an incredibly dull brick façade with no articulation other than minimal apertures as required for housing program. One could easily label it architecturally criminal given its scale and impact in its context. The 35-building complex is an aggregation of a single module which is basically based on a "plus" shape 13-story tower in plan, configured as singles and multiples depending on their site situation. There is virtually no difference in spatial experience in inhabiting a stand-alone module or joined triple module or any other permutation for that matter, as parti-walls between the modules render each module tower part isolated. The result is rather extraordinary; no matter where your interiority is within this large complex, you are always in the same building, there are 89 such instances.

Left

Yan Zheng
Mega-Block Redux-Stuyvesant Town, New York City

Kutan Ayata Urban Housing Studio with Alexander Bahr

University of Pennsylvania Weitzman School of Design, 2017

Elevated frontal view of the Communal Workplace Bubble in the live/work hybrid building transformation.

Looking up towards the integration of the Communal Workplace Bubble.

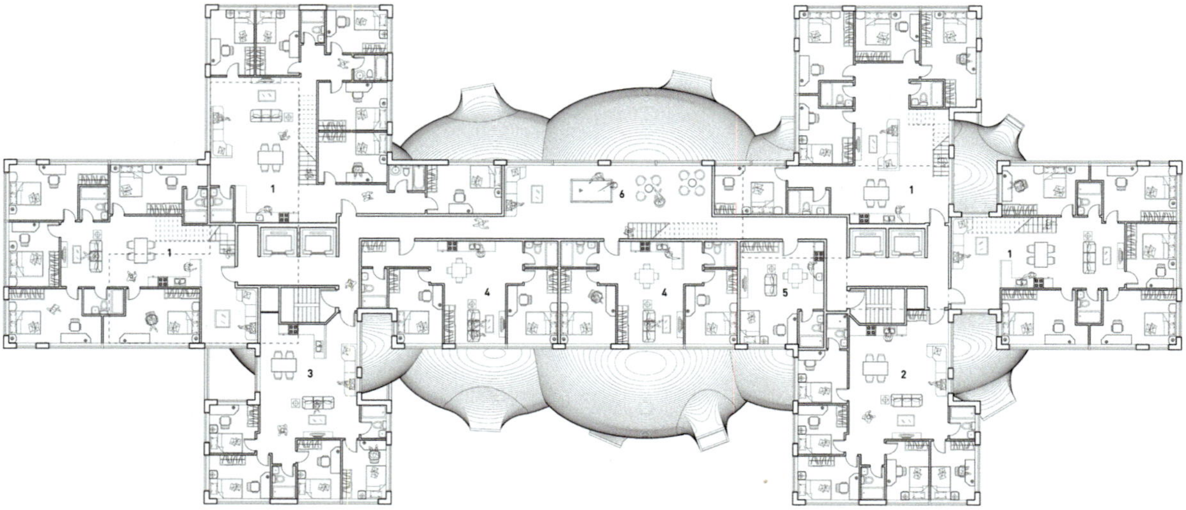

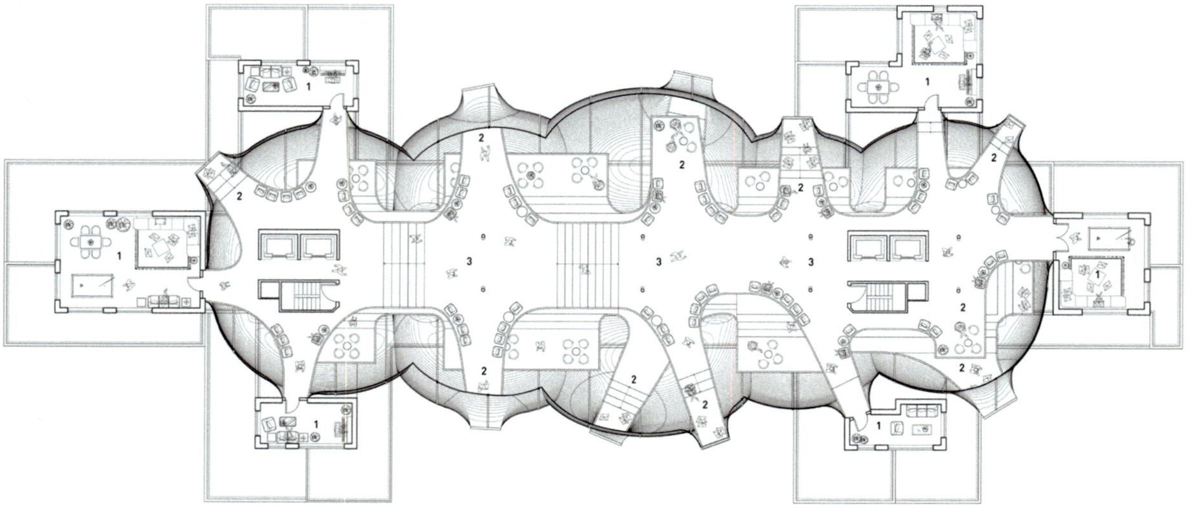

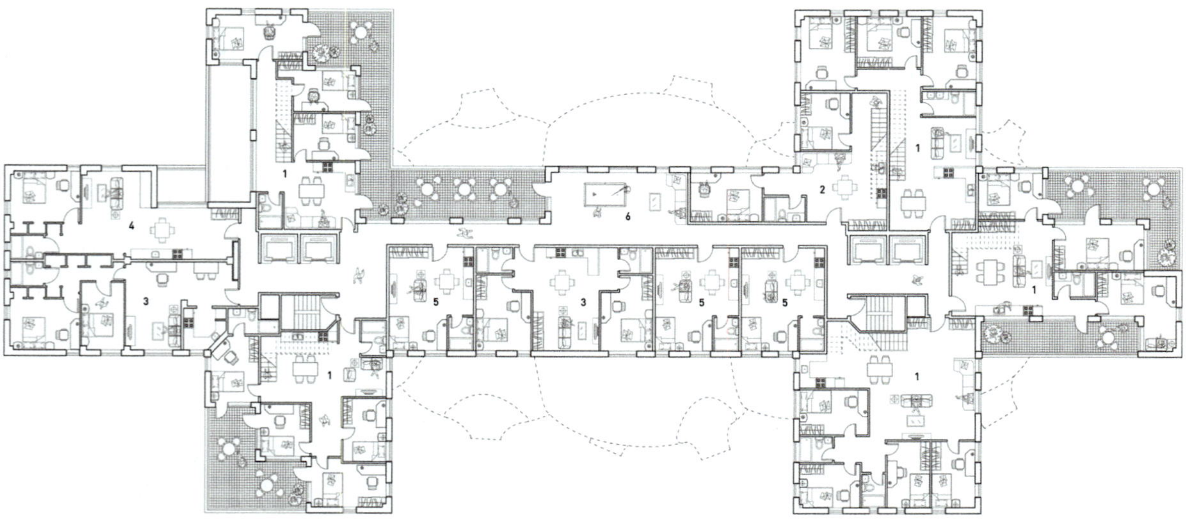

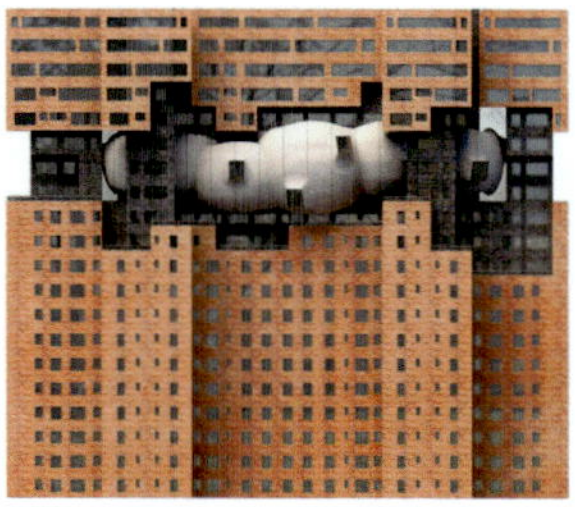

Elevation

Urbanistically, qualities are not any less grim. Stuyvesant Town defines a massive urban fortress with only handful of access points. The lateral base lining the streets and avenues either accommodates retail or car park facilities. These base buildings also completely block access into the open spaces of the complex. The periphery buildings are built to the plot line, coming straight down to the edge of the sidewalk with its less than ordinary architecture. Impact of their bluntness in the urban space, especially looking east on 14th Street, is inescapable. Once you filter through the entry points and enter the grounds (which are privately patrolled), you find yourselves in an environment which might be impossible to associate with Manhattan: tall majestic trees which are now fully grown, open spaces for recreation between buildings, various community spaces which were recently added that activate the ground level experience, the central "oval" which in many ways acts like the Sheep's Meadow of Central Park during sunny days. Interestingly, Architecture recedes to the background once one begins to meander the grounds. The lack of architectural character miraculously works towards foregrounding the organic matter and its atmosphere. On a sunny day, Le Corbusier's vague eye level sketches of Plan Voisin appear fully rendered in real material, in real life: utopia realized. That is, of course, if one chooses to ignore the history of racial segregation in the complex, and the market pressures to force out the longstanding tenants who have lived here all their lives, as well as the attempts to abolish rent control for the entire complex. Things are not as pretty as they might seem on that sunny day. The homogeneous nature of Stuyvesant Town and what it represents, as it is physically made and as it demographically trends, is far removed from our current aspirations of a just, inclusive, and diverse society.

With this picture in front of us, the studio challenges the students to alter the definitions of this homogeneous environment, towards far more heterogeneous physical and programmatic conditions. Each student is assigned a building in the complex to alter with a specific programmatic agenda which they develop in parallel to formal explorations, not fully dependent or independent, just co-evolving side by side. The formal explorations engage the literal physical conditions and constraints of the existing host buildings. Generally, these initial exercises experiment with volumetric expansion of the existing buildings laterally or vertically. Additional articulations in various scales follow as more definition is gained through maturing design process. The programmatic narratives usually operate through projections of near-future scenarios that speculate on the evolution of current realities pressuring our notions of living and working. In joint conversations with the students as a collective, we begin to develop a set of ideas about program, consciously varying from student to student, to redefine and expand the range of activities in the complex.

In Yan's case, she anticipated an architecture that represented the initial optimism and perhaps exuberance of WeWork and WeLive in the short run, which was conceived as a translucent bubble-like expressive volume squeezed into the familiar massing of the existing structure. She proposed to trim the existing building down to two-thirds of its original height to insert the co-working bubble which evolved around the proximity of the original building's footprint but expands sectionally away from the original

Left

Plans showing the organizational approach for the housing units on the levels above and below the communal workspace. Sandwiched between these is the mezzanine level of the shared workspace in the bubble.

Above

Elevation of the project, showing the integration of the bubble within the simple extrusion of the existing building.

mass. The multi-level, free-flowing space within the bubble was conceptualized as an open working space which could accommodate different scales of gathering and isolation as needed. More structured meeting spaces and offices were also defined within a recessed orthogonal volume, articulated with dark brick, also performing as a deep relief in the façade defining a physical separation between the red brick volume and the white bubble volume. The building is again capped with a brick volume, same in color and plan shape as the existing building but mildly different in aperture articulation. In a strange way the outcome is equally excessive and mute. The transformed building's formal definition oscillates between confrontational geometries which are tailored to resolve their difference at their seams. In the images on the right, the formally expressive bubble is strategically contained within the predominant orthogonal massing of the original building to keep it somewhat restrained. The change in the feel of 14th Street corridor is undeniable.

While Yan speculated on a narrative which anticipated repeated programmatic shifts within the future life of the project, she also anticipated the permanence of the architectural intervention to remain intact. This is potentially valid for all architecture. The reality is that the prevailing forces which dictate program usually subside or shift, but physical architecture remains. It is crucial to be able to calibrate the forces upon a project through a long-range anticipation, so what remains after program abandons is still good architecture.

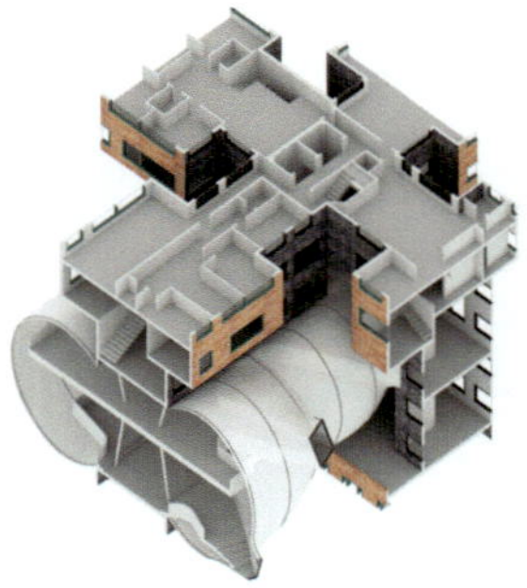

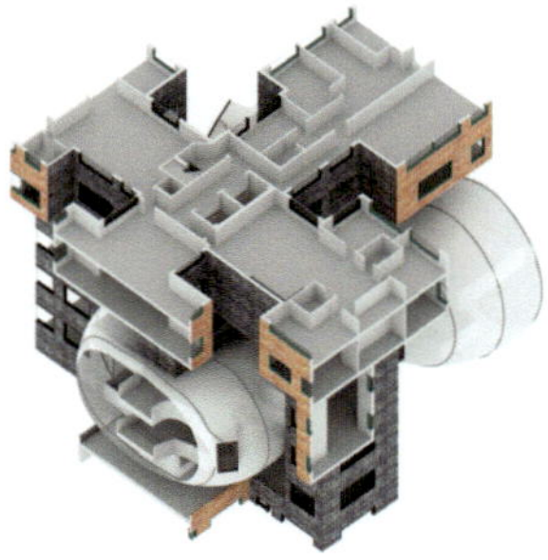

Chunk Isometrics

Above

Partial axonometric views showing the sectional conditions of the multi-story communal workspace and the planimetric condition of typical housing layouts.

Right

Elevated frontal view of the Communal Workplace Bubble in the live/work hybrid building transformation.

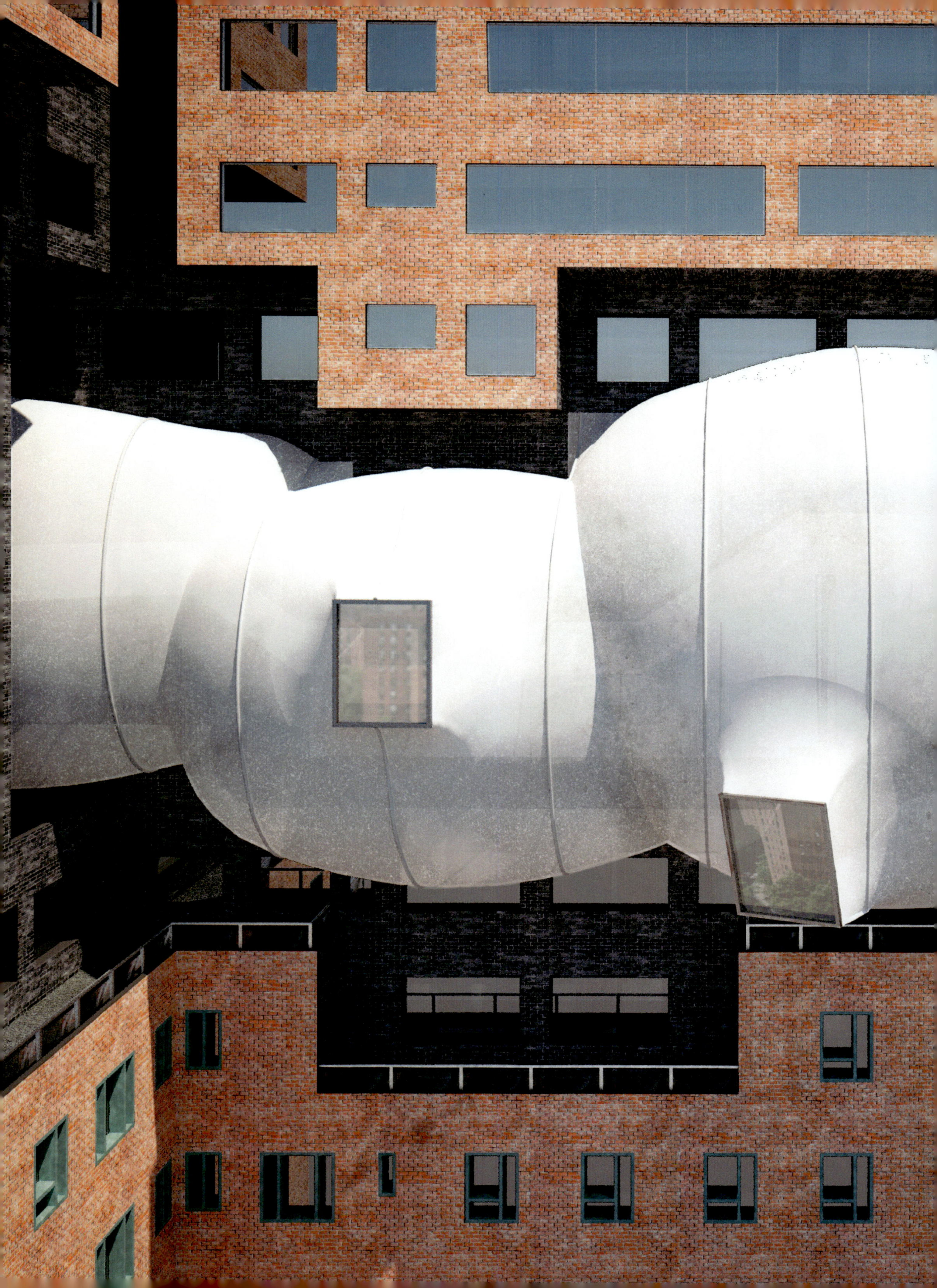

n Progress: Residential
ATLANTIC CRANE
LIEBHERR
ATLANTIC CRANE NEW YORK, NY

MICRO–MACRO LIVING

Mimi Hoang with Zachary Weimer | nARCHITECTS

The City Dweller Today

In rethinking the organization of domestic life, the micro-unit provides a larger opportunity to address how urban dwellers have changed. In cities globally, people are living greener, healthier lifestyles, and therefore living longer. They also marry later, partly due to the fact that women are studying and working more and are divorcing more. The result is evidenced by a global rise in solo living by 80 percent in the last 15 years.[1] In Manhattan, nearly half of the population lives alone and the nuclear family (traditionally characterized by two parents and children) has decreased to below 20 percent.[2] Despite this, in the United States, the size of the average house has nearly doubled since the 1950s.[3] This is partly born out of turn-of-the-century housing reforms, when the journalist Jacob Riis exposed the horrific living conditions of New York City's immigrant population. His photographs of overcrowded tenement housing without proper ventilation and daylight brought about the city's current housing regulations, which set the new standard for life safety and apartment sizes (400 square feet x 8 feet tall ceiling height minimum).[4] But these large apartments for nuclear families that the regulations encouraged are no longer in sync with the city's demographics. There are 1.8 million small households, with only 1 million suitable apartments to house them in New York City. As demand outpaces supply, the rental cost per square foot of studio apartments outstrips that of larger apartments, contributing to informal and illegal sublets and subdivisions. Crowding and density must here be distinguished—while density is beneficial to neighborhoods because it yields more amenities, services and infrastructure (such as healthcare facilities) within walkable distances, crowding, such as that within informally subdivided apartment buildings, produces unsafe and inhumane conditions.[5]

Left

nARCHITECTS
Carmel Place
New York, 2016

There are 65 modules, including the stair and elevator core. Each module encapsulates an apartment and a slice of the corridor. The financial constraints associated with a tight site required an 1/8-inch construction tolerance within the modules—a level of tolerance that would have been impossible to achieve with conventional construction.

Another important shift in urban living, which runs parallel to demographic change, lies in the transformed way we work today. Work has stretched across longer hours, intermittently invading traditionally "off" hours and creeping into informal, casual settings outside of the workplace. At the same time, the notion of "home" and its domestic armature have found physical expression in the work and public spheres. Amenities for living, recreation and social interaction have been atomized and dispersed beyond the rigid delineation of the dwelling. The concept of micro-living is thus tied to macro-pressures of population change and its corresponding housing supply challenges, as well as changes in how and when we work. As work loses its temporal and physical boundaries, increasingly overlapping with domestic space, the housing crisis is inextricably linked to changes in how we occupy private and public space.

Percentage of Single-person Households Worldwide

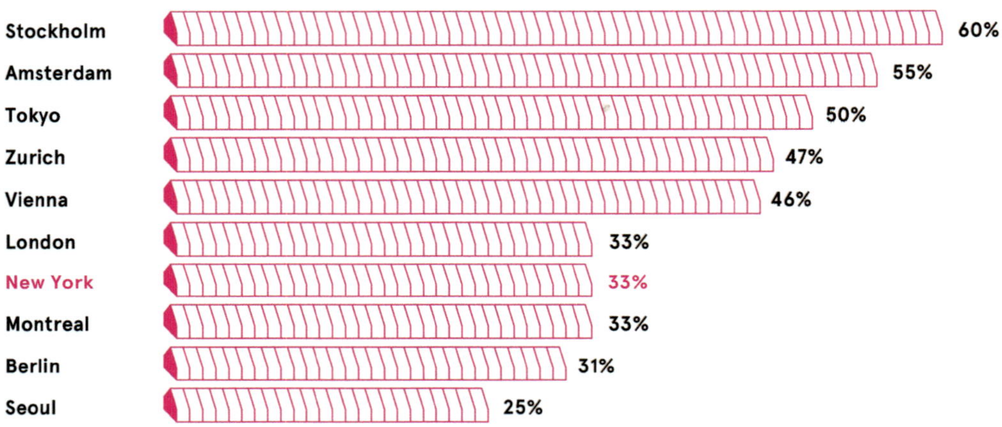

Scalable Frameworks and a Party

What are the opportunities in rethinking the delineations between private and shared space and the efficiencies of parallel use scenarios? Four approaches related to space and organization—*Shrink, Multi-Function, Share* and *Configuration*—offer different frameworks for improving housing affordability and creating better places to live. *Shrink* questions how to minimize and compact the physical size of the elements of housing. Efficiency is increased by fitting more within a limited space. *Multi-Function* encourages the design of spaces and elements for many uses and forms of inhabitation. This is accomplished either through 'transformable' elements, flexibly changing as needed, or 'blank' elements that are open for appropriation. *Share* maximizes efficiency by reducing and facilitating the sharing of spaces and resources by multiple parties. *Configuration* considers novel ways of aggregating and organizing units and spaces to gain efficiencies in duplicated spaces and functions. These approaches are designed to be applied at a range of scales, from that of objects

Above

nARCHITECTS
Percentage of Single-person Households Worldwide

Although the percentage of single-person households in New York today is considerably higher than 30 years ago and growing, other cities like Tokyo and Stockholm now comprise a majority of such households.

(e.g., small appliances, kitchenware, tools), elements (fixed appliances, showers, doors, wall partitions), domestic and shared spaces, unit aggregations, buildings and to the city itself. They offer a kind of tool-kit of spatial typologies and actions, which we explored for the Storefront for Art and Architecture's "Manhattanisms" exhibition in 2016. We were challenged to reimagine how the city might develop in response to our prevalent sharing economy model. Our contribution, Key Party, served as an extrapolation of extreme sharing in the form of micro live/work environments. With the possibilities of new configurations and sharing in mind, we explored the notion of a dispersed home. Does one have to live in a circumscribed and programmatically complete unit? If you share your kitchen, does it necessarily need to be in your home? With Key Party, we explored the possibility that the home is not defined by the four walls of your apartment—that a more radical boundary for the home might be delineated by the block, with dwelling activities dispersed across hallways and streets.

Percentage of Single-person Households Nationwide

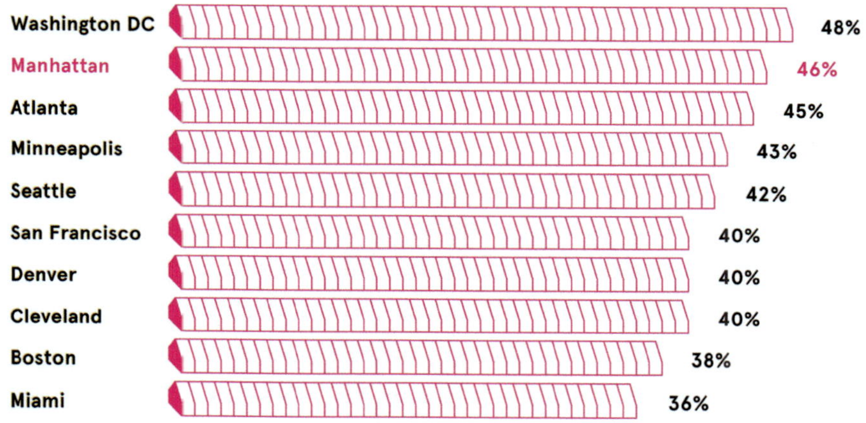

The title of Key Party (inspired by a questionable trend in the 1970s of depositing your keys in a bowl and going home with whomever picked them up) is a provocation to untether ourselves from how we have traditionally defined domestic space. Must we be so rigid in defining dwelling units, or can we detach notions from each other: the programmatic unit detached from the social unit, which is detached from the physical unit, and then detached from the economic unit? We imagined an overlapping and dispersed concept of home, comprising larger buildings that are shared, along with slender mini-homes, mini-towers that allow for solitude within the crowd. This expanded notion of living occurs within and between buildings and blocks, encouraging greater mobility and access.

Above

nARCHITECTS
Percentage of Single-person Households Nationwide

The island of Manhattan has a higher percentage of single-person households than most other large cities in the United States.

nARCHITECTS
Carmel Place, New York, 2016

Green, vibrant outdoor public space further helps in contributing to the "neighborliness" of the building. The park at the building's base creates a space for the building community and the larger neighborhood community to come together.

Planning and Design

Key Party served as a radical exercise in reconceptualizing dwelling given changes in demographics and the way we work, but it grew out of other projects in both New York and Hong Kong. In response to research highlighting the mismatch of New York City's housing stock relative to its current population, the mayor's office, the Department of Housing Preservation and Development, and the City Planning Commission launched a public competition in 2012. Entitled adAPT NYC, the competition posed the question—should the city reduce the current 400-square-foot minimum for new apartments? In response, we proposed Carmel Place, completed in 2016, as a pilot project to test what a small, livable and humane apartment might look like. Although the project received a mayoral override for the minimum apartment size under the Quality Housing Program, it still complied with all other building department rules regulating residential unit interiors. These include Americans With Disabilities Act (ADA)-accessible kitchens and bathrooms, minimum habitable room dimensions (150 square feet, with 8-foot minimum dimensions), requirements for light and air, and separation of the kitchen from the living area.

Carmel Place is the first and only building in the city consisting of 100 percent micro-units or studios. The project utilized modular construction, which offered important benefits in terms of efficiency and in implementation of sustainable best practices; structurally integrated modules not relying on a primary structural core were stacked to produce double floor/ceiling and wall assemblies. The resulting redundancy from structural self-stacking helped to protect the modules during staging and setting. To encourage modular construction in the city, the project was granted a few extra feet in height and lot coverage. Even with the extra dimension, the project relied on a construction tolerance of an 1/8 inch in certain areas in order to retain a financially viable unit count. Such a tight tolerance to ensure code compliance would not have been possible with traditional in-situ construction methods.

Objects, Elements and Spaces

The studio units in Carmel Place average 300 square feet. While reducing the previous minimum for new apartments, we considered ways to compensate for the loss of floor area. Through our research, we determined that people are far more likely to perceive subtle differences in vertical dimensions than in horizontal ones. Most people are able to notice the difference between a 5' 6" versus a 5' 9" person, whereas most would not notice the difference between a 10' 0" vs. a 10' 3" wide room. We decided this could be a place to give back: in comparison to the standard minimum of 8' 0" ceiling heights, the micro-units measure 9' 8" tall, which allows for a significant amount of extra storage space (roughly the volume of a Volkswagen Jetta trunk) above the kitchens and bathrooms. While overall unit area decreased by 25 percent, the volume was only diminished by 10 percent. We also identified unit windows as important elements that might be enlarged to offset shrinking elsewhere—by creating larger openings (minimum 8' 0" tall x 6' 0" wide sliding doors and Juliet balconies)

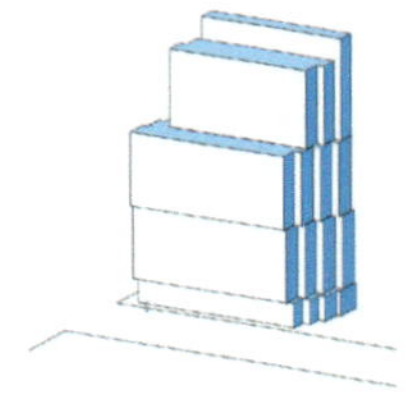

Our Micro Towers
55 units, 4 towers, 10 floors

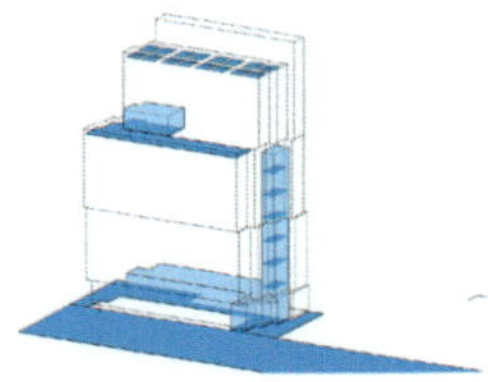

Our Shared Spaces
3525 sqft of exterior space
5470 sqft interior ammenities

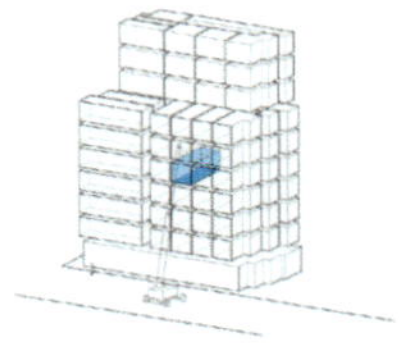

Our Micro Module
75 modules, 5 weeks to erect them

Above

nARCHITECTS
Carmel Place, New York, 2016

The building comprises individual micro-units that serve as literal building blocks, but those blocks also create a scaffold for collective living at nested scales. The prefabricated modules, together with an abundance of interior and exterior shared spaces, form a series of towers that give expression to the community life within and help give shape to a changing neighborhood.

Right

Typical floor plan. Unit layouts vary by orientation to ensure that potential residents are able to choose organizations best suited to their individual needs.

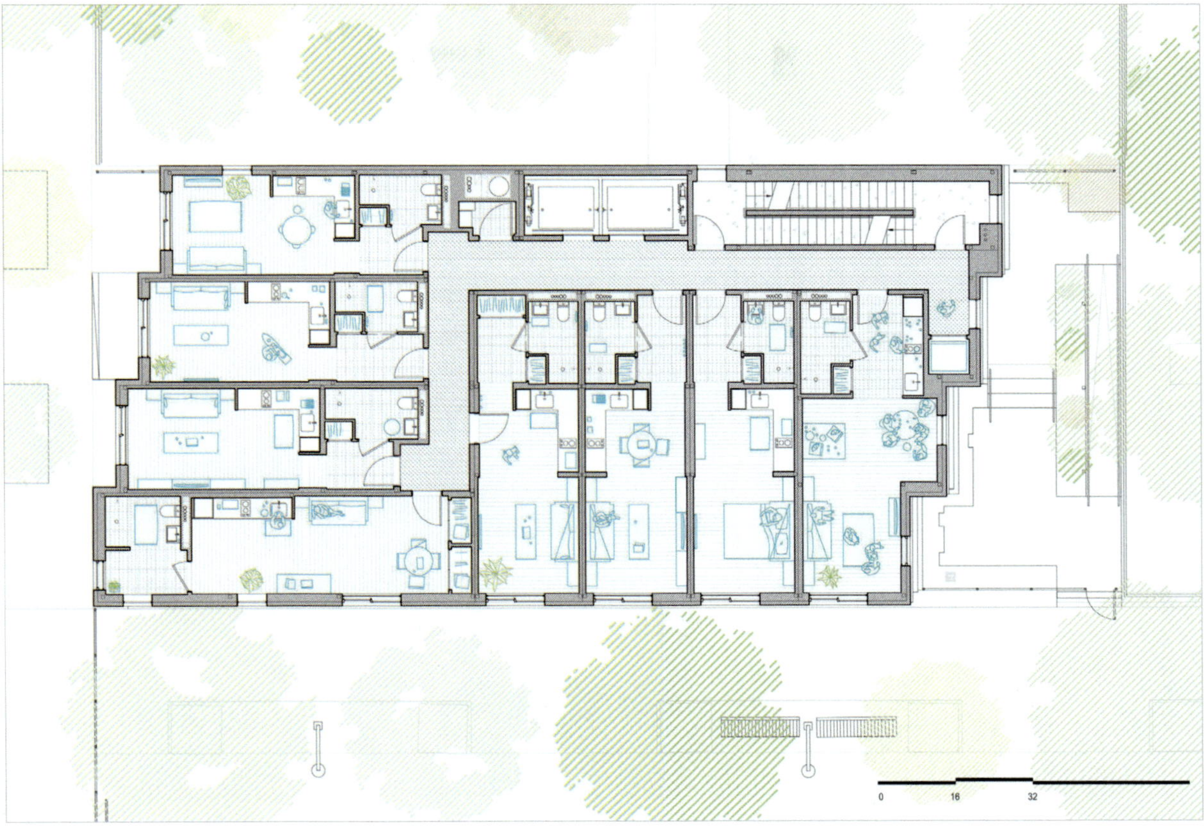

to light and air, we exceeded requirements by over 50 percent. Coupled with the ceiling height, these strategies maximized the perceived volume of space, resulting in spacious-feeling units. We also utilized transformable built-ins to ensure that spaces within units could fulfill multiple functions.

Supporting the notion of a dispersed home, we emphasized a larger-than-average ratio of shared amenities to leasable tenant space across all levels of the building. As in Key Party, we dispersed all the amenities of a typical house throughout the building. Beyond the walls of the individual apartment units, these active spaces encourage casual daily social interactions and enhance connections within the building community. Tenants have access to spaces where they can sit and work—in the spacious building lobby with defined seating areas, exterior seating areas with access to outlets, community rooms at the eighth floor level and in the cellar. A large gym highlights the changing trend for a healthier lifestyle in New York and with single people. The community rooms and terraces also provide spaces for barbequing, playing pool and table games, and watching films, and building management promotes regular social events for the building.

Building and City: Modular Construction

The building massing at Carmel Place was designed to counter the perception that micro-living constitutes a diminished living experience. Conceived as a microcosm of the city skyline where the building's exterior resembles four slender "mini towers," the concept of micro-living is thus connected to the form and identity of the building. To date, Carmel Place is the tallest modular building constructed with self-supporting units in Manhattan. A total of 65 individual steel- and concrete-framed modules make up 55 apartment units and 10 units that serve as the building's stair and elevator core. In footprint, each module delineates the boundary of an apartment unit, plus a portion of the corridor. The modules are interconnected vertically at each column, and at the floor

SHOW YOUR WORK!

level within the corridor. Building systems connections were made within the corridor. This most "raw" space of the building allowed on-site work for system connections, including plumbing, mechanical, electrical and fire safety. The stair core was fabricated without steps, which were hoisted into place as the stacking of the building proceeded. Eight residential micro-units, with five variations in size and orientation, make up a typical floor. The system allowed us to balance efficiency through repetition with variation in apartment layout, thereby broadening the spectrum of choice for small family households.

The modules were built in the Brooklyn Navy Yard and transported over the bridge to Manhattan, resulting in greatly reduced material waste and transport resources, and enabling use of local suppliers. This process also allowed for the fabrication of a complete mock-up unit prior to full production-line fabrication, to resolve potential construction issues, space or layout adjustments and to test the feasibility of extremely tight tolerances. When the modules leave the factory, most finishes, utilities, fixtures and windows were in place, leaving only appliances, finish flooring and brick work to be completed in situ. Units were stacked over the course of only three short weeks, greatly reducing neighborhood disturbance and construction time in a dense residential site.

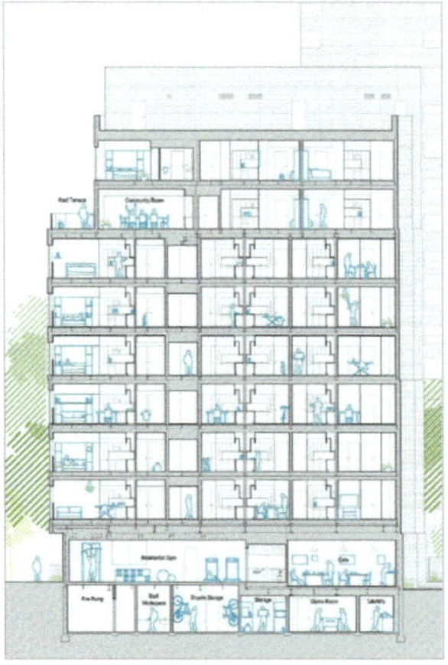

The very term "micro" triggers assumptions of impermanent, low-quality construction that invites transient tenants and poses long-term maintenance and durability issues. But modular construction offers inherent redundancies that can counter these negative associations. Double-wall and floor/ceiling assemblies provide structural rigidity and acoustic isolation within dense unit configurations, as steel posts are embedded within the thickness of the mate-line wall assembly. The apartments are designed to allow for individual retreat within light-filled, comfortable spaces while the building provides options for social interaction.

Left Top

nARCHITECTS
Carmel Place
New York, 2016

Flexible furniture, capable of performing multiple forms of work, was used as often as possible to ensure that space and efficiency were maximized in all units.

Left Bottom

Large windows, high ceilings and a restrained pallet help to maximize the perceived volume of space.

Above

The redundancy in floor and ceiling assemblies produced from stacking structurally integrated modules does not lead to compromised space—ceilings within individual micro-units are almost 10 feet high and help to create the sense of generous space.

Other Contexts: Hong Kong, City of Micro-Units

As a concurrent example of housing supply challenges, Hong Kong Island is 1.5 times the density of New York City when calculated in relation to actual buildable land area (HK Census, NYC Census). Just 2 percent of that buildable land area is dedicated to public space. Recognizing this shortage, city planning officials recently revealed the 2030 Plus vision for more public space, including transforming roads and areas under bypasses into pedestrian and performance zones. But the 2030 Plus blueprint falls short of development area needed for housing.[6] The pressures of high land cost—usually two-thirds that of the entire project (including construction cost and soft costs)—drive the density and efficiency of housing developments. Designers are not left with much room for social or public space.

The interiors of apartments in Hong Kong are not as heavily regulated as those in New York City, with no minimum area requirements and only a minimum ceiling height requirement of 2.5 meters. However, given the economic and availability pressures on area, it is more acceptable for living space to be occupied vertically, be it in overhead storage or loft spaces within residential units. The Hong Kong building department also permits a higher density within domestic buildings, at a little over twice what is permitted in New York City. Daylight requirements are comparable to New York, but the requirements for ventilation in Hong Kong exceed those of New York by 25 percent. Perhaps the most important difference between dwelling units in Hong Kong and New York is that Barrier Free Design is not required; bathrooms and kitchens are thus able to be much smaller and more efficient.

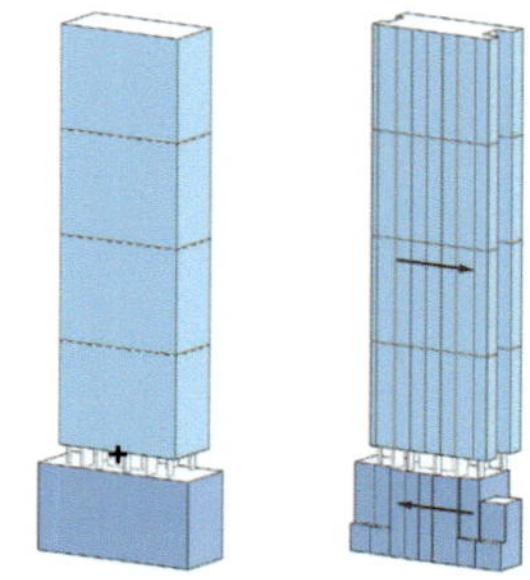

Unification and Facade Strategy

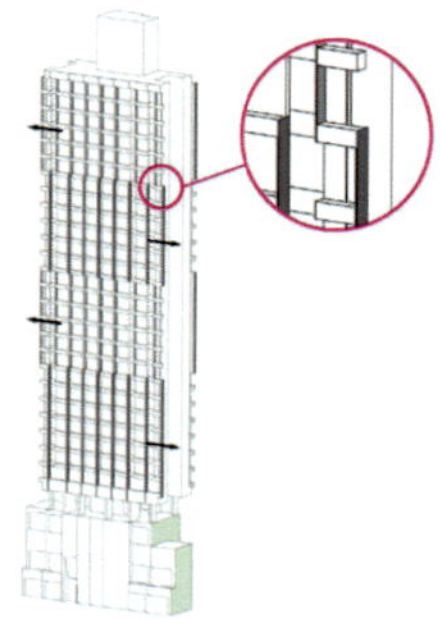

Zipper Edge

Other factors shaping the form of urban development include the practice of selling land at auction to generate government revenue. This market-driven approach, with amendments to the Buildings Ordinance, has transformed Hong Kong's urban fabric: increasingly large towers on plinths now dominate the urban landscape.[7] Older, small lots are often purchased in series by developers, and developed as a single-use complex at a monumental scale.

When we began to design a 30-floor residential tower within this context, we felt that it was important to reconcile the alienating scale of point towers with the informal, dynamic patterns of street activity for which the city is well known. At 30 floors totaling 130 meters, our Artisan House, completed in 2018, resides within a historic residential neighborhood in Sai Ying Pun that includes three-story shophouses, bulky six- to eight-story blocks and tall towers. To celebrate the history of the old neighborhood, with its narrow, low buildings and small shops, we mitigated the large scale of the podium and tower in a few ways. The podium is broken down into vertical bays, reminiscent in scale to that of historic shophouses. Extensive green walls and planters at the level of the podium help to counter the effect of extreme density and improve the street environment and air quality. While Hong Kong's humid climate is desirable for plant growth, it practically mandates concrete, rather than steel (which presents water infiltration and rust issues) as the typical construction method. To maximize interior space, a thin layer of plaster on concrete—the thinnest possible finish—is used in lieu of other wall assemblies. And the balcony soffits at each unit are clad in polished aluminum to reflect the street environment below. In this way, the building connects high-rise living with the social spaces and dynamic activities of the street.

The Social Unit

Drawing from our experiences in New York City versus Hong Kong, it is interesting to note the different pressures and contexts that result in similarly scaled residential units. Whereas solo living and small households have risen in New York City, the same trend is not evident in Hong Kong. Partly due to economics and the difficulty of finding affordable apartments, young adults stay in their parents' home for longer in Hong Kong. Additionally, in a culture that prioritizes the needs of the family over that of the individual, one's voice in society often reflects the collective voice of one's family. In contrast, in cosmopolitan western cities where one usually lives apart from one's family, the rise of the sharing economy reflects not just an attitude against ownership

Above

nARCHITECTS
Artisan House
Hong Kong, 2018

Artisan House balances the high rise's iconic blade-like volume with connections to the scale of the neighborhood through smaller articulations in its massing and materials.

Right Top

Typical floor plan. Studio apartments range from 160 to 200 sqft. Although they might be considered micro-units in other markets, in Hong Kong they are simply standard-sized, market-rate apartments.

Right Bottom

Traditional shophouses of Hong Kong provide a scale reference for the micro-unit tower.

UP
UP
UP
UP

and consumption, but also the desire for social engagement. One's social unit(s) is not necessarily circumscribed by one's family, but is rather defined by overlapping interactions defined by the individual.

The Beauty of Smallness

As we confront new challenges that arise and face down structural problems we have inherited, we must continue in our commitment to build vibrant, resilient urban communities. Technology has enabled and promoted a sharing economy, where the value of owning less and sharing tools, services and experiences has increased. Micro-living then, should be understood not only as a compact-sized residential unit, but also through the lens of the benefits of the collective experience. Designers must continue to emphasize connectivity: between shared spaces, between private units and the environment, between building and urban infrastructure. Micro-living is a crucial tool with which cities can retain their essential diversity—of their demographics, housing stock and modes of living.

Above

nARCHITECTS
Carmel Place
New York, 2016

The process of craning prefabricated units. The units stacked in three and a half weeks.

Right

When units left the factory, nearly everything was in place, including the walls, windows, lights, and plumbing mains and fixtures. Partitions were closed except for those on the corridor side of the wet walls, which remained open to allow utilities to be connected between floors. Welded at each steel post above and below, the units stacked in three and a half weeks.

References

1. Eric Klinenberg, "I Want to Be Alone: The Rise and Rise of Solo Living," *The Guardian*, March 30, 2012. https://www.theguardian.com/lifeandstyle/2012/mar/30/the-rise-of-solo-living
2. Jerilyn Perine and Sarah Watson, "One Size Fits Some." Citizen's Housing and Planning Council, 2011.
3. Mark J. Perry, "New U.S. Homes Today are 1,000 Square Feet Larger than in 1973 and Living Space per Person has Doubled," AEIdeas, June 5, 2016. https://www.aei.org/carpe-diem/new-us-homes-today-are-1000-square-feet-larger-than-in-1973-and-living-space-per-person-has-nearly-doubled/#:~:text=Over%20the%20last%2042%20years,2%2C687%20square%20feet%20last%20year
4. For more on tenement reform and the legacy of Jacob Riis, see Bonnie Yochelson and Daniel Czitrom, *Rediscovering Jacob Riis: The Reformer, His Journalism, and His Photographs*. New York: New Press, 2008.
5. Citizens Housing and Planning Council, "Density and Covid-19 in New York City," May 2020. https://chpcny.org/density-covid-19-nyc/.6. Shirley Zhao, "Planning Chiefs Reveal Vision for More Public Space in Heaving Hong Kong," *South China Morning Post*, December 31, 2016.
7. Peter Cookson Smith, *The Urban Design of Impermanence: Streets, Places and Spaces in Hong Kong*. Hong Kong: MCCM Creations, 2011.

D

CARVING NEW HOUSING ORGANIZATIONS

Ben Krone

The shift in thinking toward smaller unit types is generational and a response to changes in family demographics and the ways in which younger generations gravitate toward cities. Value is less about privately owned space and is instead geared toward shared economies, social structures, and the integration of work/life into domestic settings, an idea that I elaborate on in my previous study. There are many novel ways to achieve high efficiencies within the units themselves and the prospect of new types of spaces that are afforded by 'configurations' of stacking and shifting prefabricated micro-units.

The argument for the benefits of utilizing efficiencies by limiting the repetition of non-essential living space and giving this back to a larger, more useful shared program is undeniable. While modular construction seems to be beneficial at a certain level for micro-units due to its compactness and high degree of control, there is also a strong argument to be made for the deployment of this way of thinking into existing buildings.

Reuse vs Build New

In most cases the ratio of developable existing buildings to empty lots is high. In cities like New York, nearly all of the empty developable building sites are on the periphery of the city in non-residential zoned areas. It is for this reason that the largest percentage of construction projects in urban centers focus on the renovation and development of existing building stock.

In the last decade, incentives have evolved for greener building developments which automatically point to reuse wherever possible. Although new buildings can generally be constructed to perform better than old buildings in terms of their energy efficiency, new innovations in building materials and more aggressive city regulations make it possible for older buildings to be retrofitted to perform quite well. This is especially true when considering materials used in older buildings that are either no longer available or too expensive to deploy. In many cases these buildings have characteristics making

Left

Veronica Rosado
Co/Habitation–Red Hook

Ben Krone Urban Housing Studio with Catherine Shih

University of Pennsylvania Weitzman School of Design, 2019

The cutaway view expresses the depth of the façade and the activity that occurs at each layer. The outermost layer is a system of water gutters that become small open irrigation pools at the edges of each balcony as it makes its way down the building.

Night view detail showing the layers of carved away spaces that make up the housing units and private terraces.

them more likely to last and are naturally better insulators than the lightweight building materials of today. Performance alone is not the only factor. The amount of energy required to demolish an existing building and the material production to build new, including carbon footprints required to access materials, far outweigh the life cycle cost of performance enhancements of new buildings.

Rooms vs Units

My studios have explored housing integration into existing buildings. One of the interesting outcomes of the studio's work is that from the sectional complexity resulting from inserting into and carving out of existing building masses, a more dispersed relationship of individual rooms emerges. Rather than a defined living 'unit' which is the natural result of prefabricated construction, the integration in existing building grids resulted in the distribution of the dwelling unit into a series of private and shared rooms that are no longer defined by the traditional four walls and a roof of typical townhouse or multifamily building. The economy gained through stacking plumbing within a framework of housing units is suddenly freed. Two bathrooms or kitchens from two adjacent units can be stacked on top of one another, side by side or they may be opened and shared. The result affords a wider range of unit types and volumes, where stacking modular units tends to limit the types of adjacencies and requires a relatively defined size of unit.

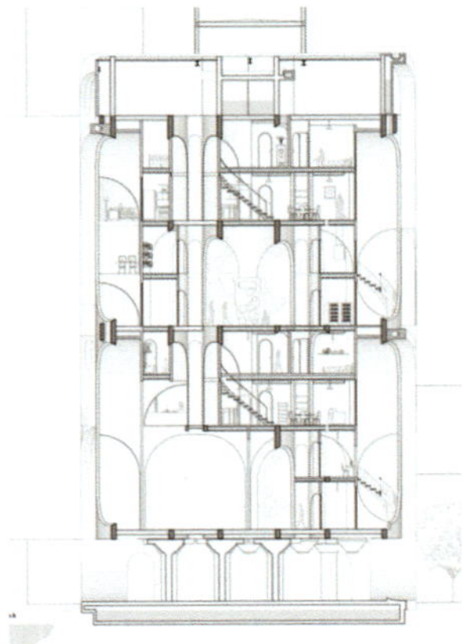

Above

East/West section shows the building's narrow depth and how the private spaces are pushed inward. The entry sequence into the building is also shown as it steps its way from the ground up into the units above.

Right Top

The plan expresses the portions of the existing grain terminal that are preserved and cut away along with the portions that are added to link multiple silo cylinders together to create larger units and shared spaces between the artist residences and the associated studio spaces.

Right Bottom

North/South section across housing and studio units expressing the relationship of the pairing of studios and housing units. In addition the system of retaining pools on the roof is expressed as they flow along the building's facade.

When considering the shifts toward new more social and shared economies of newer generations of homeowners and renters, there is an inherent advantage to having a wider range of unit sizes compared to shared common area ratios. Although it's generally true that trends are changing toward smaller units and more distributed shared common spaces, the reality is a bit more fluid. There are overlaps of several generations in the housing market, each with a different sensibility toward ownership and family size, resulting in different spatial needs for housing. It's not realistic for a young family with two kids to buy or rent a 350-square-foot apartment, even if there is a shared cafe or study in the building. One issue that makes designing housing complex is that to be economical, a high degree of generalization is required of both form and function. Something extraordinarily similar in space and volume must work for a very wide range of individuals and family types. It can be argued that modularizing and unitizing housing also narrows the market for targeted demographics. The "micro-model" will likely satisfy a narrow range of housing needs. Instead, by considering housing as a series of individually connected or isolated volumes and programs, the ability to have a more varied range of possible boundaries, sizes of units, and public vs. private shared amenities can be accommodated. The result is developing new housing approaches that can satisfy the needs of more individuals and family types.

One issue with appropriating older existing buildings for housing is having to reassign a building's organization, which was likely not originally intended to satisfy housing code requirements. For example, existing manufacturing buildings tend to have

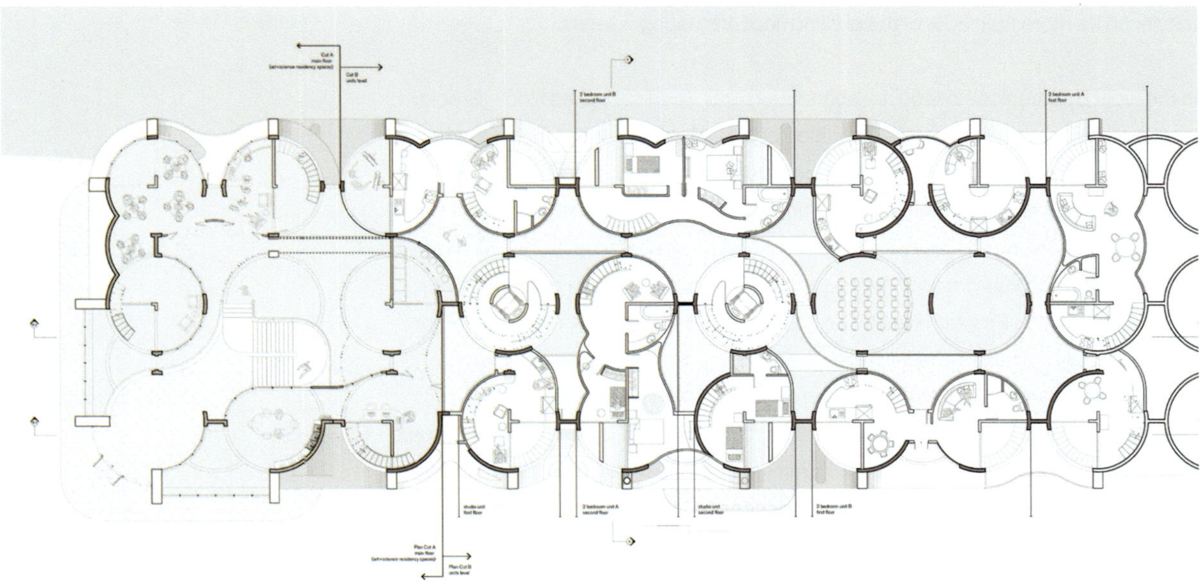

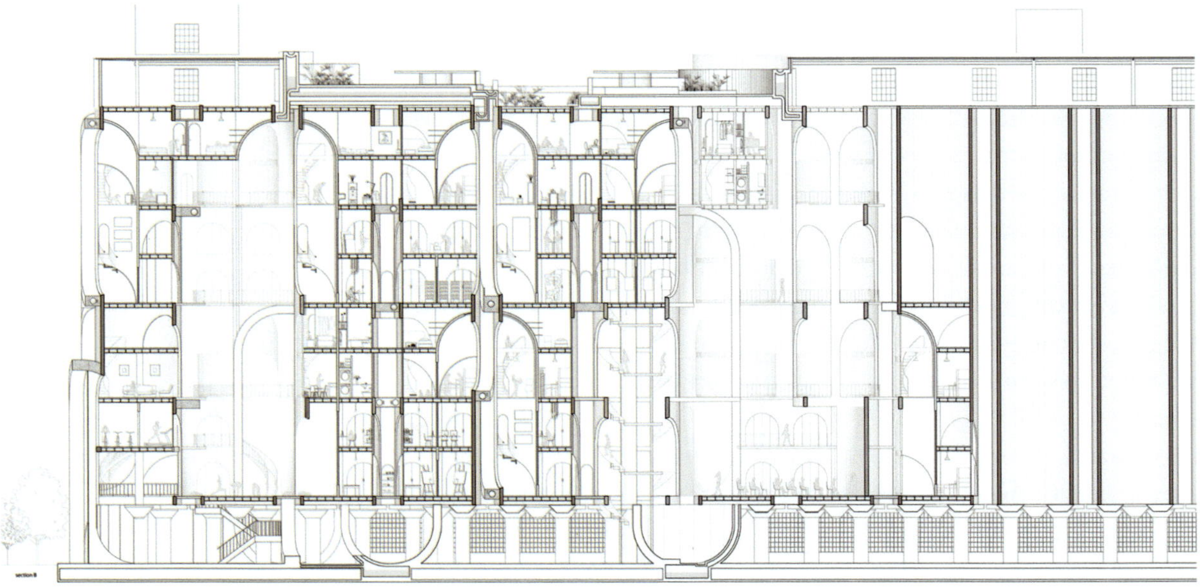

excessively deep footprints which don't meet legal light and air requirements (10% of adjacent floor area for light and 5% of area for air). There is also a maximum distance that habitable spaces can be from a window. This creates an issue for deep centralized volumes that cannot be used for living functions. Large courtyards are often cut into these buildings to get light and air deeper into the massing. This however tends to be a costly and inefficient way to resolve the conversions, and the result can be more than 30% of the existing floor area being wasted.

In the work by Veronica Rosado, an abandoned grain terminal in Red Hook, Brooklyn, was used as a case study for the integration of a new housing prototype. Community program centered around the neighborhood's strong connection to the arts. Initially the building was looked at simply as a vertical grid set by the size and offset of the grain silos and columns below. A physical model of this three-dimensional grid was constructed without its context. A singular unit size was then imagined within that existing framework. Program was dispersed into a new configuration by unraveling, cutting into, and offsetting the three-dimensional grid. Finally, the program was reinserted into the resulting spatial system and tested with new relationships of dispersed programs. This process was constantly tested and reworked until new unit mixes emerged that reimagined the program needs of the resident artists.

The housing units wrapped the edge of the building on both sides. Spaces that were left over in between units were deployed as "connective programs," operating both as private for artist residents and public facing community programs. The spatial displacement of the units was projected onto the new façade of the building. Cuts were made into the silos to create new openings. Rather than expressing the individual apartment units, the cuts linked programs bridging over multiple units. This set up a new multifaceted public-to-private spatial relationship which could forge new social and professional interactions between the artists and the public. Finally, water (a theme of Red Hook as a neighborhood) was used as connective tissue to link all the various programs. Water retention requirements of the building could be pooled in the public spaces on the roof and then slowly distributed throughout an intricate series of gutters along the building façade connecting all the units and programs together. The gutters would open onto each unit's balcony to create small pools and irrigation systems for tenant's use before being distributed back to the ground.

It is imperative as we consider the shifting attitudes toward housing that we also consider how this impacts our cities' social and physical make-up. It is not a realistic proposition to assume that all new housing can be unitized and built up new or that shifts in the family unit suggest that micro-living is the one-size-fits-all approach for future generations. There are also several freedoms and advantages that come along with working with existing building stock. Modular micro-unit construction in housing certainly has its place and economies when working with empty sites but building new also has its drawbacks. We must therefore add to the repertoire of new housing prototypes a wider range of scales, relationships between owned and shared economies, as well as how to work with the full range of existing building types.

Right Top

Detail of the corner of the building showing multiple units within the larger openings. These conditions allow for both privacy and collaboration between the occupants to occur simultaneously. The further back into the layers of the façade the more private the spaces become.

Right Bottom

Long elevation looking toward Buttermilk Channel. The right side of the terminal has been left to decay as a public park and artists' residency space with the housing and studios on the city park side of the building.

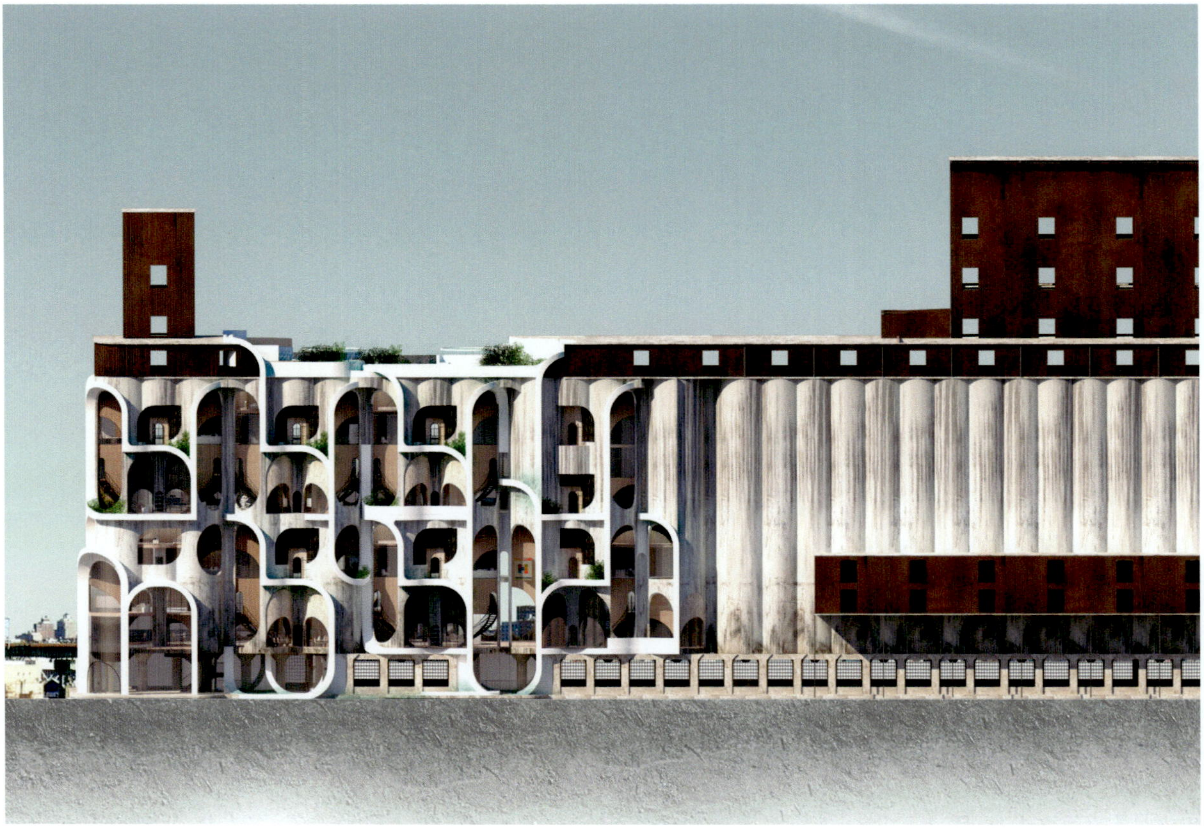

Shadow Series
Edition 3 - 4

03

HOUSING FINANCE AND POLICY

At Least 40 Percent of Renters Are Cost Burdened in Most Metro Areas Across the Country

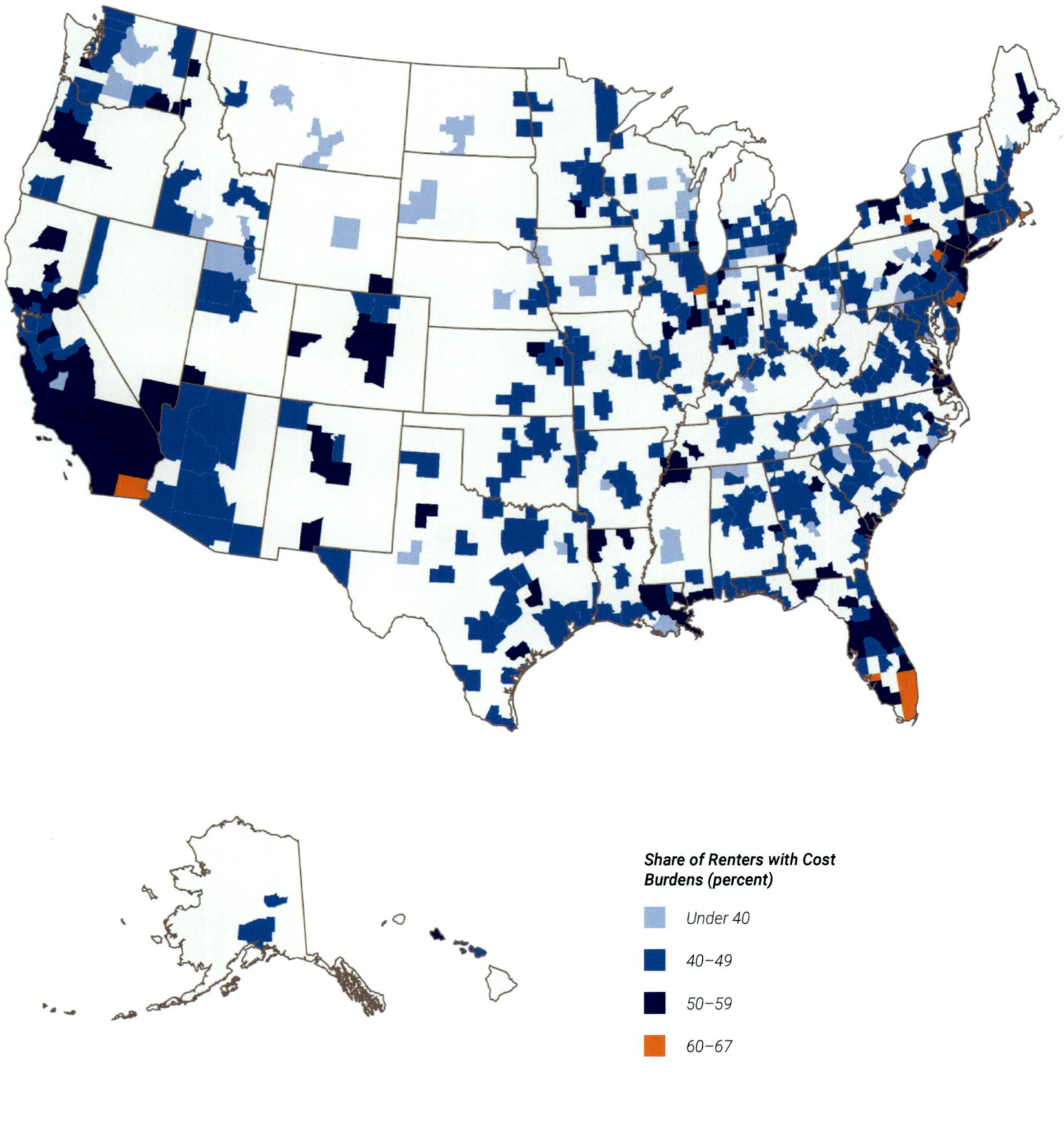

CONFRONTING AFFORDABLE HOUSING CHALLENGES
The Local Role

Mark A. Willis and Benjamin Heller | NYU Furman Center

Background

Housing affordability has become an increasing challenge for cities in the United States, though the causes vary. One driver has been the renewed popularity of urban living, particularly in city centers. In many cases, the demand for housing[1] has outstripped the local supply, resulting in skyrocketing rents and housing prices even as incomes for much of the population stagnate.[2] Other cities continue to be plagued by weak economic conditions accompanied by low wages and increased poverty, a combination that leads to affordability challenges. Both sets of problems can coexist within a single city. As if these forces were not enough, the COVID-19 pandemic is adding to the complexity of the affordability challenges many cities face. The combination of housing supply shortages and stagnating incomes have led to a mismatch between the cost of housing and what households can afford to pay. By one estimate, this mismatch has left 7 million extremely low-income renters paying rent in excess of 30 percent of their income, which is the federal benchmark for a cost-burdened household.[3] Separately, Freddie Mac has estimated that the shortfall in housing production alone has led to a nationwide shortage of 3.3 million housing units, increasing by approximately 300,000 units each year.[4] Together, these trends caused 20.8 million American households to spend more than one third of their income on rent in 2019, according to Harvard University's Joint Center for Housing Studies' 2019 State of the Nation's Housing Report.[5] A map of the United States, produced by the Joint Center, shows just how pervasive affordability issues are, as measured by the share of renters paying more than 30 percent of their income for housing.

Left

Joint Center for Housing Studies of Harvard University
"At Least 40 Percent of Renters are Cost Burdened in Most Metro Areas Across the Country"
America's Rental Housing: 2020 Report, 2020

Most metropolitan areas across the country face affordability issues although the causes may vary.

Even as the affordability challenges facing cities have grown, the federal government has stepped back. Federally funded public housing peaked at 1.4 million units in the mid-1990s and had fallen by 18 percent by 2012 while total housing units in the U.S. grew to more than 130 million.[6] In fact, the U.S. Department of Housing and Urban Development's overall budget has fallen over time in real terms, resulting in less and less federal funding of affordable units.[7] Moreover, since 1986, the value of the Low Income Housing Tax Credit—the federal government's primary vehicle for subsidizing the construction and preservation of affordable housing—has struggled even to keep up with inflation.[8] In this chapter, we argue that because the United States' affordability crisis manifests itself in many different ways, cities and towns need to be proactive in developing and implementing well-tailored local housing strategies, taking advantage of the knowledge and expertise of groups who understand local housing needs and market conditions. Local stakeholders such as for-profit and not-for-profit developers, architects, planners, advocates, and other interested and concerned members of the community are well-positioned to help. This chapter lays out a framework for identifying the best set of programs and policies each locality can and should take.

S&P/Case-Shiller U.S. National Home Price Index

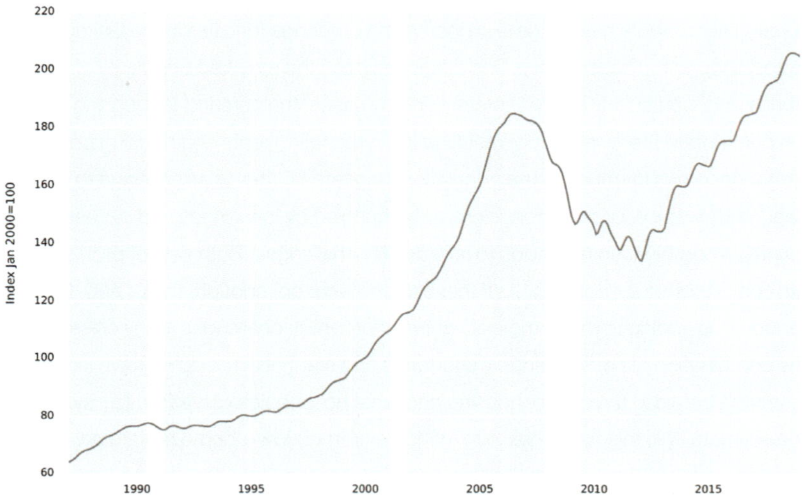

Finally, we present two examples of very different approaches to addressing local affordable housing challenges in a comprehensive and balanced way. Our first example is a city in America, New York City, which harnesses multiple of local, state, and federal resources to support an array of programs, generally built on public–private partnerships. The other, the city-state of Singapore, which has a different political structure and uses a model based almost entirely on public housing.

The United States' Growing Affordability Crisis

The housing bubble of the early 2000s sparked the 2008 Great Recession, when housing prices plummeted and millions of homes across the United States went into foreclosure. According to the S&P Case-Shiller U.S. National Home Price Index, while the national home price index fell from 184.6 to 134 between July 2006 and February 2012, it has since risen nationally, surpassing by 2019 its peak from before the

Left

S&P Dow Jones Indices LLC, S&P/ Case-Shiller U.S. National Home Price Index [CSUSHPINSA]

While home prices fell nationally during the Great Recession, they have now surpassed their pre-crisis peak.

Great Recession, but the local story is more nuanced. Freddie Mac data, seasonally adjusted and indexed in December 2000, show the variation across metro areas. Since the Great Recession, Detroit's housing prices, which were hardly holding their own before 2008, have barely recovered even in nominal terms (110.2 in January 2006, compared to 121.2 in December 2019). Washington, D.C., where housing prices rose sharply before the crash, has regained its previous high (217 to 231.4). By contrast, Seattle (159.4 to 254) and San Francisco (176.1 to 232) have more than recovered; both cities' housing prices far exceed their pre-recession highs.

Analyzing the trend over time in the affordability of rental units is somewhat complicated by the increasing share of high-income rental households. Between 2010 and 2018, high-income households have driven more than three-quarters of growth in rental markets, according to Harvard University's Joint Center for Housing Studies.[9] For many renters, however, the stagnation of wages has made it increasingly difficult to make ends meet, even in low-cost cities where rents have not risen steeply. According to the National Low Income Housing Coalition, in no state in America can a renter earning minimum wage for a 40-hour work week afford a two-bedroom rental.[10] As a result of these trends, more and more cities have felt the need to address their local housing challenges, especially as the federal government has stepped back. However, there is no universally applicable mix of policies suitable for all cities, just as there is no national housing market. Rather, every city needs to compile their own set of policies and priorities tailored to local needs and market conditions—that is, create their own, unique local housing strategy.

Developing and Implementing a Local Housing Strategy

A local housing strategy lays out the approach for a city, town, or county to meet its housing objectives in a comprehensive and balanced manner. Ideally, it should reflect a consensus among stakeholders as to the housing problems that need to be solved, as well as the mechanisms to solve them. A critical first step is to analyze available data to understand and document what is driving local affordability issues. Local housing goals require more than just a single numerical goal for affordable unit production; what is required is a more holistic and nuanced view of the policy interventions and programs needed to address the breadth of the affordability problems. Possible objectives include increasing homeownership rates; promoting stability, quality, and safety; meeting the housing and services needs of older persons or persons with disabilities; and reducing housing discrimination.

Local jurisdictions also need to assess trade-offs to decide how to allocate limited resources across competing objectives. For example, local strategies for cities with high housing demand and costs might consider the trade-offs of building and preserving dedicated affordable housing units with increasing the overall supply of housing; of expanding resources in low-income areas with building affordable housing in higher-income areas; of accommodating growth while protecting individuals from displacement; and balancing increases in rental housing with homeownership.

Three Key Elements

Three elements critical for a successful local housing strategy are coordination, coalition, and consistent multi-year legislative support. As for coordination, a local strategy needs to knit together many sources of funding and relevant policy strands into a single, coordinated plan. Moving from a written document to action requires coordination across local government agencies and divisions that administer policies and programs affecting housing, from the department of housing to the planning department, buildings department, department of finance, local housing authority, and homeless services agency. Local jurisdictions are also more successful when they actively involve key partners throughout the planning and implementation process.

As for coalition, the locality needs to build and maintain a political coalition, which it can do by engaging with the public to develop strategies that reflect shared objectives. Providing residents with an understanding of how proposed developments contribute to broader, jurisdiction-wide goals can help minimize community resistance to individual affordable housing developments, which has been an increasingly formidable challenge to addressing our housing shortage. As for multi-year, legislative support, local housing strategies cannot succeed without multi-year funding and consistent programmatic support by federal, state, and local governments. State government has the power to provide localities with additional resources and with greater legal and regulatory flexibility to address local affordable housing issues. State housing agencies may need to be active partners, too, in both planning and implementation phases.

Four Policy Areas Critical for a Comprehensive and Balanced Local Housing Policy
LocalHousingSolutions.org, Housing Policy Framework, Housing Policy Library, 2020.

1. ***Creating and preserving dedicated affordable housing units***
2. ***Aligning housing supply market and neighborhood conditions***
3. ***Helping Households access and afford private-market homes***
4. ***Protecting against displacement and poor housing conditions***

A Housing Policy Framework and Monitoring System

An effective framework for developing a local housing strategy spans four different policy areas (see Four Policy Areas Critical for a Comprehensive and Balanced Local Housing Policy figure): creating and preserving dedicated affordable units; aligning housing supply with market and neighborhood housing conditions; helping households access and afford private-market homes; and protecting households against displacement and poor housing conditions. In addition are complementary policy areas (e.g., health, education, and environment) which make possible expanded, and hence stronger, coalitions, focused on issues of affordable housing, and more comprehensive solutions that address multiple local priorities at once.

Of course, monitoring the progress of programs and policies is essential for keeping them on track, including detecting the need to adjust the allocation of resources, goals, and priorities based on the pace of progress. Such monitoring also allows for transparency, which helps to build trust and maintain support across government agencies, private stakeholders, and the public.

What does it Mean to Be Comprehensive and Balanced?

A comprehensive and balanced local housing strategy draws on the full array of tools that local governments have at their disposal. Comprehensiveness refers to the breadth of a jurisdiction's involvement in carrying out its local strategy. Strategies that access programs and policies from multiple domains and agencies are likely to be more effective than those that are more narrowly based on one particular program, policy, or agency. Relying solely on the powers granted directly to the housing department, for example, misses out on the powers that other agencies, such as local tax authorities and planning and building departments, can bring to the table. A strategy that focuses only on providing subsidies for dedicated affordable housing is less comprehensive than one that combines subsidies with tax incentives, zoning incentives or requirements, and permitting reforms. While it can be challenging at times to foster the interagency collaboration needed for this approach to succeed, the more comprehensive a local housing strategy is, the stronger its potential for impact.

Balance is equally important for a local housing strategy to succeed. By balancing different dimensions of housing policy, a local strategy is more likely to create an effective approach that meets the full range of a jurisdiction's needs. For example, preserving and expanding the supply of dedicated affordable housing is critical, but research shows that aligning housing demand and supply is also critical. When overall demand is increasing, for example, reducing barriers to new construction is also essential to constrain rises in housing prices and rents. There is immense value in taking a holistic approach that balances different housing challenges and solutions, rather than addressing problems in isolation.

Local Housing Strategies in Action

Perhaps the easiest way to understand the impact of having comprehensive local housing strategies is to see them in action. Two case studies—New York City and Singapore—illustrate different approaches to deal with the challenges of providing affordable housing.

New York City

New York City's "Ten-Year Capital Plan," announced in 1985 by Mayor Edward Koch, was the largest municipally supported housing production plan in the history of the United States. Initially proposed as a five-year, $4.2 billion program targeting 100,000 units for middle- and low-income families, after three years, the program's budget grew to $5.1 billion and the goal expanded to 253,000 homes. In actuality the Ten-Year housing plan has never ended, even as it has continued to evolve and expand. Mayors since Koch have made the creation and preservation of affordable housing a key priority. Between 1987 and 2000 alone, the city used over 100 different programs to build or renovate over 182,000 private-sector units for renters and homeowners.[11]

Key to the success of the Ten-Year housing plan was its range of stakeholders; the plan harnessed the skills and expertise both inside and outside government. For example, the number of community-based not-for-profit organizations involved grew from 12 at the plan's inception to over 100. Community development corporations, local financial institutions, and other government agencies also helped to execute the ambitious plan. Some 81 percent of funding for the plan came primarily from the city's capital budget, with state and federal sources providing the rest.[12]

The most recent incarnation of New York City's housing plan, "Housing New York 2.0," was launched by the De Blasio administration in 2017. Built upon Mayor De Blasio's original housing plan of 2014, its aim is to create or preserve 300,000 new affordable units in the private sector by 2026 (only approximately 176,000 rental housing units out of approximately 3.2 million are publicly owned).[13] This overall goal comprises a number of comprehensive sub-goals, which focus on serving specific populations including low-income renters, homeowners, and seniors. It also includes such non-numerical goals as combating the displacement of existing residents in neighborhoods with rapidly changing demographics.[14]

While the Koch plan grew out of concerns for growing homelessness and the need to rebuild devastated neighborhoods, New York City's current housing plan has eight guiding principles reflecting major changes in the economic condition of the city. After losing a million in population, dropping from almost 8 to 7 million between 1970 and 1980, the city has rebounded, reaching all-time highs in population, now approximately 8.4 million, as well as record high employment rates.[15]

The latest plan aims to expand the range of households served by affordable development programs and encourage greater economic diversity by including the production of affordable housing as part of comprehensive neighborhood rezoning plans. It pledges to revamp existing planning and land-use processes to incorporate early and frequent feedback from neighborhoods into its plans to balance density with livability. It seeks to safeguard the legacy of previous investments and eliminate inefficiencies in incentive programs and regulatory processes. Another principle of the

New York

33%

Home Ownership Rate

8%

Percentage of Housing Units that are Government-Owned

12%

Percentage of Other Subsidized Housing

Above and Right

Mark Willis
Key Facts About New York City and Singapore, 2017

New York City and Singapore show two approaches to managing local affordability challenges.

Singapore

91%

Home Ownership Rate

80%

Percentage of Housing Units that are Government-Owned

0%

Percentage of Other Subsidized Housing

plan is to protect tenants in rent-regulated units, which account for approximately half of the rental stock in New York City, as well as capitalize on low interest rates while remaining able to adapt to future market downturns.[16]

Between 2014 and 2019, Housing New York 2.0 led to over 147,000 newly constructed or preserved units; specifically, over 98,000 units preserved and 49,000 constructed. Forty-one percent of the units were for low-income households earning 51 to 80 percent of Area Median Income (AMI); 24 percent were for very low-income households earning 31 to 50 percent AMI; 17 percent were for extremely low-income households earning 0 to 30 percent AMI; and the rest for households earning 81 percent and above of AMI. Over 12,000 units were set aside for the formerly homeless, and over 9,000 were set aside for seniors.[17]

Singapore

The city-state of Singapore has taken a very different approach to dealing with housing affordability by comprehensively addressing the issue via the housing market as a whole. While New York City has addressed housing affordability mainly through public–private partnerships, Singapore relies almost totally on public housing. From the time of its independence from the British Empire in 1959, its government made housing a priority. In 1960, the Housing & Development Act empowered Singapore's Housing & Development Board (HDB) to take a leading role in producing low-cost rental housing units. Four years later, the focus began to turn toward homeownership.

The HDB offers subsidies and grants, which cover home purchases, 100 percent of required home repairs, and up to 95 percent of optional renovations.[18] As a result, as of 2017, 80 percent of Singaporeans live in government-built homes and the overall homeownership rate in Singapore is 91 percent, among the highest rate in the world.

Singapore's public housing strategy has been successful because of four main components: a neighborhood-driven plan, careful use of density, an integrated approach from land acquisition to property maintenance, and long-term political commitment. First, the government designs large apartment blocks with mixed-income housing and easy access to an extensive public transport network. Second, because Singapore has relatively little land, it has built vertically, leading to a high degree of density throughout the country. Third, in 1967, the Land Acquisition Act enabled the government to acquire land at low cost for public use. In addition to its ability to acquire land cheaply (the state now owns 90 percent of the land in Singapore), the HDB incentivizes efficient construction and management; contractors are rewarded for good work, and neighborhoods elect their own representatives to oversee the public housing estates. Fourth, because so many Singaporeans benefit from public housing, the Housing & Development Board has enjoyed public support and a stable budget: almost $1.2 billion in 2017.[19]

Context Matters When Addressing Local Affordable Housing Challenges

When addressing affordability challenges, context matters, as evidenced by the difference in approaches between Singapore and New York City. The former, a city-state, has been able to rely extensively on public housing. With its multiple levels of government and wide variations in local affordable housing challenges, the United States necessitates that each locality tailor its own housing strategy. Regardless of government structure, however, a successful local housing strategy is one that responds to local housing needs and market conditions. It will also benefit from broad-based political support and by mobilizing the talents of stakeholders both within and outside of government. Perhaps most importantly, such a strategy needs to address the affordability challenges in a comprehensive and balanced way.

Right

NYU Furman Center
Freddie Mac House Prince Index 1975–2019, 2020

While Seattle's and San Francisco's house prices now far exceed their pre-2008 highs, other cities like Detroit have seen hardly any rise in dollar value (not adjusted for inflation) since 2000.

References

1. University of Michigan Center for Sustainable Systems, "U.S. Cities." http://css.umich.edu/sites/default/files/US%20Cities_CSS09-06_e2019.pdf
2. Congressional Research Service, "Real Wage Trends, 1979 to 2018," July 23, 2019, p. 2. https://fas.org/sgp/crs/misc/R45090.pdf
3. The U.S. has a shortage of 7 million rental homes affordable and available to extremely low-income renters, whose household incomes are at or below the poverty guideline or 30% of their area median income. See National Low Income Housing Coalition, "The Gap: A Shortage of Affordable Rental Homes," 2020. https://reports.nlihc.org/gap
4. Kathleen Howley, "U.S. Housing Market is Missing 3.3 Million Homes, Freddie Mac Says," HousingWire, March 02, 2020. https://www.housingwire.com/articles/u-s-housing-market-is-missing-3-3-million-homes-freddie-mac-says/
5. Joint Center for Housing Studies of Harvard University, "The State of the Nation's Housing," 2019, p. 26. https://www.jchs.harvard.edu/sites/default/files/Harvard_JCHS_State_of_the_Nations_Housing_2019.pdf
6. Alex E. Schwartz, *Housing Policy in the United States*. New York: Routledge, 2015, p. 164.
7. Cushing N. Dolbeare and Sheila Crowley, "Changing Priorities: The Federal Budget and Housing Assistance 1976–2007," August 2002. https://nlihc.org/sites/default/files/Changing-Priorities-Report_August-2002.pdf
8. The amount of Low Income Housing Tax Credits allocated to the states on a per capita basis was capped initially at $1.25 from 1986 to 2002/3 when it was increased to $1.75 (an increase short of inflation over the same period of time). Since 2003 the per capita credit has been adjusted for inflation. See Congressional Research Service, *An Introduction to the Low-Income Housing Tax Credit*, updated February 27, 2019, footnote 4. https://fas.org/sgp/crs/misc/RS22389.pdf
9. Joint Center for Housing Studies of Harvard University, "The State of the Nation's Housing," 2019, pp. 25–26. https://www.jchs.harvard.edu/sites/default/files/Harvard_JCHS_State_of_the_Nations_Housing_2019.pdf
10. National Low Income Housing Coalition, *Out of Reach* 2019, p. 1. https://reports.nlihc.org/sites/default/files/oor/OOR_2019.pdf
11. Michael H. Schill, Ingrid Gould Ellen, Amy Ellen Schwartz, and Ioan Voicu, "Revitalizing Inner-City Neighborhoods: New York City's Ten-Year Plan," *Housing Policy Debate* 13(3), 2002, pp. 533–540.
12. Ibid
13. NYC Housing, "Our Plan—Housing New York." https://www1.nyc.gov/site/housing/about/our-plan.page
14. NYC Housing, "Housing New York." https://www1.nyc.gov/site/housing/action/housing.page
15. NYC Planning, "Total Population: New York City & Boroughs, 1900 to 2010." https://www1.nyc.gov/assets/planning/download/pdf/planning-level/nyc-population/historical-population/nyc_total_pop_1900-2010.pdf; NYC Planning, "Current Estimates of New York City's Population for July 2018." https://www1.nyc.gov/site/planning/planning-level/nyc-population/current-future-populations.page
16. NYC Housing, "Our Principles." https://www1.nyc.gov/site/housing/about/our-principles.page
17. NYC Housing, "Housing By the Numbers." https://www1.nyc.gov/site/housing/action/by-the-numbers.page
18. Singapore Housing & Development Board, "Housing Benefits for Singapore Citizens Versus Singapore PR." https://www.hdb.gov.sg/cs/infoweb/hdbspeaks/housing-benefits-for-singapore-citizens-versus-singapore-pr
19. Abas Jha, "But What About Singapore?' Lessons from the Best Public Housing Program in the World," January 31, 2018. https://blogs.worldbank.org/sustainablecities/what-about-singapore-lessons-best-public-housing-program-world

Freddie Mac House Price Index, 2000–2019

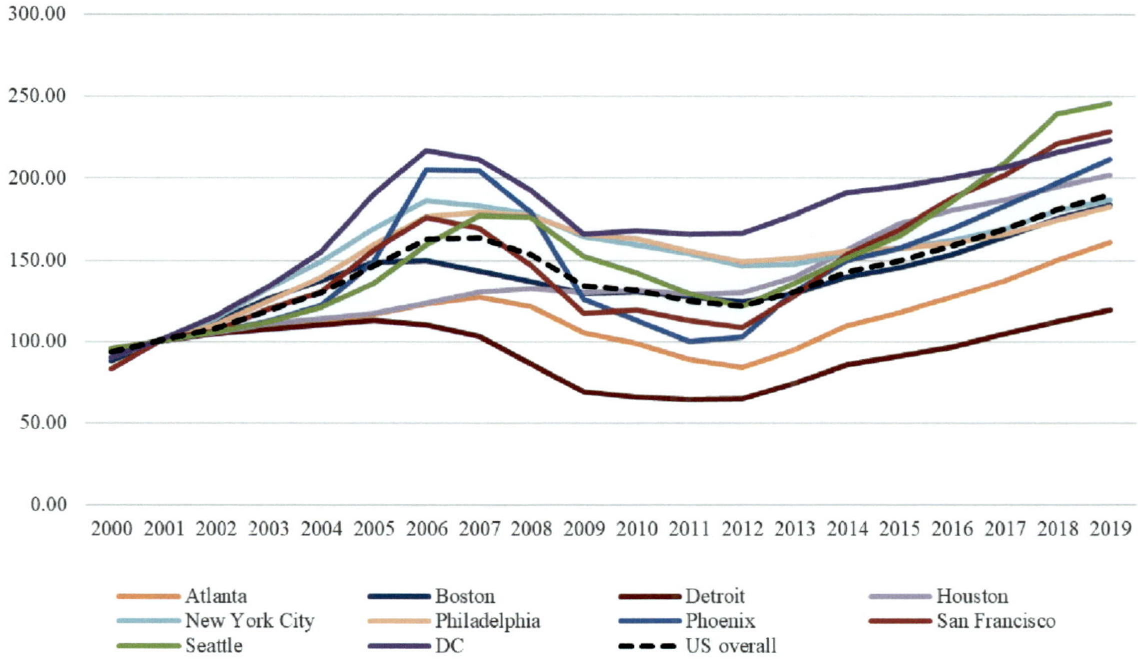

FRONTLINE

Brian Phillips

Cities are constantly changing. Some change is physical, as with the addition of new buildings and activities, but some is less visible, embedded in social and economic conditions that can be difficult to detect. The *Frontline* studio encouraged students to tackle issues of affordability through the lens of resource sharing and resisting gentrification. Daniel Silverman's project focused on the emotional and programmatic overlapping needs of both young and older residents who together define the cultural context of the neighborhood.

In *Frontline*, students were asked to catalog both visible and invisible forces on the studio project site. Contextual research was focused through the lenses of six broad topics: mobility, history, people, money, program and environment. Documentation included maps, infographics, photography and interviews unpacking the spatial, statistical and social stories of Philadelphia's Fishtown neighborhood.

In an era of information overload, editing data is essential to creating a useful tool for design. As a way to filter the studio research, students were asked to create a physical deck of cards organized by topic—each containing a key piece of data. This editorial process produced a studio-wide research deck of 16 cards per topic, for a total of 96 cards for the whole studio. Committing the data to physical cards required students to go on record with assertions that each statement was worthy of attention and might prove important for the design process. This exercise uncovered key drivers for urban, architectural and programmatic inputs while simultaneously fostering a sensitivity to local context.

The Fishtown neighborhood is an example of the shifting demographics of American cities. As young, creative class pioneers search for affordable housing and workspaces near dynamic cultural centers, an urban transformation has occurred along edges of working-class immigrant neighborhoods. *Frontline* looked at a site along Fishtown's emerging Front Street corridor, exploring the nascent reciprocity between neighborhood newcomers and the old guard.

Left

Daniel Silverman
Golden Age

Brian Phillips Urban Housing Studio with Alex Tahinos

University of Pennsylvania Weitzman School of Design, 2017

Section perspective showing interior organization of building as well as its relationship to the surrounding context.

Above

Perspective view showing screened south façade with adjacent elevated train line.

Golden Age / Daniel Silverman Studio Project

Situated within Fishtown's dynamic context, the *Golden Age* project explores the potential for amplifying multi-generational social engagement. The neighborhood's demographic trends include both an aging population and a recent influx of young people. Presently the two groups coexist in parallel with minimal day-to-day interaction. The project suggests that people in their 20s and 60s have more in common than one might think and the housing proposal encourages residents to explore, discover and socialize in ways that forge new links of mutual interest and support.

The project's 16-story tower makes use of the modestly scaled site, positioned near a train station, to provide spaces for mixing and interaction. Social spaces at the top and bottom of the building are imagined as co-located, multi-generational experiences. At street level there is a public plaza space for building tenants and neighborhood residents that includes spaces for skateboarding and chess, and on the roof a social terrace is programmed for ping-pong and laundry.

The building itself radicalizes the familiar form of the housing tower. The corridor is expanded to become extra wide, creating spaces for social interaction accessible to all ages. It is single-loaded with a gallery wall along the side opposite the apartments inspired by the idea of the curio cabinet. This collective display casework allows residents to curate personal and family objects creating a shared repository for social history. Unit entries at the shared hallway include a small sitting zone—a porch-like moment bridging the gap between public and private zones and encouraging informal exchanges as a way for those living alone to combat loneliness. This social stoop is inspired, in part, by the prevailing street condition in the surrounding neighborhood.

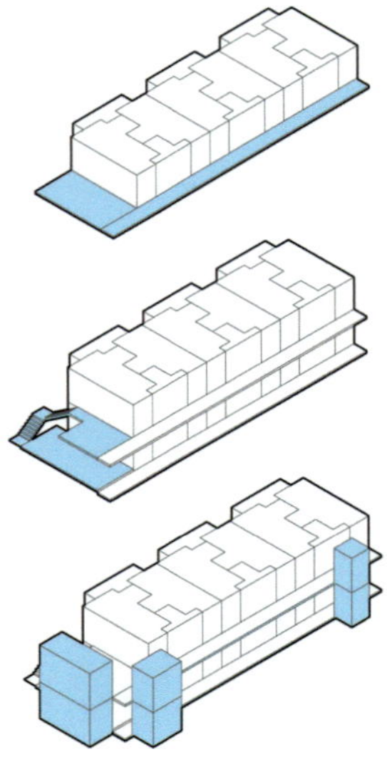

Unit Configurations

Conventional

Engaged

Above

Unit configurations, with diagrams juxtaposing conventional scenario of limited shared circulation and expansive private units with expanded circulation and social space with minimized private units.

Right

Interior elevations showing public and private sides of interactive wall and typical floor plan at apartment level.

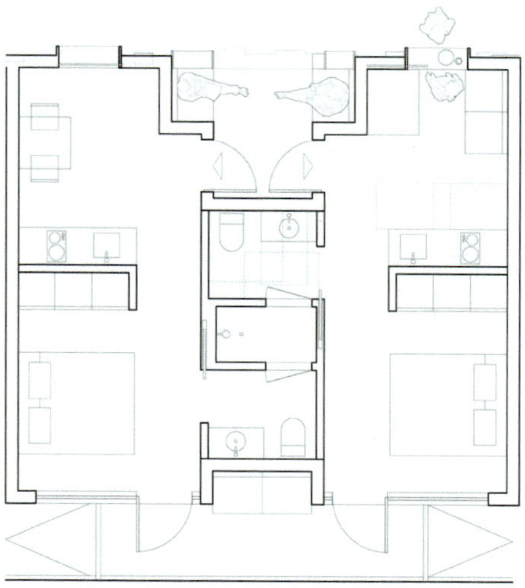

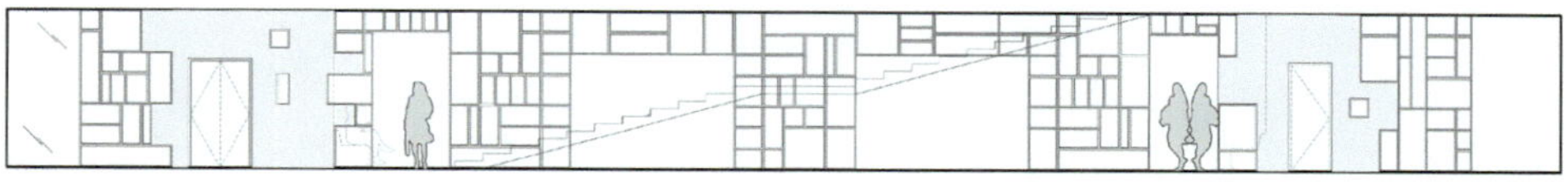

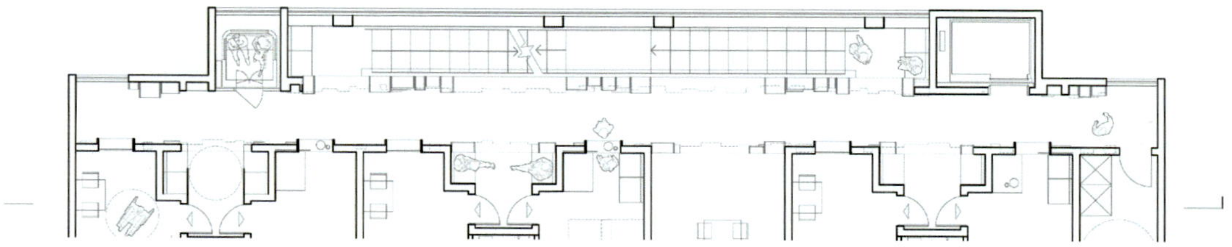

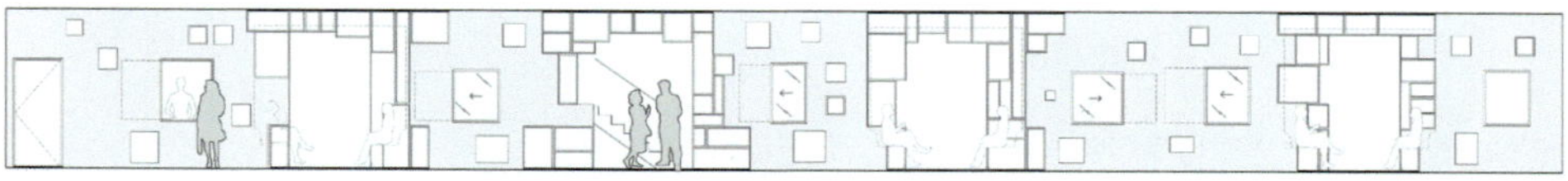

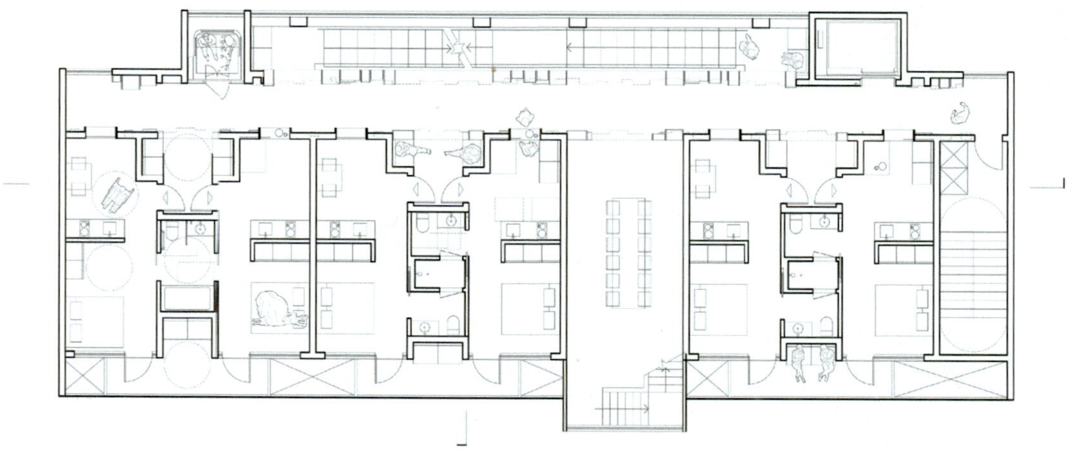

NYC
X
NYC
DESIGN
MAY 3–17
NYCXDESIGN.COM
[WANTED DESIGN]
ONE WAY
HUDSON ST
DOWNTOWN
WINE & LIQUORS
DOWNTOWN
WINE & LIQUORS
WARBURG

URBAN HOUSING AND THE VALUE OF THE ARCHITECT

Martha Kelley | Goldman Sachs

As a real estate investor, the lens through which I study urban housing differs from my colleagues in the architectural community. I start with a series of questions related to the supply and demand of people and jobs, because, ultimately, people are the users of housing, and jobs are a driving factor as it relates to people's decisions about where they live. The basic questions that help to frame the discussion on urban housing for a real estate investor are therefore: where do people have to or want to live; in which cities are both population and employment growing; what is the existing housing stock in those cities; what is the availability of land in those cities; and, finally, is there an imbalance between supply of housing and demand for housing that creates an opportunity for an investor to build, or buy, urban housing?

In addition to the supply and demand analysis that we do as investors, there is also a question related to preferences. If a hypothetical city has 100,000 residents and 150,000 housing units, the math would tell us that that city has a supply problem. But imagine that 50% of those housing units no longer fit the needs of the residents for one reason or another—all of a sudden that city has a demand problem and needs new housing units to be built to better serve the community. This gets to a question of preferences, and how the housing stock evolves in response to changing user preferences. Sometimes preferences change because of improvements in technology; other times because of social or societal changes. Consider the 21st-century trend of millennials, among other demographic profiles, choosing to rent apartments rather than buy apartments or houses—this change in user preference has fundamentally altered the landscape of urban housing by creating a new asset class—the multifamily apartment building—to respond to changes in user demand. The shift in ownership of urban housing from the individual to the investor created opportunities for investors to not only build housing for individuals to buy (condos), but also to build, buy, and own housing for the long term (multifamily apartment buildings). I revisit this topic below.

Left

Herzog de Meuron
56 Leonard Street
New York City, 2017

56 Leonard Street as seen from the corner of Leonard and Hudson Streets in TriBeCa. The building occupies a land site that was formerly owned by the New York Law School, which allowed for density in an otherwise height-restricted and historic neighborhood.

Herzog de Meuron
56 Leonard Street
New York City, 2017

Herzog & de Meuron offset the vertical stack to disaggregate the individual apartments and relate the building to its residential neighborhood, and in so doing created the illusion of a building disintegrating as it climbs higher.

Evaluating real estate investment opportunities through the lens of supply and demand and other principles of economic theory is certainly step one, but investors also have to deal with the reality of actual economic, political, and social conditions in real places, and those conditions don't always align with textbook theories. San Francisco is a good example of this. The economic rationale for building housing in San Francisco is divorced from the reality of building housing there. Specifically, the supply and demand equation works in that city because demand for housing vastly outweighs supply of housing. Yet local conditions also include strict, if necessary, affordable housing requirements and vocal community groups that make building housing difficult and often cost prohibitive, despite the market opportunity. Therefore, as much as we want to focus on the San Francisco market opportunity as investors, we have to weigh the real-world political constraints of such an endeavor.

Annual Home Ownership Rates for the United States by Age Group 1982–2020

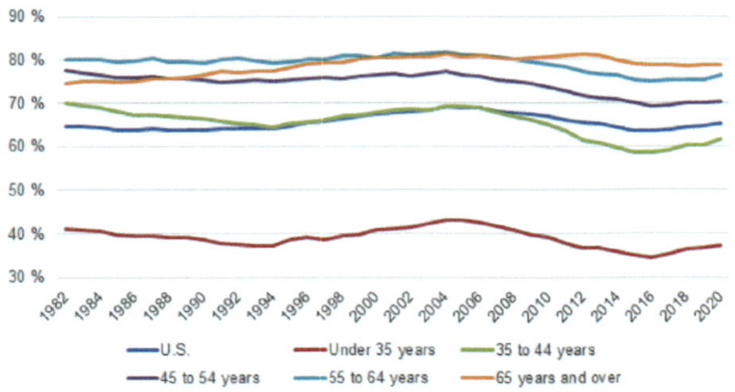

Manhattan Average Condo Price Per Square Foot–Last 25 Years

While real-world conditions can sometimes thwart housing development in cities that otherwise have clear supply/demand imbalances, they can also be the catalyst for real estate deals getting done. Consider the land deal at 56 Leonard Street in New York City, which I will cover in more detail later in this essay. In that case, a real estate deal came together because the land owner, the New York Law School, needed capital to build a new academic facility. Their site sits in a historically designated district with height restrictions, but owing to their ownership it was carved out of the zoning map,

Left Top

U.S. Census Bureau
Current Population Survey/Housing Vacancy Survey, March 10, 2020

Note: 2020 Data represents first quarter.

Declining rates of homeownership, especially among younger people, indicates that housing preferences may be changing in favor of rentals. This trend has altered the housing landscape and created a new class of real estate: the multifamily apartment building.

Left Bottom

Corcoran Sunshine
Manhattan State of the Market Update, May 18, 2020

Note: Figures represent contracts signed during the quarter, and exclude some new developments not publicly disclosing individual sales figures, as well as unknown credits.

New York City is one of several US cities that has seen a substantial increase in condo prices over the last few decades, which has spurred a wave of new development.

which meant that it had significant value. By selling part of their land to a housing developer, to whom the land was worth more, the school was able to fund the construction of a 235,000-square-foot academic building on one corner of the block, while an architecturally significant condo tower was erected on the other corner. In this instance, specific zoning conditions actually facilitated the development.

Textbook economics and real-world dynamics shape the conversation around urban housing for a real estate investor. But what do we mean when we say "urban housing"? I bifurcate urban housing into two different types of asset classes: multifamily, which is for-rent housing, and condo, which is for-sale housing. These asset classes, while both considered as housing, have very different risk profiles for an investor, and are treated differently in the capital markets.

Volatility and Average Annnual Return by Asset Class–Last 25 Years

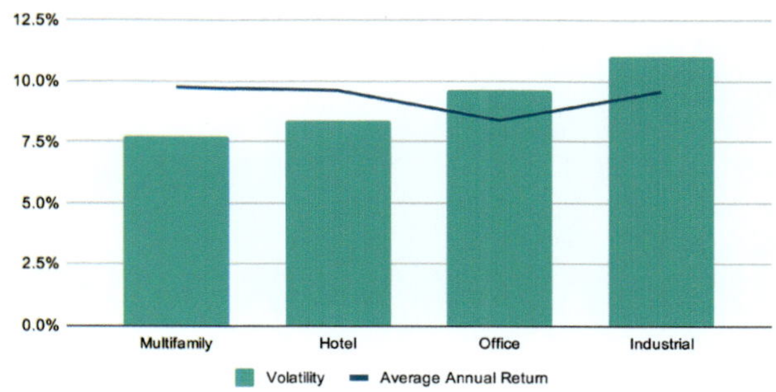

Multifamily housing is generally thought of as the most stable asset class within commercial real estate. During an economic downturn, real estate that is most closely tied to consumer spending—such as retail and hospitality—is generally impacted first and most severely. As the contraction continues, office and industrial real estate become impacted as well. Multifamily is typically the asset class that is least impacted by an economic downturn, because people will always need places to live, and also because rental apartments are less impacted by individual-level leverage than apartments or houses that are owned and encumbered by personal home mortgages. Multifamily properties will see an increase in vacancy or credit losses during a recession, but relative to other real estate asset classes they remain somewhat stable.

Right

CBRE Research
NCREIF, Q3 2017

Notes:
Based on trailing four-quarter total returns (Q3 1992–Q3 2017). Volatility as represented by Standard Deviation in Annual Return Multifamily housing is generally thought of as the most stable asset class within commercial real estate, with the lowest level of volatility in returns over economic cycles.

As a result of this relative resilience to economic changes, multifamily housing is particularly attractive to institutional investors seeking stable cash flows. And higher demand for multifamily housing among investors drives up its value in the capital markets. Over this past economic cycle, investors have chased multifamily acquisition and development opportunities in traditional gateway markets, but also in high-growth secondary markets—cities such as Denver, Seattle, Dallas, Austin, Atlanta, and Silicon Valley, where job and population growth are outpacing the US average. These cities

have seen new and growing demand for apartment product amongst a group of people who prefer to rent in urban areas than own in suburban areas. These are also places in which, generally speaking, the low cost of land has allowed investors to build multifamily housing below replacement cost (the cost to buy comparable product). This dynamic has spurred a wave of multifamily development across the country.

For-sale condo development represents a completely different risk profile, and value proposition, for an investor than multifamily development (let alone acquisitions). As outlined above, multifamily housing is fairly low risk, because of the stability of cash flows generated by multifamily assets. Condos, on the other hand, are high risk—the value of a condo development project is entirely dependent on the market conditions at the time that the project is delivered, as well as entirely dependent on there being a group of individuals who are willing to buy the condos at pricing that is above the cost to build them. It is the uncertainty around the "exit value" that makes condo development a high-risk investment relative to other real estate asset classes.

Investors who choose to develop for-sale housing are aware of the risks inherent in the asset class, and typically will only choose to invest in condo development projects if those risks are "priced-in" to the deal. Said differently, an investor will only choose to develop condo if the expected return from that investment is higher than the return it would expect to generate from a lower risk project (such as multifamily development). This rationale is no different than any other investor rationale—the higher the risk, the higher the reward. If some investors choose to pursue condo development because it yields a higher return, let's consider where. The wave of condo development that occurred in the US over the last 20 years was concentrated in gateway markets: New York City, Los Angeles, Chicago, Miami, Washington DC, Boston, Seattle and, to some extent, San Francisco. These cities have seen a confluence of events: demand drivers such as population and job growth driving housing development more broadly, user preferences creating a new class of urban luxury condo product heavily sought after by buyers, and price trends in most of these cities causing more and more developers to choose to build condo product.

As these cities have experienced increased levels of condo development, there has been a growing focus on the architecture of such projects. This is not to say that architecture is not valued and considered in all real estate asset classes—it is. However, luxury condo places a particular emphasis on the architect and interior designer, in part because the design of the project has become a prominent selling feature amongst competing condo projects. If condo projects are inherently risky, investors feel that one way to de-risk a project is to build something that will attract buyers because it is different than everything else in the market—more beautifully designed, with better amenities and higher quality materials and finishes. Investors cannot control the economic conditions at the time of delivery, but they can control the quality of the project that they build, and hope that building something better will allow them to optimize value in a strong economic environment or a weak one.

Left

Herzog de Meuron
56 Leonard Street
New York City, 2017

The project includes generous amenities for residents, in spaces designed by Herzog & de Meuron. As luxury condo projects have become common in New York City, buildings often differentiate themselves with the amenity packages that they offer to residents.

In addition to de-risking their projects, investors often do care about design, and want to build beautiful projects that enhance the built environment. In the case of my firm, we have chosen to work with premier architectural firms such as Herzog & de Meuron, Jean Nouvel, Pelli Clarke Pelli, among many others, on some of our large-scale urban condo projects, because we know that they will design beautiful, high-quality buildings both inside and out.

Our project with Herzog & de Meuron—56 Leonard Street in Manhattan—elucidates several aspects of condo development that I have outlined above. First, it demonstrates how economic cycles can impact condo development projects. Second, it highlights the important role of the architect in designing a building that can attract buyers irrespective of economic conditions. Finally, it shows how successful projects are entirely dependent on the teams of professionals who are involved in their creation, from investors to architects. The development at 56 Leonard Street is a 57-story, 810-foot-tall condo tower located at the corner of Leonard Street and Church Street in the TriBeCa neighborhood of downtown Manhattan. Goldman Sachs partnered with Dune Real Estate Partners, Alexico Group and Hines to develop the tower between 2006, when we purchased the land from the neighboring New York Law School, and 2017, when the tower was completed. Over this 11-year period, the world experienced one of the worst recessions in recent history, the Global Financial Crisis, which delayed the project by over half a decade and resulted in massive cost increases. Notwithstanding those challenges, the project has been a success for all of the firms involved and is considered by some to be one of the more architecturally significant projects delivered in Manhattan in the last few years.

The team's decision to work with Herzog & de Meuron was influenced by the residential landscape in New York City in the early 2000s, when we conceived of the project. The for-sale residential market in New York was changing rapidly during that time, particularly at the highest end. World-class architects such as Jean Nouvel, Robert Stern, and Richard Meier were starting to become involved in large-scale luxury condo development projects, and the term "starchitect" was born. Buyers became aware of these designers and were paying a premium for buildings that were designed by well-known architects. When the team began searching for an architect for the project the starchitect phenomenon was a consideration, but more importantly, we needed to select an architect to solve a design challenge related to the site. Specifically, we needed to find an architect who could manage the scale of the building within its context, and design a 350,000-square-foot tower that complemented, rather than contradicted, the height-restricted and historically designated neighborhood of TriBeCa, which is filled with 7–10-story boutique buildings.

Herzog & de Meuron clearly understood the scale problem of the 56 Leonard project, and designed a project that solves two important contextual issues. First, they created a tower that was large without being dense. By offsetting the vertical stack, they designed a building with important voids of space, that break up the monolithic

Right Top

Herzog de Meuron
56 Leonard Street
New York City, 2017

A hand-poured concrete staircase connects the two amenity floors on 9 and 10, which total over 17,000 sqft of amenity space.

Right Bottom

A shared resident lounge features a private dining room and adjoining screening room. Other building amenities include a 75-foot pool, sauna, sun deck, fitness center, yoga studio, and children's playroom.

tower and relate the building to its lower-density neighbors. The building rises 810 feet out of a sea of cast iron low-rises, but it also disintegrates into the sky, receding as it gets higher. The staggered stack of units also allows for individual apartments to be identifiable within the form. Looking up at the tower, an owner can see his or her unit as a distinct component of the form—separate but within—and that makes it special.

Second, they created a tower that "lives" like a boutique building. The 145-unit building has seven elevators, which allows for a layout with no more than two units per elevator landing. In fact, more than 50 units have direct apartment access from the elevator. This was a major selling feature of the building because it allowed owners to feel as though they were buying into a boutique building. Another important design feature is the outdoor space, which is paramount in luxury condo projects. Herzog & de Meuron's cantilevered design allowed for 45,000 square feet of terraces, or approximately 300 square feet per apartment. The large amount of outdoor space contributed to the attractiveness of the project because buyers could walk outside of their apartments and literally stand in the Manhattan skyline.

As a result of its design, 56 Leonard became the best of both worlds for a buyer looking to live in TriBeCa—it has the features, amenities, and views that one would expect from a large-scale luxury condo tower, but the living experience for an owner is much more intimate than your average condo project by virtue of the design, both interior and exterior, of the project. The uniqueness of this project contributed to its success—when the economy recovered post-financial crisis and the building was finally completed, it sold quickly. As an investor you cannot predict how a project will perform—all you can do is try to minimize and mitigate the known risks. One way to mitigate risk in condo development—one of the riskiest forms of real estate investing—is to build something that people want to own. In the case of 56 Leonard Street, our team of professionals, led by Herzog & de Meuron, artfully did just that.

The landscape of urban housing is constantly changing. The evolution of investor-owned multifamily buildings and starchitect-designed condo projects are two examples of how urban housing has evolved in the last 20 years, and there will no doubt be further evolutions and refinements to come. Several examples of new trends that are emerging are co-living, micro-housing, and other responses to the increasing cost of urban living—a theme that will continue to require collaboration between designers and financiers to effectively solve. I can't help but wonder if, as new challenges in urban housing emerge, the role of the architect can be widened, to enable enhanced collaboration among all constituents from an earlier stage in a project's lifecycle. The technology firm Envelope, which is a breakaway from SHoP Architects, is one interesting example of how architects can contribute to yet another part of the value chain. However our respective roles might evolve or merge, it is evident that new opportunities will continue to materialize within the urban fabric. When evaluating those opportunities, we revisit the intersection of textbook economics and real-world conditions, to determine where we focus next.

Right

Herzog de Meuron
56 Leonard Street
New York City, 2017

The building has over 45,000 sqft of outdoor space with sweeping views of Manhattan in all directions. The offset stack created ample terrace space, as the ceiling of one apartment becomes the terrace of another.

INCLUSIONARY HOUSING AND INNOVATIVE REUSE

Hina Jamelle

Evaluating real estate opportunities involves an amalgam of economic, political, and social factors. Inclusionary housing—where developers are incentivized to provide a stipulated number of units at below-market rates in exchange for tax credits and relaxed zoning regulations—has had two primary benefits. First, it expands the issue of substandard living and income inequality from being strictly a governmental issue and opens it to private sector investment, where there is funding for large-scale housing and aggressive competition. Second, it moderates housing shortages onset by the rapid gentrification of traditionally low-income neighborhoods. On its surface, inclusionary housing strategies appear to be able to achieve results with sensitivities toward issues of segregation and class inequality by mixing disparate income groups; however, inclusionary housing has not been implemented without controversy. One big issue with mixed-income developments has been the details of how "integration" is achieved. A pressing topic has been how to design buildings where space is shared between low- and high-income tenants without marginalizing one group or the other. One solution advanced by developers has been coined "the poor door"—a separate entrance often on an adjacent street that services below-market units. This move has been criticized and deemed by many to be a form of segregation.

There are a host of anti-segregation laws in place that may be able to prevent such practices; however, greater questions still exist regarding how developers should navigate these issues. Governmental authorities are faced with shrinking budgets, which force them to figure out how to do more with limited vacant land and fewer capital resources. New York City has proven to be a pioneer in housing policy in the past; today's challenges once again call for innovative strategies, approaches, and ways to attract a diverse mix of incomes, households, and lifestyles. The question for architecture is whether design can become a catalyst for bringing numerous stakeholders and vocal communities together in support of such projects. The reuse of existing buildings for new purposes offers one compelling such catalyst and warrants further inquiry.

Left

Madison Green
Shifting Hybrids: Adaptive Reuse of the Sunshine Theater on the Lower East Side, New York City

Hina Jamelle Urban Housing Studio with Caleb Ehly

University of Pennsylvania Weitzman School of Design, 2019.

Façade view from the street. The Sunshine Theater's existing façade materials are seamlessly extended upward to the new residential construction above.

SHINE

Façade Strategy Diagrams

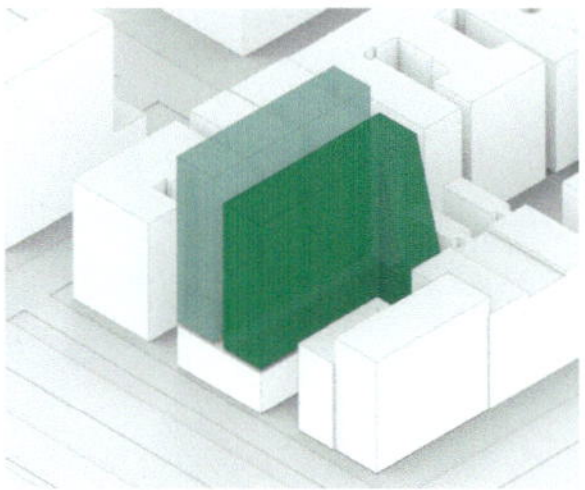

Massing

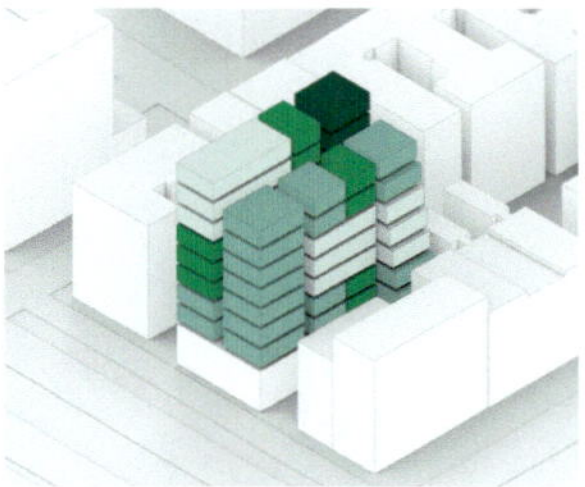

Unit Distribution

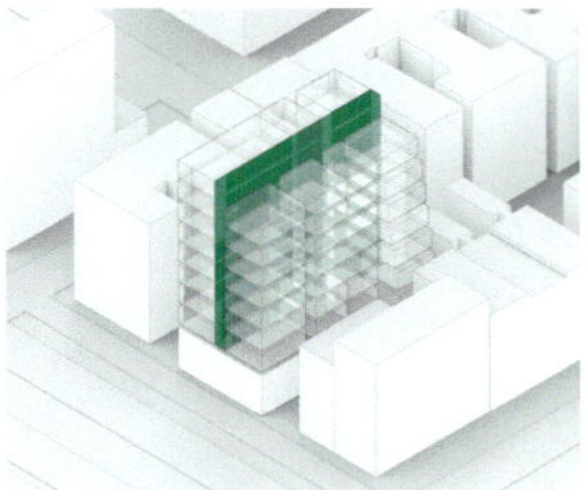

Circulation

Left

Transverse building section.

Above

Diagrams of existing Sunshine Theater façade (right) and proposed new construction (left).

Massing diagram. Two split volumes above the original theater create vertical shafts that bring light down to the lower levels of the building. Unit distribution along the naturally lit corridors. The central corridor design organizes the housing units into two vertical zones. Each corridor ends with open views of the city.

The adaptive reuse of buildings has several advantages over demolition and reconstruction. It can support and benefit local culture, especially in cases where a building is rooted in city or neighborhood identity, history, and culture and offers inspiring spaces. It can be used as a tool for leveraging and streamlining investment, particularly if there is support from vocal community groups. Additionally, new buildings require tremendous amounts of energy and resources to construct. Reuse is often a more environmentally friendly solution, or as a 2005 National Trust for Historic Preservation campaign put it, "the greenest building is the one that is already built." Finally, reuse can strengthen a community by positively linking a city or neighborhood's past to its future.

Despite its many benefits, adaptive reuse projects are often criticized for hastening gentrification. Urban development can displace longtime residents, particularly when it does not include affordable housing. However, repurposing an existing building can act as a catalyst for attracting and retaining a diverse mix of households through unique spaces and structures and can be critical to the character of a neighborhood. Reusing a beloved local building also usually requires and brings with it a great deal of local support necessary for the building's ultimate success. When combined with the principles of inclusionary housing, reuse has the potential to stave off criticisms while enhancing its acknowledged positive aspects.

The Sunshine Theater, formerly located at 143 E. Houston Street between Eldridge and Forsyth streets in the Lower East Side of Manhattan, is an intriguing architectural reuse case study—both for its storied 175-year history and its eventual demolition. Its architecture reflected a mishmash history, with two symmetrical church towers, a central arched span punctuated by windows, and a theater marquee with a neon sign. The building began as a Dutch Reformed Church in 1844. In its lifespan, it served as a church, an immigrant meeting hall, a boxing venue, a nickelodeon, a Yiddish vaudeville house, a hardware warehouse, a graffiti showcase, and an indie-rock playroom. The building's last chapter as an independent art-house movie theater operated by Landmark Theaters began in only 2001. It stood at the center of daily life for generations of Lower East Side residents before it was sold on January 21, 2018 and demolished the following year.

Madison Green's project, "Shifting Hybrids: Adaptive Reuse of the Sunshine Theater on the Lower East Side, New York City," proposes an alternative reality where the Sunshine Theater was not demolished; instead, it reimagines the beloved venue as the site of a new residential building. Engaging inclusionary housing within the context of adaptive reuse, the project leverages the building's unique historical qualities to ensure and create added property value while procuring additional space through new construction. Instead of a standard split between reduced and market rate housing, one-third of the project engages directly with the historic Sunshine Theater, and the other two-thirds are devoted to newly constructed residential units. The large, street-facing neon "Sunshine" marquee is preserved, and the rich brick and metal façade work of the original building is carefully restored and extended upward as part

View of the city from the multi-level roof terrace.

of the new construction. These and other rich material crossovers create an intricate relationship between old and new that blurs where the existing building ends and the new intervention begins.

Likewise, thresholds between private, shared, and public areas highlight the project's unique attitude towards commonly underutilized space. Often, new housing projects seek to minimize circulation space in order to maximize sellable square footage. This can often compromise the quality of communal spaces, despite their daily use by residents. The proposal here to adapt and reuse the Sunshine Theater seeks to add value to both the property and the experience of residents through communal spaces that engage with the historic building's architecture. The project does this in three ways. First, a small plaza is created along the side of the building by removing a previous addition to the original structure. This defines a new, more private, yet communal entry corridor sequence for all residents offset from the busy street. Second, the volumes above the original theater are subdivided to create light wells. These wells serve to funnel light to skylights in lower units and illuminate horizontal shared corridors on each unit level. Shared corridors terminate in glazing and communal space at each end, capitalizing on continuity, light, and atmosphere within the building's urban context as well as views out to the city. Third, interest in fostering community is maintained in the vertical organization of units into zones that take advantage of the site's four open façades. The roof is composed of multi-level terraces that create a landscape of completely open or partially enclosed spaces for residents to gather, socialize, and connect back to the surrounding urban environment of the Lower East Side.

By focusing on enhancing and harnessing the building's historic and cultural character, the project shifts the origin of value from unit amenities to shared identity. This effectively displaces potential tensions between residents by enabling them to all take part in the iconicity and communal spaces of the building without diminishing day-to-day experience or property value. Further synergies between building reuse and inclusionary housing policy as well as new construction that harness the value of localized identity should be explored to better understand the capacity of design to mediate between stakeholders and promote meaningful forms of inclusion, integration, and community.

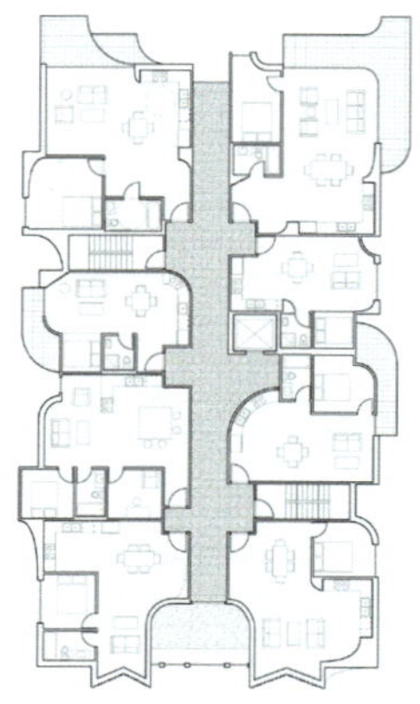

Level 7 Plan

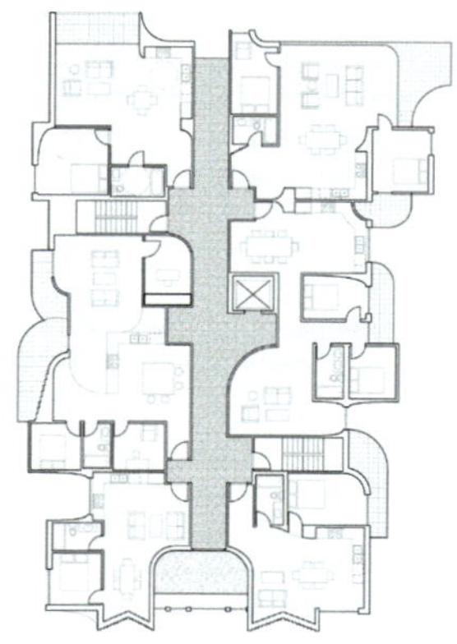

Level 5 Plan

Above

Unit level plans.

Right Top

Studio unit configuration.

Right Bottom

Grand Stair and public interior viewed through the Sunshine Theater's existing neon sign.

References

The New York Times. https://www.nytimes.com/2018/01/21/nyregion/sunshine-movie-theater-closing.html

http://cinematreasures.org/theaters/1907

https://furmancenter.org/files/publications/AHistoryofHousingPolicycombined0601_000.pdf

Matteo Robiglio, *The Adaptive Reuse Toolkit. How Cities Can Turn their Industrial Legacy into Infrastructure for Innovation and Growth*. Washington, DC: German Marshall Fund of the United States, 2016.

Erasing 70 Years of Progress in Five Years
Bell - Seong

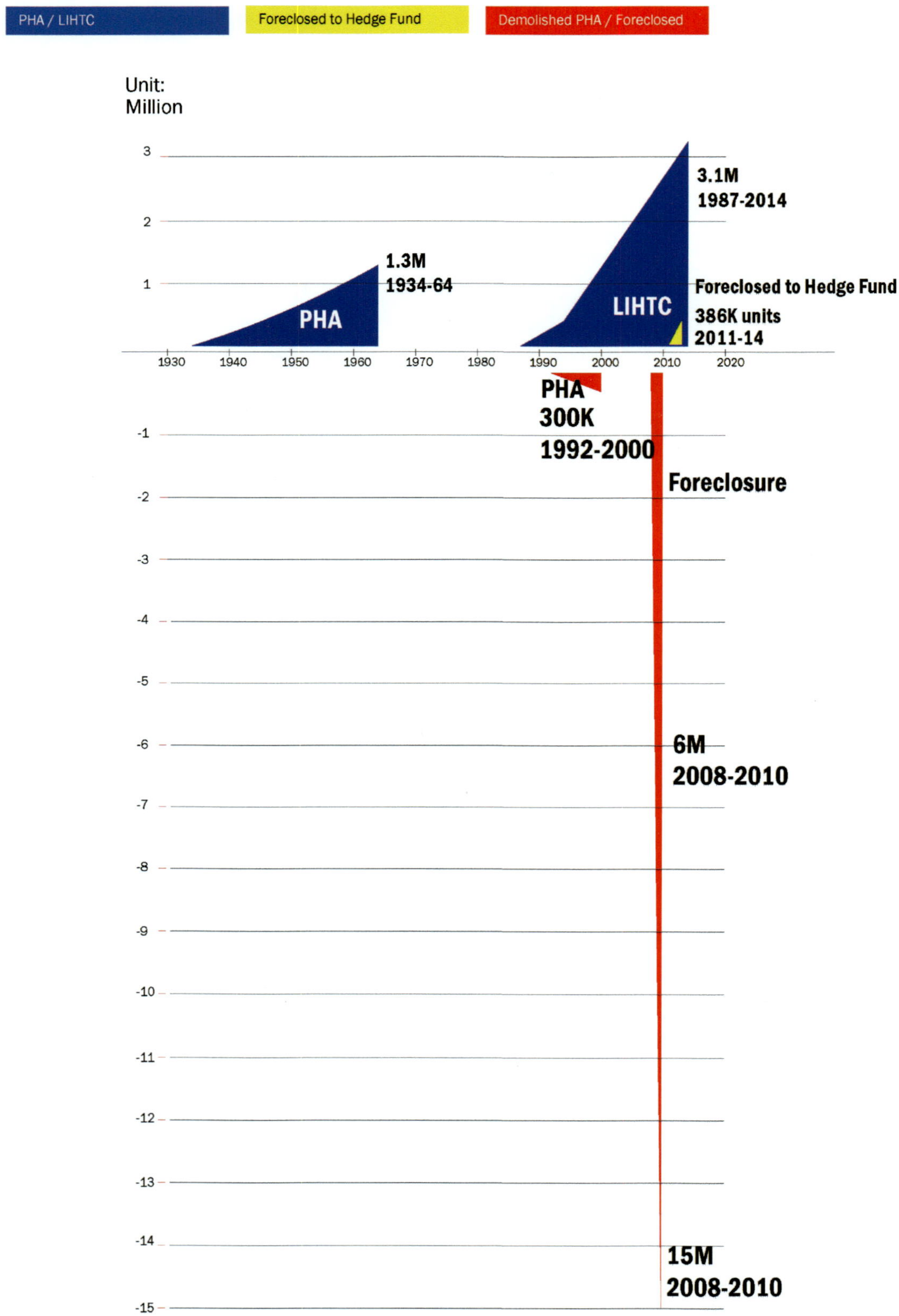

TEN POINTS ON A PROJECTIVE ECONOMY AND ARCHITECTURE

Michael Bell and Eunjeong Seong | Bell - Seong Architecture

Architects have been using data, mapping myriad extra-architectural concerns and making use of diagrams in ways that are often seen as undermining the disciplinary qualities of architecture. We propose that architects have skills that allow us to see plastic qualities and temporal aspects of space in economic and financial means—in ways that could instigate new architectures without being a derivative of or subservient to economics.

One: Accelerating Debt Peaks: In 1947 United States households held housing debt equivalent to 17% of gross domestic product (GDP). Three years after the signing of the Bretton Woods Treaty, two years after the conclusion of World War II, the US began a steady rise in homeownership and an accrual of long-term debt. By 2006 housing debt had reached virtually 100% of GDP. The growth was not in a steadily increasing line: it increased dramatically between 1971 and 1990, more rapidly in the 1990s, and then explosively between 1999 and 2006. Before crashing.

In the aftermath of the 2008 Great Recession the world's ten largest central banks took an immense amount of illiquid housing debt. A Bloomberg analysis shows the banks quadrupling their holdings between 2006 and 2016.[1] A study by the Bank of International Settlements shows the world's top six central banks quintupling holding by 2019.[2] The past 20 years deeply accelerated the uses of leverage in housing; central banks and households have worked aggressively to mask this but today debt of all kinds is increasingly seen as untenable. We think it's shoring up assets whose time is past.

Two: Architecture Can't Solve Affordability: In 2005—as the housing financial markets began to fail—land accounted for 77% of housing costs in California. In West Virginia the ratio was closer to 11%. In Nevada land accounted for 53% of a housing transaction. Land, over this past 40 years, has proved to be far more volatile as a component in the pricing of housing—far more than architectural construction in valuation.[3] During a crash, land also falls further and faster. Plentiful job markets attract

Left

Bell - Seong
Erasing 70 Years of Progress in Five Years

Since Public Housing Authorities (PHA's) were founded in 1937 the United States has realized approximately 1.3 million hard-units of federal/state/city owned apartments. The 1986, Reagan era, Low Income Housing Tax Credit (LIHTC) laws have financed as many as 3.1 million soft-units (developed by non-profits) of affordable housing. In the 1990s the Clinton Administration reduced the PHA count by more than 300,000 hard units. The 2008 financial crisis threw as many as 16 million private homes into foreclosure proceedings; more than 6 million were fully foreclosed. As the 08 crisis ebbed hundreds of thousands of single-family homes were purchased by hedge funds in an immense wealth transfer. More homes were foreclosed in the post-08 period than had been built in nearly a century of federally assisted low-income housing construction.

people to expensive cities where everyone becomes a speculator in the midst of a deeper, more volatile form of risk. Affordability in expensive housing markets is by necessity achieved as a matter of increased density; an architectural form of spatial arbitrage to spread land values over more owners. But stacked against globally traded housing debt—financial instruments—the arithmetic density of architecture is no match for the calculus of derivatives. Credit default swaps (CDS), mortgage-backed securities (MBS): these demand more return—even more leverage. Density, long sold as cultural capital, may today be irretrievably financial; cloaked as a form of culture—an architectural mask enabling the ever hyper financialization of homes.

United States Household Debt to GDP, 1947–2019
Bell - Seong

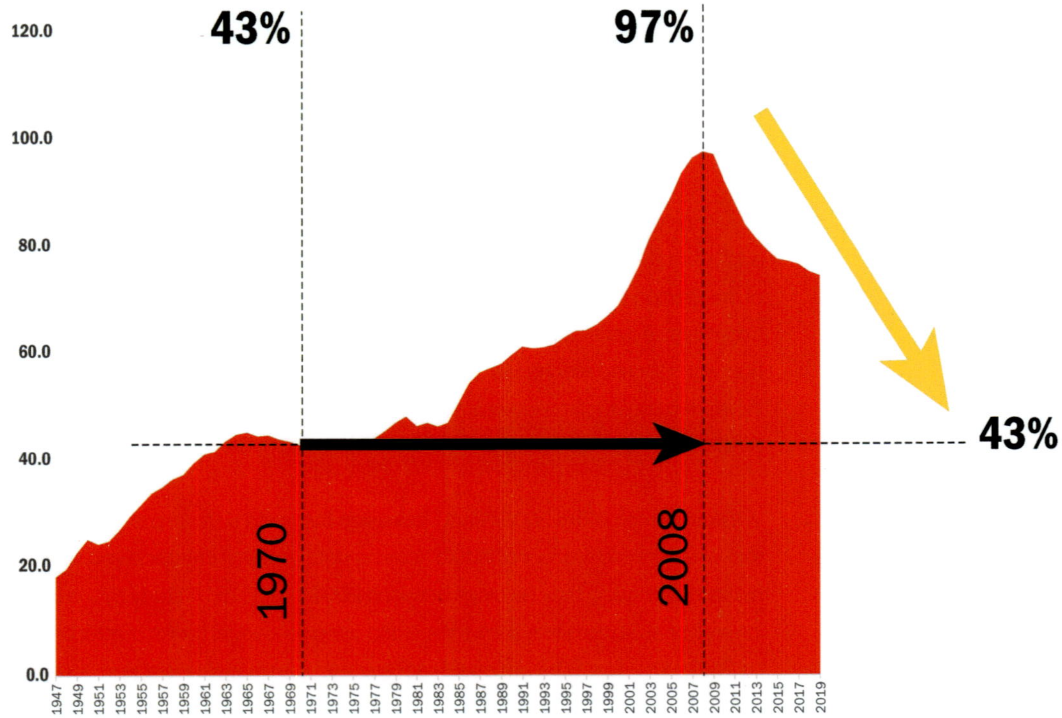

Three: Aggregate Scale: In the run-up of housing valuations prior to the 2008 crash US residential real estate valuations had peaked, in 2006, at more than $25 trillion.[4] In 2000, the value was $13.531 trillion. The six-year period leading up to the liquidity and banking collapse constituted a 185% increase in aggregate housing valuation. As the "recovery" emerged, aggregate values were well above the year 2000, but the uneven distribution of equity and date of tenure (when purchased) meant that US households had in many regions entered years of negative equity. In the past two decades, housing values in the US have fluctuated violently. The increased valuations between 2000 to 2006 were unprecedented, but nothing in our history has approached the loss of housing tenure that followed the credit seizure. More homes were foreclosed after 2008 than had ever been realized in the collective forms of 80 years of government-sponsored Public Housing, Affordable Housing, and inclusive of every form of city-or municipal-based subsidized housing. We have seen in 19 short years profound forms of instability that should awaken in us a willingness to think differently; to incorporate more into what we imagine is needed or possible. It suggests that the system is broken and needs to be replaced, but the inevitable amnesia of the recovery eclipses reason. The Financial Accounts of the United States, Flow of Funds (FOF), Balance Sheets, and Integrated Macroeconomic Accounts, published by the US Federal Reserve in the first quarter of 2017, showed the aggregate valuation of US residential real estate held by households as $26.866 trillion, or more than $77,000 per capita. We are a rich nation in terms of housing—but a simple scalar relation of housing debt to value does not show the uneven distribution of equity or entire regions left behind. Why are so many people deeply underwater or housing costs stressed?

The Federal Reserve's attempts to value the aggregate of residential real estate are crucial to understanding the financial health of the nation. In a post-1970s economy housing accounts for approximately half of household total net worth. Tied directly to consumption, mobility, amortized debt, and jobs, the contours of wealth as real estate directly correspond with urban form—urban form is a form of money. Architecture or at least buildings in this equation are the collateral: it could do so much more. But to what extent is the economy we know the economy of even the near future? We can't project the future on a failing past.

Four: A Retreating State + Existential Architect: In the published archive, *Team 10, 1953–1981*,[5] editors Max Risselada and Dirk van den Heuvel share interviews, letters, meeting photographs, and texts from an array of Team 10 members. These fragments of information illuminate Team 10 confronting a shrinking welfare state in France. They form a parallel to events in the United States as the United States deconstructed New Deal public housing programs and laid the grounds for a more privatized form of affordable housing.

The archive brings Team 10 up to 1981, but it is doubts that are revealed in the late 1960s and early 1970s that are still unresolved today. Archival notes show George Candilis addressing an emerging, but overt sense of vulnerability. In the late 1960s the housing project at Toulouse le Mirail—still under construction—forms a backdrop for Candilis imagining his exiting of the scene. Largely, but not fully realized, it now could house a significant portion of the 20,000 people it was designed for. There was a burgeoning awareness that the work had taken a decade to build—was possibly obsolete even under construction—and that the post-war reconstruction and then welfare state that propelled such works was waning.

Left

Bell - Seong
United States Household Debt to GDP, 1947–2019

Household debt as a percentage of United States GDP since the end of World War II falls in three eras. It expanded after World War II as homeownership grew. After the Bretton Woods Agreement was dismantled in 1971 the uses of debt at the private level accelerated. Mortgages traded as derivatives and securities enabled and sustained a deeper leveraging of housing markets before it collapsed under the exploding prices between 2000–2007.

Data source: Board of Governors of the Federal Reserve System (US), Households and Nonprofit Organizations; Debt Securities and Loans; Liability, Level [CMDEBT], retrieved from FRED, Federal Reserve Bank of St. Louis: https://fred.stlouisfed.org/series/CMDEBT, June 25, 2020 and U.S. Bureau of Economic Analysis, Gross Domestic Product [GDP], retrieved from FRED, Federal Reserve Bank of St. Louis: https://fred.stlouisfed.org/series/GDP, June 25, 2020.

Protesters called for less central control over development; students castigated professors and asked them to disengage from work so centrally controlled. Aldo van Eyck and Jacob Bakema were censured by TU Delft for acting as a "lackey of capitalism." Candilis in an interview speaks of people having more to contribute to the design of where they live—of them having some hand in building it. Candilis was asking Team 10 to face the literal scale and social ambition of their work, but also their own viability in the politically contracting welfare state that had been their patron and a form of conscience. That welfare state was under duress, it was shrinking, but also Candilis was doubting the scale of the role he played in thousands of people's lives.

The state retreated from housing and so did architects. A kind of evolved endgame emerged—one we are still in today.

Five: Architecture and Climate Change after Jobs and after Consumption: Housing need is about to be exacerbated in unprecedented ways as automation reduces work opportunities. In some regions of the United States 40% or more of jobs will be lost or deeply altered by automation. In large parts of the nation post-war housing is now on average 80 years old. On aggregate the United States housing industry already only serves a narrow percentage of the population, producing new housing only in markets that can sustain a high price point. Vast portions of the market are simply not served; immense amounts of people in the United States and worldwide occupy housing they cannot afford or will never be able to afford. Even as the markets leave so many underwater, or unhoused, the US housing market routinely builds as many as 1 million housing units per year. More than 25% of the existing housing stock today was built since 1985.

The housing and mobility world we live in today is still shaped by the rise of the single-family house and suburbs—the house and automobile. In the post-1970s era it came to be characterized by steep levels of debt and dramatic rise in personal consumption. The near future of this matrix instigates a set of new interrelated pressures: climate change, as an already declared denominator, will couple with the advanced automation of labor. We are by many accounts approaching a peak-labor society, a peak-automobile society, a peak-debt society, and a peak-consumption society. Each of these supply chains will face immense pressure.[6] Conflating home and jobs—and by extension the potential for automation of jobs—quickly undoes any secure sense of what the next two decades hold for development. The post-war matrix of housing, mobility, and jobs is unraveling—a median income portioned out over a 30-year mortgage and 12 cars is far from certain anymore. We are 50 years past the 42% of GDP housing debt levels of 1971—when post-Bretton Woods globalization began.

The recent past should still scare us to think hard about this: if climate change is a barely acknowledged horizon what can we say of climate change in an automated—jobless—era? What pays for housing? What funds climate innovation?

Right

Morris A. Davis and Jonathan Heathcote Residential Land, Homes, Structures, Price Index, 1975–2005

In the post 1975 period residential land cost in the United States has risen at a rate that far outpaces growth in the cost of residential structures. Land costs are also shown to be more volatile and high land costs diminish the role architecture plays in the provision of affordable housing. See data sets by Morris A. Davis, Jonathan Heathcote. See: The Price and Quantity of Residential Land in the United States, p. 40, Real Land, Home, and Structures Prices (Log Scale). http://www.jonathanheathcote.com/land-final.pdf

Residential Land, Homes, Structures, Price Index, 1975–2005
Morris A. Davis and Jonathan Heathcote

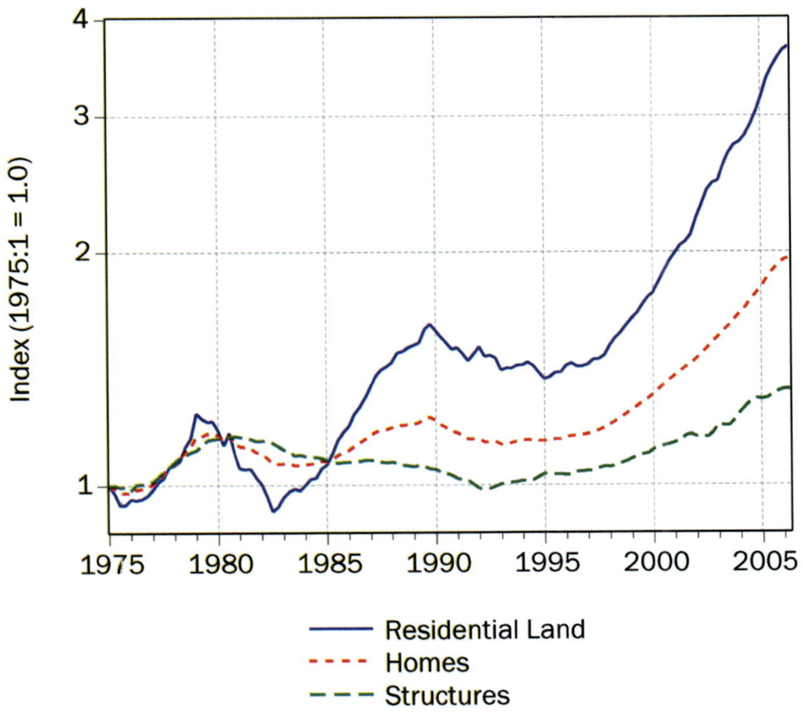

Six: Post Commodity Housing: Most architects will tell you housing has become a rote product; often a low-level commodity with little financial incentive to improve design. A case study we took on in Houston, Texas, in 1998, as HOPE VI programs were taking hold, found speculative houses (in this case, single-family houses typical for Houston) were built with virtually no architectural engagement. In one case we chronicled a $12 per house design fee and several thousand dollars in fees for several hundred standardized houses. The percentage of construction costs for architecture fees: .028%. In the United States housing standardization has meant low or nonexistent design fees, but it has also meant little if any research and development. While the debates of New Urbanism in this era drew immense attention it ultimately deflected the more urgent debate: what role does architecture play in housing when the market is the denominator and the federal government has instigated a quasi-privatized role for its economic contributions—has disaggregated its role in development. In hoping to incentivize entrepreneurial aspects of capital markets this had the side effect of diminishing the role of architects. There is no direct path to regain that in the current market unless we show design as a wealth mechanism. We'd propose to not take this path—what if housing was instead de-commoditized?

Home Value–Structure Cost–Land Value: California, 1975–2016

Bell - Seong

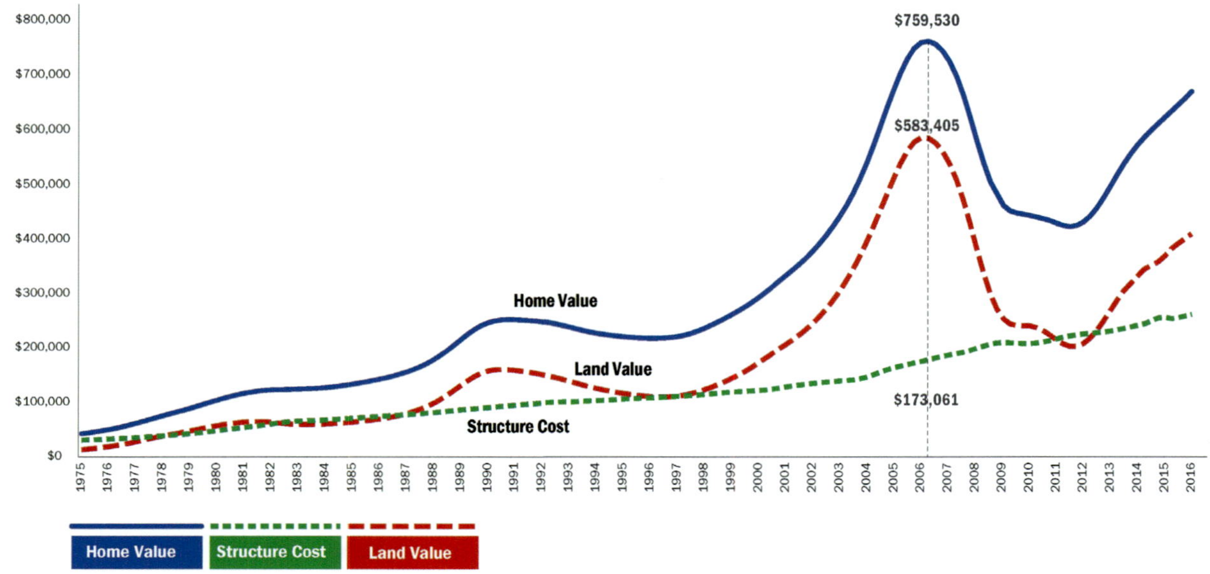

Seven: Density Sustains Leverage: 2008 and its aftermath had introduced the public to an array of algorithmic leverage mechanisms in banking: collateralized debt obligations (CDOs), mortgage-backed securities (MBS), credit default swaps (CDS) ... to tranches of debt. It revealed how little research went into housing itself; but how exotic and expansive its financialization had become. In light of accelerated costs, we commonly hear that density is needed—an assurance of affordability that also portends sustainability. But density is, in effect, a form of leverage and the public at large often recoils from this. So, what is possible otherwise? Especially in the wake of shocks that momentarily open a possible door to something other. Whatever it is it should begin with apprising the role of debt; it also cannot expect direct government engagement in reducing cost. It can expect innovation in renewable energy.

Eight: Not Scarce: Regimes of scarcity have been built into federal housing programs since the New Deal. The 1937 Housing Act was rife with political (ethical) conflict as it called for housing for the nation's working poor. The 1937 Housing Act outlined the formation of the nation's first Housing Authorities. It formed Public Housing. A federally instigated, manifest, owned, and operated mass housing project—in partnership with states and cities—spanned much of the country but was nonetheless tremendously lopsided in its emergence in New York City, Chicago, and Philadelphia. More than 1,300,000 units of public housing were built since 1937, realized on more than 3,000 sites. As placed on the president's desk the document was only 13 pages long and

Above

Bell - Seong
Home Value–Structure Cost–Land Value: California, 1975–2016

In the post-1970s economy land became an increasing percentage of housing costs in jobs-rich states. Increasing density to offset land value turns architecture into a form of spatial arbitrage–a form of leverage. In California land accounted for 77% of a residential real estate transaction in the pre-crash market leaving only 23% of housing cost for actual building. Davis has ceased updating this work to focus on metropolitan areas with a tighter control over variables. The state work gives a view to larger regions of government but also territory and geographic regions.

Graphics on pp. 206 and 207 are generated from data sets by Morris A. Davis. See: . See: https://www.fhfa.gov/PolicyProgramsResearch/Research/Pages/wp1901.aspx# and https://www.lincolninst.edu/news/press-releases/online-data-land-property-values-lincoln-institute-web-site

it enunciated a very precise demand. No apartment built as public housing was to exceed $4,000 or $1,000 per room. The document for the president's approval notes that land, development, and community costs were excluded from this price limit, and in cities that exceed 500,000 people the provision per apartment was set at $5,000 and $1,250 per room. The actions were to build housing. The reason, however, was to provide for the health of the nation. Not the individual. The wording was intended to say "we are not giving hand-outs; we are not a developer, and we are not competing with the market."

Home Value–Structure Cost–Land Value: West Virginia, 1975–2016
Bell - Seong

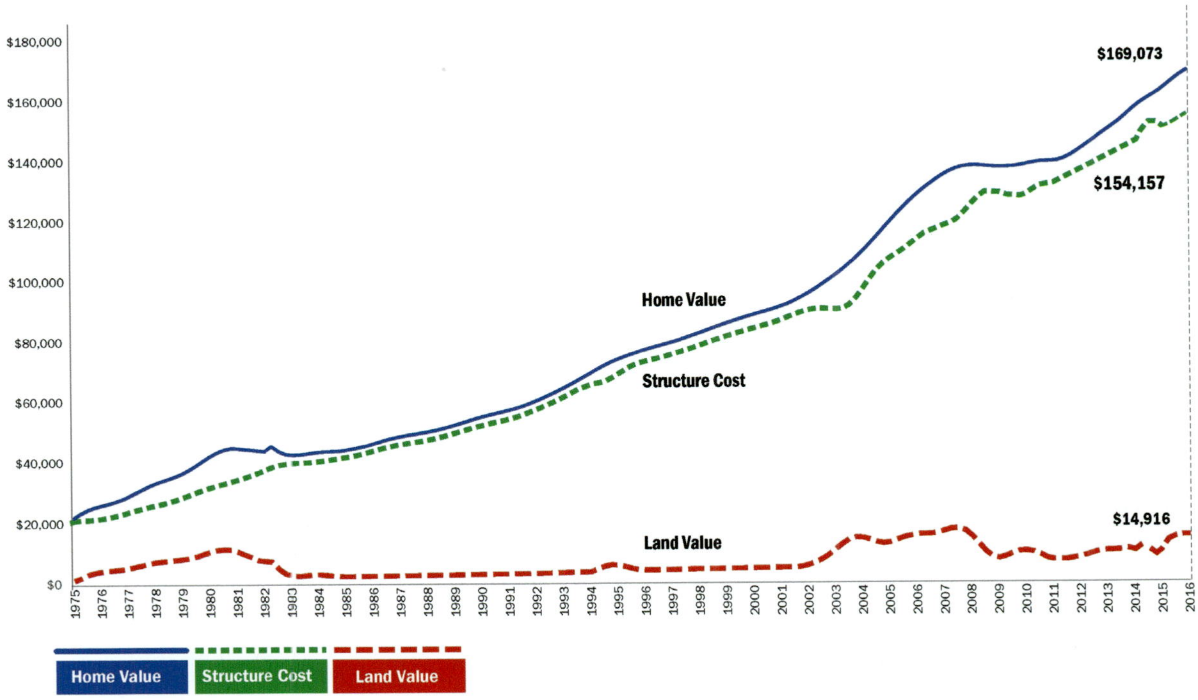

Above

Bell - Seong
Home Value–Structure Cost–Land Value: West Virginia, 1975–2016

In West Virginia the ratios form a doppelgänger to California. Land values accounted for 11% of a residential real estate transaction. If one were to resettle in lower cost land areas the vast proportion of housing cost could be attributed to architecture.

If the page count of the Act was surprisingly spare it was not without long-lasting complex political and ethical dimension. The Housing Act in unleashing as much at $5,000,000 per annum at the outset would instigate a literal construction project; housing for the country's working poor, mostly its urban poor, but the legal cause of the "act-ion" was not for construction of housing, per se, but in a more circumscribed way to promote the "general welfare of the Nation." It "declared policy" in which the United States would "promote the general welfare of the Nation by employing its funds and credit" "to assist the several States and their political subdivisions to alleviate present and recurring unemployment and to remedy the unsafe and insanitary housing conditions and the acute shortage of decent, safe, and sanitary dwellings." Housing here becomes less a building than a governmental action—a sustained role to in effect reduce poverty. In calling public housing a "governmental function" rather than a building an Ohio Housing Authority sought to limit its liability for a death that occurred in a fire in one of its buildings.[7] Housing is scarce, so scarce that it can be barely called real as architecture.

Nine: Non-Denumerable: Renewable energy, if removed from sustainability parameters, is an indicator of something that is *not scarce*. It is, in effect, hardly measurable in its *excess*—it becomes non-denumerable.[8] Energy from the Sun arrives at the Earth's surface in eight minutes. Fossil fuels formed 250 to 350 million years ago contrast to energy newly manifest in eight-minute intervals. This is not abstract in nature and is rapidly becoming a matter of our future economy. The cost to produce a solar cell capable of producing a watt of electricity has dropped during the past 40 years—from 77 dollars to 53 cents per watt. This is the emergence of a new asset class and it points to a form of excess rather than scarce energy. But can we save it from becoming a new form of leverage; a new way to prop up the old economy of scarcity?

In India the prospect of a universal wage expanded in 2016. The Indian government's proposals included references to Thomas Paine, the Revolutionary War American pamphleteer and author of The Rights of Man. Paine proposed a universal wage at the near founding of the United States recognizing within state-based rights to property a guaranteed displacement or seeming exile of some people. Property-less, placeless, constituencies. Household debt as a percentage of GDP here becomes evidence: GDP barely grew in the centuries prior to the industrialization and democratization of the world's modern nations. Paine saw an inevitable manifestation of property-less people within new property law (despite a massive rise in national and private wealth).

Ten: Post-Scarcity: Today housing as debt, density as the dilution of property cost to lower housing costs—all of this presumes a future of increased GDP, increased land values, perpetuation of jobs to fund that debt. The risk assessments measured in relation to residential real estate are often quite straightforward. Since 2017 UBS has published an annual "Real Estate Bubble Index." The study looks at a global array of cities and uses simple ratios of annual income to dwelling space: how many years does a skilled worker need to work to pay for an apartment. For many this is not a job, but several jobs; a de facto lack of affordability that does not even factor into a bubble. A constituency simply not served—not measured. While the UBS studies are indicative of simple ability to service debt, they do speak to a multi-decade window within which cities benefited from a jobs expansion and a technology-driven wealth accumulation that benefited enough to fuel exorbitant real estate prices. Today, instead we must cast the emergence of a reverse flow: artificial intelligence and machine learning—automation—as easing the rush to urban land and as running parallel to emergent forms of renewable energy. To, in effect, draw the future of housing as a renewed—inverted—extrapolation of jobs and energy. This time the jobs are (partially) erased, but we are paid anyway; and energy is abundant not scarce.

Right

Bell - Seong
Aggregate Value of Residential Real Estate, Mortgage Debt Outstanding, Consumer Credit

The aggregate value of residential real estate in the United States and the mortgages that underwrite it give an impression of significant equity in housing. But equity has fluctuated severely in the past 12 years. In the fourth quarter of 2008 Core Logic estimated 18% of homes had negative equity. By 2010 this rose to 24%. Today the national average stands at approximately 9%, but regional variations are still significant or worse. In Brooke County, Illinois, for example, nearly 40% of mortgages are underwater.

Data sources:
https://www.census.gov/content/dam/Census/programs-surveys/ahs/publications/Drowning_in_Debt.pdf

https://www.reuters.com/article/us-usa-housing-underwater-insight/millions-of-americans-still-trapped-in-debt-logged-homes-ten-years-after-crisis-idUSKCN1LU0EP

Modified sources:
Federal Reserve Bank of St. Louis

Mortgage Debt Outstanding by Type of Property: Multifamily Residences, Millions of Dollars, Annual, Not Seasonally Adjusted: https://fred.stlouisfed.org/series/MDOTPMFR#0

Mortgage Debt Outstanding by Type of Property: One- to Four-Family Residences, Millions of Dollars, Annual, Not Seasonally Adjusted: https://fred.stlouisfed.org/series/MDOTP1T4FR#0

Households and Nonprofit Organizations; Consumer Credit; Liability, Level, Billions of Dollars, Annual, Seasonally Adjusted: https://fred.stlouisfed.org/series/HCCSDODNS#0

Households and Nonprofit Organizations; Real Estate at Market Value, Billions of Dollars, Annual, Not Seasonally Adjusted: https://fred.stlouisfed.org/series/HNOREMV

This is not a form of sustainability, but actually excess. It is not a taking of development off the grid but instead *never having been on the grid.* Housing could become a downstream byproduct of renewable energy; not monetized by square footage, but instead a form of economic stability and a post-capital form of energy as housing.

Aggregate Value of Residential Real Estate, Mortgage Debt Outstanding, Consumer Credit
Bell - Seong

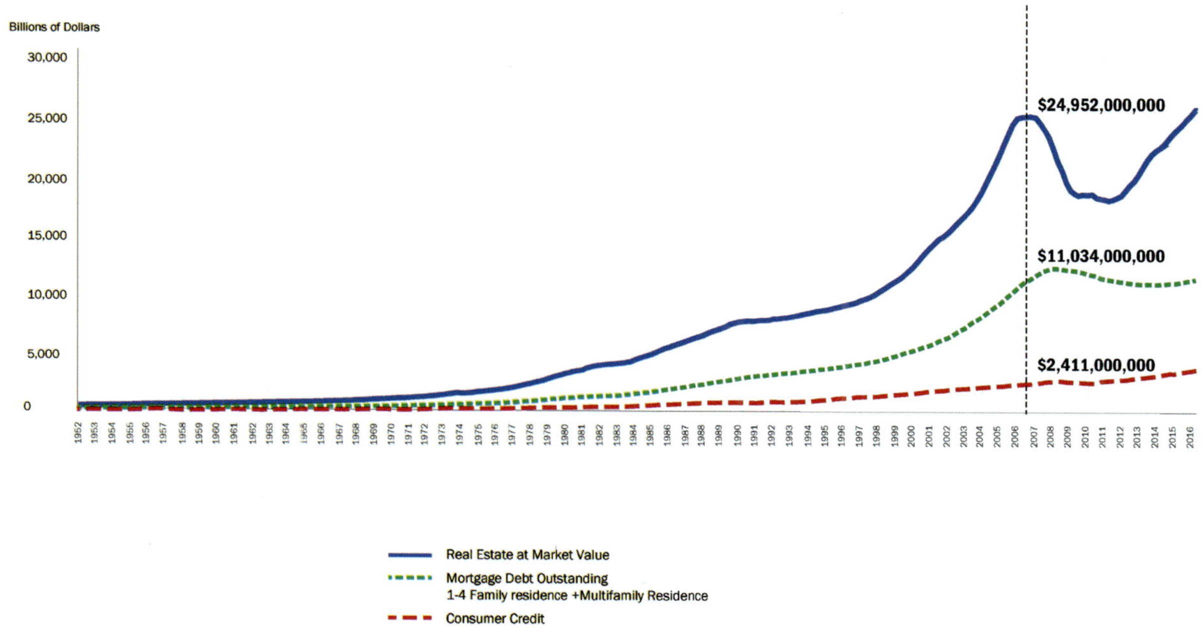

The spatial imagination to draw this will not come from banking, but without a view to economics we in effect don't know our own history. We have been living in a pressurized space that cannot fathom architecture without money; we might begin to see an exit. Despite the evidence of economic oppression everywhere, one can imagine a kind of dissipated plasticity—a recapitulation of 2008 as debt cycles meet labor automation meet climate change. A collapse of economic pressures that would leave renewable energy as the origin and a reason and means to construct. We, in effect, must address climate change in an increasingly jobless society.

Photons arriving from the Sun in eight minutes. And we are all staying home. In ways we never imagined possible—in ways not experienced since pre-industrial agrarian life. The financial pressure on future housing markets does not have to be—it will surely persist as long as we trade space as a commodity, but the question is who will pay for it and with what income? What value does an un-tradable asset have? A migration away from high cost metropolitan land is one step; a move to localize the production and even sale of excess renewable energy is another. The mind set—a theory of excess, even—would in effect place the pressure of economy as a new imaginary. Far from anti-capitalism, it is instead an evolution of what is traded, what is withheld, and what is secured by architecture.

Right Top

Bell - Seong
Personal Consumption Expenditures, 1959–2019

Personal Consumption in the United States has risen dramatically since 1970. It is historically tied to the house and automobile, but after the 1970s it was fueled by equity and leverage afforded by housing equity. On a per capita basis and accounting for population growth the acceleration is far more dramatic.

Retrieved from FRED, Federal Reserve Bank of St. Louis: https://fred.stlouisfed.org/series/PCE, June 27, 2020. Annotations by Bell-Seong.

Data source:
U.S. Bureau of Economic Analysis, Personal Consumption Expenditures

Right Bottom

Bell - Seong
Silicon Photovoltaic Cell Cost per Watt and Solar Energy Consumption

A declining logarithmic curve depicts Silicon PV cell pricing (dollar/watt). Lower prices are possible but they will arrive at slower pace. A rising exponential curve in solar energy consumption could accelerate but what relation will that curve have to PV panel pricing? When does housing cease to be a real-estate asset and instead become a downstream product of an energy asset.

PV cost data source: https://www.economist.com/news/2012/11/21/sunny-uplands (Geoffrey Carr, 'The World in 2013, "Alternative Energy will no Longer be Alternative",' The Economist, 21 November, 2012)

Solar consumption data source: "Energy Consumed by the Residential Sector," September 27, 2016. https://www.eia.gov/totalenergy/data/monthly/pdf/sec10_4.pdf

Renewable Energy Production and Consumption by Source: Solar Energy Consumption, September 27, 2016. https://www.eia.gov/totalenergy/data/monthly/pdf/sec10_3.pdf

References

1. https://www.bloomberg.com/news/articles/2016-10-16/big-central-bank-assets-jump-fastest-in-5-years-to-21-trillion
2. https://www.bis.org/publ/mktc11.pdf
3. See Morris A. Davis and Jonathan Heathcote, "The Price and Quantity of Residential Land in the United States," *Journal of Monetary Economics* 54(8), November 2007. http://www.jonathanheathcote.com/land-final.pdf
4. Board of Governors of the Federal Reserve System, "Flow of Funds Accounts of the United States," December 9, 2010.
5. Rotterdam: NAI Publishers, 2006.
6. https://www.rethinkx.com/transportation-executive-summary
7. https://www.sconet.state.oh.us/PIO/summaries/2009/0325/072106_080030.asp
8. The term "non-denumerable" comes from mathematics and can be understood to mean uncountable within natural numbers. Thanks to A. Tepper and S. Cooke for assistance with the term.

Personal Consumption Expenditures, 1959–2019

Bell - Seong

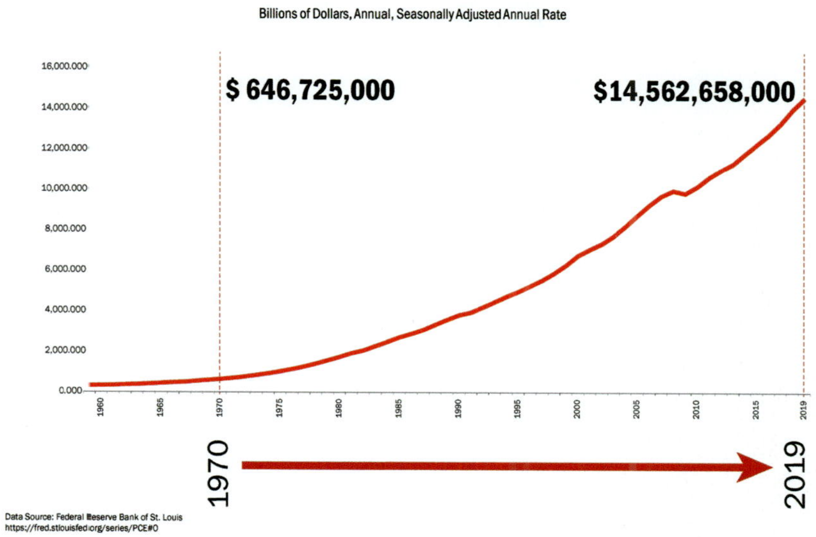

Silicon Photovoltaic Cell Cost per Watt and Solar Energy Consumption

Bell - Seong

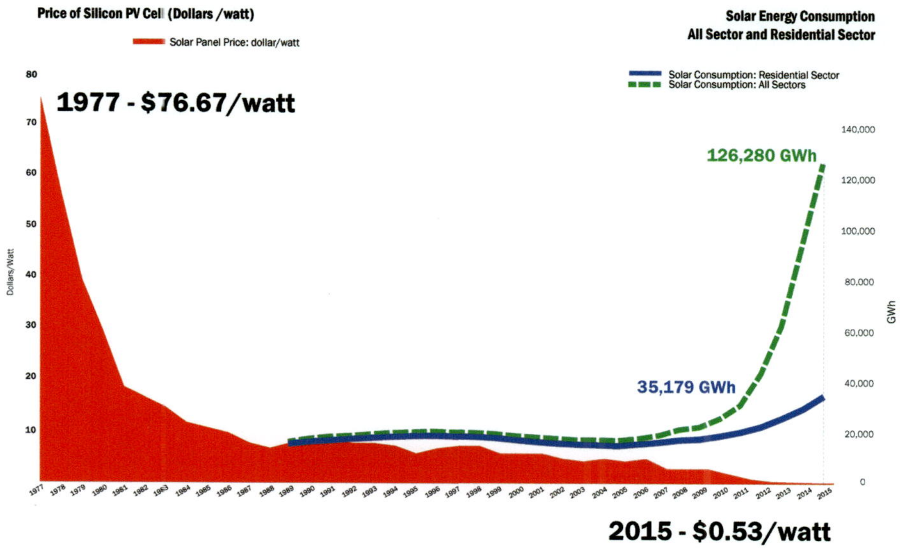

LOLUX: HYBRID DENSITY

Jonas Coersmeier

"LoLux: Hybrid Density" explores the relationship between low-income and luxury housing and proposes a building complex of hybrid density for the megacity. It simultaneously focuses on the two primary growth markets of New York City real estate—luxury condominiums and low-income apartments—and systematically works out areas of synergy between these disparate segments. Envisioning a future for the urban housing environment under pressure, the project aims at developing a new model for densification, recognizing that cities need to grow inward, not just for ecological sustainability, but for social and economic sustainability as well.

The project initiates from two parallel investigations. On one hand, a comprehensive study on urban housing precedents informs the project's take on housing typologies. Among several precedents studied, the Barbican development in London illustrates that a well-orchestrated mixed-use building complex benefits both inhabitants and the community at large. On the other hand, research on the urban context of the site in Dumbo, Brooklyn, informs the project's hybrid program and its urban strategy. A creative environment to work, live, and play in is essential for the growth of the energetic tech industry in downtown Brooklyn. The property's as-of-right entitlements for more than 1.2 million square feet of development could, if developed as fully residential, drastically increase Dumbo's current population. Meanwhile the site is adjacent to the Brooklyn Bridge Park and could potentially act as connective tissue for a larger continuous public space in Downtown Brooklyn. The project responds to these opportunities with an integrated model for urban landscape and architectural densification.

On an urban scale, the project creates a new ground that extends horizontally and links to the open and green spaces between the riverside and Downtown Brooklyn, which are currently disconnected by bridges and highways. The elevated new ground, as part of a continuous urban landscape, provides a public destination for the densifying neighborhood. Furthermore, based on the analysis of the socio-economic context, the project addresses the unique needs of the tech industry in the area

Left

Shih-Kai Lin
Hybrid Density

Jonas Coersmeier LoLux Studio with Chao Liu

University of Pennsylvania Weitzman School of Design, 2017

Physical model showing Finer Tectonic System of the building façade.

through its mixed-use programs. The plinth, whose roof becomes the new ground, is designed to be a coworking campus where neighbors share spaces and amenities, as well as ideas and experiences. Suspended above the new ground, horizontal housing wings complete the block edge formation, and at the eastern end of the site they merge and rise up as tall housing towers. The sculpted form of the proposed complex maximizes density while defining diverse spatial conditions for public and communal engagement on two urban levels.

On a local scale, the spatial organization provides new possibilities for the relationship between living and working as well as the public and private domains. The junction within the building complex, which is illustrated on the physical model, demonstrates a smooth transition from a common working space on the ground to private living units above. Amenities that support both, such as community auditorium or vertical bike-parking space, are arranged around the junction, which connects the coworking space at the plinth, residential wings, and residential towers. Supported by the junction and plinth below, the residential towers comprise a variety of housing units. The standard unit types are studio, one-bedroom, two-bedroom, three-bedroom, and duplex. Unlike conventional stacked floor plate arrangements, the housing units are aggregated in a way that creates a variety of niches either within units or between units. Within a unit, those niches can accommodate double-height living spaces or balconies. And between units, they can accommodate amenities, such as shared lounges, kitchens, or working spaces facilitating work-from-home mode. This spatial organization allows for various forms of living and could integrate a spectrum of needs and desires for low-income and luxury housing.

"LoLux: Hybrid Density" addresses socio-economic issues in urban housing and how they relate to the architectural mandate. It acknowledges that architecture alone cannot solve systemic inequity, but it assumes agency for the design disciplines in these matters. It insists that architecture provides cultural content, creates spatial, material, and aesthetic value, and thus holds the potential for improving human coexistence and the urban condition. The project is deeply invested in the concerns of adjacent disciplines, especially those analyzing the larger economic framework it is operating in. Yet it aims at complementing rather than adopting their narratives, as it focuses on core architectural expertise in its argument.

The project's search for new forms of densification is driven as much by the urgent need to create affordable and resilient space for habitation, as by the desire for density itself. It considers density an architectural quality that registers in one part as spatial sensation, and in another through the frequency of diverse urban encounters. The project pursues this quality and proposes a model for densification that increases the city's capacity to simultaneously absorb internal and external pressures caused by global warming and urbanization.

Above

Physical section model showing live/work spaces connecting to shared amenities.

Right

Physical section model showing the transition from plinth to new ground and tower.

Shadow Series
Edition 4 - 4

04

DESIGN AND MATERIAL INNOVATION

VOIDS AND OTHER INVISIBLE OBJECTS

Marcelo Spina | PATTERNS

Persistent notions of type, scalar repetition, material form, building image and legibility in the context of recent residential and mix-use developments suggest that the larger the size, the greater the moves that architecture has to make in order to both adapt to internal typological pressures and external financial constraints while proposing a progressive and engaging agenda for building organization, form, and urban presence in the city.

PATTERNS's recent experience suggests a play on extremes. On the one hand, the ambitions of material plasticity at the scale of the unit and the formal posture at the scale of the whole,[1] on the other, the need to distribute and mute large portions of undifferentiated volume and mass while strategically and meaningfully articulating (often interstitial) voids. By concentrating on the specifics of recent and ongoing projects of the office ranging dramatically in size and scale, the following notes and thoughts reflect retroactively and propositionally imagine a realist and speculative approach to the problem of urban housing, in Los Angeles and elsewhere.

Cuts and Outward Voids[2]

If, at least at the most visceral level, we understand architecture as primarily a matter of volume and mass, then articulation or the lack thereof becomes essential. Voids and other interruptions to mass are fundamental. Cuts are sources for shaping volumes, adding crystalline features at times or simple holes at others. Voids are a different matter altogether; they are dimensional subtractions destined to negatively emphasize that which is not there, or sometimes, that which came before or will come after. In these instances, illustrated in projects such as *Olympia, Split Block* and *1099 Grand* to a lesser extent, voids are connective separators. They reveal depth and create opportunities for other even contrasting articulations, either at the scale of volume, system, or material. Individual or collective, centralized or linear, static or dynamic, voids are the invisible spatial and volumetric substance that interacts with building mass internally or externally.

Left

PATTERNS
1099 Grand
Downtown Los Angeles, 2018–2020

1099 Grand, worm's eye isometric view.

PATTERNS in collaboration with SOM
Olympia Towers
Downtown Los Angeles, 2016–2026

Olympia Towers isometric view within Downtown Los Angeles context. The project sits right in front of the 110th freeway, shaping the iconic skyline of Downtown Los Angeles.

Cuts and voids are fundamental assets in the articulation of architectural volume and mass. In the tradition of solidity, constructing a gap can also create new features within a mass. While a building can demonstrate coherence in its silhouette, its internal cuts, with depth and shadow as resulting characteristics, can imply either fragmentation of mass or volumetric assembly.

Displacements and Disarticulations[3]

Displacements, shifting, and other forms of disarticulation are the opposite of volume and mass and, at the same time, a direct reversal of articulation. Removing parts from whole, creating dissonances that are sudden, unexpected, and local, can lead to the production of fuzziness within otherwise legible objects. This is where the "glitch" becomes conceptually interesting, in its ability to introduce qualities and features within a given object that were, a priori, completely outside its original genealogy.

A glitch is a momentary deviation from what is considered conclusive; it is information that is almost correct but displaced in a critical way. System glitches suggest a specific failure in computation, manufacturing, or any other similar production. It is an undesired outcome in the production of efficiency, often a momentary mistake. There are qualities of the glitch that are aesthetically productive for the mute icon, leading to clumsy forms and pixelated tectonics. A glitch has limits; there is a tolerance point at which the glitch stops being an anomaly and starts becoming new. The glitch is not an incorrect representation of conclusive form; it still refers to conclusive form, though it flickers somewhere in between completeness and incompleteness. When controlled, these momentary displacements and disarticulations reveal a plausible and productive alternative to strong form and legible aesthetics. The shifting displacements and disarticulations of floors, balconies and entire trays in Olympia Towers is an example of this approach.

Glass Mass

The dichotomy between transparency and opacity has long haunted architectural history and theory. In his seminal essay entitled "Transparency: Literal and Phenomenal," Colin Rowe formulated the basis of formal and material aesthetics for much of modern architecture, departing from the most common understanding of transparency as "that which is easily detected, perfectly evident, and free of dissimulation."[4] In describing transparency, he made clear very early on, the very own paradox at the basis of the term.

If one sees two or more figures overlapping one another, and each of them claims for itself the overlapped part, then one is confronted with a contradiction of spatial dimensions. To resolve this contradiction, one must assume the presence of a new optical quality. The figures are endowed with transparency, that is, they are able to interpenetrate without an optical destruction of each other. Transparency, however, implies more than an optical characteristic. It implies a broader spatial

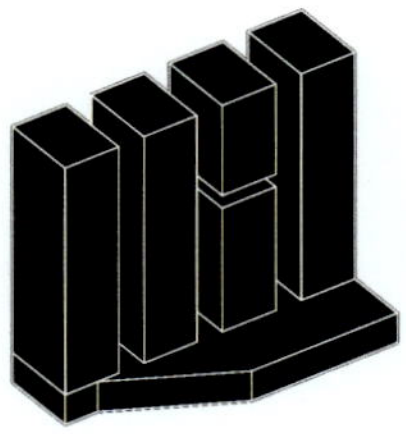

01 Primary Programs

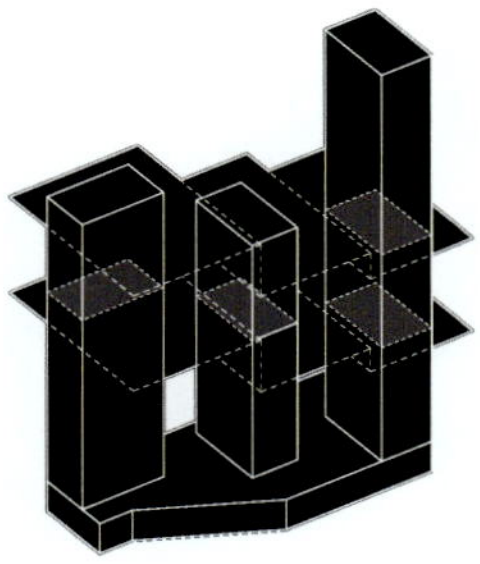

03 Slicing

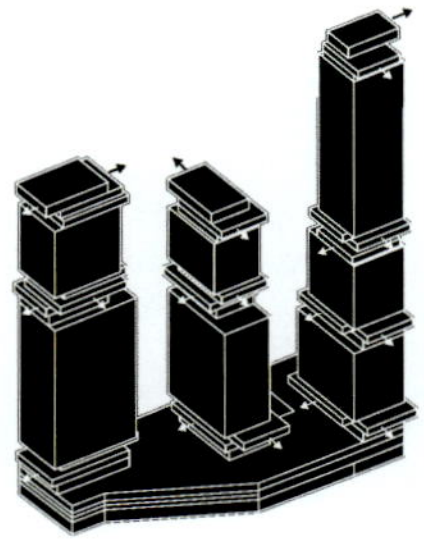

05 Shifting

Above and Right

PATTERNS in collaboration with SOM
Olympia Towers
Downtown Los Angeles, 2016–2026

Diagrams showing design sequence and void articulation as well as displacements and disarticulations across the entire complex of three towers.

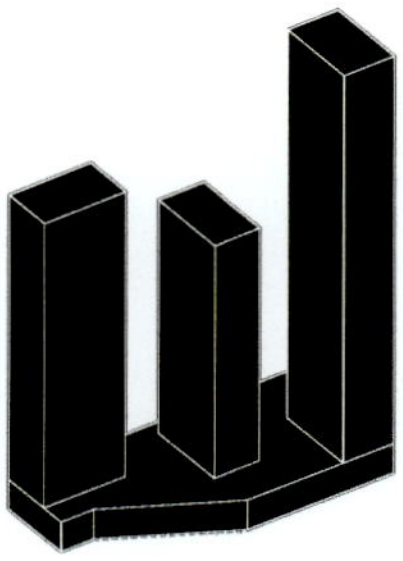

02 Program Distribution

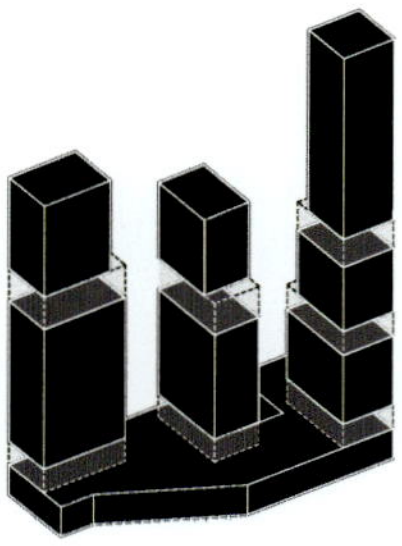

04 Void

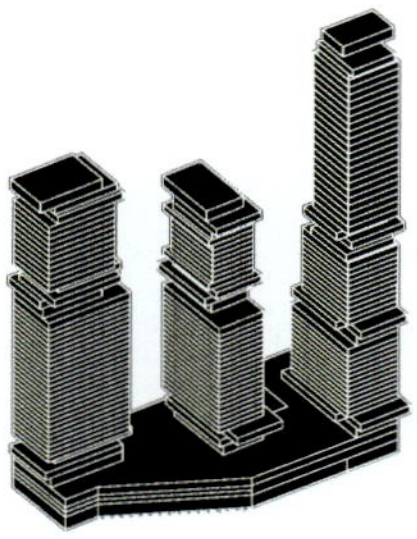

06 Floors

order. Transparency means a simultaneous perception of different spatial locations. Space not only recedes but fluctuates in a continuous activity. By this definition, transparency ceases to be that which is perfectly clear and instead becomes that which is clearly ambiguous. In fact, Mies van der Rohe's sequence of photomontages for Berlin's *Friederichtrasse Skyscraper* depicting the building first opaque and then transparent, conveys precisely the ambivalence of the architect towards these seemingly oppositional notions of describing glass mass. When surfaces are opaque, mass is clearly readable but relations between interior and exterior are very much discontinuous. On the contrary, transparency implies the partial erasure of mass, in pursuit of clarity of vision as well as views. While this dichotomy is still very much present, the possibilities offered by color, UV values, tints, ceramic frit, digitally printed and self-shading glass nowadays, allow for more nuanced possibilities when it comes to material aesthetics.[4]

As glass becomes the predominant material for a large array of medium and large projects for a variety of climates, regions and cultures, its aesthetic conception and formal sensibility, long associated to the rise of corporate modernism in America, needs to be expanded and reconceived. For efficiency and aesthetic reasons, architectural projects of a certain size, located within dense and increasingly developing urban cores of American cities, need to rely in unitized curtain wall construction with some variation of glazing envelope.

As environmental control systems become more and more integrated within building envelopes, the need to articulate transparent façades as well as to reduce heat gain becomes ever more pressing. For instance, the energy code in California, one of the most advanced and stringent in the world, allows for only 40 percent of a given façade to be actually transparent [vision glass], therefore affording buildings with a newfound level of conceptual and literal opacity through either the use of more solid opaque surfaces or actual shadow on transparent surfaces. The reason this is significant nowadays, is because it brings back the material and aesthetic dichotomy of glass, long associated with the notion of transparency which confounded the rise of corporate modernism in America.

The three projects featured here speculate on the mute and robust aesthetics [material, tectonic and aesthetic] of glass mass, wherein the glass, purposely rendered dark, vibrates between transparency, opacity and reflectivity. By focusing on and expanding upon the possibilities offered by contemporary fritted ceramic glass, these projects aim to construct vague and brutal prisms. With volumes defined by strong and yet fuzzy silhouettes, reflective monolithic envelopes, relief articulation and contrasting textures, these projects aim to develop a nuanced approach to architectural volume using glass. Much like in Gerhard Richter's Eight Grey. The use of glass aims to imitate our relationship with the real, by constantly replacing and distorting the image of the building with that of the context and "emphasizing the viewer's individual perceptions, rejecting a predetermined collective unified experience."[5]

The Case of Olympia Towers, Downtown Los Angeles

Poised to become one of the largest high-rise developments in Downtown Los Angeles, Olympia Towers consists of three mixed-use towers of 65, 53, and 43 stories each. Consisting of residences, apartments, hotels, and amenities such as retail, restaurants, pools, and parking, the project occupies a unique site within South Park district and will create a strong link to LA Live, Staples Center, and the Convention Center. Collectively, the proposal traces a distinctly new silhouette on the Los Angeles skyline, defined by vertical masses, horizontally displaced volumes, and stacked terraces that create visually interconnected places for leisure, entertainment, and urban life. Conceived as a "vertical neighborhood," the project articulates communal space across three discrete towers creating a diagonal sequence of horizontal "voids." Through local subtractions and displacements, these "voids" visually unify the composition while creating a radically distinct scale of legibility and experience for high-rise typology in the city.

The façades of the towers are articulated with stacked terraces and intercalated bands of vision and fritted glass, allowing residents to have framed horizontal vistas of Los Angeles while enjoying the indoor/outdoor lifestyle of Southern California living. In addition, the overlapping of the two bands of vision and fritted glass allows the curtain wall system to provide additional solar shading and improve insulation in the interior. To be clear, in Olympia, the voids are full of activities. Throughout the height of each tower, terraces and gardens are concentrated around communal activities within the amenities level. Consisting of an outdoor pool, a gym, restaurant/café as well as terraces and gardens, these indoor–outdoor spaces provide residents and visitors alike with opportunities to interact while taking in dramatic views of the city. Materially, these spaces are perceived and experienced in continuity and contrast to the glass envelope of the rest of the building, with soffits being clearly highlighted with a shimmering texture of embossed stainless steel ceiling tiles.

Higher than the rest of the floors, the displacement produced in the amenities floor is also supported and followed right above by two levels of special apartments. Considered penthouses and designed to be occupied by a younger demographic, these residences would enjoy a maximum proximity to the shared communal areas and include generous outdoor balconies facing right down to them. The programmatic, spatial and aesthetic attributes of these spaces, in combination with their user-driven, close-up experience as well as their public legibility from far away, makes them a significant quality not only for a large project, but also and more importantly, for the surrounding urban milieu of the city at large.

Form as Void

In a context of urban densification and development guided by both local city ordinances and private capital, volume and to a certain extent form are directed as much by zoning codes such as FAR[6] maximum heights, setbacks, building envelope

Right Top

PATTERNS in collaboration with SOM
Olympia Towers
Downtown Los Angeles, 2016–2026

Olympia Towers, worm's eye isometric view describes displacements and disarticulations produced by local voids cut diagonally across three towers.

Right Bottom

Worm's eye isometric of single tower depicting amenities level and special residences surrounding communal areas overlooking into garden and terraces.

01 Primary Form

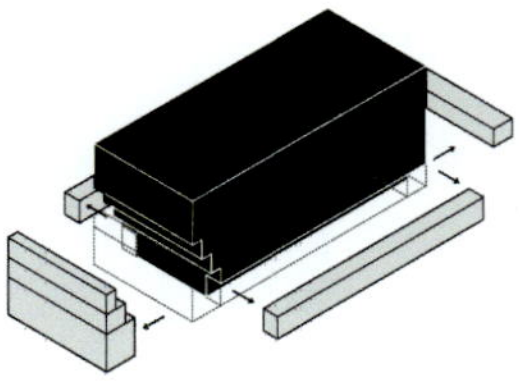

02 Subtracting

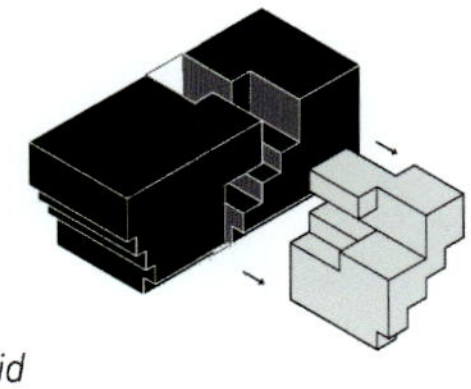

3.1 Void

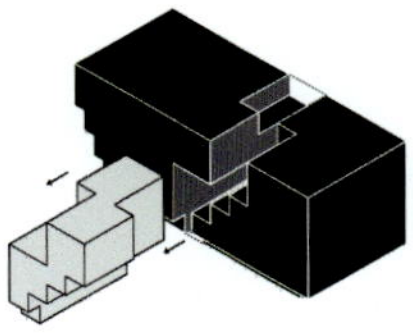

3.2 Void

and open space to name just a few, as they are designed by architects. In such context, managing void is as important as managing form, for formal reasons but also, and even more importantly, for urban reasons. In the hollowness of voids, lies the opportunity for amplification of depth and the possibility of meaningfully breaking with both the often-endless flatness of urban façades as well as the suffocating fixity of the city grid.

When it comes to housing, size matters in a different way than any other architectural type. The larger and denser the building, the less its unit exposure and expression, and the more muting of some of the elements that in smaller scales could have been the source of determining the external appearance. In a denser and more compact context, the unit's capacity to yield substantial formal and volumetric results at the scale of the whole is clearly diminished. In these situations, it can be said that the unit withdraws, seemingly extracting itself from any apparent formal and aesthetic role at the scale of the whole urban object. Once this size threshold is understood, the possibilities for housing are of an utterly different nature. In the projects featured here, the housing units, long thought to be the drivers of residential development, withdraw into larger and quieter volumes, distinctly cut or displaced to produce legible and yet unexpected urban silhouettes.

The difference between strictly residential programs and mixed-use is of significance here. While the typological mixture is barely affected, residential units as apartments (units for rent) or condominium (units for sale) make up to 90 percent of a project's entire program. The combination does change enough so as to, hypothetically, generate new and distinct[7] forms of inhabitation. Considering this context, void is the insertion of otherness, the possibility of semi-private or even communal, semi-public space and urban connectivity. Void is also a way of splitting and breaking down mass, for compositional, contextual and even safety purposes. Void is and must be programmed, and in its formal specificity as well as in its lack of structural determination, allows for the possibility of distinct and unforeseen uses and activities to unfold over time.

Void is what's not there rather than what's there. An invisible object. As the antithesis of mass, void is the perfect complement for it: it makes solids more monolithic and mute, but also, depending on the feature-giving capability of the void, more iconic. Voids are cuts, interruptions or simple omissions, and in this series of projects, voids are made of aesthetically alluring contrasts and structural challenges. Using dark tinted glass in combination with embossed shiny gold metallic panels, their mass is reflective and mute. These are some of the aesthetic reasons for articulating voids. In their apparent emptiness, there is a possibility of inserting conflicting contrasts, and even new aesthetic regimes. As a result, void is about legibility and image: the image of an object or objects, and urban images of those objects estranging their context. When it comes to economy, void is benefit, and certainly not for free. Since according to zoning codes, void counts towards FAR, when it comes to efficiency and finance, void is (added) value. This value is often seen in the quality and quantity of community

Left Top

PATTERNS
Split Block
Arts District, Los Angeles, 2018

Split Block, isometric view.

Left Bottom

Worm's eye perspective view.

Above

Subtraction diagrams.

and shared spaces and the way these they are integrated within a given project. It is precisely this dichotomy between the compact solidity of units and the collective void of communal space that comes to define these projects. Following from this, voids can also be politically radical. Clients, especially developers, are often afraid of this word (void), much like little kids are afraid of the dark. In the over-deterministic tendency to define, program, maximize, and monetize space, it appears that the possibility of leaving area undecided is frightening.

But voids are not just absences. Voids are hidden negative parts. Their employment doesn't necessarily follow a simple and linear process wherein form is carved out from a single volume. While this can be the case, voids can also connect across separate parts and objects or exist as gaps, creating a complex relationship between many disconnected larger parts or objects, or a multiply broken whole. Given a certain scale, they articulate as much form as void. So, retroactively, in these projects, form is void. Considering the social-distancing measures still in effect in much of the world as a result of COVID-19 and the subsequent global pandemic, void is not only space, but therapeutic distance and healing time, exterior surfaces for leisure, play and human interaction.

This proposition is not intended to be a universal formula, and is certainly as speculative as it is provisional. Likewise, this is not even a housing proposition, but one that may find, within the ever-tightening and complexing territory of urban housing, vast possibilities for advancing an architecture that, operating in close proximity to the real, can insert otherworldly formal, spatial, social and aesthetic conditions within the cities we currently inhabit.

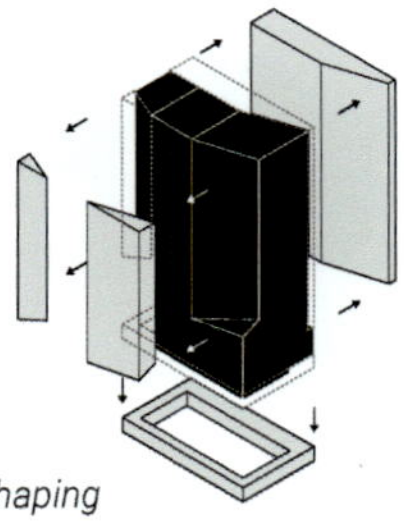

02 Shaping

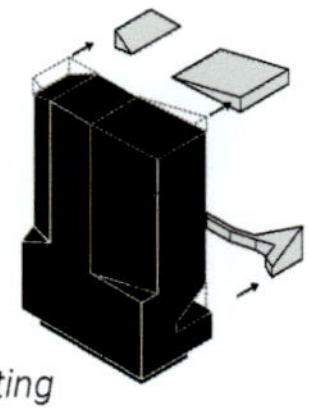

03 Subtracting

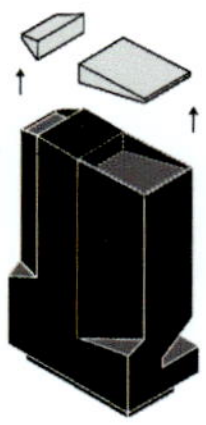

04 Void

Above

PATTERNS
1099 Grand
Downtown Los Angeles, 2018–2020

Process diagrams.

Right

Isometric view in context.

References

1. Jujuy Redux, 2012, is an award-winning 14-unit apartment building in Rosario, Argentina, designed by PATTERNS and MSA. The project was based on this design assumption wherein housing units as well as elements such as balconies and windows play a fundamental role in shaping a subtle and delineated mass that operates both at the scale of the entire mass as well as the scale of each apartment.
2. Marcelo Spina and Georgina Huljich, PATTERNS. Originally published in "Discipline: Current Dichotomies and Their Disciplinary Implications," *Mute Icons, and other Dichotomies of the Real in Architecture*. Barcelona: ACTAR Press, 2020, pp. 162–163.
3. Ibid., pp.
4. Colin Rowe and Robert Slutzky, "Transparency: Literal and Phenomenal," *Perspecta* 8, 1963, pp. 45–54.
5. Eight Grey, Gerhard Richter, 2002, is a series of tinted [enamel glass] panels which reflect a shadowy perpetually shifting image. As spectators move in and out of the picture plane, they re-create the random cropping of a snapshot, adding a heightened element of chance. Continuously transforming, the mirrors reproduce the always fleeting moment in front of us and thus remain open, boundless. Though monumental in scale, this series of identical, individual panels surprisingly resists a single coherent vision. Richter's mirrored panels emphasize the viewer's individual perceptions, rejecting a predetermined program or collective, unified experience.
6. FAR, Floor Area Ratio, is one of the most precious assets and driving forces behind current residential and mix-use development in the US, affecting not only the land value but also the potential for up-zoning of many urban sites.
7. Albeit formulaic if one considers what is currently being built in many American cities in the name of "mixed-use" typologies. Shoehi OMA has referred to the mix-use type as the new "Bento Box of food."

SOCIAL VOID

Scott Erdy

The Social Void sits at the border between the Fairmount and Poplar sections of Philadelphia. Buildings on the east side of Broad Street are technically in Poplar, but look westward toward the more affluent Fairmount neighborhood. Fairmount has a long and storied history. It was named by William Penn because it was the largest hill in the area. During the American Revolution, British soldiers utilized the hill as a means of defense when they were fighting against American soldiers under George Washington's command. The Fairmount Dam and Water Works organization would later utilize the large hill as a natural pump, using gravity to provide water to homes and businesses within the city from the reservoir above. The area was also home to the Baldwin Locomotive Works, an American manufacturer of railroad locomotives from 1825 to 1956. The company was for decades the largest producer of steam locomotives in the world. Fairmount benefited greatly from industrialization, which brought breweries and other factories into the neighborhood, spurring residential development. The Eastern State Penitentiary, built in the early 19th century, is a prominent landmark in the neighborhood. The area is probably best known for the historic and symbolic Philadelphia Art Museum, the site where Penn had planned to build his country house and where later Rocky would cement Philadelphia's position in history by his hopefully triumphant climb of the museum steps.

Poplar is different. After the Great Depression the area fell into disrepair and abandonment, leading the city to raze a large portion of the neighborhood in the late 1930s to build Richard Allen Homes, a massive public housing project that replaced blighted urban areas with low density semi-urban public housing. Budget cuts and neglect by the city hastened deterioration of the homes, and poorly planned open spaces encouraged crime, and made it the center for homelessness, crime and drug trafficking by the 1970s and 1980s. Most recently, the semi-urban apartments are being systematically replaced by true suburban-style single family detached homes, with front yards and private driveways in the heart of the city. The construction and subsequent dereliction of Richard Allen Homes defined Poplar's physical characteristic for decades, creating a void in the fabric of the city that still exists today.

Left

Jiateng Wang
Trans-Urban Dwelling

Scott Erdy Urban Housing Studio with Ruo Wang

University of Pennsylvania Weitzman School of Design, 2015

Axonometric section illustrating relationship between the exterior building enclosure (fortress) and the interior volumes of transition space.

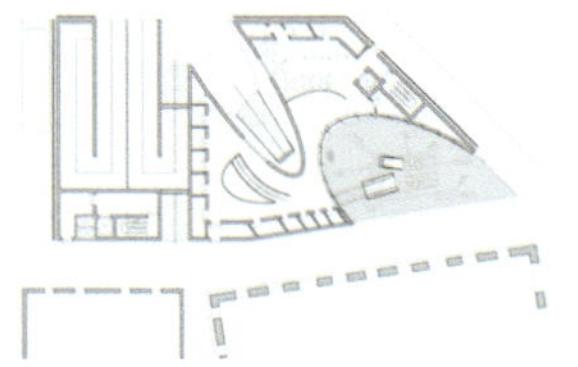

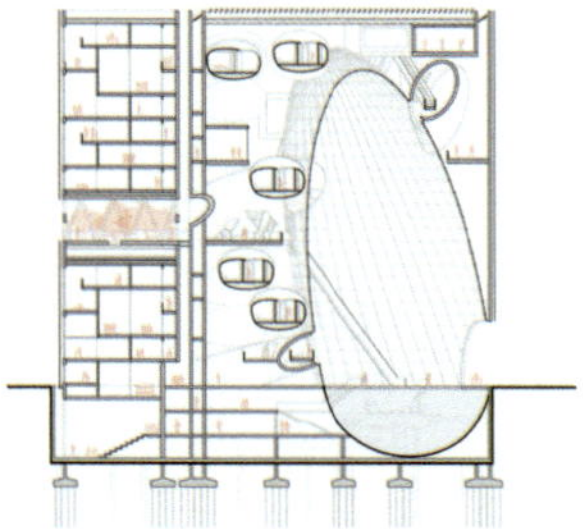

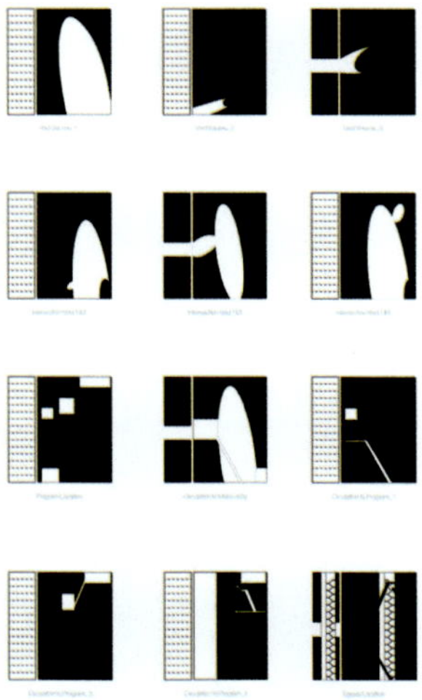

Left

Physical model.

Above

Based on the traditional Chinese Tulou typology, Jiateng's building presents a fortified perimeter with a single access point that leads into a large void that becomes the transcendental space in the project.

Serial section diagrams studying the spatial sequence of public spaces through the building indicating the transitional voids between public and private spaces.

Jiateng's proposal translates physical and cultural differences of the site and makes them visible. The monumentality of his building stands in solidarity with the adjacent Divine Lorraine Hotel immediately to the north, continuing its history as Civil Rights advocate and comforter of the poor.

The mission of the project is to empower individuals to break the cycle of homelessness and poverty by providing temporary, transitional and emergency housing for the homeless as well as education and healthcare. Job training is accomplished through its café and thrift store. To help the residents navigate the complex US legal system, there is a Legal Aid and Advocacy Center that will assist in getting their legal affairs in order and guide them through the process of obtaining permanent housing.

As with most northern cities, homelessness becomes urgent in the winter when temperatures drop below freezing and sleeping on the street can be deadly. To respond to this acute need, the program calls for emergency housing which can take in large numbers at a moment's notice. The transitional housing program is defined by three discernable housing types. Family and elderly units are housed in simple block forms connected in section by an elevated outdoor garden. The single occupants, who are the most transient by nature, are located just inside the exterior envelope and are enclosed by a diaphanous membrane which creates a transitional temperature range for the occupant. These pod-type units are visible from the entry hall as a way to draw the homeless in from the street.

Based on the traditional Chinese Tulou typology, Jiateng's building presents a fortified perimeter with a single access point that leads into a large void. Vertical in nature, and lined with a semi-transparent scrim that reads as either solid in the day, or semi-transparent at night based on interior illumination, it is the transcendental space in the project. Unlocked and open each day and night of the year it becomes the salon of the neighborhood. At the base of the void, the café serves meals while the thrift store provides clothing to those in need. The ovate structure speaks in broader spiritual terms. Both a void and an invisible object, it becomes the public indoor room of the neighborhood. Lit during the day by a single oculus, it becomes a sanctuary from poverty, homelessness, addiction and crime. At night, the dome's diaphanous structure becomes more transparent, softly revealing the transitional housing and other programs there to help the impoverished.

The overall building is heated and cooled by a grid of geothermal wells that take advantage of a consistent year-round ground water temperature of 52°–57° Fahrenheit. Slicing through the void is a horizontal plane of tightly spaced grating at street level. Below the slice the void becomes a solid concrete radiant shell with embedded hydronic coils that either heat or cool the space based on average outdoor temperature. During the humid summer, condensation is collected at the bottom of the shell and pumped to the top of the building to irrigate the green roof. In winter, the mid-50s° temperature of the lower shell creates a more habitable microclimate, making it more tolerable sleeping environment for those who would otherwise be sleeping on the street. Facing up from the floor the bud-like transitional housing cells can be seen floating within the overall volume. These membrane-enclosed structures benefit from the tempered microclimate of the overall container, requiring only a minimal increase in temperature for comfort. Their pliant skins expand or contract depending on temperature differential—in winter they become larger like a hot air balloon whose volume is defined by the warmer air inside. This change in volume is visually significant as these cells become larger and more noticeable from the primary void below, and when viewed become a welcoming enticement to those below to then take the next step of enrolling into the program and benefiting from the offered social services.

Much like a Tulou, the building exterior mass appears solid. The vertical aluminum ribs of the building's exterior resemble a fortification during the day and reveal its transparency at night as the interior spaces become illuminated. The perimeter creates a boundary condition that demarks a safe place for the impoverished citizens of the Poplar neighborhood to the east. Cutting through this seemingly impenetrable solid are a series of Boolean voids. Beginning with the entry salon, these social voids slice through the primary mass to reveal the inner functions of the building and articulate their purpose. These operational cuts provide the connective spaces for access and circulation in the building.

By penetrating the exterior wall, these voids reconnect to the outside and to the neighborhood. They provide a momentary glimpse for the transient residents back to the neighborhood, while from the neighborhood they provide a brief look into the building and the social programs that the voids provide.

Above

Exterior view.

Right

Exterior close-up showing the interstitial circulation, aperture point of the building, and transparency among the spaces.

(RE)CONFIGURING TYPOLOGY

Hina Jamelle | Contemporary Architecture Practice

Left

Contemporary Architecture Practice
NY SH
Samsung Haan River Masterplan
Façade detail view
Seoul, South Korea, 2015–2018

A flat-type building showing connection details between the window and frame types. The façade is created using ten window types that are arranged to create maximum difference for each residential tower in the masterplan.

Above

Existing apartment buildings and blocks in central Seoul, South Korea.

Large-scale housing projects in Seoul are relentlessly homogeneous due to the standardization of each building form and material assembly. Rigid standardization is driven by the low-cost construction and maximum profit seeking by builders, developers, and housing associations.

Large-scale urban housing design is bedeviled by countless conundrums and contradictions: how to preserve design integrity while maintaining cost-effectivity and efficient construction, how to create collective form without suppressing individual identity, how to create flexibility and difference in a repetitive program, and so on. Design is wedged between these issues as a process of negotiating between different agendas. Housing typologies serve as useful aids in this process by providing established precedents for programmatic, construction, and regulatory considerations, which allow projects to move forward and be realized projects in time- and cost-efficient ways. Their abstraction, however, always creates a false relation to context, as every project requires different needs and a design approach to match. The negative consequences of a hammer to nail typological approach range from the seemingly benign mediocrity and sameness of suburban sprawl to more devastating alienation and segregation of whole urban areas and segments of the population, often along lines of race and class. On another level, typologies serve to perpetuate, deepen, and ingrain past standards—architectural and social—that may be flawed to begin with or have nothing to do with the present (not to mention the future).

Mass housing design in Seoul, South Korea, is driven by standardized, replicable typologies with predetermined setbacks, sun angles, building orientations, and views. These rules and regulations guide the overall forms of masterplans, and building forms are further determined by plan efficiency, building core locations, shaft locations, views, and natural light. The results are generally predictable: each building looks the same and is replicated multiple times in one masterplan organized around a boulevard that connects all the buildings at the plinth level with parking below. The main difference between these masterplans is their locations within the city and whether the plinth is above or at grade level. Without even speaking to its architectural or social drawbacks, repetitive, identical modular construction is no longer necessarily technically more efficient or cost-effective, especially on the scale of such mass housing. Technological developments in design, fabrication, and construction processes can raise critical questions about such existing typologies and instigate

Contemporary Architecture Practice
NY SH
Samsung Haan River Masterplan
Façade detail view
Seoul, South Korea, 2015–2018

We were given five building types: Flat, L, Butterfly, Y, and A shapes. By reorienting the elevators, emergency stairs, and chases for mechanical systems and plumbing, we were able to develop a system in which the unit, size of unit, and façade could vary. The unit orientation shifts depending on the unit configuration on either side of each building. The unit sizes per floor change in each building, and the elevations of each building are different.

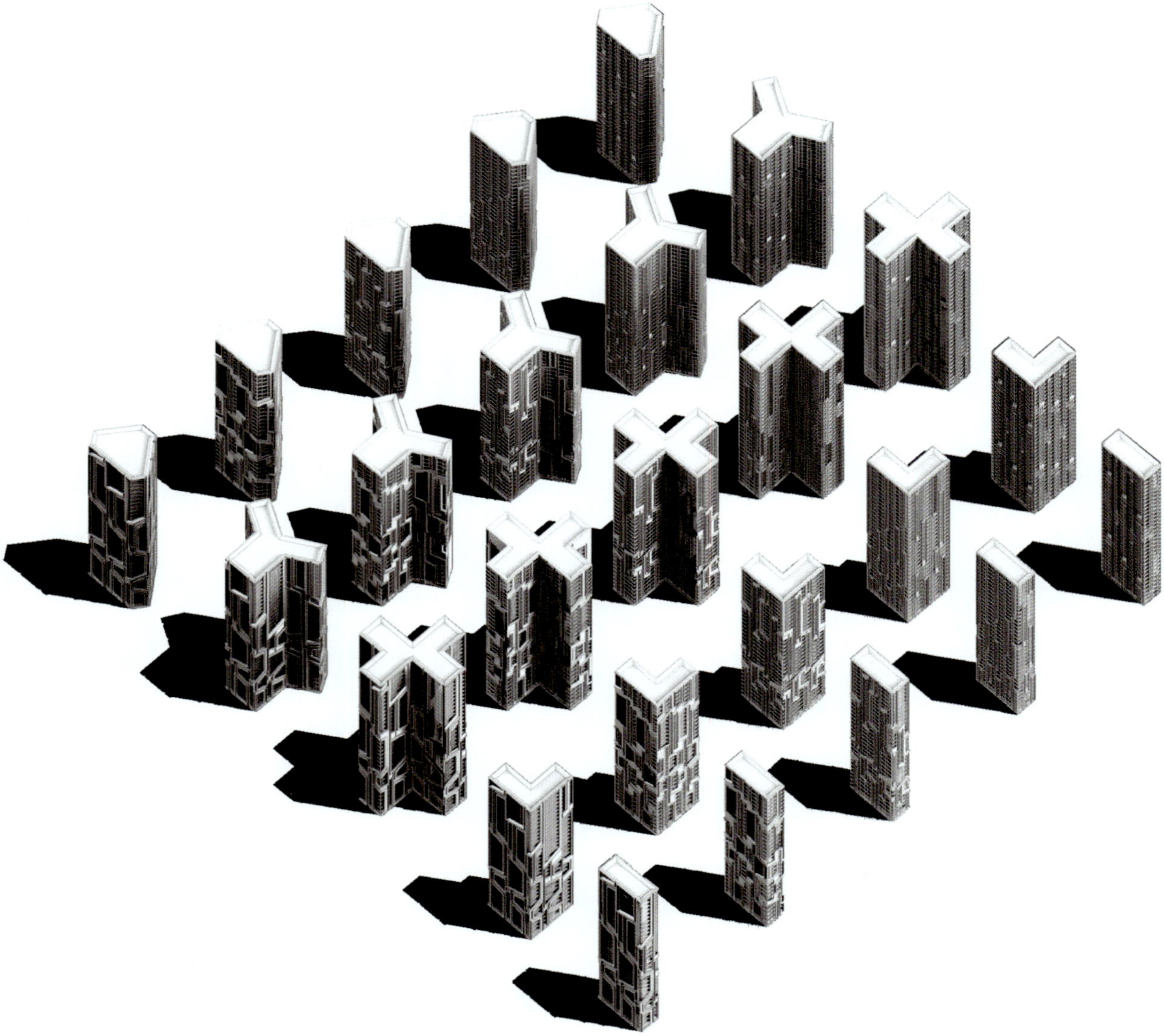

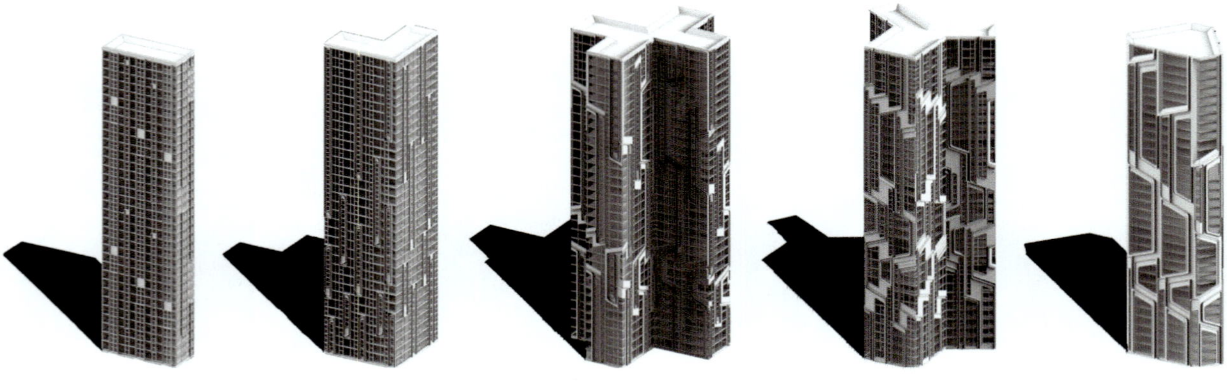

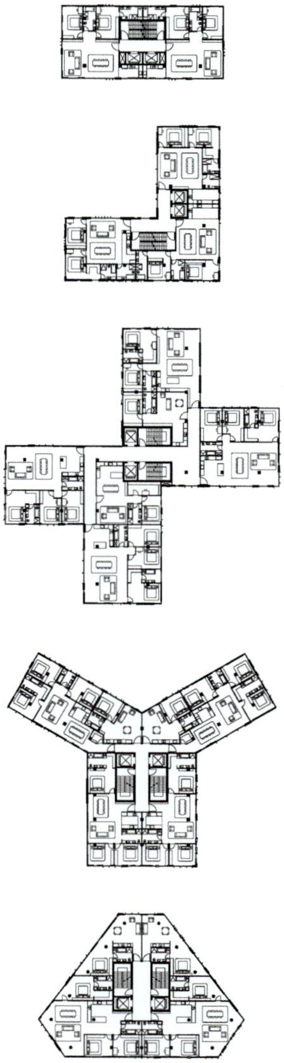

Left

Contemporary Architecture Practice
NY SH
Samsung Haan River Masterplan
Façade detail view
Seoul, South Korea, 2015–2018

The efficiencies of mass production are enhanced by using ten different cost-effective window frame types, which, when assembled in different ways, create different aesthetics for each tower.

One of each building type, showing façade variations. Customization was tailored to construction costs and limitations.

Above

Typical floor plans for each building type.

new opportunities for design. Building codes and regulations, however, are less malleable and represent significant challenges. With an intricate understanding of how typology responds effectively to specific pressures and policy contexts, contemporary architecture can reconfigure and vastly improve upon existing typologies by intervening with technological approaches that harness new techniques in mass customization, prefabrication, and logistics. The results can shift ideas about the aesthetics of mass urban housing and its position as a signifier of local, regional, and global identity as well as initiate new workflows in manufacturing and construction.

Seoul's replicable masterplans are the result of a series of government-led housing initiatives implemented starting in the aftermath of the Korean War to rebuild Seoul and modernize its infrastructure. In the 1970s and 1980s under the Land Readjustment Program, large-scale housing developments such as the Hangang Mansion (1970) and the Yeouido Pilot Apartment (1970) were constructed to house Seoul's booming population, which more than doubled between 1960 and 1970 from 2.45 million to 5.43 million.[1,2] The dominant housing stock that emerged consisted primarily of replicable 8–15-story housing blocks inspired by Soviet housing standards and typically organized in rows with an east–west orientation.

By 1990, with a population of over 10 million people, the city paved the way for new private developments and higher buildings. Major construction companies quickly pivoted toward developing larger-scale communities for new construction. For example, Samsung Construction and Technology launched the Raemian brand to create comfortable, futuristic living environments for city dwellers. Raemian masterplans repeat quantitatively different floor plans in different building typologies including a Flat-Type, L-Type, Two-L Butterfly Type, and A-Type building plans. In many cases, the only differentiating feature between such buildings is a serial number painted on the exterior. When public lands ran out, companies turned towards existing housing communities for redevelopment. Each housing community is led by a union of its owners, and, if over 50 percent of the union votes for a new building to be built in the location of their current dwelling, the union is compelled to hire a construction company to develop and construct a new masterplan and building design. Once built, the residents are able to move back in to the higher floors of the new construction and split profits on the sale of new units. This development model, with its threefold capacity to simultaneously increase density and curb affordability issues while turning profits, revolutionized housing and real estate development in Seoul. In August 2020, the government further reinforced this model when it announced numerous new measures to increase housing density and suppress demand, including eased rules for redevelopment projects such as stretching floor-to-area (FAR) ratios to 500 percent and raising the cap on the number of allowed residential floors from 35 to 50.[3] Irrespective of its drawbacks, this typology will remain a powerful force in Seoul's housing morphology, and a key question for architects now and in the future will be how to reconfigure and work with it in ways that invigorate, diversify, and deepen its potential spatial relationships.

Confronting chronic and ongoing housing shortages and affordability issues over the past five decades, Seoul's repetitive masterplans have been effective in adding massive numbers of units to a city whose population density is now double that of New York City. Architecturally speaking, however, the city's development model has led to homogeneity in aesthetics and circulation with little added value to urban life on more social and cultural levels. The building strategy runs counter to many aspects that make cities and urban life dynamic and vibrant; drawbacks include a lack of programmatic and formal diversity, a sense of urban alienation through repetition, and a scalar disconnect from the greater urban context. Mass housing schemes in such cases have at times become described as urban "blight." This derives from the aesthetic contrast between heavy-handed modernist urbanism and older urban fabrics and is inflected with conservative aversion to publicly financed housing. Local strategies to ameliorate the negative impacts of this housing type have ranged from outright demolition—as with Pruitt–Igoe—to aesthetic interventions—as in, for instance, the painting of a megagraphic on the façade of Gustavo-Haus in Lichtenberg, East Berlin. In the latter example, the building achieves a new status as a public art work, a neighborhood signifier, and as a building to call one's home as differentiated from the housing across the street. In 2009, recognizing these issues, the Mayor of Seoul signed a law stating that if there were more than two buildings on the same development site, they must be distinguishable from each other. Initially, developers circumvented this decree by altering building heights while maintaining the same building morphology. Later, the ordinance was clarified to include a requirement for a change in look and feel in each building. These policy changes forced companies to rethink and devise new cost-effective alternatives that could adhere to strict systems of plan configurations while producing variations between buildings.

In 2015, Contemporary Architecture Practice (CAP) was tasked by Samsung Construction and Technology with formulating one such alternative in developing a masterplan, floor plans, and façade designs for an 18-building development along the Haan River in central Seoul using predetermined building types initially created for their Raemian design. The challenge was to create significant differences between buildings across the masterplan while maintaining specified building forms. We had several constraints including zoning codes, unit sizes based on tax codes, and the need to create a unique façade for each building. All three components—unit, façade, and masterplan—had to be cost-effective. In the spirit of aesthetic intervention, we sought to use a highly graphic and variable façade strategy with a deep investment in architectural performance to reconfigure the typology; a novel approach to detailing and prefabrication was essential in this respect. Within our practice, we have always been interested in the role of the detail in the production of an aesthetic goal. Focusing on the design of the detail allows us to circumvent building form (which in this case was already predetermined) and produce highly intricate and varied assemblies composed of advanced materials. We find that it enables a more nuanced and in-depth engagement with materiality and assembly as well as manufacturing and fabrication processes. The goal of this approach is to achieve diversity in a singular, overall expression, or what we call "disjunctive continuity."[4] Disjunctive continuity

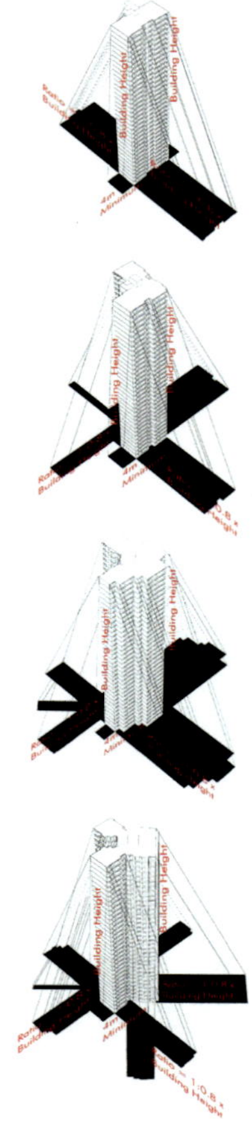

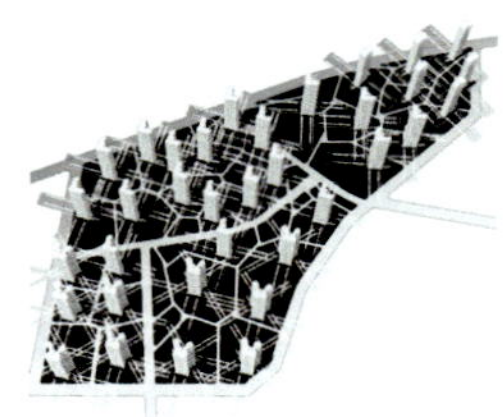

Above

Contemporary Architecture Practice
NY SH
Samsung Haan River Masterplan
Façade detail view
Seoul, South Korea, 2015–2018

The Masterplan needed to comply with several regulations determined by building codes. Each type of building had different sun angle tolerances. These angles are determined by the maximum sunlight on each building in each season of the year.

Right

The landscape is spatially and materially varied using hard- and softscapes including plantings, water features, benches, and lighting elements.

frees us to move from detail to form, rather than the other way around, a design sequence that breaks with the homogeneity of the original Raemian design while enhancing its attractiveness in terms of cost-effectivity and construction efficiency.

Disjunctive continuity is developed at several scales in the project including that of the detail, the material, the unit, and the masterplan itself. We used different methods to achieve our goals including the development of façade assembly details that work to conceal or reveal the building and create variations in transparency. Details control the aesthetics of material assemblies and formal attributes. Details are developed into framing devices, and these frames are inserted into larger assembly logics controlled by specific spatial, aesthetic, and programmatic qualities. Seams are calibrated to accentuate or diminish assemblies. Materials nest into and layer on top of one another. The exact techniques of assembly vary, but the goal is always the same: to achieve a visually cohesive aesthetic composed of details that enable different performance and programmatic criteria. This goal was achieved in five ways ranging from façade details to the overall masterplan.

To start, the façades are composed of ten unique prefabricated frames, each with its own architectural detailing. Frames sit flush, are recessed, or protrude from the façade. The edges of each frame are either wide, narrow, or bend and become an angle. Some frames contain a seam making them appear bifurcated. Other frames sit adjacent to or on top of one another creating a reveal between frames of different widths. Multiple frames are also grouped together in larger frames to create a nesting effect. Further, the materiality of each frame changes depending on its width relative to other parts of the façade. If the frame is extremely wide, there is a seam that is carved into it to give it a narrower reading while enhancing the metal on the façade. When we group multiple wider frames together, we use metal as the façade material, making the building more opaque. At the other extreme, we use very thin frames assembled next to each other to develop the most transparent parts of the façade. As frames oscillate in width, the glass to metal ratio is altered, which is aimed at giving an overall sense of cohesion and aesthetics to the building. Frame components and glazing articulate movement across the façade to enliven and enrich the generic form of the building footprint.

All of these different façade arrangements and material transitions are enabled by a single detailing and design system. The frame components worked well within the limitations of Samsung's production strategies and utilized their manufacturing techniques. This knowledge set the limits of the amount of variation possible yet allowed for a tremendous amount of variation and customization in each building. By integrating and optimizing the frame design with prefabrication processes and limitations from the outset of the project, we were able to achieve cost-effective, mass-customized results. The typology, here, because of the need for repetition actually opens up an opportunity to push forward new design processes with effects for both the housing typology itself (in terms of new configurative and performative capacities), as well as the manufacturing and construction (in terms of implementation of new technology). By asserting mass customization on such a large scale, architecture can put pressure on the construction industry to implement technologies that it might otherwise be slow to adapt. Instead of one detail, there are ten, which—at least in a public housing context—might be a tall even if readily achievable system. But because there are not one but 18 buildings, the project is able to achieve an economy of scale. The typology provides a grounded scenario for adapting an automotive model of manufacturing to housing. Customizable options at different scales can be swapped in and out while maintaining a basic design system and processing line. This creates opportunities to vary materials in ways that enable higher level performance, whether programmatic, phenomenological, or environmental in nature. By prefabricating components and assemblies in off-site manufacturing facilities, agency and expression are given back to multiple stakeholders: to the city in terms of aesthetics, builders in terms of how they work, and residents in terms of the feel and performance of their homes.

Variations in framing details are echoed in larger scale configurations of units and relations between buildings throughout the project. For instance, with only minor alterations to the core and chase locations, we transformed the unit organization from a static repetition of residential units into dynamic layouts with enough flexibility that they can change in plan location as needed. The buildings adhere to strict regulations including unit size while maximizing the amount of variation of views and interior space within the plan configurations. Configurations were determined primarily by the locations of vertical building systems including circulation as well as dry and wet shafts. In some cases, there are living rooms in the corner of the buildings and at other times there are bedrooms. Also, the locations of one-bedroom units and two-bedroom units change, mediating between efficiency of layout and quality of space with views. Starting from two types of units in the Flat-type building we created six variations across each building. These unit types were developed per building, and there

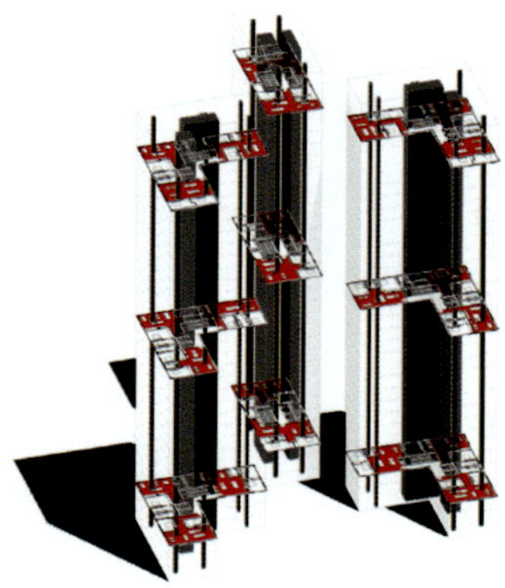

Above

Contemporary Architecture Practice
NY SH
Samsung Haan River Masterplan
Façade detail view
Seoul, South Korea, 2015–2018

The living spaces and bedroom spaces change in location according to three variables: the configuration of units per floor, the unit size, and the unit orientation in the adjacent building.

Right

Flat- and L-type floor plans for multiple levels. These drawings are to be read vertically and adjacent to each other, they are taken at the same floor levels from two different buildings, illustrating how adjacent buildings relate in terms of program and configuration.

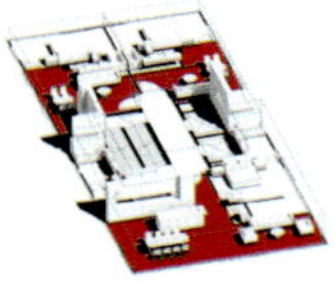

Flat Type 01 / 34F / 3 Units
1 Bed x 2, 2 Beds x 1

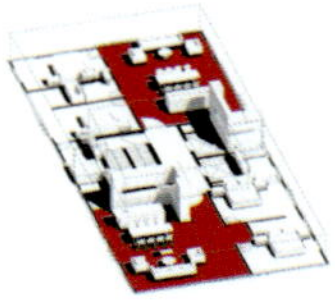

Flat Type 02 / 19F / 2 Units
2 Beds x 2

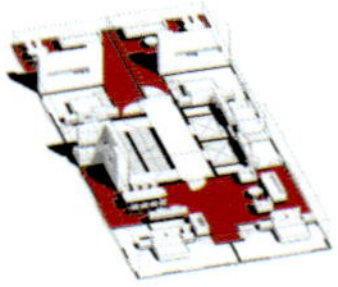

Flat Type 03 / 4F / 3 Units
1 Bed x 2, 2 Beds x 1

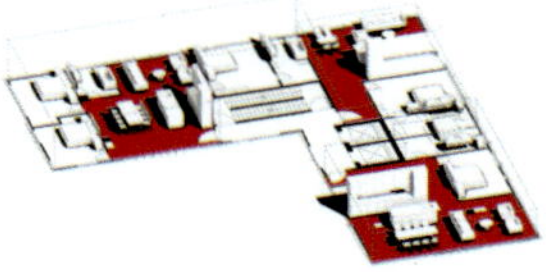

L-Shape Type 01 / 34F / 3 Units
1 Bed x 1, 2 Beds x 1, 3 Beds x 1

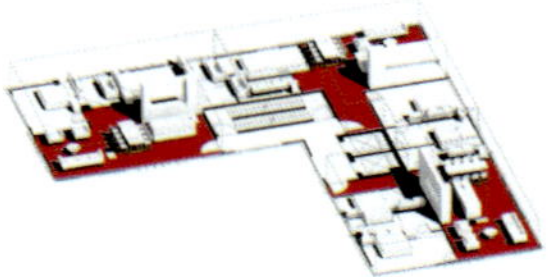

L-Shape Type 02 / 19F / 3 Units
2 Beds x 3

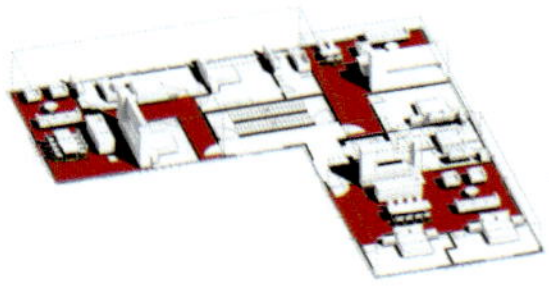

L-Shape Type 03 / 4F / 3 Units
1 Bed x 1, 2 Beds x 1, 3 Beds x 1

are dislocations in the plan correlated to core and shaft location and design. Plan configurations also shift across multiple buildings. In particular, unit configurations correspond to the proximity of adjacent buildings to create dialogue between buildings and maximize both views and privacy. The location of chases provided us with opportunities to alter kitchen and bathroom layouts, maximizing views for each residential unit. In sum, the tectonic design gave Samsung flexibility in how they located units without adding additional cost to the overall project.

The interaction between the façade and the variation of units developed nuance for each residential unit in orientation, elevation, and window performance. The façade brings in light in different ways, frames specific views, and makes strategic areas of the unit more opaque or transparent than others. The combination of strategies gave us 64 unique façades and plans per building. This enables the resident to select from a menu of features for each unit as well as height above ground, unit orientation, and unique window features. Each unit affects the location of the layout of the building next to it. This produces a masterplan with a look and feel based on floor by floor regulations and repeatable customized components rather than generic mass-produced building to building relations. The plans and elevations appear disjunct, yet they are tied together by the underlying tectonic and aesthetic logic of the building as a whole.

Finally, at the scale of the 18 high-rise building masterplan, our solution utilized all of Samsung's research on housing and complied with strict zoning regulations in Seoul. There are five building types that were given to us. The Flat-type (rectangular in shape) is the most commonly used, followed by the L-types and the Two-L or Butterfly type. The A-type is the least commonly used. The masterplan had to meet zoning and setback codes and each building had to maintain two hours of sunlight per day. There were a host of other minor adjustments at the building level. On the parking level, a ratio of cars needed to be near the core for security and there was a specified number of parking spots allocated for women owners. The building types and parking below set up the relationships required for the final masterplan and incorporated amenity spaces in the basement near the green areas. Our strategy was to use these constraints and develop the most efficient masterplan possible, tying the discontinuity between building forms together with landscapes of similar elements at different scales. The masterplan incorporates all the programmatic and zoning codes required to maximize views and quality of light for mid- to high-rise development. We reassessed the value of a large central recreation area for the entire community and developed several micro-community recreation areas around smaller zones. This reflects the effort to create more localized architectural moments in the façade and layout design. The micro-community areas likewise acquire their own particular qualities and identities in relation to the building and landscape variations around them. This type of fine-grain tailoring and coordination benefits exponentially from customized algorithms and software that is not only able to account for multiple interrelated variables linked to production but also develop design intelligence through rapid iterations and computation.

In summation, the Haan River masterplan uses a complex system of rules and program code to generate masterplan opportunities that adhere to all required regulations while producing diverse architectural effects. Our approach of disjunctive continuity adds value to the client, as the pressures of building codes and costs are taken into account at the beginning of the design process, helping the design to develop a nuanced masterplan with innovative buildings using cost-effective variation. The project recognizes that certain efficiencies and building construction workflows are needed in order to meet the pressures of urbanization, affordability, densification. It shows that deeper understandings of typology and its material and social performance can be achieved by engaging it with more intelligent and nuanced design systems and procedures. It allows for a diversity of localized architectural experiences and individual expressions of identity while putting forward an overall expression of technology at urban and global scales. While the replicated masterplans of Seoul may trace their origins to tenets of socialist housing established in the 1920s, the pitfalls of their realization can be upturned with a contemporary approach. With a 21st-century approach to prefabrication, units of material can be modulated, and joinery can be engineered in ways that were previously impossible. Incessant repetition that leads to monotony in architecture and urban life can be replaced with heterogeneous assemblies that enable a range of experiences and activities. This implies a turn toward design approaches which attune prefabrication processes to variable tectonics, a reinvigoration of architectural detailing as a generative tool, and new synergies between aesthetics and performance. It instigates new graphic or aesthetic conceptions of architecture invested in building performance.

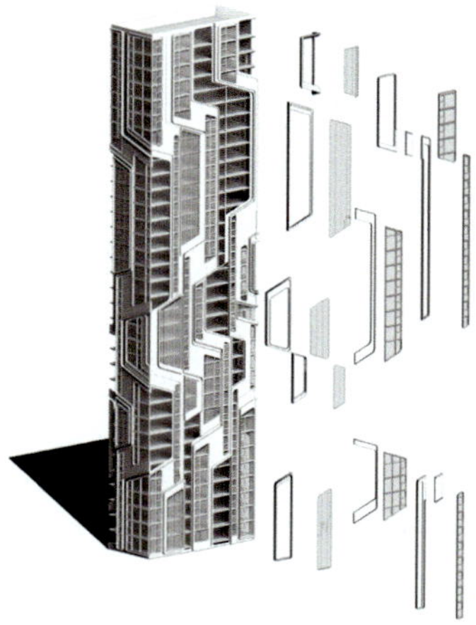

Above

Contemporary Architecture Practice
NY SH
Samsung Haan River Masterplan
Façade detail view
Seoul, South Korea, 2015–2018

Our design combines ten unique window frames that are prefabricated to develop each of the 18 buildings that we were commissioned to design. The ten designed window frames are assembled in many ways, providing a cost benefit for Samsung while bringing difference in qualities across the masterplan.

Right

The program has moments of continuity and discontinuity. In this view the living rooms stack upon each other for eight floors and then there is a switch to living rooms for 12 floors, as determined by the overall configurations of the program in the masterplan.

References

1. https://seoulsolution.kr/en/node/3448
2. https://seoulsolution.kr/en/node/3446
3. Lee Eun-joo, "Korea to Stretch Floor Space, Highrise Height to Add 132,000 Housing Units in Seoul," Pulse by *Maeil Business Newspaper* and mk.co.kr, August 4, 2020. https://m.pulsenews.co.kr/view.php?sc=30800022&year=2020&no=797518
4. "Disjunctive Continuity," see H. Jamelle and A. Rahim, eds, "Disjunctive Continuity and the Aesthetics of the Seam," *IMPACT Architectural Design AD*, November 2020.

PREFABRICATION AND DIFFERENTIAL HOUSING

H na Jamelle

The construction industry has long lagged behind other sectors in technological innovation, and construction methods themselves have by and large not changed in decades. As one of the largest global economic sectors, a profound shift in the construction industry can have major impacts. Prefabricated construction, though not a new concept, is attracting a fresh wave of interest and investment following digital advancements. Recent prefabricated projects have already established a solid track record of accelerating project timelines by 20–50%, and, in the right circumstances, prefabrication can reduce costs by 20%—a particularly important prospect in the context of housing shortages and constrained city budgets. Today, prefabrication offers opportunities for change by shifting many aspects of building activity away from project sites to off-site manufacturing.

Historically, prefabricated construction has gained traction in markets where demand for housing is strong but labor in the building trade is in short supply. Housing lends itself very well to prefabrication methods because units serving the same basic functions can be easily repeated and reproduced. Prefabricated housing has been in and out of favor in markets such as the United States and the United Kingdom since the post-war era, yet there is reason to believe the current revival could be different. The industry is adopting new materials as well as digital technologies to enhance design capabilities and variability, improve precision and productivity in manufacturing, and facilitate complex logistics. Countering its old reputation as an ugly, cheap, and poor-quality option, new prefabricated housing focuses on environmental-friendliness, aesthetics, and function. Moreover, it has achieved a sustainable foothold in places including Scandinavia and Japan.

Prefabricated construction involves producing the standardized components of a structure in an off-site facility, then transporting and assembling them on the building site. Terms such as off-site construction, prefabrication, and modular construction are used interchangeably and cover a range of different approaches and systems. These systems vary depending on the complexity of the elements being brought together.

Left

Bumjin Park
Shifting Hybrids: New Hotel and Residential Building
TriBeCa, New York City

Hina Jamelle Urban Housing Studio with Fei Chen

University of Pennsylvania
Weitzman School of Design, 2013

Exterior view. Prefabricated standardized components are assembled differently from unit to unit, producing a customized end result.

View of the prefabricated 2D panelized systems consisting of glazing and metal frames across the building façade.

The simplest are single elements that are clipped together using standard connections and interfaces. It is worth noting that repeatability does not mean that all products need to look the same. Instead, a variety of standardized components can be assembled in different configurations to produce a customized end result. Likewise, prefabrication does not denote quality and can be used to produce a range of options from the most cost-effective to the most luxurious. In Japan, for instance, the industry has capitalized on synergies with other manufacturing industries to achieve very high quality results that sell at higher premiums than those produced by traditional means. The automotive industry is a useful analogy in this respect. Car manufacturers use the same chassis in multiple car models but swap out various features to make different models look and feel distinct. Even within these models, customers are given personalized options, all of which can be achieved in the manufacturing process. In this way, the design is open-ended enough to maintain a processing line that can be modified and deliver custom features.[1]

Architecturally speaking, most part to whole organizations share common characteristics including structure and units defined as parts and their composition and interconnectivity in a system that has coherent functional, structural, and spatial relationships. Prefabricated parts can be used to produce architectural formations that vary, accumulate, and are subject to changes that may shift spatial experiences, scale, and materials. Program, space, structure, and enclosure can be incorporated into singular formations that enable and encompass formal variations of gradated intensities and patterns. While housing projects are defined by the singular and general program of "housing," this undercuts the simple fact that housing's basic function is to cater to an extraordinarily diverse set of needs, desires, and lifestyles of different individuals and groups of individuals. Prefabrication offers a toolset for mediating these extremes.

Bumjin Park's project "Shifting Hybrids: New Hotel and Residential Building in TriBeCa, New York City," a proposal for a hybrid hotel and residential building in the TriBeCa neighborhood of New York City, asks how one can create individualization and uniqueness in an urban housing project using repeatable prefabricated parts. The project explores the architectural variability of a single aspect that is critical to city living and differs greatly between individuals: the need for privacy. While housing offers the most private and personal of architectural experiences, in urban hotel settings there is also a desire to have immediate access to all of the city's amenities.

This project brings both experiences together in a new hybrid dwelling typology. The studio and one-bedroom housing units as well as variable-scaled hotel units are all different yet related. Each of the seven-unit plans comprises five unique and carefully optimized prefabricated 2D paneling systems. The paneling systems consist of glazing and metal frames, which determine the greater system of units across the entire building façade. Each housing and hotel unit transforms based on new orientations, which not only affect neighboring units but also create new configurations and clusters of units. As a result, the system of units shifts from a relatively rigid residential

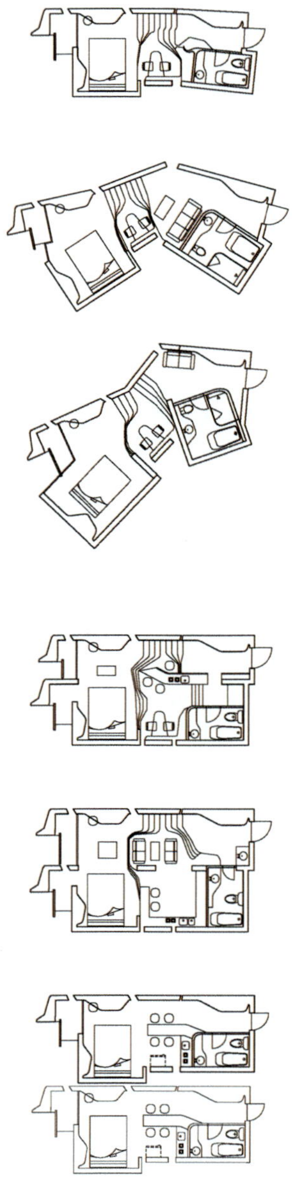

Above

Residential (above) and hotel (below) unit plans.

Right

Typical and third-floor plans. The long façade along a side street is more suitable for residential units which demand the highest levels of privacy and quiet. Turning the corner onto Greenwich Street, a more public thoroughfare, units become multidirectional and provide hotel guests with multiple framed urban views.

Typical Floor Plan

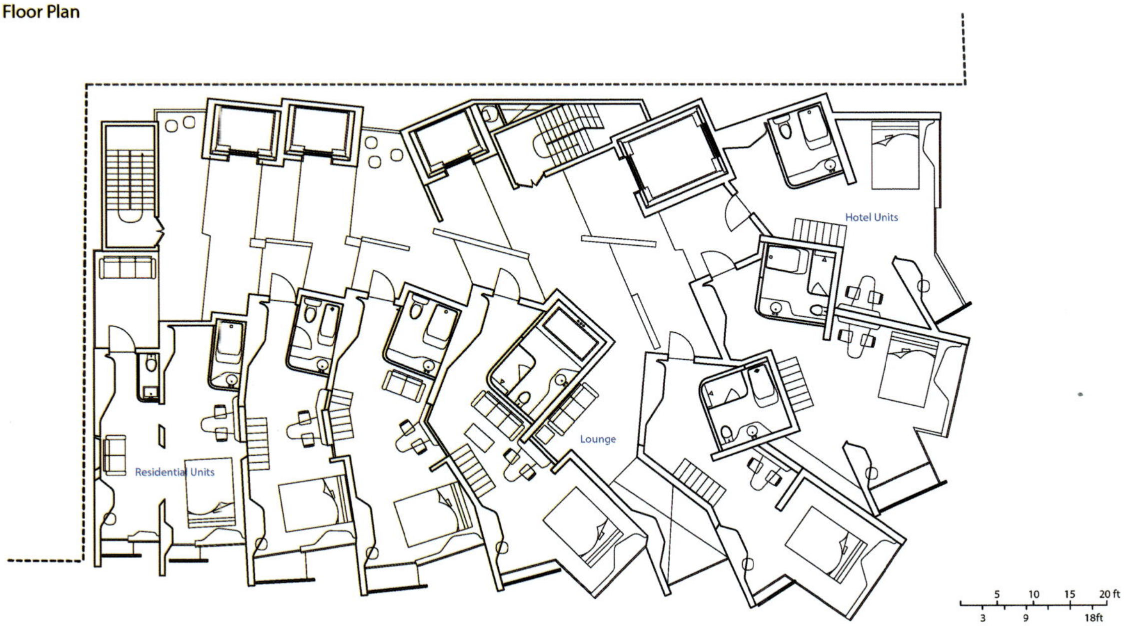

3rd Floor Plan

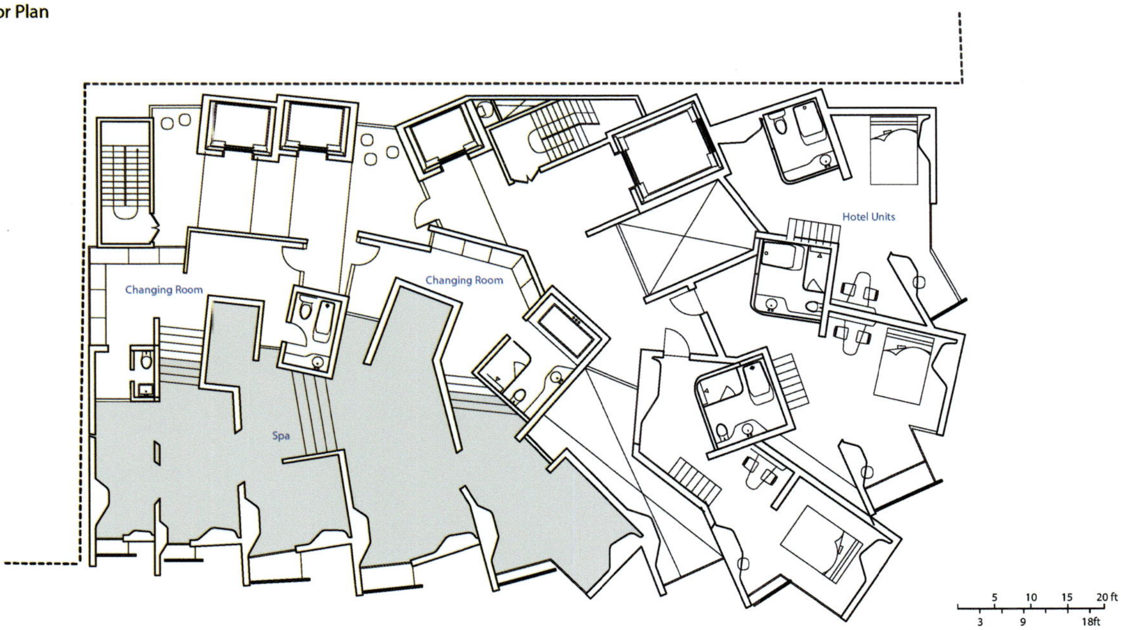

structure to a flexible open hospitality scheme, accomplishing diverse effects in terms of transparency, scale, and orientation within the city. The rigid unit is more suitable for residential life, which demands the highest level of privacy. As material fragmentation proceeds and unfolds through the construction system, units become multidirectional and provide hotel dwellers with unique city views. The result is a project exhibiting innovative architectural organizations using topological surfaces, unit arrangements, and patterns scaling from individual rooms to the entire building with different spatial and material qualities that contribute to a new customized approach to prefabrication in architecture.

More broadly speaking, the project highlights how designs that thoroughly incorporate prefabrication from conception through realization can work to increase efficiencies in housing construction while simultaneously diversifying housing stocks. In this way, prefabrication can address pressure on cities to increase housing while adapting to and servicing rapidly changing economies, demographics, and domestic relations. To be clear, this does not imply a return or "final realization" of the speculative modular architecture of the 1960s and 1970s; it also does not mean that whole housing units will or should be swapped out on a regular basis. It does imply, however, that multiple, highly differential units can be coordinated in singular building systems through manufacturing processes without becoming prohibitively expensive or technically challenging. Moreover, by centering prefabrication in design processes, dramatic changes in configuration, materiality, and assembly can be realized from one building to the next without being limited by economies of scale.

Above

Building view at corner.

Right

Cutaway section perspective.

References

1. https://www.mckinsey.com/~/media/mckinsey/industries/capital%20projects%20and%20infrastructure/our%20insights/modular%20construction%20from%20projects%20to%20products%20new/modular-construction-from-projects-to-products-full-report-new.pdf

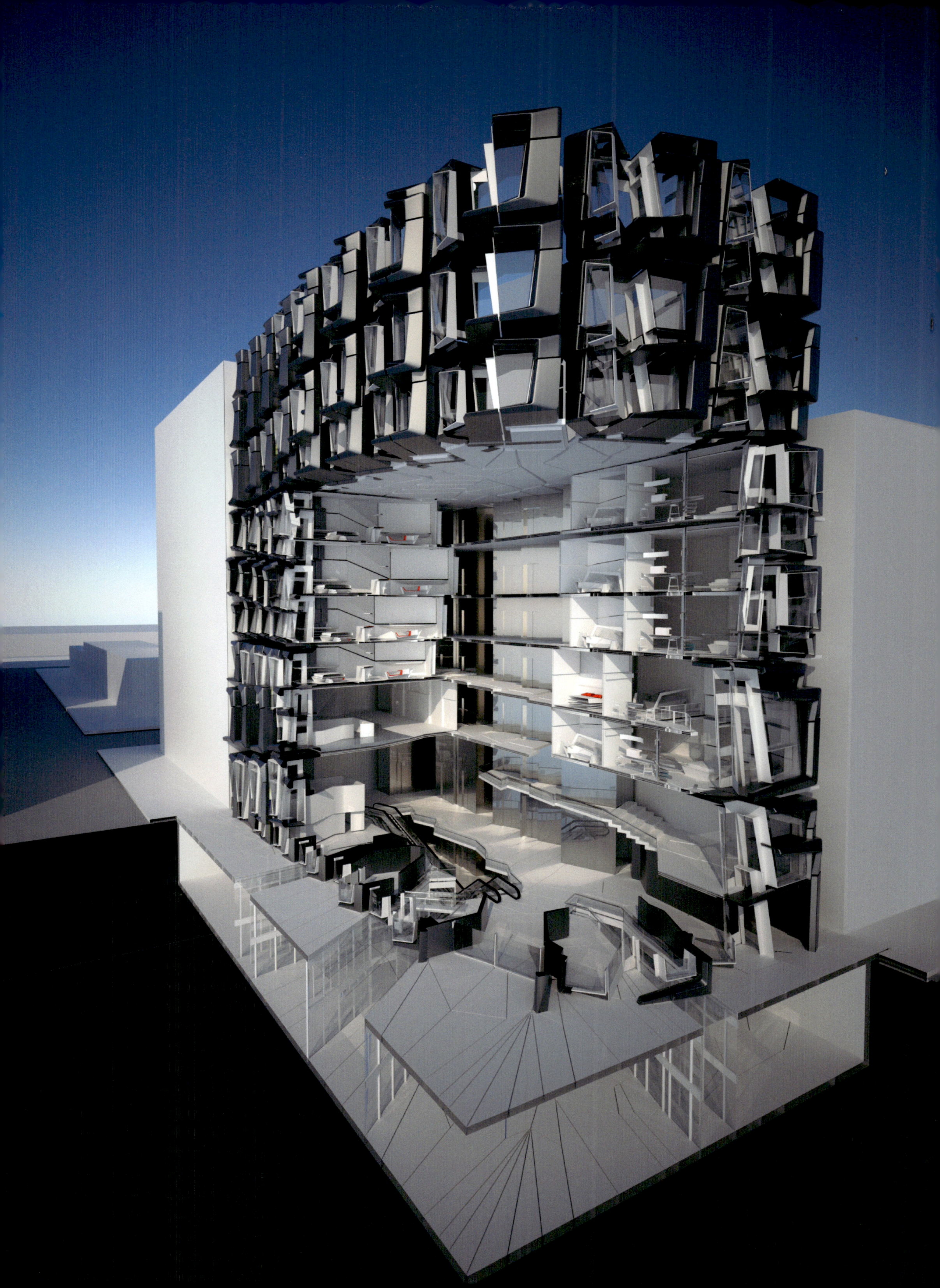

MATERIAL SPECULATION
A Science and Craft

Laia Mogas-Soldevila | MIT Media Lab & Tufts Silklab

Materials Under Pressure

Most of the housing materials used today such as glass, metal, ceramics, and concrete use enormous amounts of energy, during extraction, processing, and recycling. There is concerning exponential use in regions where population is fast growing and housing is a primary demand. Substituting only a few unsustainable building material parts with, for instance, biopolymers, reverse-engineered proteins, or bio-composites, could alleviate waste, energy, and health problems derived from the construction of typical building envelopes. Architects have turned to nature's building solutions in search for effective sustainable alternatives. As an example, the Living Future Institute and their Living Building Challenge (LBC) compares buildings to flowers as they collect energy from the sun, protect the soil beneath as it provides them water to function, and ultimately decay by increasing available nutrients for a new cycle. The LBC guides development of buildings that not only have less negative environmental impact, but actively contribute to the wellbeing of people and the Earth. Projects that are solar-powered, net-positive, waste-processing, and fossil-fuel free prepare the field for the advent of biomaterials in building construction. Once "living building" certifications are in place that create a new paradigm in deeper sustainability considerations, the progress towards bio-derived materials in building construction is foreseeable. Pioneering examples include brick towers made by mushrooms and straw, hygro-responsive wood for façade self-actuated shading, living concrete walls repaired by crack-filling bacteria, mechanically and optically tunable skins derived from shrimp, fruit, and cellulose, or silk protein sensing tapestries that report on the health of our living spaces.

Left

Laia Mogas-Soldevila, Jorge Duro-Royo, Daniel Lizardo, and Prof. Oxman
Ocean Pavilion, Media Lab
MIT, Cambridge, Massachusetts, 2015

Four self-supporting fully biodegradable leaf-like structures formed for the Ocean Pavilion display at the MIT Media Lab in 2014. Made by robotic extrusion of a water-based solution derived from shrimp shells and self-assembled in contact with air, they represent the first steps towards large-scale manufacturing of biomaterial parts.

A Short Survey of Biomaterial Architectures

Biologically improved or fiber-reinforced concrete has been used since the early 1990s as an alternative to the expansion–contraction issues that lime-based mixes undergo. Hemp in particular is a fast-growing and CO_2-sequestrating plant used in building

Laia Mogas-Soldevila, Jorge Duro-Royo, Daniel Lizardo, and Prof. Oxman
Ocean Pavilion, Media Lab
MIT, Cambridge, Massachusetts, 2015

A lightweight and strong beam-like construct is made of chitin biopolymer found in shrimp shells. Its programmed structural inertia is given by geometric patterning of stress lines that generate three-dimensional self-folding while the printed structure dehydrates.

structures since Roman times. Hempcrete was already widespread in France in the 1990s as a technology using a mixture of hemp shives and lime, sand, or pozzolans, and can be employed today for loaded construction, insulation, and moisture regulation performance. Modern companies are working towards a certification of Hempcrete as a regulated material, to increase its use in the industry without architects having to request a building code exemption.

In other efforts to improve the properties of concrete, microorganisms have been promisingly used for cleaning and healing cracks to prevent steel rebars from corroding. Certain strains of bacteria mediate the precipitation of minerals such as limestone remediating cracks in concrete. In order to industrially certify "living concrete" for widespread use, more research needs to elucidate robust bacteria able to withstand construction duration, and evaluate if their bio-precipitation significantly decreases water permeability through cracked concrete in order to protect reinforcement corrosion and increase durability.[1]

BioMASON in 2012 invented a new way of making construction materials with microorganisms. Their bio-cements are assembled and cured at ambient conditions by bacteria, reducing energy costs and resulting in zero carbon emissions. In particular, the technology uses sand, certain robust bacteria strands, and additives in an aqueous solution. Bricks or parts are allowed to harden to ASTM specification. Interestingly, matter can be tailored to different requirements of porosity, lightness, or insulation, and still maintain properties comparable to traditional masonry materials.[2]

Architecture studios like TerreformONE have started looking at borrowing principles of synthetic biology to prototype 100% compostable furniture in their Mycoform research from 2014.[3] Instead of looking at molding a brick, the studio generated 3D-printed constructs containing a combination of fungal mycelia with varying types of organic substrates. They asked: Can we direct organisms to assemble matter into free-form structures? Expansion of the living mixture was carefully controlled within molds towards a potential catalogue of infinite shapes. A first explorative example into grown forms was a modular piece of furniture called Gen2Seat. The Gen2Seat was shown at the International Genetically Engineered Machines (iGEM) conference and combined bacterial cellulose to form its skin and mycelium roots assembling discarded wood chips, gypsum, and oat bran to form its filler. At the end of its use cycle, it was placed in a garden to feed other organisms.

Since 2015, the Institute for Computational Design at the University of Stuttgart are partnering with the Self-Assembly Lab at MIT to reinterpret wood and ask: Can an ancestral building material be re-designed to become isotropic? And, can it be active and adaptive within buildings? Can it activate with the building's needs and surrounding environment? Work is progressing towards certification of printed water-responsive augmented wood for applications in canopy and façade systems.[4]

Right

Laia Mogas-Soldevila, Jorge Duro-Royo, Daniel Lizardo, and Prof. Oxman
Ocean Pavilion, Media Lab
MIT, Cambridge, Massachusetts, 2015

The degrees of opacity in these water-based fabrications combine a narrative that is ecologically friendly with bioinspired geometric material distribution patterns that generate self-folding behavior and tunable mechanical performance.

Architects have used instances of bio-based materials in larger scales. An example is the "Hy-Fi Pavilion" at MoMA PS1 gallery in 2014, a partnership of The Living design studio with Ecovative, a biotech company making products and parts out of fungi. They have successfully certified mycelium agglomerated agricultural waste for applications in packaging, skincare, textiles, apparel, and food.[5] Hy-Fi was a temporary gigantic structure out of mushroom-grown bricks, demonstrating that these materials can perform at large scales and produce new aesthetics. Even if combined with a primary wood structure to ensure stability, the pavilion represents a big step towards a dialogue with industry for a change in regulations.

Water-Based Digital Fabrication

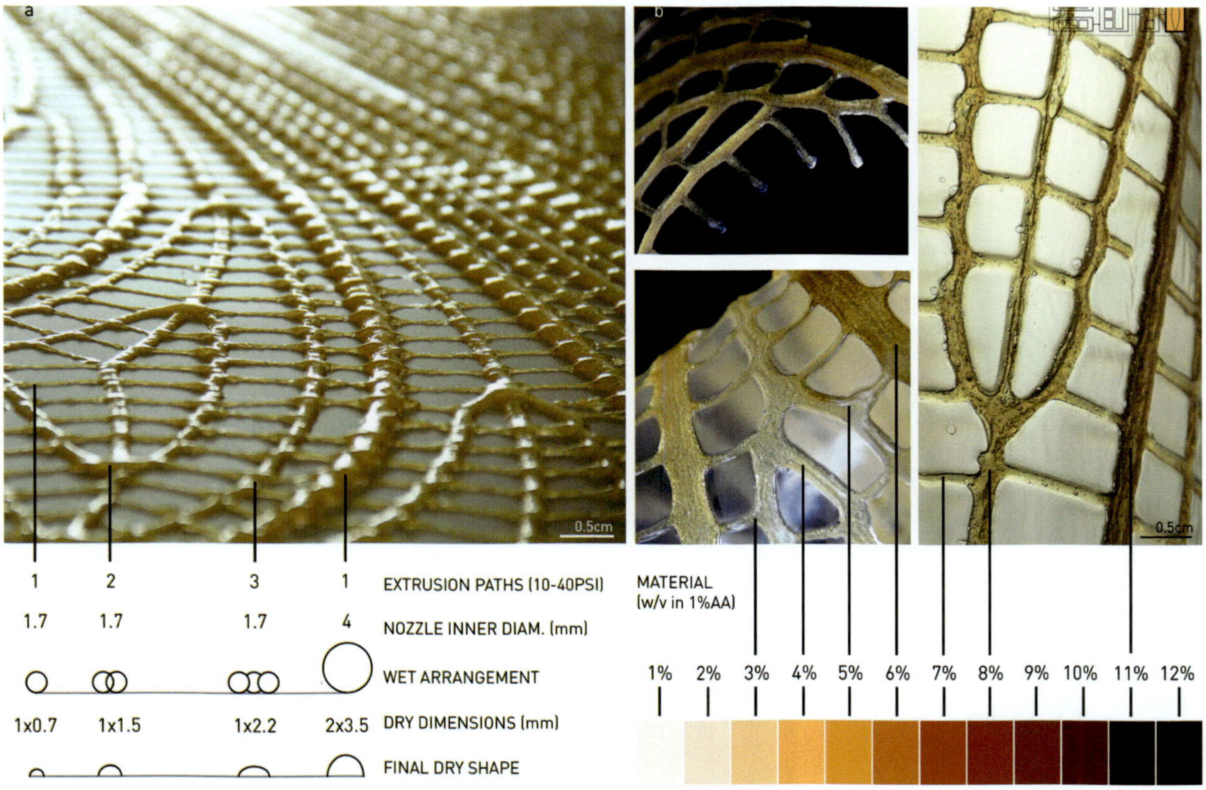

Obstructions to Implementation

Current limitations to the use of biomaterials in architecture are obstructions faced to maintain "living-like" properties throughout use cycles. For instance, bacteria powering self-healing concrete must wait in a dormant state for years, perhaps decades, before being activated by water penetrating the cracks and survive within a harsh and dry alkaline rock-like environment.

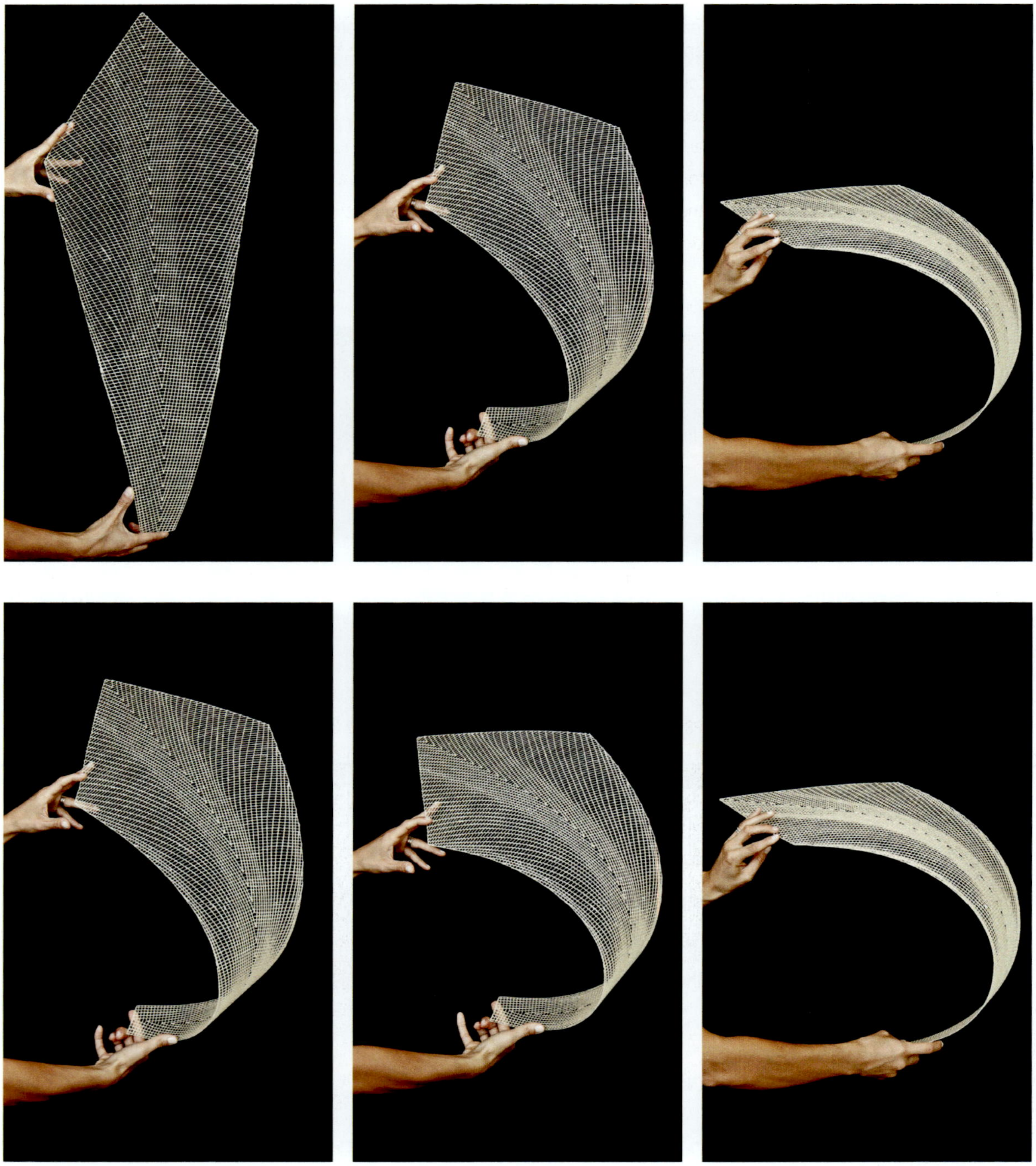

Another obstacle is sustaining biomaterial solutions to traditional testing methods and compliance rates in deformation, fire, or water resistance. Paradoxically, one of the most interesting properties of biomaterials is their water responsiveness. It enables them to autonomously hydrate and dehydrate according to seasonal changes so that, for instance, cellulose fibrils within laminar wood surfaces can curl and relax depending on atmospheric humidity. This can be harnessed to tune light incidence through building skins[6] or perhaps deploy protective rain canopies when needed as environmental humidity allows hygro-responsive joinery to swell. Deformation and adaptation to changes in loading pressures are also crucial in these materials, and generally penalized in building code. However, this property could help existing building structures, for instance, "grow" more matter where highest wind or traffic forces are applied. Such beneficial dynamics are yet to be regulated in architectural handbooks, but they are becoming within reach as designers and architects push for their implementation.

From Materials Science to Experimental Design

A partnership with recent scientific discoveries can help overcome issues to market. Fundamental changes are influencing how materials science and experimental design relate. The field of materials science is transforming from theory-focused to innovation-seeking and materials are designed to fulfill vanguard needs. Experimental design is increasingly pushing computation and advanced fabrication to new domains and larger scales beyond engineering applications. This results in traditional building materials being redesigned from the bottom up responding to shared interests between scientists and designers and strengthening the case for industrial adoption of biomaterial solutions.

In 2017, architect Martin Bechthold and scientist James Weaver embarked on a review to demonstrate such overlap. They follow developments for hydro-actuated wood, tunable-porosity ceramics, actuatable shape-memory metals, functionally graded or translucent concrete, bendable and printable glass, robotically woven flexible composites, and auxetic or responsive ultra-tough polymers.[7] Within these advances, a few mentions of reliable approaches to bio-derived and biological material systems promise interesting steps towards new interpretations beyond improving existing solutions. Either as supplements or alternatives to conventional building materials, biomaterials seem the best suited to accommodate energy-reducing, adaptive, and biodegradable material synthesis strategies borrowed from the natural world.

Context in Biomaterials Engineering

Biomaterials, like cellulose, collagen, nacre, or bone, are abundantly produced by organisms and exhibit multiple functions responding to diverse environmental requirements.[8,9] Such performance has long been a goal for synthetic materials research with an aim to be introduced into future products and ultimately the building

Left

Laia Mogas-Soldevila, Jorge Duro-Royo, Daniel Lizardo, and Prof. Oxman
Ocean Pavilion, Media Lab
MIT, Cambridge, Massachusetts, 2015

Additively manufactured cellulose-biopolymer composites with the Water-Based Digital Fabrication platform. The structure combines geometrically graded bending capacity and strength conferred by cellulose fibers semi-aligned within the biopolymer matrix. This opens up implementations in flexible paneling or interior partitions in housing applications.

industry. Nontoxic, extremely high-tech living material elements are specifically designed with tunable elasticity, porosity, density or toughness rates very comparable to technical ceramics or even Kevlar and epoxies, but contrarily to man-made materials, they fully biodegrade after use.[10]

Pharmaceutical and medical fields do commercialize biomaterials in implants and drug delivery devices that are digestible, dissolvable, and compatible with our bodies. The pioneers in reinterpreting biomaterials towards new functions are biomedical research groups. They investigate very small-scale tissue scaffolds where a biomaterial construct made of algae, silk, chitin, or cellulose, for instance, is geometrically organized in a lattice-like 3D shape. Forms inspired by cellulose fibrils or shell platelets are populated with living cells and allowed to grow into, for example, muscle or bone tissue replacements. Another big research topic in biomedical fields is drug delivery research. It derives devices like bioplastic containers that can be swallowed and digested along with therapies without causing harm to the stomach, or biomaterial-based disappearing bandages providing drugs through our skin and wounds as they are absorbed.[11]

What's very interesting about biomaterials is not only how sustainable, benign, nontoxic, and biodegradable they are while still maintaining amazing mechanical properties, but the way they are grown and assembled by nature. This is something that in science is called self-assembly.[12] Consider molecules that assemble into bundles of microfibrils that align into packed rods that can then form honeycomb lattices and result in a multi-scale material that has different properties along its structure.[13] Because of such organization, we observe functionally graded porosity in wood, or differential flexibility in chitin, or varying rates of calcification within shell. Current research strives to program such complexity within synthetic materials similar to the way nano-to-macro hierarchies grow in nature; with simple building blocks, mostly hydrogen, carbon, and oxygen, assembled in a very clever way.[14]

The Water-Based Fabrication Challenge

Questions remain for architectural design constraints. Can we scale materials that typically form tiny tissue scaffolds or soft drug delivery pills into the matrixes of a giant extruder? How would they need to be tuned in order to be fabricated with digital tools used in cutting-edge architectural research? And, how would the virtual tools that we know and love in architecture, need to be transformed to design with water-based natural matter? In 2013, our collaborators at the Harvard Wyss Institute for Bioinspired Engineering[15] were able to manually mold cups and eggshell containers out of hydrogel materials they were using for their biomedical applications. That sparked questions in our team at MIT.[16]

A challenge was in place to define water-based fabrication. Biopolymers were explored from the lenses of digital design and fabrication, which entailed structuring them, blending them with other natural additives, and distributing them through a

Right

Laia Mogas-Soldevila, Jorge Duro Royo, Daniel Lizardo, and Prof. Oxman
Ocean Pavilion, Media Lab
MIT, Cambridge, Massachusetts, 2015

Bioplastic-based fully recyclable products. Created with the Water-Based Digital Fabrication platform, these hold the promise of waste-free packaging that dissolves providing nutrients to the earth with the right environmental conditions. They also map a surprising new aesthetic integrating natural dyes or even sensing chemistries within their printed surfaces.

robotic arm's system to produce demonstrative parts. The "Water-Based Fabrication Platform"[17] was created as a novel digital design and manufacturing tool and process to further the understanding of large-scale manufacturing of biomaterial products exhibiting the complexity and advantages of natural assembly. Water is instrumental in all steps of the process; mixing agent, property mediator, and decay initiator as constructs are re-dissolved at the end of their life.

Shrimp shells were at the base of material design, which are a byproduct of the fish industry and make for an incredible biopolymer called chitin that can be made soluble and dries in plastic-like sheets.[8] Chitin also comes from insect wings, fungi, and shells. It's the second most abundant polymer on earth and can be made soluble by deacetylation into a substance called chitosan. Chitosan is easy to process. Using mildly acidic water, gels are formed from chitosan flakes and can be tuned in different concentrations.[15] Interestingly, color of gel concentration directly maps onto mechanical properties once dry and allows observers to interpret performance just by looking at the color of material blends.

First results were 4-meter tall self-supportive structures made entirely of biomaterial gels responding to the question: Can new material function be "designed" through fabrication?[18] Extruded biopolymer hierarchies were built similar to the way dragonfly wings or leaf venations are structured in nature, not only in terms of biomimetic shape inspiration, but in terms of material distribution and molecular bonding. For that, different extrusion pressures, distribution densities, and material concentrations were employed so that 2D wet structures would fold into 3D dry structural leaf-like parts as their water content evaporated. To our initial question, this process did affect the material at the nano-scale; polymers within the gel became aligned, ordered in the direction of printing, consequently informing folding patterns. For instance, a dry construct forms a beam that is very light but exhibits high structural inertia given by geometric patterning which induces its 2D and 3D folding along its medial axis. Final shape and function were effectively induced and self-produced, contrarily to what we observe in top-down methods such as concrete casting or metal extrusion.

In nature chitin is rarely found by itself, it is generally structured in organisms with minerals, proteins, and other types of biomaterials. Chitosan-based blends can be then designed to observe new emerging properties. One of the best outcomes of such exercise is plasticizing these materials, making them flexible so they are performative in elongation, and foldable without break. Packaging that composts in the backyard can then be produced, or a plastic bag to be dissolved in the sink with a bit of vinegar. Other interesting outcomes are blending biopolymer matrixes with fibrous fillers and obtaining materials with programmable deformations comparable to man-made composites of fiber-glass and epoxy, but that fully biodegrade after use.[19] Importantly, a consequence of designers' quest for understanding matter and fully controlling a material design and fabrication platform, outputs results that would initially escape imagination. For instance, color-rich surfaces that drape can emerge by tuning geometric, mechanic, and chemical properties by design.

LACHESIS 2019
silklab

A Protein-based Augmentation Opportunity

At the Silklab within Biomedical Engineering at Tufts University, research is based on silk protein from cocoons made by silkworms. Fibers are dissolved into "liquid silk" that can be molded, extruded, patterned, etc. The Silklab looks at many manifestations of silk as a polymorphic material. It examines microneedles, hollow tubes, electronics that can dissolve into the body, antennas to track food properties, implants, microspheres, opals, to name a few. As a designer in the lab, I investigated how scientific progress in biomaterials can contribute to the field of product design and architecture.[20]

Biomaterials can substitute both matrixes and fillers in today's unsustainable fiberglass-epoxy composites; by rapid dehydration they can form non-toxic foams for cushioning or insulation, and through careful control of evaporation dynamics at ambient temperatures they become ceramics able to withstand repeated loading and climate-resistance requirements of everyday use and without the energy-intensive issues of their mineral counterparts. Moreover, when silk fibroin enters design with biomaterials, a new augmentation dimension can be explored.[21]

Fibroin is the protein that makes the fibrous part of silkworm cocoons. It assembles into a hierarchical structure which leads to superior stability and mechanical strength and that can be used to form materials with controlled unexpected functionalities. Fibroin in solution can be digitally distributed with water-based fabrication platforms such as the one mentioned above, and in dry state can be machined to any shape in computer-controlled milling environments. While wet, silk fibroin and its derived blends can stabilize myriad active compounds providing matter with new functional dimensions that make it a reporter of the world around it. Solid silk blocks can make glass frames and also be programmed to change color when withstanding high mechanical stresses as monitors of structural performance. Very thin silk composites can be printed and become both tough and flexible and form basket-like lattices or translucent leather-like surfaces that not only elegantly drape, but also signal surrounding heat changes.[20] Silk inks, as discussed later in this text, can be made bio-active so that they sense and respond to human health and environmental chemicals.[22–24] High-resolution digitally structured, mechanically performative, chemically active, and optically tuned fibroin-based material systems are key contributors to the future of augmented matter and bespoke products and structures.

A Living Buildings Future

Everything discussed so far are inert material opportunities to design sustainably. However, biomaterials are never inert in nature, in fact they are the best suited to support life, hence the medical and pharma efforts to better understand them. What if we designed with materials that are living themselves? In 2016, DARPA, the defense agency in the United States issued an extremely important grant call for their Engineered Living Materials program. It urged builders and architects to unite

Left Top

Laia Mogas-Soldevila, Giusy Matzeu, and Prof. Omenetto Lachesis, Athens Opera House, Nostos Summer Festival, 2019

Lachesis, named after the weaver goddess of destiny, are giant tapestries made of silk fabric and silk protein inks able to sense and respond to their environment. Living material inks are processed so that they encapsulate chemical sensors originally developed for medical diagnostics and infused here for the first time into soft architectural-scale surfaces.

Left Bottom

Chemical sensors that track health can be redesigned to diagnose the quality of living spaces. Bioderived inks composed of silk protein and environmental reporters of air quality, for instance, sustain traditional screen-printing methods onto wall paper, textile canopies, or curtain systems in housing. Rich palettes of colorimetric transformations follow digitally designed patterns such as this one inspired by the intricacy of silk cocoon fibers under the microscope.

with scientists and respond to: How to make living materials for housing? Housing materials that have the properties of traditional building materials, but with the attributes of living systems? Buildings that can regenerate, that can self-heal, that can sense and respond to their surroundings? This question was posed to our community for the first time and very relevant for what's to come.

Since then, efforts have been fruitful in designing tools and methods for creating programmable, adaptable, sensing, self-healing, living materials for products and buildings. For instance, "Living building materials" (LBMs) use biology to confer multiple functionalities to materials for the built environment. The Srubar Research Group at UC Boulder has recently engineered LBM bricks to become capable of both biological and structural functions. In particular, regeneration of the living component in response to physical switches, and precipitation of calcium carbonate to confer bricks with high fracture toughness.[25] This research emphasizes one of the most challenging issues of living buildings and products, which is ensuring survival or replenishment of the system's living part so that it can continue performing its designed functions.

Taking a chemically active instead of metabolically active perspective, at the Silklab we proposed living materials based on bio-inks able to perform living-like functions without the containment and survival challenges that wet microorganism culture systems pose to design of functional objects and architectures. Reverse-engineered silk protein is used as a matrix to stabilize all sorts of biologically active labile compounds such as pH sensing dyes, thermochromic molecules, vaccines, or customized therapeutics.[26]

A new category of sensing inks was developed to be screen printed on large textiles, paper, and other conformal substrates. Bio-reactive colorimetric patterns of varying size can be designed with micro-scale geometric resolution all the way up to meter scales, opening a giant opportunity in passive sensing for apparel or architectural parts. Medium-scale demonstrations via bracelets, scarfs, or athletic T-shirt prototypes are developed to illustrate the utility that such formats could add to the wearable interface space. Image analysis allows to track performance and health parameters variation in human sweat in real-time yielding a map-like format of distributed biophysical response.[22] With this technique, first-of-their-kind larger-than-human bio-sensors were deployed as the "Lachesis Series."[27] Three-meter tall environmental-sensing tapestries were successfully printed and withstood manipulation from thousands of visitors at international exhibits. Such novel formats enabled by silk-based living materials could take the form of drapes, canopies, wall paper, internal partitions, façade shading systems, or other large architectural surfaces for distributed monitoring of concerning metrics such as rainfall acidity, toxic spills, air quality, or pollution ranges, and become useful signals and material partners in our daily life.

Right Top

Laia Mogas-Soldevila
Additively manufactured and screen-printed biomaterial blends
MIT and Tufts University, 2015–2019

Digitally fabricated biomaterial constructs ranging from half to three meters in length and made of cellulose microfibers, chitin biopolymers, and silk protein, encapsulating molecules able to sense and react to their environments. These experimental large-scale structures have a minimal ecological footprint and are fully biodegradable yet highly technical, aiming to tackle pressing unsustainable material needs.

Right Bottom L–R

The Living
HyFi, MoMA PS1
NYC, 2014

ICD
Hygro-responsive Wood
Stuttgart, 2013

Prof. Jonkers
Self-healing Concrete
TuDelft, 2011

Progress towards bio-derived materials in building construction is pioneered by groundbreaking projects. Recent developments are The Living's HyFi brick tower made by mushrooms and straw, ICD Stuttgart's hygro-responsive wood systems, and Prof. Henk Jonker's self-healing concrete walls with crack-filling bacteria.

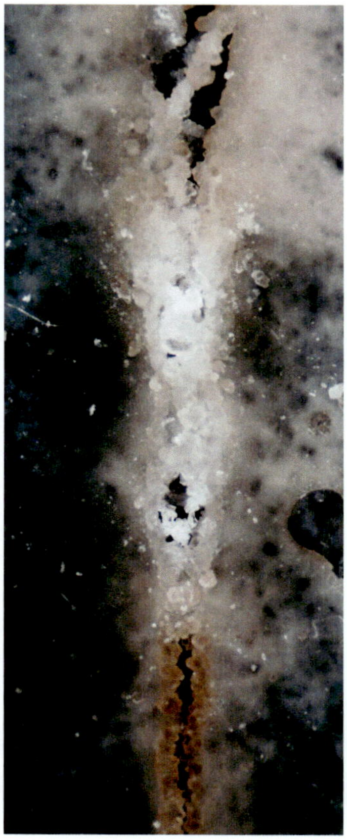

We are soon to witness, at an exponential pace, material solutions that critically respond to bodily, cultural, productive, and habitat-related needs of sustainability, scalability, and economic viability, crucial to the pressures of our time. Being through mushroom brick walls that digest waste, self-healing concrete infused with calcifying bacteria, fishery byproduct shrimp shells printed into beams, thin wood brise-soleils that curl up with air humidity, or silk inks monitoring health and distributed on walls and shades, near future housing regulations will adapt to welcome biomaterial solutions alleviating a wasteful and energy-intensive building industry and proposing myriad novel augmenting functions and unprecedented aesthetics.

Right

Laia Mogas-Soldevila, Jorge Duro-Royo, Daniel Lizardo, and Prof. Oxman
Water-Based Digital Fabrication
Media Lab, MIT, Cambridge, Massachusetts, 2015

Digital manufacturing of large-scale biomaterials creates new opportunities for sustainable production and aesthetics. Depicted are structured biodegradable blends derived from shrimp shells.

References

1. Henk M. Jonkers, *Self Healing Concrete: A Biological Approach*. Dordrecht: Springer, 2007, pp. 195–204.
2. Ginger Krieg Dosier, "Methods for Making Construction Material Using Enzyme Producing Bacteria," US Patent, 2011.
3. Mitchell Joachim and Maria Aiolova, *Design with Life: Biotech Architecture and Resilient Cities*, edited by TerreformONE. New York: ACTAR Publishers, 2020.
4. David Correa, Athina Papadopoulou, Christophe Guberan, Nynika Jhaveri, Steffen Reichert, Achim Menges, and Skylar Tibbits, "3D-Printed Wood: Programming Hygroscopic Material Transformations," *3D Printing and Additive Manufacturing* 2(3), 2015, pp. 106–116.
5. Eben Bayer and Gavin McIntyre, "Method for Making Dehydrated Mycelium Elements and Product Made Thereby," US Patent, 2012.
6. Achim Menges and Steffen Reichert, "Performative Wood: Physically Programming the Responsive Architecture of the HygroScope and HygroSkin Projects," *Architectural Design – Special Issue Material Synthesis* 85(5), 2015, pp. 66–73.
7. Martin Bechthold and James C. Weaver, "Materials Science and Architecture," *Nature Reviews Materials* 2(12), 2017, p. 17082.
8. Julian Vincent, *Structural Biomaterials*. Princeton, NJ: Princeton University Press, 2012.
9. Marc Andre Meyers, Joanna Mckittrick, and Po-Yu Chen, "Structural Biological Materials: Critical Mechanics-Materials Connections," *Science* 335(6065), 2012, pp. 199–204.
10. M.F. Ashby, L.J. Gibson, U. Wegst, and R. Olive, "The Mechanical Properties of Natural Materials. I. Material Property Charts." In *Proceedings of the Royal Society of London A: Mathematical, Physical and Engineering Sciences*, 450. London: The Royal Society, 1995, pp. 123–140.
11. Buddy D. Ratner, *Biomaterials Science : An Introduction to Materials in Medicine*. Cambridge, MA: Academic Press, 2013.
12. George M. Whitesides and Bartosz Grzybowski, "Self-Assembly at All Scales," *Science* 295(5564), 2002, pp. 2418–2421.
13. André R. Studart, Randall M Erb, Rafael Libanori, A.R. Studart, and R.M. Erb, *Bioinspired Hierarchical Composites*. Dordrecht: Springer, 2015.
14. Ulrike G.K. Wegst, Hao Bai, Eduardo Saiz, Antoni P. Tomsia, and Robert O. Ritchie, "Bioinspired Structural Materials," *Nature Materials* 14(1), 2015, pp. 23–36.
15. Javier G. Fernandez and Donald E. Ingber, "Bioinspired Chitinous Material Solutions for Environmental Sustainability and Medicine," *Advanced Functional Materials* 23(36), 2013, pp. 4454–4466.
16. Laia Mogas, Jorge Duro, and Neri Oxman, "Water-Based Robotic Fabrication: Large-Scale Additive Manufacturing of Functionally Graded Hydrogel Composites via Multichamber Extrusion," *3D Printing and Additive Manufacturing* 1(3), 2014, pp. 141–152.
17. Jorge Duro, Laia Mogas, and Neri Oxman, "Methods and Apparatus for Additive Manufacturing Along User-Specified Tool-Paths," US Patent, 2019.
18. Laia Mogas, Jorge Duro, Markus Kayser, Daniel Lizardo, Will Patrick, Sunanda Sharma, Steven Keating, John Klein, Chikara Inamura, and Neri Oxman, "DESIGNING THE OCEAN PAVILION: Biomaterial Templating of Structural, Manufacturing, and Environmental Performance." In *Proceedings of the International Association for Shell and Spatial Structures (IASS) Symposium*. Amsterdam: International Association for Shell and Spatial Structures, 2015.
19. Laia Mogas, "Water-Based Digital Design and Fabrication: Material, Product, and Architectural Explorations in Printing Chitosan and Its Composites," Masters Thesis, Massachusetts Institute of Technology, Cambridge, MA, 2015.
20. Laia Mogas, "Reviving Matter: Design Companions in the Science of Life," PhD Thesis, Tufts University, Medford, MA, 2020.
21. Laia Mogas, "Formalizing Infinite Properties: Beyond Functionalism in Design," ACTAR UrbanNEXT, no. Designing Matter, 2018. https://urbannext.net/formalizing-infinite-properties/
22. Giusy Matzeu, Laia Mogas, Wenyi Li, Arin Naidu, Trent H. Turner, Roger Gu, Patricia R. Blumeris, et al., "Large-Scale Patterning of Reactive Surfaces for Wearable and Environmentally Distributed Sensing," *Advanced Materials* 2020.
23. Benedetto Marelli, Nereus Patel, Thomas Duggan, Giovanni Perotto, Elijah Shirman, Chunmei Li, David L. Kaplan, and Fiorenzo G. Omenetto, "Programming Function into Mechanical Forms by Directed Assembly of Silk Bulk Materials," *Proceedings of the National Academy of Sciences of the United States of America* 114(3), 2017, pp. 451–456.
24. L. Mogas-Soldevila, Giusy Matzeu, M. Lo Presti, and F.G. Omenetto, "Additively Manufactured Leather-like Silk Protein Materials," *Materials & Design* 203, 2021, p. 109631.
25. Chelsea M. Heveran, Sarah L. Williams, Jishen Qiu, Juliana Artier, Mija H. Hubler, Sherri M. Cook, Jeffrey C. Cameron, and Wil V. Srubar, "Biomineralization and Successive Regeneration of Engineered Living Building Materials," *Matter* 2(2), 2020, 481–494.
26. Fiorenzo G. Omenetto and David L. Kaplan. 2010. "New Opportunities for an Ancient Material," *Science* 329(5991), pp. 528–531.
27. Laia Mogas, Giusy Matzeu, and Fiorenzo Omenetto, *W*. https://vimeo.com/304908228

2
1
5
6

LOLUX: MATERIAL URBANISM

Jonas Coersmeier

"LoLux: Material Urbanism" is based on organizational and aesthetic principles found in the study of aleatory material expression. It ascribes design intelligence to the behavior of material composite models and is concurrently invested in the materiality of the urban condition itself. The project produces unplanned urban fabrics that operate across various scales—super block, building and housing cluster. It takes an inclusive approach to media, fostering a continuous transposition between analog and digital matter. Agency is assumed for both the routines of the universal machine and the performance of the material engine. With material alchemy playing an active part in its conception, "LoLux: Material Urbanism" engages with the city in crisis, and proposes a new form of densification and resilience.

The project critically discusses a notion of context that does not rely on past conventions of contextualism, and it takes an active approach to the problem of adaptive reuse. It proposes a radical intervention into an existing housing estate, a forward-looking and sustainable form of preservation that creates a new life cycle for the old building structure. The project studies models of densification that are invested in the autonomous reality of the city. The urban intervention is assessed by the architectural quality it produces, not merely by the degree to which it sustains the city's current condition or its historical continuity. A novel urban artifact arrives as a peculiarity in the city fabric and suggests a new kind of urbanism at the scale of a Brooklyn superblock. The existing building structure on the site, located directly adjacent to the Brooklyn–Queens Expressway, is a 1940s public housing estate that is managed by the New York City Housing Authority (NYCHA) and represents many of the challenges the agency faces today. How does one adapt post-war public housing developments, known colloquially and often pejoratively as "projects," to a drastically changed socio-economic environment, with new demands and desires for amenities, access and public space? What are economic models that allow for such transformation in times of no public funding for public housing development? And how does one inspire, through design, a positive identity for, and identification with, stigmatized old structures of this kind?

Left

Saina Xiang
Material Urbanism

Jonas Coersmeier LoLux Studio
with David Forero

University of Pennsylvania
Weitzman School of Design 2019

3D-print-cast composite material study informing programmatic organization and aesthetic repertoire of the project.

Section rendering showing micro vertical courtyards of multigenerational housing.

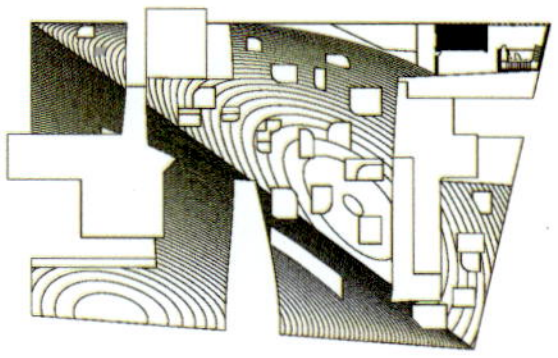

Upper Level Plan

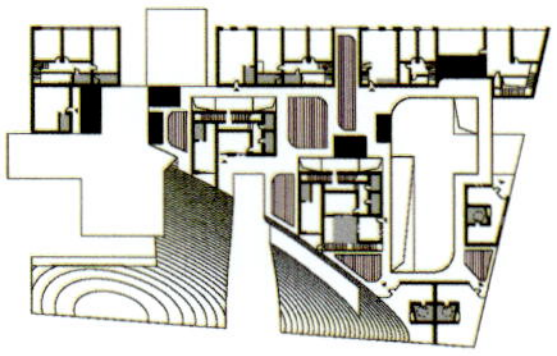

Mid Level Plan

Lower Level Plan

The larger study site between the Brooklyn–Queens Expressway (BQE) and the Brooklyn Navy Yard defines an urban corridor of near-future massive development. The project studies current planning initiatives including infrastructure and urban design proposals and considers the direct link between densification and infrastructural growth, such as new transportation systems and recreation in conjunction with new development. The Cross Downtown Brooklyn Tunnel, a project that is being studied by the NYC Department of Transportation to relieve the BQE from serving as a congested thoroughfare, is assumed to be in place. The left-over BQE structure adjacent to the site is speculatively adapted towards a scenario that includes partial or full recreational use (elevated park). The project proposes a transit hub on the site near the Eastern portal of the new tunnel as a complementary program to urban housing.

"LoLux: Material Urbanism" simultaneously focuses on two primary growth markets of New York City real estate: luxury condominiums and low-income housing. It discusses these two extreme segments in context, probes into their interaction and systematically works out areas of synergy in order to add value for various stakeholders and for the community at large. The project encourages the discussion of socio-economic and political issues of urban housing, and how they relate to architectural responsibilities and desires. It promotes the idea that design holds the potential for improving human coexistence, and that it does so through the production of core architectural qualities. Architecture itself provides cultural content, it adds spatial, material, and aesthetic value and thus improves the urban condition. The aim of the proposed project is to provide people who would typically lead separate lives in separate urban quarters the opportunity to live in shared environments, focusing on students, young families, and the elderly as occupants.

The project proposes a new hybrid that is based on the study of primary housing types and their organizational principles in relation to building form. The hybrid-type development is driven by the integration of diverse user groups (LoLux occupants of different generations) as well as by the mixed programmatic profile (housing, communal programs, and transit hub). The apartment complex hybridizes four different housing types: single-loaded corridor, double-loaded corridor, urban mat building, and tower. These types interlock to provide intimate relationships between the different user groups. Boundaries and overlaps of the different housing types accommodate community programs or dedicated spaces for specific groups or communities. For instance, where student housing meets with housing for the elderly, a shared amenity, the library, promotes intergenerational exchange and the idea of life-long learning.

Material experiments inform the organizational, programmatic, and aesthetic repertoire of the project. Triggered by the fluctuating density of cast composite materials and the sequence in which they are poured, the process creates conditions of relinquished control, where aggregated substances nest within one another. Varying porosities and scales within the composite inform compounds of mini-

Left Top

Physical section models at two scales showing vertical courtyards and shared amenity spaces.

Left Bottom

Close-up of physical section model.

Above

Schematic building floor plans showing hybrid housing typology, integrating single-, double-loaded corridor, micro courtyard, and tower types.

courtyard housing units which are nestled next to single-loaded corridor apartments. The material experiments also instruct program differentiations, such as the public market hall that is situated amongst the apartment clusters. Porosities of various dimensions allow light to filter into the depths of the urban massif, generating large cavernous spaces, vertical courtyards and plaza-like openings reminiscent of the idiosyncrasy of medieval villages. The granular texture of the cast composite engenders an aesthetic language for the mega complex, it finds manifestation in both the exterior large building façade, as well as the inner façades of the small-scale courtyards.

The urban envelope sets up a gentle curvature tailored to the rectilinear existing building. Challenging the skyline of the Brooklyn Navy Yard and employing traditional brick textures, the complex aims to both celebrate and challenge the historic context. The typological hybridization that provides a high degree of housing diversity settles into a novel urban form. An intricate, sculpted super block presents itself as a strange aberration in the urban fabric; at certain moments, however, it reveals its lineage of canonical urban housing types and appears eerily familiar.

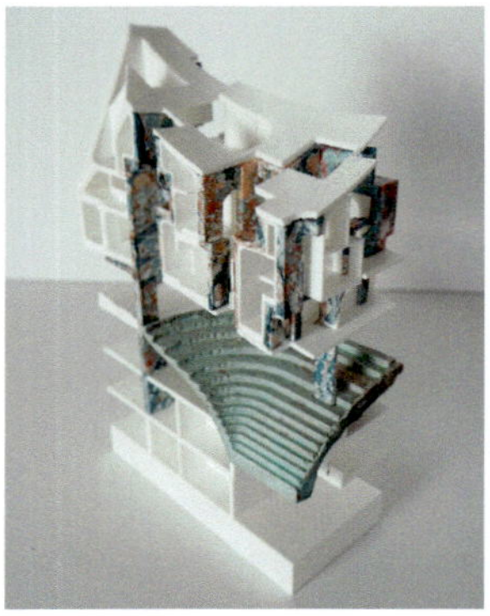

Above

Building section showing multigenerational housing in relation to market hall and transport hub.

Right

Schematic elevation showing material expression and opening strategy for various housing types.

SPECULATING WITH CONSTRAINTS

Nader Tehrani | NADAAA & Cooper Union

The design of housing remains one of the most neglected areas of inquiry in the United States over the past decades. With only pockets of significant work in practice and the academy, the discipline has mirrored a shift towards neo-liberal tendencies that have impacted American practices over the past 40 years. With much of housing being relegated to private initiatives, even much of public work has been restructured around joint venture partnerships that seek economic viability as the driving measure of success in housing proposals. For this reason, most housing developments and proposals have revolved around known typologies and configurations, with little research or risk incurred. Often, the academic context has followed suit, adopting two dominant approaches, the first being mere acquiescence to the evolving commercial model (as witnessed mostly through urban design and real estate programs) and a second being a robust design research model, but rooted in formalism and often disengaged with the programmatic intricacies that make housing distinct from other architectural practices. There is, of course, a third evolving model that gains its agency through social engagement, participatory design processes and community development, but that is often not paired with a design agenda. Indeed, without necessarily assuming that these positions are mutually exclusive, they are unfortunately an apt reflection of the relativism of practices today; they coexist with sense of alienation, instead of forcing a productive friction in the interest of advancing a cause larger than the sum of their parts. This essay speaks to the book's commitment to bringing these different disciplinary spheres into productive conversation.

Despite this, or maybe because of it, there is a dire need for housing in most American cities in a variety of sectors, economic groups and communities. A brief encounter with the range of demographic groups would also reveal that the way in which people live today varies vastly from the nuclear family; for this reason, most housing types do not directly address the evolving circumstances of programmatic, configurational or functional needs. Having said that, one of the salient aspects of housing, in general, deals with the question of flexibility, in great part because of the dynamic changes

Left

NADAAA
The Macallen Building
Boston, 2007

The Macallen Building viewed from the Fourth Street Bridge.

NADAAA
The Macallen Building
Boston, 2007

The ascending massing of the Macallen Building from Dorchester Avenue's Live/Work units to the Skyline Units on the west.

19 89

in society over years, decades and centuries. It is no accident that communities continue to thrive in forms of housing from the 17th century to the present with marginal needs for change. Most change comes in the form of the infrastructure of electricity, plumbing and environmental systems which are often encrypted into the logic of the age-old structures without significant challenges. Still, if those very technical contingencies are taken with a measure of disciplinary gravity, they have also proven to be defining in terms of degrees of possible invention, if only because they are measured against the very constraints that provide for the necessary friction. As such, new building types have evolved directly from the balance of optimization of certain technical systems on the one hand, in tandem with formal and organizational play on the other.

It is important to note that there are, in fact, a range of architects—both practitioners and academics—undertaking significant work in this area; among them Pier Vittorio Aureli has made the most compelling argument for the discrete challenges to typologies rooted in the principle of collective thinking. Jonathan Tate has engaged the potentials that are encrypted in the zoning and code bylaws of Louisiana to develop a host of dwelling innovations. In California both Michael Maltzan and Brooks & Scarpa have extended the experimental traditions of LA culture towards housing for under-served communities. Of course, there are other East Coast universities still tackling the question of housing in their curricula, but with a dispersed set of agendas that do not always speak to the political challenges we face today. This book, as an extension of the eponymous symposium at University of Pennsylvania, draws from the many facets of these and other practices to address such divergent themes as historical lessons, the changing nature of domesticity, the finance and policy behind housing initiatives, and of course the material manifestation of all themes ideas as they converge onto buildings.

This essay, then, will attempt to outline some of the theoretical tenets against which NADAAA has been able to test housing as a contemporary architectural discipline. It is, by no means, a thorough enough body of work as it draws from one case study, the Macallen Building; however, insofar as this building set forth certain ambitious agendas, it is also a good measure of how we might redirect our efforts going forward. As outline, I will appeal to certain paradigmatic ideas that have driven this work, and how those may become relevant to other projects in the future. The first area of focus deals with the question of urbanism, the city and its landscapes, and how various scales of community are implicated in the definition of housing complexes; here, the unit, the cluster, the building and the neighborhood comes into conversation with an idea about the city—making housing respondent to externalities and part of a civic obligation. The second deals with the necessity of assessing emerging programmatic needs and how that may impact new building organizations, typologies and hybrids. The third inspects the infrastructure of buildings, the systems that drive organization and their capacity to impact flexibility, what is often seen as ancillary, hidden, or in deference to the discipline of architecture; here, I will argue that speculative approaches towards the structural, mechanical and conveying systems become indispensable for the possibility of invention.

Duplexes and Triplexes

Skyline Units

Live/Work Units

Above

NADAAA
The Macallen Building
Boston, 2007

1. Duplexes and triplexes are sited atop the building, configured as row houses typical of the South End and South Boston. Accordingly, they also take advantage of sectional interconnections with double-height spaces and decks that open up towards the eastern view.

2. The Skyline units on the western edge of the building take advantage of the height of the building to gain panoramic views from downtown Boston all the way to the Back Bay and Fenway neighborhoods.

3. The Live/Work units take advantage of their adjacency to Dorchester Avenue to allow for retail and storefront access, while reserving domestic space on the second floor via private access.

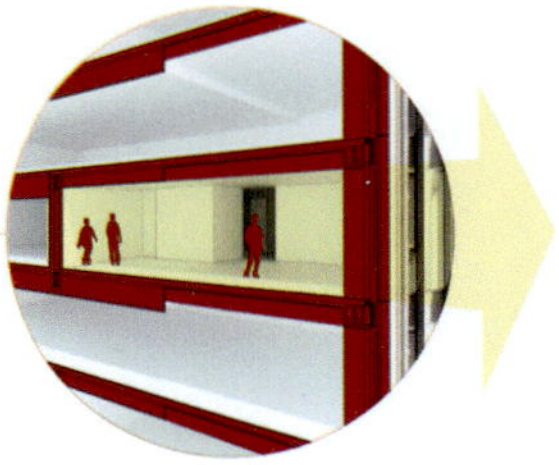

Scaling Urbanisms: From the Unit of the Community

It is with a certain Hippocratic Oath that an architect comes to engage the city: perchance, not only to do no harm, but indeed to catalyze urban opportunities and ameliorate conditions. How we achieve that differs vastly, and yet housing provides us a scaled approach to urbanism that touches on the individual, the family, the community and the entire city. Beyond the private realm of the house, or apartment unit, the role of public space looms large in this responsibility, allowing for many scales of interaction between the private and the public. As such, architectural gestures such as balconies, decks, courts and plazas are all indications of a scalar ambition of interaction, because each identify a slightly different dimensional threshold between the individual and the collective. The Macallen offers a few, but important arenas in which this urbanism gets played out.

Located on Dorchester Avenue, a traditionally light industrial stretch of South Boston, the Macallen Building was to be the first of several buildings to encourage smart development next to the Broadway Red Line subway station. With the Fourth Street Bridge to its southern edge, the sidewalk ascends about 20 feet to cross over the railway lines to the west, setting up a sectional predicament with respect to the existing zoning ordinances, which as of right, only permitted a three-story height building on the plot. The Court Square Press building, located to the north of the site, was the only veritable architectural context, an industrial historic brick structure that, through adaptive re-use, was renovated into lofts. Thus, the site did not offer any easy triggers to which to respond, and as such, opened up opportunities to explore massing strategies that violated the zoning restrictions, yet opened up a strategic approach towards housing on the site. The Sphinx-like figure of the building, thus, emerges as an interpretation of the site, with a tall tower on the west facing the skyline of Boston at its own scale, and a lower tail on the east, tangent to the triple-deckers of South Boston. A large raised courtyard on the north offers a relief from the Court Square Press building, allowing the two buildings to come together with shared amenities including parking, a gymnasium, two common rooms, a screening room, a swimming pool, and a public deck for barbeques and gatherings. The same raised deck has individual garden units located on it, and this offers an opportunity to develop landscape thresholds between the public and private areas of the deck. At street level on the north, a paved plaza serves as a daily drop-off area, while maintaining the tactility and semantics of a plaza: on weekends serving for markets and street events. Maybe most importantly, on Dorchester Avenue, the strategic placement of live/work units are accessible from both the street as well as the building lobby on the interior, linking the retail to the dwelling as a unique type. In this way, Dorchester Avenue is activated as a pedestrian street for the first time, and now in retrospect, has led the development of ten new buildings that are following suit. The green mane of the sloped roof contains a punctuated series of large decks, belonging to the immediate units to which they are conjoined; these look out over the long distance into the harbor towards the archipelago of islands. On Fourth Street, smaller balconies populate the depth of the woven façade, and offer added shade

and acoustic remediation to the south-facing façade. In tandem, all these spaces of encounter define scales of the public realm, from the individual to the family, and from cluster to the community at large. For a building of ample urban challenges, they also attempt to create a sufficient buffer, and a deepened threshold, extending the inside out, and absorbing the outside in.

Programmatic Transformations: Typological Hybrids

Whereas the rationalist 20th-century housing structure is often characterized by notions of efficiency, repetition, optimization and standardization, it also developed an ideal family unit around which to project organizations of houses and apartments. Recent data demonstrates that at least 50 percent of marriages result in divorce today, but further that many family units are more diverse in their organization than the nuclear family would suggest. For this reason, many households may include an in-law, a caretaker, a renter or other such assistants. Other family structures are informed by different cultural lifestyles, be they part of LBGTQIA thinking, immigrant groups, or communal partnerships who share common facilities. In recent years with the rise of the internet, the role of the home-office has taken root, and now with the pandemic it has de facto even become the required convention; few dwellings have actually been designed to accommodate the actual necessities for work, nor the decorum that might be necessary for hybrid activities. With the rising costs of living, micro-units have offered an alternative to the excesses of the conventional apartment. Co-housing has also offered an alternative to the excesses of independent programs, and with ample shared space external to the unit, they offer the type of social engagement that can be provided by commons such as shared kitchens, dining facilities, gymnasia, screening rooms, decks and other such spaces. Among other types, these are just a few of the organizational structures that are beginning to impact buildings, but almost never within one structure, as the culture and legal frameworks of buildings—whether as rentals, coops, or condos, defy the types of mixtures that is a fair depiction of our society.

Most importantly, what is often forgotten is the tacit acceptance of ideological biases that drive political decisions in the making of cities, and subsequently their housing. The process of districting, gerrymandering and redlining all play a critical role in the definition of communities long before a building is even put to design. If communities were not already conceived around cultural, racial and economic divisions, policies and laws often reinforce those divisions such that they forbid the kind of social exchange that might better advance the health of the city. Among other things, this is one of the most poignant reasons why American society suffers from racial inequities: indeed, these are as much legislated as they are culturally assumed. Architecture alone cannot address this, but insofar as formal, spatial and material practices can embody certain values, and instigate ways of occupying space, the built environment serves as an index of who we are. The commission for the Macallen Building emerged from a program that was conventional at best. The developer had already completed a proposal for two buildings that would work in tandem with each other: a tower on the west edge of the site and a lower bar building on the east, with a shared court in between. Naturally, as separate buildings, they would each require their own infrastructure of elevators, stairs and services. The tower would contain most of the one- and two-bedroom units, while the bar would also include some three-bedroom units. In contrast, our proposal conjoined the tower and bar building, and in doing so effectively eliminated the redundancy of infrastructures. By doing so, we also gained added space for the elaboration of more units, and more variations in unit types such that the building caters to a wider array of housing needs. In effect, by minimizing the net to gross losses, we were able to internalize the gains towards better units, and a more sophisticated typological hybrid.

Left

NADAAA
the Macallen Building
Boston, 2007

The eastern edge of the Macallen Building seen from the fabric of South Boston against the skyline of the Back Bay.

Above

The staggered truss during construction, from top to bottom: with metal decking, with vertical chases and rebar, and with concrete deck.

The law also mandates 20% affordable units to be included with the building, usually achieved through downgraded finishes. However, on closer inspection of the neighborhood, the community and the potentials of the site, we were able to achieve three significant things: first to imagine a building figure that responds to the urban situation in a critical light, second to revise the zoning envelope as a result, and third to develop over a dozen unit types with the possibility of radicalizing its social mix. As a result, we were able to aggregate live/work units, lofts, efficiencies, one-bedroom, two-bedroom, three-bedroom units, skyline units, sky-deck units, garden units along with duplexes and triplexes. As a development idea, it took a few risks in that it offered a wider range of low cost and high cost units, a mix that would not normatively be seen as favorable to the integrity of a building brand. Still, the marginal site of the building on the railroad tracks, next to the Red Line station and on the edge of historic South Boston, had a sufficient heterogeneity to be able to speak to different constituencies, defying traditional monolithic tendencies. As a hybrid organization, it also imagined that tenants of varied economic reach might be able to coexist within the same building, with units as low as $500 to as high as $1,000 per square foot. The cost variations were a result of predictable variables: space, views, height and finishes. For this reason, the units atop the green mane formed maybe the most desired of the types. Those are arranged as duplexes and triplexes taking advantage of the sloped roofline to create large open decks with eastern views. Much

Plan Organization and Unit Plans

like row house organizations, these units smuggle typologies found in South Boston into the building, giving it a familiar semblance, offering it the best combination of independent and collective inhabitation. Other units towards the base of the building gave other advantages at more accessible costs: open loft spaces without distant views, and a more engaged relationship with the noise of the street. However, it is this variation that defines the interesting results of the building, something that was further amplified by the economic meltdown of 2008. Indeed, it was precisely the flexibility of its infrastructure that allowed for new architectural accommodations and a new organization of parts of the building.

Catalytic Structures: The Infrastructure of Flexibility

The organization of the Macallen Building derives from both top-down thinking, as well as bottom-up. The sloped figure of its profile is tall on the western edge as part of the city skyline, but as low as a row house on the east as it meets the South Boston neighborhood fabric. The internal configuration of apartments within this larger figure is anything but conventional: standard units are not stacked on top of each other, as would be in a modern structure. Instead, units are mixed on seemingly unorthodox stackings throughout: adopting a Tetris stacking system, the apartment units nest into each other in both plan and section, allowing for the programmatic and typological range we thought might enhance the opportunities of the building. More importantly, these units worked in dialogue with an infrastructural strategy that was unprecedented of this type, drawing on structural and mechanical approaches. From a structural perspective, we adopted a 'staggered-truss system' to achieve several goals: lighting the structure, prefabricating all trusses off-site, minimizing the amount of footings, and ensuring a faster construction schedule than any other type of construction system. In turn, these strategies ensured lateral stability in both the longitudinal and lateral axes of the building without the introduction of sheer walls, thus allowing the

Left

NADAAA
the Macallen Building
Boston, 2007

The typical unit types are nested into an infrastructure composed of two cores and a staggered truss system allowing for 72' open spans. This allows for a flexibility of unit types that are not restricted by an overburdened structural system.

Right

View of triplex decks on the mane of the Macallen Building.

passage of cars under the building within the garage. The space between each truss was 72 feet, allowing for unprecedented spans within which even long lofts could be placed. With short span beams tying into the top and bottom cords of trusses each 36 feet, the module of the structure tied directly into the parking bays below the deck, allowing for three cars, every structural bay. In turn, the 72-foot open bay above allowed for the liberal insertion of any unit type, as long as they complied with the mechanical mandates. The mechanical strategy was as precise as the structural: all plumbing, wet walls and major duct-work was restricted to the inner corridor edge, adopting an absolute adherence to the vertical shafts to which they were assigned. As such, while light gauge steel studs can be re-situated to expand and compact unit types, the plumbing chases need to be respected with absolute fidelity. Metaphorically, the chases serve as a skewer that holds the varied meat and vegetables of a kebab intact in a linear sectional arrangement.

Flexibility emerges as a significant theme in this building, much as its legacy has sparked debate and experiments during the modern era. The decade that has passed since the construction of the Macallen Building has also revealed a few lessons. Originally conceived as a condominium project, the developer was slated to sell all of it units by the time of its completion. Indeed, it did succeed to sell 50% of them before 2008, but with the economic crash, a radical shift in plan was necessitated: the remaining units needed to be rented for a period of time, making for an economic hybrid model as much as a spatial one. Because of the unique nature of the building's infrastructure, especially its structural and mechanical layout, it became easy to make immediate transformations to the units. Light gauge steel partitions were summarily moved around for various units to add and subtract rooms in rental units, all while respecting the staggered truss system that was the building's main structure. The rental period only lasted about three years, and during that time, all the remaining units were sold as the economy gathered steam. Other metrics proved telling also. As the first gold LEED rated building of its type, it was designed with ambitions to build a community around sustainable ethics. With a calculated support of the developer, the project built its audiences, further enhanced by the management practices of the building. The pattern of interest in the building's units are predictable: all units with views, outdoor spaces and special amenities were the ones most sought after, and hence the most expensive. Most were sold beforehand, and the others soon after. The units in the 'core' of the building became the most economical ones: the south-facing ones due to the traffic on Fourth Street, and the northern ones with no direct sunlight. These were also the ones most prone to rentals during the transition period and with further turnaround subsequently. However, critical to these differences was a sense of orchestrated variety that ensured a wide range in its occupancy, ensuring a demographic profile with varied age groups, racial and ethnic backgrounds, as well as economic reach. More importantly, later post-occupancy narratives center around the inevitable schism between the projection of architectural intentions and the administration of governance by its evolving user groups; with the early years being characterized by diversity, the eventual condo trustee group was to be overtaken by a majority of empty-nesters, whose main political initiatives were to limit the use of the public spaces, to curb the times of their use, and to mostly disallow use of many facilities by children—rooted in principles of liability, but in effect to bring bias to a dominant user group within the building, something that would eventually challenge the very diversity on which it was conceived.

Still, from an architectural standpoint, whereas one interpretation of flexibility is rooted in the idea of the generic, this building is characterized by two simultaneous approaches. The first is the distinction between heavy and light structural systems: that which is the main scaffolding and that which is temporary and kinetic. The second involves the sheer diversity of unit types, creating flexibility through fundamental choices of program, view, size, access to outdoor space, and a variety of amenities that demonstrate that we do not all desire the same things: flexibility through difference. This is a building whose programmatic potential is delivered on the ability to design, a priori, an approach to its infrastructural systems to catalyze a hybrid organization.

In closing, there seems to be a critical need to bridge practical and conceptual cultures, and housing can serve as a major instrument for this opportunity. With emerging challenges today, between the phenomenon of social distancing during the pandemic and the reinvocation of the long-standing social and racial inequities, housing stands to pose significant opportunities for formal, spatial and material research. This case study interrogates some of the more seemingly benign elements of housing to reveal their instrumentality: that is, their agency to effect change. The Macallen Building is but a development, and certainly does not cast itself as a public housing project; and yet, it offers certain pointed attitudes towards disciplinary internalities that have the ability to impact the politics of collective living.

Right

NADAAA
The Macallen Building
Boston, 2007

The southern face with impressions of the staggered truss and balconies carved out of the folded façade.

THE ICE AT

MATERIAL ESTRANGEMENT

Kutan Ayata

The masterplan development of large-scale modernist housing projects typically ventured into two distinct directions: dispersal of buildings as abstract figuration in the field or relentless repetition of buildings in a strict geometric order. In both cases the distributed building objects suppress any kind of apparent hierarchy of planimetric organization, as though they are just severed instances of infinite fields. However, Stuyvesant Town's layout of the buildings is highly figural and organized symmetrically around an open central space, which in return gives different weight to different buildings, regardless of their identical architectural definitions. As the periphery buildings negotiate the pressures of an urban edge, the central buildings deal with flows and orientation within the complex towards and through its center.

Yang's project was about the transformation of a building in the middle of the housing complex facing the Oval, which is the main central open space. The building is a stand-alone volume with pathway circulations all around it, oriented towards the central open space. This open space also contains a farmer's market, seasonal ice-skating ring, communal shared programs, and multiple playgrounds. Additionally, the building is next to one of the access roads with parking along one of its longer edges. Its symmetrical plan might be suggestive of indifference to its context, but there are weighted sides to this location that could allow one to consider varying articulations all around the building.

Yang's project early on recognized this sidedness in this specific location and began to explore volumetric strategies to break the object's initial symmetry. Considering its situation at the center of the complex, the intuition was to cap the height of the building at its current condition and expand the building laterally. The end faces of what we called the "arms" or "appendages," basically the tips of the square modules in plan, were expanded in various ways to begin this experiment. Initial studies focused on deviating the open-ended and terracing tips away from their orthogonal trajectories which attempted to redefine the ground around the building and the housing types within. Once we pushed the tips further where they began to wrap around and

Left

Yang Li
Mega-Block Redux-Stuyvesant Town, New York City

Kutan Ayata Urban Housing Studio with Alexander Bahr

University of Pennsylvania Weitzman School of Design, 2017

View showing the project hovering in the background. Seen from the ice ring.

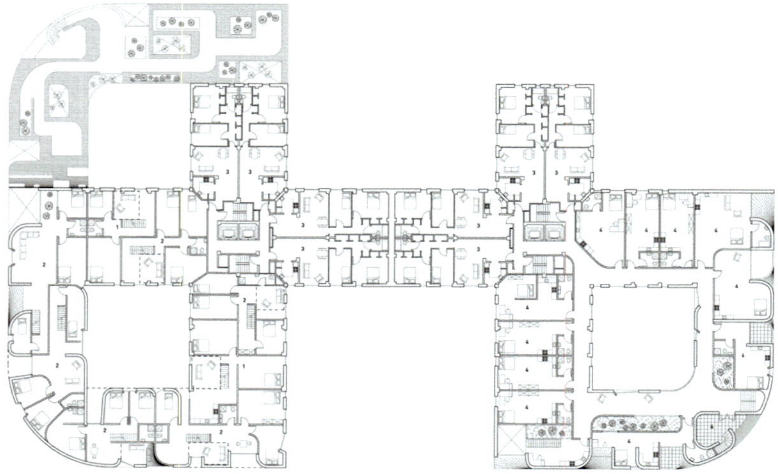

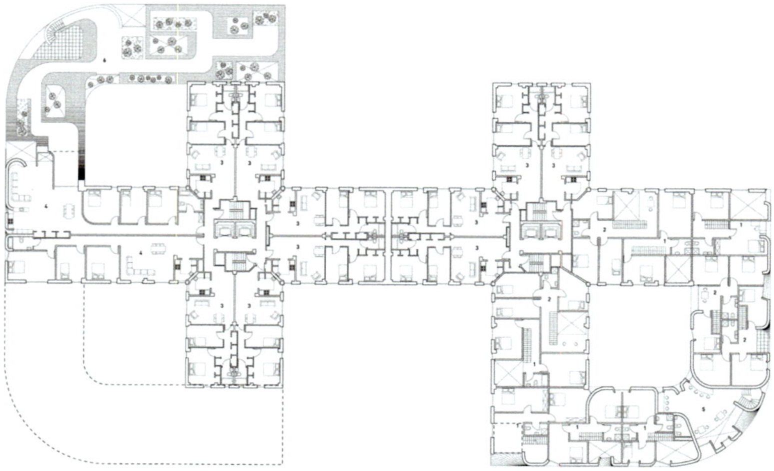

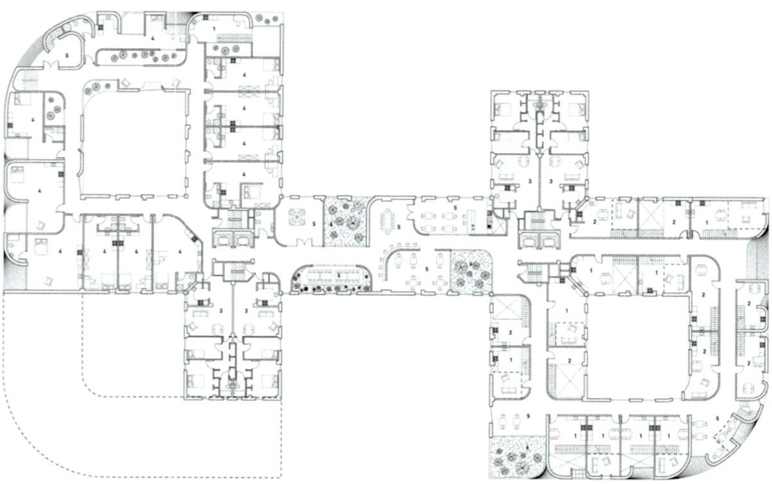

Chunk Isometric

reengage the two other arms of itself, interesting conditions began to emerge with regards to how the building started to posture towards the center, above the service road and towards the meandering pathways. At the end, two considerably basic loops across two ends at different heights crisscrossed the short ends of the building. These cantilevering volumes began to impose the building towards the different circumstances surrounding it. More of a frontality and surface area, along with multiple communal terraces developed facing the Oval. A cantilevered hovering volume over the service road redefined the "backside" of the building.

These hovering additions resulted in unit organizations which began to gain multiple orientations radiating out of the building, as well as inverted orientations looking into the middle of the loop, back towards the existing building, promoting a sense of density as an alternative to the openly spaced buildings of the complex. To make sure that the plan of these hovering parts did not result in units which face either one side or the other, an interlocking duplex strategy was implemented. Just like the section in Le Corbusier's Unite d'habitation, circulation runs every three floors, around which two duplexes interlock. This way, it was guaranteed that every unit in these loops would have double exposure, one oriented towards the openness of the field and one towards the existing building, defining a more intimate rear window condition. Additionally, the terracing which follows the direction of the loops results in rotation of the units resulting in another condition of orientation to the end units.

It is one thing to define a volumetric expansion that begins to articulate new potentials of massing and organization, it is another challenge to articulate this massing to push a project over from the territory of abstraction towards the territory of plausible. Yang's project undertakes this challenge with two specific strategies to ensure what is implied as an idea of volumetric continuity is articulated in its surface definitions, both materially and in terms of aperture articulation. The overwhelming presence of the red brick is inescapable in Stuyvesant Town. The choice to steer clear from it in any new addition would emphasize the fact that it is an addition. To stay with the red brick might be misunderstood as a nostalgic approach to context and its historic registry. Contemplating these two poles, Yang's project pushed the existing brick color into the expansion, further reinforcing the reading of the volumetric growth of the original building by erasing the seam between the existing and the addition. Additionally, the aperture articulation begins to redefine how brick performs in the project. As the hovering volumes gain distance from the existing buildings, apertures, which start as extensions of existing windows, begin to laterally expand to increase their sizes and also push deeper into the envelope to define more relief in the surface. As surfaces negotiate this depth from the outer face to the position of the aperture, various formal conditions emerge as ruled surfaces, curved extrusions, and peeled surfaces. This also begins to delineate the edges of the hovering volumes which are extensions of the existing edges of the original building's corners. It is not only the surface, but also the edges which begin to gain depth, both in plan and section, resulting in series of mini-corners that begin to emulate the large cantilevered corners. Not only do these

Left

Plans of three successive levels showing the development of the sectionally interlocking duplex units.

Above

Partial axonometric showing the sectional arrangement of interlocking units, as well as the façade articulation.

formal articulations begin to define the characteristics of the new addition, they also begin to alter the manner in which the brick is deployed on the surface, ensuring the use of the material escapes the classification of nostalgia and perhaps gains an aesthetic definition of estrangement.

This aesthetics of estrangement, both with regards to the building's formal and material qualities, is registered within existing photographs. This is of course intentional to further amplify the sense of estrangement by representing the project realistically in its context. Perhaps, these images should be understood as future-past documentations of a present speculation. Often, the original photograph is not centered or focused on the building the student designs. They are photographs of other things, perhaps people, perhaps fountains, perhaps skating rings, perhaps cars, perhaps other buildings. The goal is to slip the plausibility of the proposals to the background of reality, to let them just be without calling attention to their architectural innovation or genius, to let them quietly seek our close attention. One of the interesting outcomes of Yang's project is that once you accept its realism and plausibility through the way it is domesticated within the convention of photography, it makes you take another look at Stuyvesant Town itself. If Architecture, by stepping back, could make one contemplate the nature of its context, then it is onto something interesting.

Above

Elevations showing the extension and articulation of the existing building.

Right

View from the driveway/parking, showing the cantilevered hovering corner.

THE ARCHITECT'S AGENCY IN A DEVELOPERS' MARKET

Patrik Schumacher | Zaha Hadid Architects

A Pressing Political Problem

Housing is one of our most essential and most cherished commodities and makes all the difference to our well-being. Urban housing provision is under pressure in the prosperous metropolitan centers of the world. This so-called "housing crisis" has been going on unabatedly for quite a number of years, despite attempts at corrective political intervention. The thesis of this essay is that the housing markets in the troubled cities are not working, not despite but because of massive political interventions. These regulations and interventions block the self-regulation mechanisms that would otherwise assure supply improvements together with affordability improvements, as they do in all the other product categories that are less subject to political regulation and intervention.

The underlying demand side pressure originates in the social and economic attractiveness of urban centers where the agglomeration economies and synergies of our post-Fordist network society are increasingly garnered via knowledge work like R&D, marketing, and finance, work that requires a dense integration of diverse workers. These workers, and the entrepreneurs that employ them, must continuously reconfigure their collaboration patterns. This implies their co-location in large, dense urban clusters that represent large and liquid labor markets. This density of agglomeration is not only vital for everybody's career optimization within this labor market but also a necessity in the daily routines of communicative interaction, within and across firms.

Left

Zaha Hadid Architects
520 West 28th Street
New York, 2018

The balconies protrude differentially to individuate the apartments. The blackened stainless steel resonates with the materiality of the High Line steel structure.

The supply of accommodation to bring people together in the desired way is unable to catch up with the demand. The consequence is an acute scarcity and rising prices in the major high productivity hub cities. This inability to match the demand with supply, however, is not due to an inherent lack of land, but it is due to political barriers raised. Permitting a development is always more controversial than rejecting it. It is a matter of debate to what extent the rising house prices are the conscious purpose of these barriers. In any event, home- and land-owners are the winners of this market dysfunction, at least in the short to medium term. To the extent that this blockage of a possible and desired urban concentration and productive urban flourishing implies a general long-term loss of otherwise likely productivity and prosperity gains for these cities and societies, everybody will be a loser in the long run. However, these are invisible losses based on a counterfactual argument and thus unlikely to mobilize as much as the prospect of more immediate gains or losses.

The affordability crisis is socially divisive and diminishes overall prosperity. The immediate losers are all those mostly young workers who are trying to join these knowledge production hubs and have to put up with historically extraordinary rents and house prices that cut deep into their current living standards. The alternative to stay in the unproductive province should be out of the question, although some make this choice to the detriment of their careers and thereby to the detriment of overall societal productivity. The compromise to live suburban and commute for hours into the hub is also increasingly unattractive. Increasingly the choice taken is to pay "an arm and a leg" for a small patch in the center. Career development and the career-relevant full participation in urban life and culture takes precedence over the comfort of a larger home. Therefore the pressure keeps building up. Politicians, although they are the real perpetrators of the young workers' plight, take up the issue and pose with prima facie plausible, apparently self-evident "solutions" that leave the incumbent home- and land-owners' interests untouched. These "solutions," namely the requisitioning and political distribution of an increasing part of the new housing supply under the label of "affordable housing," are only making the remaining market supply more expensive, i.e., matters are made worse for all those who do not receive the subsidized and rationed supply.

The key problem is the political imposition of supply restrictions that take the form of restrictive land allocation, the restriction of the overall quantum of construction allowed on each parcel, i.e., density restrictions, as well as detailed prescriptions about the characteristics of the permitted product, the so-called housing standards. The fact that these standards have to be enforced implies that they do not match up with the actual market demands and customer priorities. These standards, especially minimum unit sizes, are a major contributing factor in this affordability crisis.

One Possible Interim Architectural Solution: Co-living

Currently the detailed political prescription of housing specifications prevents developers from supplying what the market is demanding. This implies that many potentially beneficial trades cannot take place and people have to live with older, inadequate stock that is already in the market or with what is now allowed into the market, often unaffordable without subsidies. If creative developers and their architects were truly free to develop a response, then many more urban dwellers could be serviced much better with offerings tailored to their needs and purchasing power.

Above

Zaha Hadid Architects
Concept Design for The Collective
North London, 2016

The clustering of varied micro-apartment modules expresses that co-living is a way of life for people who value individuality and privacy as much as community. The gaps in the modular façade indicate the presence of larger shared spaces.

Right

The micro-apartments cluster around courtyards and atria thus clearly articulating the larger communal communication spaces.

Through the creative exploitation of a loophole some urban entrepreneurs discovered a new form of urban living that is both more economical and more communicative than traditional apartment blocks: co-living. The loophole in the UK that allows the circumvention of apartment sizes is the "house in multiple occupation" (HMO) where three or more inhabitants share facilities like living rooms, kitchens and bathrooms without forming a household. The individual rooms can here be much smaller than the mandated minimal apartment sizes. HMOs with five or more unrelated inhabitants are termed "large" HMOs. While there seems to be no upper bound the authorities did not expect to see this concept stretched to 500 inhabitants as is the case with "The Collective" in London. The Collective is a co-living development company with a first completed and successfully operated co-living project in West London called "The Collective Old Oak." This project offers self-contained 10sqm units for rent, fully fitted with integrated bathroom, shower and kitchenette, thereby offering more privacy than the usual flat-shares that the Collective's residents would otherwise be left with. Social spaces like shared kitchens with dining rooms, TV and party rooms, etc. are offered on each floor plus a free co-working zone, lobby, restaurant with terrace and a programmed lecture hall, all shared by the whole building. Since the success of Old Oak, the Collective has planned four further projects in more central London locations. However, all are stuck in the planning process with uncertain prospects.

Zaha Hadid Architects planned another building for The Collective in North London, with a similar programming concept but with slightly larger individual units. Here the units are 16sqm rather than 10sqm, still less than half the size of the currently mandated minimum apartment size. Our concept was premised on modular construction, and is expressing the apartment units and their clustering around shared social spaces.

Co-living is a winning value-for-money proposition for single professionals in the city, a group that most urgently requires central accommodation and is neglected by the

Bürofläche
zu mieten

political authorities privileging families. The co-working offering as well as the lecture program focusing on start-up entrepreneurship implies that a congenial rather than random sample of tenants is coming together here and thus giving the emergence of a genuine community a real chance. Spatial offerings alone would not be enough. The fact that planners prevent many co-living projects in London—supposedly to protect tenants from substandard accommodation—is a scandal hiding behind an obfuscating rhetoric. The alternative for these tenants is to live outside the city or to take up old flat-shares in the city with a far lower standard of privacy and comfort. The shift from 10sqm to 16sqm as base unit shows that there is an ongoing learning process with respect to offering and market feedback. Unfortunately, this experimentation in the market as discovery process will be shut down as soon as co-living will be officially recognized. The price of recognition will be a much too detailed regulation. Freedom of entrepreneurship and freedom of contracting has lost a lot of ground. By implication, this also applies to the architectural design freedom to find viable new solutions for developers and end users.

Zaha Hadid Architects have recently completed an innovative project with small units in Austria, a cluster of small short-term serviced apartments in the historical city center of Graz. This building operates via online bookings that deliver QR keys to unlock the rented apartments. The apartments are varied in size and each is represented by one or two uniquely tailored cocoon-like bay windows. This façade articulation is meant to express individuality and inspire the desire to stay.

Left

Zaha Hadid Architects
Argos-Short Term
Serviced Apartments
Graz, 2020

This corner block is inserted within the historical center of Graz, picking up the urban grain in 21st-century architectural translation.

Above

Interior view.

The Opportunity for Architectural Aspirations

This article started with the assertion that the quality and location of our dwellings makes a massive difference to our well-being and productivity. In recent years, Zaha Hadid Architects have had many opportunities to engage and innovate in the realm of urban housing. All our work is market rate housing. The previous two projects focus on market-based affordability. The following two projects now focus on new concepts for luxury urban living, both located in the US, in New York and Miami respectively. All four projects, whether small or large, economical or luxurious, are expressive of our 21st-century style and urbanity, developed within the same architectural paradigm.

Our New York project is located in Manhattan, at 520 West 28th Street. It is a boutique luxury condominium building located directly on the High Line in Chelsea. As 520 West 28th Street is our first project in Manhattan we were very eager to make a mark. We were confronted with a lot of highly determinate requirements that presented both challenges and opportunities. Initially, we received from the client a list of units with various fixed room sizes. We also knew that there would be numerous sales personnel and firms involved in the interior layout. Such limitations raised concerns for our ability to build a successful architectural contribution to this critical urban landscape. In fact, even the building's massing was highly predetermined due to the strict zoning envelope that we had to adhere to while trying to maximize the usable floor area. This zoning envelope, an L-shape with various setbacks, was an amorphous lump

Zaha Hadid Architects
520 West 28th Street
New York, 2018

The massing and façade articulation fits into the urban fabric of Chelsea. The façade articulation identifies and projects the spacious, elegant apartments over the High Line.

Bar & Grill
315
OPEN

without a recognizable form or figure. So first we needed to forge a volumetric unity, an identity, a character which was recognizable as a unit of interaction and as a destination.

Our first sketches were based on the concept of setting the envelope a little bit loose to find a figure that we could later tighten again into the envelope. We used a lot of fillets to smooth out all the corners of the L-shape. With respect to the High Line, we tried to contextualize with the materiality of blackened stainless steel. The significant chevron detail that, together with the cantilevering balconies, gives character and identity to the building comes from the idea of shifting levels to match adjacent back levels, which in turn gives the entrance hall a lift of half a story. This play with half levels provides interesting scissor-section apartments on the inside. The stepping back due to the zoning setbacks was absorbed into a play of varied cantilevering balconies.

Then we convinced the client, Related Companies, to let us design the interiors as well. In recent years, architects have become façade designers. The expectation, particularly in commercial projects, is whether it's office, retail, hotel or residential, that there will be interior specialists separate from the architect. We've managed to insist on doing interiors as well and this was very important for us in order to execute a holistic architectural experience, both spatially and aesthetically. The marketing idea was to bring residents to Chelsea who like the grittiness and atmosphere of the neighborhood but who could afford and might otherwise have chosen the Upper East Side. Our building provides this group with a comfortable place with many social spaces that can serve as high-powered networking areas for these rather special residents. The aesthetic expression of a building, together with the urban location, becomes part of the self-expression of the residents. This is why buildings have the capacity to collect a group of people with a certain shared sensibility and outlook on life. Our building signifies that we have arrived in the 21st century and value contemporary urban culture, decidedly without any sense of nostalgia. There are 39 units across 11 levels, but since we have split levels, there are truly 21 levels. The size of the units range between 1,700 to 6,400 square feet, with prices going from $5 million to $50 million.

In addition to the interior execution, we controlled the subtleties and complexities of surfaces and geometries throughout the building. Critical to this was the interesting execution and detailing process, which included a lot of handcrafted elements. In fact, we conceived that the entire building be filled with sculptures. Interestingly, exterior features are also expressed in the interior. We used different window features, types of balconies, and terraces that connect the exterior expression with the interior expression. We wanted to make sure that users can feel the building's special beauty and character in every space, rather than allowing a generic condition to take over.

The building has shared amenity spaces that consume 15 percent of the overall structure. There are some outdoor shared spaces as well as lobbies, club rooms, a beautiful lap pool with a big bright skylight, a gym, spa areas, outdoor gardens.

Right Top

Zaha Hadid Architects
520 West 28th Street
New York, 2018

The iconic chevron signature feature of the building results from a level shift in the building that allows for a higher lobby space as well as for interesting scissor-section apartments. This also allows for more elevator stops thus giving each apartment its own exclusive stop.

Right Bottom

The balconies protrude differentially to individuate the apartments. The blackened stainless steel resonates with the materiality of the High Line steel structure.

Our critical approach with these spaces was to find the in-between of something innovative and unique, but also something comforting with the iconography of the contemporary. This unique 21st-century quality also translates into the units. Initially, we wanted to make every single bedroom, bathroom, and kitchen special. This got out of hand because then everybody was arguing about every detail in every room. So we thought maybe the bedrooms should be relatively neutral. We focused on a particular moment of identity within each unit, namely a glossy, soft object which collects some of the secondary spaces, bathrooms, and kitchens into a sculptural volume. The more neutral rooms spin around this delicious element that to some extent, again, represents the exterior on the interior. So we concluded that we didn't have to impose ourselves too much after all, but rather concentrate the identity into the envelope, organization, and the select interior nuggets.

Our tactic then was to reduce complexity and control where we provided that identity. This also offered more freedom of articulation with the users coming in and appropriating their rooms individually. So the architectural identity is concentrated in each apartment at one or two points where the façade geometry is imprinted and via the polished objects in the center of the apartments. For example, one unit has an L-shaped glossy object encompassing the kitchen, i.e., this object is a "reminiscence" of the overall building form, like a building copied back into itself as an identifier. The bedrooms have beautiful curved glass at the corners, while the floor-to-ceiling high openable glass elements are a rather sophisticated piece of technology from Austria. It's interesting that there is now a global chain of suppliers who can provide products competitively. The windows open with a press of a button and the entire window pushes out gently. The building is a friendly machine for living in.

In fact, we created a showroom where we tested the materiality of the floor and kitchen block, as well as some of our own furnishings. We're pleased that we established ourselves as mature interior designers who can deliver to a sophisticated market and our product is indeed selling well. In fact, we opened an interior design department and hired some specialists to make ourselves credible competitors for fitting out our own buildings. The design of 520 West 28th has generated a whole new value level in this part of Manhattan.

The same area value upgrade effect can be observed with respect to the effect of our Miami tower, One Thousand Museum. The sales prices achieved with these condominiums on Biscayne Boulevard are exceeding records on that side of Miami. Our approach with respect to the audience approached for this project is similar to 520 West 28th.

The architecture is very different, but like with our Manhattan project, units are expressed via their balconies. The top ten floors have an uninterrupted balcony overlooking the Museum Park, indicating that these apartments take up a whole floor each.

Left

Zaha Hadid Architects
One Thousand Museum
Miami, 2019

The iconicity of the tower is not invented but emerges from the structural morphology of the skeleton. The skeleton logically changes along the vertical axis and sponsors a variation in apartment articulation.

Above

At the top of the tower the structure is the lightest. The corner columns split open. Here is the third occasion within the tower for a grand social space.

The overall aesthetic identity of the tower is given via a striking structural expression. A well-articulated exoskeleton provides character and an unmistakable identity. The skeleton differentiates along the vertical axis, sponsoring different conditions for balconies and apartment subdivision. In the bottom part of the tower reside social spaces, parking spaces and generous amenity spaces. Then follow four floors with double-height "town houses." Then the tower allows for a division into three apartments per floor, then two apartments per floor, finally the top with a single apartment per floor. There are ten "penthouses" and a double penthouse at the very top, available at $50 million.

This variation in product correlates with the variation in façade articulation via the exoskeleton. Thus, rather than offering an endless repetition of a single façade and product condition, we used the structural logic to differentiate both appearance and product. At the very top we have an exclusive double-height amenity space for the large top penthouses, with a second pool, as well as a heli-pad.

Technological innovation is also at play. We have employed an innovative way of constructing a skeleton. We have integrated a lost formwork made by fiber concrete and then filled these elements with reinforced concrete. This was a global first time that this technology was used, and it was a success. This method allowed for prefabricated and thus beautifully sculpted skeleton elements that are also present on the inside as well as on the balconies.

Throughout both of these projects, 520 West 28th in Manhattan and the Miami Tower, it is our objective not only to lend a quality and a character to the architecture but to innovate in ways that move us far beyond the usual tropes of the developer market. The ambition is not to follow the market but to create a new market. The market rate housing segment has often been an arena for experimentation and for the development of new aspirations in urban living that might then influence the desires of a broader stratum of urbanites. This is the ambition of Zaha Hadid Architects.

Right

Zaha Hadid Architects
One Thousand Museum
Miami, 2019

The corner detail is demonstrating how the skeleton allows for a gradual variation in balcony configuration.

References

Patrik Schumacher, "Only Capitalism Can Save the Housing Crisis," The Adam Smith Institute, April 25, 2018., https://www.adamsmith.org/capitalismcansolvethehousingcrisis/

Patrik Schumacher, "Smaller Living Spaces in Cities Could Help Solve Britain's Housing Crisis," *The Guardian* Housing Opinion, May 1, 2018.https://www.theguardian.com/commentisfree/2018/may/01/smaller-living-spaces-cities-housing-crisis

CONTEMPORARY LIVE/WORK HYBRIDS

H na Jamelle

In 2019 alone, the United States Department of Labor estimates that approximately 6.5 million people started a business, just over half-a-million people each month. Even though only a small amount of these businesses survive more than five years, the picture is quite clear: a staggering number of new entrepreneurs and a substantial percentage of businesses are moving out of typical office environments to work from home or in more informal communal environments with shared resources. More than half of the American workforce will experience self-employment at some point in their careers, and many will cycle back and forth between self-employment and traditional employment. According to the Advocacy Office of the Small Business Administration, 50% of American small businesses are based from home. According to projections from Statista,[1] by 2028, over 53% of the entire U.S. workforce, or about 90 million people (up from 62.2 million in 2019), will be composed of solopreneurs, independent contractors, or freelancers, most of whom will desire ergonomic, inspiring, and fitted-out workspace.

Being an entrepreneur is about the ability to seize new opportunities. It requires tremendous drive but also flexibility. It additionally means defining risk-taking as a value, being able to adapt to change, and being able to innovate and leverage new ideas. Equally important is the need to build networks and have access to structured financing. Millennials and Gen Zs have a natural affinity for adopting new technologies, and their web-savvy allows young firms to make the most of the Internet's economic opportunities. The accelerating pace of new technologies—web-based technologies in particular—changes the way businesses operate locally and globally. The Internet has become a major enabler of growth and performance, and companies that can master their usage of it can stimulate opportunities for high economic growth.

A hybrid live/work housing model for entrepreneurs is attractive in this context, as it can be a burden on individuals to spend money on both a home and an office at the critical stage of starting a business. Entrepreneurs may not be able to devote additional resources to growing their business while managing both home and

Left

Andre Stiles
Shifting Hybrids: A New Live Work Building
North TriBeCa, New York City

Hina Jamelle
Urban Housing Studio
with Miguel Abaunza

University of Pennsylvania
Weitzman School of Design, 2016

Exterior view of façade. Unit clusters are registered in differentiated façade apertures and coordinated with programmatic performance.

Exterior view of ground level.

6TH FLOOR

1. STUDIO APT. 100%
2. WORK 50%
3. 1 BEDROOM 50%
4. STUDIO APT. 100%
5. WORK 50%
6. WORK 100%
7. STUDIO 50%
8. WORK 100%
9. WORK 50% - ADA
10 CONFERENCE

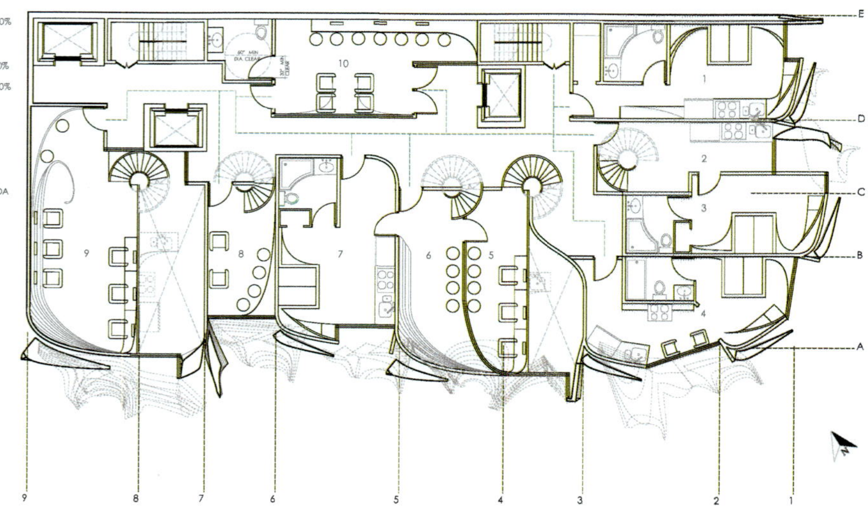

5th FLOOR

1. STUDIO APT. 100%
2. STUDIO APT. 100%
3. POP UP 100%
4. STUDIO APT. 50%
5. WORK 50%
6. 1 BEDROOM 50%
7. STUDIO 100%
8. STUDIO 50%
9. WORK 50% - ADA
10 1 BEDROOM 50% - ADA
11. CONFERENCE

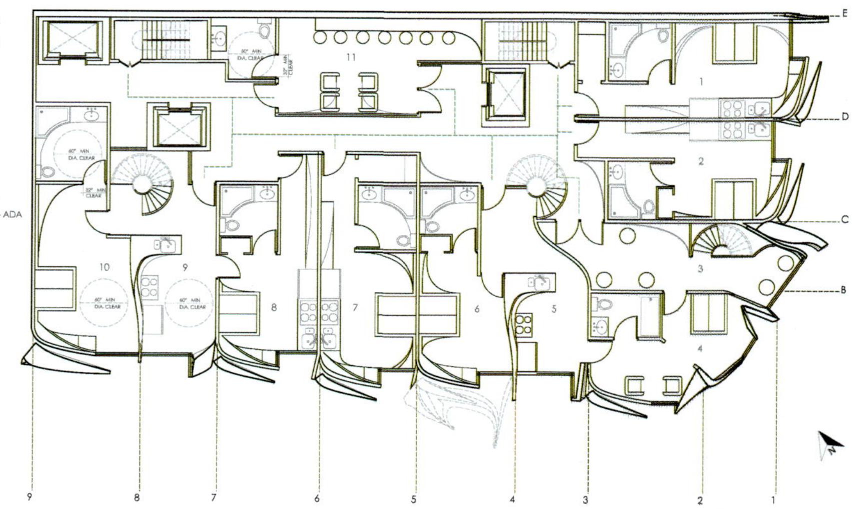

GROUND FLOOR

1. CENTRAL MARKET
2. POP-UP VENUE
3. VESTRY ENTRANCE
4. BAR
5. AUDITORIUM
6. GREENWHICH ENTRANCE
7. POP-UP VENUE

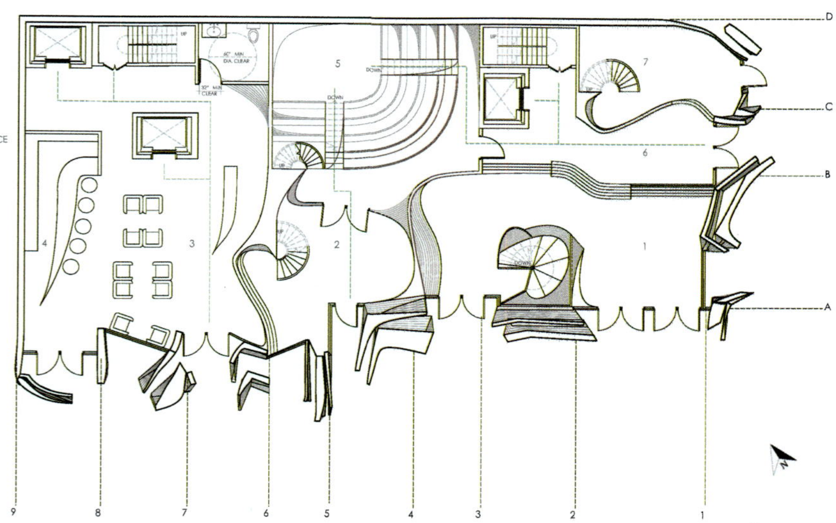

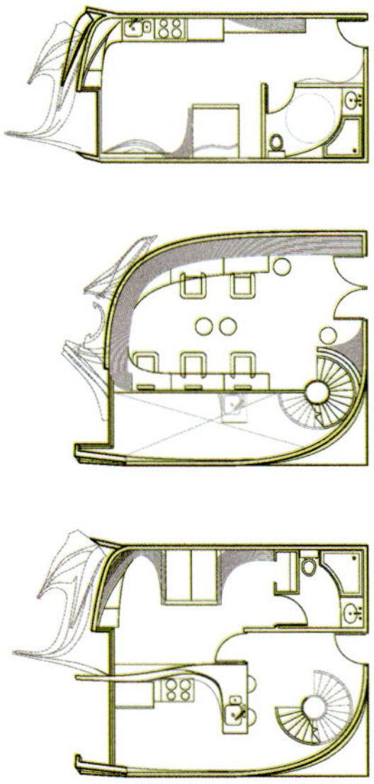

office expenses. Andre Stiles's project, "Shifting Hybrids," proposes a new live/work building on the corner of Hudson and Vestry Streets in the North TriBeCa neighborhood of New York City. The site is geographically linked to important business and industry centers like Wall Street, yet it occupies a quiet neighborhood advantageous for home life and more solitary work.

The neighborhood features cobblestoned streets, iconic 19th-century loft buildings, and numerous other features that reflect its notable history. In the 1850s, the Industrial Revolution transformed TriBeCa into a major commercial center. In the late-19th and early-20th centuries, the neighborhood became a center of textile manufacturing and trade. By the 1960s, the neighborhood's industrial base had all but vanished. Slowdowns in factory work during the 20th century left behind the large warehouses and lofts that typify much of TriBeCa's architecture today. The surplus of large empty commercial spaces attracted artists and creative types alike, who were drawn to large lofts that could serve as excellent studios and blank canvases for non-traditional living arrangements and lifestyles. During this period, there was a movement to legalize the live/work housing arrangements of artists and residents in the fledgling area south of Chambers Street. A group of passionate artists looking to gain more traction for their cause named their group the Triangle Below Canal Block Association, where "TriBeCa" gets its name.

Today, the majority of TriBeCa's buildings fall into one of five official historic districts overseen by New York City's Landmarks Preservation Commission. Much of the neighborhood has established itself into further subdivisions of historic districts, with each cluster designated because of its associations with specific events, people, architectural styles, and other characteristics.

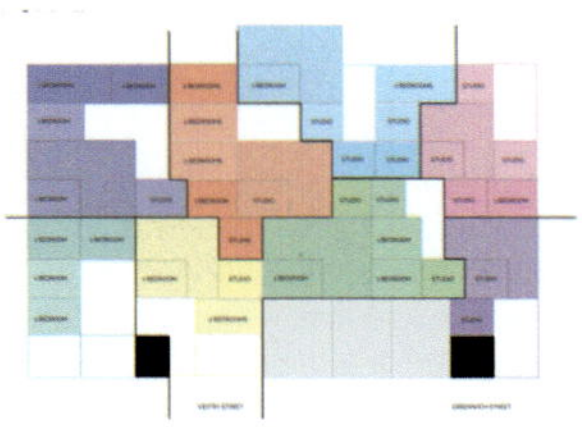

Andre Stiles's design proposal in "Shifting Hybrids: A New Live/Work Building in North TriBeCa, New York City" builds upon historic aspects of the neighborhood's past and incorporates eight interrelated clusters inspired by TriBeCa's historic districts into a single structure. These clusters are each represented by different trades and consist of studios, one-bedroom apartments, and duplexes that range in program from 100% work to 100% live. Depending on one's business needs and lifestyle, there are residential units with either separate or combined workspaces and entrances within the same unit and in different clusters of the building. Duplexes for instance are laid out with office space on one level and private bedrooms and bathrooms on another; the kitchen often serves as an intermediary threshold between public and private spaces and offering both informal meeting space as well as shared amenities.

Left

Floor plans.

Above T–B

Unit plans.

Cluster concept and program diagram.

The variation in unit clusters reinvigorates the diverse historic functionality of spaces that characterize TriBeCa and creates a self-sufficient building in which all the units reinforce and support each other. Some 100% work units are located on each floor and foster interaction between each work cluster and the broader public. This is reflected in the building's façade, whose unique apertures modulate in conjunction with unit clusters and programmatic performance, allowing for a variation of visual dialogues between the building's interior spaces and the city outside. The public nature of the design cumulates on the ground floor where the exhibition hall serves as a forum and public showcase for the building's population of live/workers.

The project's focus on an ever more prevalent entrepreneurial constituency underscores the need for both new typological considerations as well as modifications to existing home and office typologies that can serve the changing nature of work and domesticity. Shared spatial resources offer flexible solutions that can meet a variety of needs and adapt to change while providing opportunities for cultural shifts that support new models of inspiring entrepreneurship.

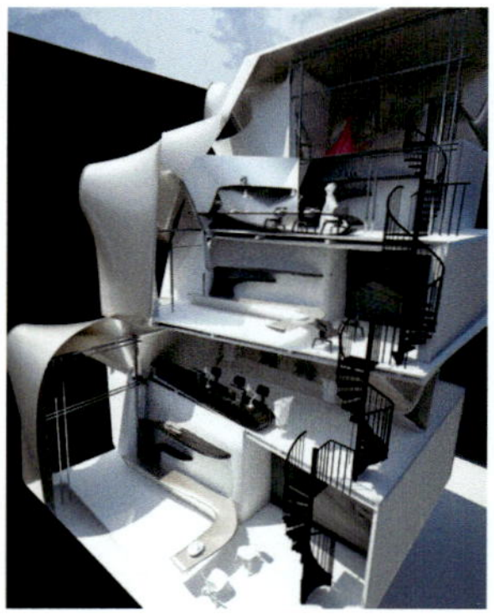

Above

Detail view of a live/work unit cluster. Two duplex units with loft-style workspace are connected to private residences with spiral stairs. The design is reminiscent of 1960s use of loft spaces as artist studios.

Right

3D cutaway section showing the live/work unit cluster organizations.

References

1. https://www.statista.com/statistics/921593/gig-economy-number-of-freelancers-us/

01

KUTAN AYATA

Ayata is a founding partner of Young & Ayata, an award-winning practice based in New York City and Los Angeles. He is an Associate Professor in the Department of Architecture and Urban Design at UCLA, also serving as Vice Chair. His previous teaching appointments include positions at the University of Pennsylvania, Pratt Institute, Cornell University and Columbia University. He received his Master of Architecture from Princeton University in 2004 and his Bachelor of Fine Arts in Architecture from Massachusetts College of Art in 1999.

02

SCOTT ERDY

Scott's work pursues a methodology where form embodies purpose, and sense of place is revealed through the careful intersection of program, site and culture. Since establishing Erdy McHenry Architecture with David McHenry, Scott's design work has received many accolades from the local and national press as well as his peers and has received more than 30 state, local and national awards. His design for St. Aloysius Church was recognized by ArchDaily as one of the Top 100 Architectural Projects in the US and as one of the Five Best Churches of the World by WorldBuild365. Beginning with the September 2001 cover story of Architectural Record featuring the Southern Poverty Law Center in Montgomery, Alabama, and most recently the July 2013 cover of highlighting the Cornell Teaching Dairy Barn, Ithaca New York, Scott's work has been recognized for the embodiment of both its cultural significance and utilitarian beauty.

His award-winning projects celebrate place, program and cultural relevancy while exploiting the conceptual potential of practicality and constructability. The strength of Scott's work is its ability to translate normative programs into architecture of poetic beauty and cultural significance. Scott received his undergraduate degree from the Ohio State University and his master's degree from Syracuse, where he studied under the stalwart modernist Werner Seligmann. He currently teaches a Graduate Housing Studio at the University of Pennsylvania and lectures widely on his work.

03

BRIAN PHILLIPS

Brian Phillips is founding principal and creative director of ISA, a design and research office based in Philadelphia. Brian earned his Master of Architecture from the University of Pennsylvania where is currently a Lecturer. He was awarded a 2011 Pew Fellowship in the Arts, and was named an Emerging Voice by the Architectural League of New York in 2015. ISA has won over 50 local, regional, and national design citations, including the Philadelphia AIA Silver and Gold Medals, and five AIA National Housing Awards. The firm's work has been featured in Architect, Architectural Record, The Boston Globe, The Philadelphia Inquirer, The New York Times, and on NPR.

04

NEIL DENARI

Neil Denari is principal of NMDA, Inc. and Professor of Architecture at UCLA. He received his M.Arch from Harvard in 1982. In 2015, he was elected to the College of Fellows of AIA. He is the recipient of the 2019 AIA-LA Educator of the Year, the 2011 AIA-LA Gold Medal, 2005 and 2007 National AIA Awards, 2005 Progressive Architecture citation, and eight AIA Honor Awards, among others. He lectures worldwide and has been a Visiting Professor at Harvard, Princeton, Columbia, and UC Berkeley among other schools. From 1997 to 2002, he was the Director of SCI-Arc. Denari is the author of Interrupted Projections (1996), Gyroscopic Horizons (1999), and Mass X (2018).

05

CLIFFORD PEARSON

Clifford Pearson is a writer and editor focusing on architecture and culture. From 2016 to 2018, he was the director of the University of Southern California's American Academy in China and a lecturer at the USC School of Architecture. From 1989 through 2015, he was an editor at Architectural Record. He is the co-author (with A. Eugene Kohn) of The World by Design, author of Indonesia: Design and Culture, and the editor of Modern American Houses. Mr. Pearson holds a master's degree in architectural history from Columbia University and a bachelor's degree in urban studies from Cornell University.

06

SIMONE TARANTINO

Boasting more than 25 years of entrepreneurial and business experience, Simone started his career with companies like Intel and Acer. In 2001, he launched a management consulting and marketing advisory company focused on creating new intersections between technology and the workplace to create smarter and more efficient ways to conduct business (then sold it to a bigger conglomerate). After that, in addition to raising money and founding InspectManager, a cloud-based testing infrastructure, he also invested in and co-founded AudioBox.fm, one of the most advanced media platforms in the cloud, invested in and expanded the disruptive co-living concept of StartupHome from the UK to the US, refocusing it towards underrepresented founders, launched a B2B Podcast company, and EdTech nonprofit for adult literacy, and other successful ventures. He is a lead mentor for the ERA Global accelerator in NY, a consultant for the Italian Trade Agency, and Senior Advisor to several international startups.

07

MIMI HOANG

Mimi Hoang co-founded nARCHITECTS with Eric Bunge with a belief in architecture as an agent of positive change, responding to and connecting people to their environment in unexpected ways. Their work instigates interactions between buildings and their dynamically changing contexts—architecture for a world in flux. nARCHITECTS is tackling the most pressing issues that our cities face—how we live, work and activate public spaces in response to social and environmental change. The practice was honored with an American Academy of Arts and Letters Award in Architecture and AIANY's Andrew J. Thomson Award for Pioneering in Housing. Mimi received a Master of Architecture from Harvard Graduate School of Design, a BSc in Architecture from MIT and teaches at Columbia University's GSAPP (Graduate School of Architecture, Planning and Preservation) as an Adjunct Associate Professor.

ZACHARY WEIMER

Zach hails from the Appalachian Mountain area near Pittsburgh, where he developed his deep love of nature and conviction in the architect's role as good stewards of their urban and natural environments. He brings his passion for positively transforming the public realm to his work. Zach received his Master in Architecture (with Distinction) from the Harvard University Graduate School of Design and his Bachelor of Architecture from Carnegie Mellon.

08

MARK A. WILLIS

Mark A. Willis is the Senior Policy Fellow at New York University's Furman Center for Real Estate and Urban Policy. Before joining Furman, Dr. Willis was a Visiting Scholar at the Ford Foundation following a 19-year career developing and overseeing JPMorgan Chase's programs and products to help strengthen low- and moderate-income communities. Before joining Chase, Dr. Willis held various positions with the City of New York in housing, economic development, and tax policy and was an urban economist at the Federal Reserve Bank of New York. He serves on the boards of a wide range of banking and community-oriented organizations. He is a frequent participant on panels at academic, industry, and government conferences/convenings, and his recent publications have focused on affordable housing, national housing finance reform, and the Community Reinvestment Act. Dr. Willis has taught Housing and Community Development Policy at New York University's Law and Wagner Schools. He has a JD degree from Harvard Law School and a PhD degree in urban economics and industrial organization from Yale University.

BENJAMIN HELLER

Benjamin Heller is a Master's student at New York University's Robert F. Wagner School of Public Service and a Graduate Researcher at the NYU Furman Center. Before pursuing his Master's degree, Benjamin worked for Ernst & Young's UK Financial Services Advisory practice and London's Metropolitan Police. He holds a Bachelor of Arts in Political Science from the University of Chicago.

09

MARTHA KELLEY

Martha is a Vice President in the Merchant Banking Division of Goldman Sachs, which serves as the private investing arm of the bank. Her group has invested in real estate assets totaling over $50 billion in equity across more than 800 investments. In the housing space, the team is currently active in multifamily development and acquisitions, and is also building several luxury condo projects in major urban markets. Martha has led investments across the residential, retail, office, hospitality, and self-storage sectors in her time at Goldman Sachs, and is currently leading the Northeast investing platform. Prior to joining Goldman Sachs, Martha worked in the investment banking sector. She has an AB from Princeton University and an MBA from the Wharton School of Business.

10

MICHAEL BELL

Michael Bell, Professor at Columbia University, is founding Chair of the Columbia Conference on Architecture, Engineering and Materials. Bell's architectural design has been commissioned by the Museum of Modern Art and is included in the Permanent Collection of SFMoMA. Bell has taught at UC Berkeley, Rice and held visiting professorships at Harvard, Cornell, and the University of Michigan as Saarinen Visiting Professor of Architecture, and Berkeley as the Howard A. Friedman Professor of Practice. Bell was a Fellow at the Joint Center Housing Studies at Harvard and a Visiting Professor at the Stanford School of Engineering / Center for Design Research.

EUNJEONG SEONG

Eunjeong Seong, R.A., is an Adjunct Associate Professor at Pratt Institute. Seong's architectural work has been exhibited at the Museum of Modern Art and in galleries in Shanghai and Beijing. Seong is the author of the forthcoming book, Housing after Banking, with Michael Bell. Seong was a lead designer at SHoP and the founding director of a New York City design office for Yamasaki Associates. Seong has written for SPACE and work has been featured on MSNBC, Fox Business News and Reuters. Seong holds a Master of Architecture, Columbia University, and has taught at RPI, RISD, and Cornell.

11

MARCELO SPINA

Born in Rosario, Argentina, Marcelo Spina is an internationally renowned architect and educator. Along with Georgina Huljich, he is a partner at PATTERNS, an award-winning architectural practice based in Los Angeles and recognized worldwide. He is a Design Faculty at SCI-Arc since 2001 and has been a Visiting Professor at Penn, Yale, Syracuse, Harvard, Berkeley, and Di Tella among others. He is the co-author of the forthcoming Mute Icons & Other Dichotomies of the Real in Architecture (2020), Material Beyond Materials (2012), PATTERNS Embedded (2010), and co-curator of Matters of Sensation (Artists Space, 2008).

12

HINA JAMELLE

Hina Jamelle teaches Architectural Design at the University of Pennsylvania Weitzman School of Design, where she is the Director of Urban Housing and teaches final year Graduate Option Studios. She has held the Visiting Schaffer Practice Professorship at the University of Michigan. Jamelle has co-edited two issues of , titled IMPACT [2020] and Elegance [2007]. She has lectured widely in North America, Europe, and Asia. Jamelle is co-director of the New York and Shanghai-based firm Contemporary Architecture Practice. Founded in 1999, the firm has been known for its futuristic designs using digital techniques and the latest technologies for the design and manufacturing of architecture. Funded research projects include Dupont, ARUP, Z-Corporation, ABT Manufacturing, and the Wharton Business School. Commissioned projects include Lutron Electronics, the Museum of Modern Art [MoMA] in New York, Reebok, Wenjin Hotels, NJCTTQ Pharmaceuticals, Tencent, AMEC Technologies [China], the Viceroy Hotel [Abu Dhabi], Samsung [South Korea], and IWI Orthodontics [Japan]. Contemporary Architecture Practice's projects have been exhibited extensively at MoMA; the London, Beijing, and Shanghai Biennales; and the Tel Aviv Museum of Art, among others. They also have been featured in more than 250 major publications around the world. The firm has been awarded the Architecture Record Product of the Month for the fixture titled "Opale" for Ivalo as well as the Outstanding Award for FEIDAD [Far Eastern Digital Architecture Design]. Jamelle has won the Architectural Design Vanguard Award and was featured in Phaidon's 10x10x2 as one of the world's top 100 emerging architects. The firm's project, IWI Orthodontics in Tokyo, Japan, was featured in Record Interiors and Phaidon's ROOM 100 as one of the most creative interior design projects of the year. In 2015 she was recognized in the 50 Under 50 Innovators of the 21st Century.

13

LAIA MOGAS-SOLDEVILA

Laia Mogas-Soldevila is an Architect and Assistant Professor at the University of Pennsylvania Weitzman School of Design interested in novel material practices. She holds an interdisciplinary doctorate within Tufts Biomedical Engineering and has worked and taught at MIT and Cornell University. Her team and solo work have been published in science and design journals and shared in cross-field venues such as MRS, IASS, eCAADe, Biofabricate, and ACADIA, and at the MoMa, the Copper Hewitt Design Museum, the New Lab, the Lisbon Architecture Triennial, the Istanbul Design Biennial, and the Pompidou Center in Paris. Since 2008, she co-directs DumoLab.

14

NADER TEHRANI

Nader Tehrani is founding principal of NADAAA and Dean of the Cooper Union's Irwin S. Chanin School of Architecture. For his contributions to architecture as an art, Nader Tehrani was the recipient of the American Academy of Arts and Letters' 2020 Arnold W. Brunner Memorial Prize. His research focuses on the transformation of the building industry, innovative material applications, and the development of new means and methods of construction, especially through digital fabrication. Tehrani's work has received many prestigious awards, including the Cooper-Hewitt National Design Award in Architecture, the American Academy of Arts and Letters Architecture Award, and 18 Progressive Architecture Awards. Prior to becoming Dean at the Cooper Union, he taught at RISD, Harvard GSD, Georgia Institute of Technology, and MIT.

15

PATRIK SCHUMACHER

Patrik Schumacher is principal of Zaha Hadid Architects and is leading the firm since Zaha Hadid's passing in 2016. He joined her in 1988 and was seminal in developing Zaha Hadid Architects to become a global brand. Patrik Schumacher studied philosophy, mathematics and architecture in Bonn, Stuttgart and London and received his PhD at the Institute for Cultural Science in Klagenfurt. In 1996 he founded the Design Research Laboratory at the AA in London where he continues to teach. He taught design studios at the Angewandte with Zaha Hadid from 2000 to 2015 and is currently teaching a PhD group there.

BEN KRONE

Since founding Gradient in 2006, Ben has designed and constructed a wide range of projects and exhibitions, including art installations, high end residences, restaurants, parks and boutique hotels. Previous to establishing Gradient, Ben spent seven years with SHoP Architects where he held a leading role on a number of high profile projects including the Virgin Atlantic First Class Lounge at JFK and three residential developments in New York City ranging in size from 15,000 to 50,000 square feet. Ben holds a Master of Architecture from Columbia University, where he was the recipient of the McKim Prize for Excellence in Design and the Sol Kaplan Traveling Fellowship. He also holds a Bachelor of Architecture from the University of Florida. Ben currently teaches at the University of Pennsylvania's Graduate School of Design and has also taught at Columbia University's Graduate School of Architecture, Preservation and Planning. In 2018 Ben was the recipient of Penn Design's Perkins Teaching Award recognizing outstanding teaching for non-standing facility member. He is a registered architect in the State of New York.

JONAS COERSMEIER

Jonas Coersmeier, Dipl.-Ing MS-AAD, is an award-winning architect, educator and partner of the design practice Büro NY based in New York and Berlin. He previously worked as a management consultant for McKinsey & Company. He studied at TU-Darmstadt, the Massachusetts Institute of Technology, and Columbia University, where he was awarded the Honor Award for Excellence in Design, the Kinne Fellows Prize, and the Lowenfish Prize for Design.

Coersmeier teaches housing studios at the University of Pennsylvania Weitzman School of Design. He is an Associate Professor with CCE at Pratt Institute, and previously was chair of the Digital Design Department at the University of Kassel, Germany. He has received design awards by the Empire State Development Corporation for his 9/11 Memorial design, the Foundation for the Arts and Culture of the State of North Rhine-Westphalia, and the Van Alen Institute, among others, and he was a fellow of the German Academic Exchange Service. His work has been published and exhibited internationally.

Embossed Series
Edition 6 - 7

PUBLICATION TEAM

Assistant Editor
Leon Yi-Liang Ko

Assistant Editor
Katie McBride

Book and Cover Design
Madison Green

FEATURED STUDENTS

Andre Sties
Bumjin Park
Daniel Silverman
Ian Pangburn
Jiateng Wang
Jingyi Zhou
Kerry Hohenstein
Madison Green
Paul Germaine McCoy
Peik Shelton
Saina Xiang
Shih-Kai Lin
Siyi Wang
Veronica Rosado
Xinyu Wang
Yang Li
Yuheng Ouyang

GRADUATE ASSISTANTS

Adrian Subagyo
Alexander Bahr
Alex Tahinos
Ariel Cooke-Zamora
Caleb Ehly
Catherine Shih
Chao Liu
David Forero
Fei Chen
Graham Nelson
Miguel Abaunza
Ruo Wang
Ryan Henriksen

FEATURED OFFICES

Contemporary Architecture Practice
Herzog & de Meuron
Interface Studio Architects
MINI LIVING
NADAAA
nARCHITECTS
Neil M Denari Architects
P-A-T-T-E-R-N-S
SsD
Startup Home London
Universal Design Studio
WOHA Architects
Zaha Hadid Architects

BOOK GRAPHICS

Madison Green

Embossed Series
Editions 1–7
pp. ii–iii, 5–6, 8, 10, 338–339

Shadow Series
Editions 1–4
pp. 22–23, 102–103, 164–165, 216–217

Color Edition
Cover

Andre Stiles
Façade image used in each Series and Cover
pp. 314–315

INTRODUCTION

Kerry Hohenstein
Shifting Hybrids: Adaptive Reuse of the Sunshine Theater, Lower East Side, New York City
p. 12

© Hina Jamelle Urban Housing Studio with Caleb Ehly

University of Pennsylvania Weitzman School of Design, 2019

© Shutterstock
NYC Skyline Post 9/11
Photography by Stefan Ugljevarevic
p. 15

© Shutterstock
Construction fabrication and assembly facilities
Photography by Pavel L Photo and video by Paparazzza, Nordroden, and Moreno Soppelsa
p. 17

© Shutterstock
Urban density, New York
Photography by View Apart
p. 18

© Shutterstock
Urban density, Tokyo
Photography by f11photo
p. 21

01

ESSAY

© Shutterstock
Aerial view of Hong Kong City, Hong Kong
Photography by Lee Yiu Tung
p. 24

U.S. Department of Housing and Urban Development
Minoru Yamasaki
Pruitt-Igoe Housing Complex
Completed 1955, demolished 1972
p. 27

© Zaha Hadid Architects
Zaha Hadid
IBA Housing
Berlin, 1986–1993
p. 29

© Shutterstock
Rem Koolhaas
Checkpoint Charlie Apartments
Berlin, 1980–1990
Photography by Dinosmichail
p. 29

© Eisenman Architects
Peter Eisenman
IBA Housing
Berlin,1981–1985
p. 29

© Shutterstock
Ricardo Boffill
Les Espaces d'Abraxas
Noisy-le-Grand, 1982
Photography by Victor Ramon
p. 31

STUDY

Studio Collective
Mega-Block Redux-Roundhouse, Moscow
pp. 32, 37

Jingyi Zhou
Block Redux-Roundhouse, Moscow
pp. 34–35

Paul McCoy
Block Redux-Roundhouse, Moscow
p. 36

Peik Shelton
Block Redux-Roundhouse, Moscow
pp. 36, 39

© Kutan Ayata Urban Housing Studio with Ryan Henriksen

University of Pennsylvania Weitzman School of Design, 2019

02

ESSAY

Library of Congress, Prints and Photographs Division, John C.H. Grabill Collection
A young Oglala girl sitting in front of her tipi, 1891
Photography by John C.H. Grabill
p. 40

NASA
Gemini 9 and Earth Limb, 1966
Photography by Eugene Cernan
p. 42

© Shutterstock
Tent City
SFWeekly, 2016
Photography by Matt Gush and Philip Pilosian
p. 43

© F.L.C. / ADAGP, Paris / Artists Rights Society (ARS), New York 2020
Le Corbusier
Sketch of the Certosa di Firenze, cell plan and section, 1907
p. 44

© F.L.C. / ADAGP, Paris / Artists Rights Society (ARS), New York 2020
Le Corbusier
Village Radieux, model, 1937
p. 45

© F.L.C. / ADAGP, Paris / Artists Rights Society (ARS), New York 2020
Le Corbusier
Garden City Honeycomb Housing, 1925
Cellular Housing System, 1925
p. 47

© F.L.C. / ADAGP, Paris / Artists Rights Society (ARS) New York 2020
Le Corbusier and Pierre Jeanneret
Pavilion de L'Esprit Nouveau
Paris,1925
p. 48

© F.L.C. / ADAGP, Paris / Artists Rights Society (ARS), New York 2020
Le Corbusier
Ville Contemporaine, 1922
Housing Scheme with Honeycomb Principle, 1925
p. 51

STUDY

Ian Pangburn
Living off the Land
pp. 52–57

© Scott Erdy Urban Housing Studio with Graham Nelson

University of Pennsylvania Weitzman School of Design, 2017

03

ESSAY

© Free Library of Philadelphia, Print and Picture Collection
Aerial Views
Kensington area of Northeast Philadelphia, 1951
Photography by Charles Higgins
p. 58

© Free Library of Philadelphia, Map Collection
Thomas Holme
A Portraiture of the City of Philadelphia
Philadelphia, 1683
pp. 60–61

© ISA, LLC
ISA
100K House
Philadelphia, 2007
Photography by Sam Oberter
pp. 63–65

© ISA, LLC
ISA
Tiny Tower
Philadelphia, 2018
Photography by Sam Oberter
pp. 66–67

© ISA, LLC
ISA
XS House,
Philadelphia, 2019
Photography by Sam Oberter
pp. 68–69, 71

STUDY

Siyi Wang
Adaptive Misuse
pp. 72–79

© Brian Phillips Urban Housing Studio with Ariel Cooke-Zamora

University of Pennsylvania Weitzman School of Design, 2018

04

ESSAY

Irma and Paul Milstein Division of United States History, Local History and Genealogy, The New York Public Library
Gordon Bunshaft
SOM
Manhattan House
New York City, 1951
Photography by Wurts Bros.
p. 80

© Shutterstock
Philip Johnson
Johnson and Burgee
AT&T Headquarters model, 1979
Photography by A G Baxter
p. 82

© Flickr
Richard Meier & Partners
173/176 Perry Street and 165 Charles Street
New York City, 2002 and 2004
Photography by Peter Guthrie
p. 83

© Neil M. Denari Architects, Inc
© 2012 Benny Chan / Fotoworks
Neil M. Denari Architects
HL23
New York City, 2012
Photography by Benny Chan / Fotoworks
pp. 84, 88, 90–93

STUDY

Yuheng Ouyang
Trans-Urban Dwelling
pp. 94–101

© Scott Erdy Urban Housing Studio with Ruo Wang

University of Pennsylvania Weitzman School of Design, 2015

05

ESSAY

© SsD Architecture
SsD
Songpa Micro Housing
Seoul, 2014
pp. 104, 108–113

© BMW AG, München, Deutschland
MINI LIVING and Universal Design Studio
MINI Living
Shanghai, 2020
p. 106

© Patrick Bingham-Hall
WOHA
Kampung Admiralty
Singapore, 2017
Photography by Patrick Bingham-Hall
p. 115

STUDY

Xinyu Wang
Co/Habitation–Red Hook
pp. 116–123

© Ben Krone Urban Housing Studio with Adrian Subagyo

University of Pennsylvania Weitzman School of Design, 2016

06

ESSAY

© Simone Tarantino
Percentage of freelance workers per age group, 2020
p. 124

© Simone Tarantino
Number of freelancers in the US, 2020
p. 127

© Simone Tarantino
Simone Tarantino
WeLive studio apartment, 2018
p. 128

© Simone Tarantino
Deal volume for female founders, 2020
p. 130

© StartupHome.org
StartupHome London, 2016
p. 132

StartupHome London, 2017
p. 133

STUDY

Yan Zheng
Mega-Block Redux-Stuyvesant Town, New York City
pp. 134–141

© Kutan Ayata Urban Housing Studio with Alexander Bahr

University of Pennsylvania Weitzman School of Design, 2017

07

ESSAY

© nARCHITECTS
© Iwan Baan
© Pablo Enriquez
nARCHITECTS
Carmel Place
New York, 2016
Photography by Iwan Baan
Photography by Pablo Enriquez
pp. 142, 146–151, 154–155

© nARCHITECTS
nARCHITECTS
Artisan House
Hong Kong, 2018
pp. 152–153

STUDY

Veronica Rosado
Co/Habitation–Red Hook
pp. 156–163

© Ben Krone Urban Housing Studio with Catherine Shih

University of Pennsylvania Weitzman School of Design, 2019

08

ESSAY

© Harvard Joint Center for Housing Studies
Joint Center for Housing Studies of Harvard University
"At Least 40 Percent of Renters are Cost Burdened in Most Metro Areas Across the Country" America's Rental Housing: 2020 Report, 2020
p. 166

© 2017 by S&P Dow Jones Indices LLC, its affiliates and/or its licensors
S&P Dow Jones Indices LLC, S&P/Case-Shiller
U.S. National Home Price Index [CSUSHPINSA], retrieved from FRED, Federal Reserve Bank of St. Louis: https://fred.stlouisfed.org/series/CSUSHPINSA
p. 168

© NYU Furman Center
Provided by Freddie Mac®, Freddie Mac House Price Index, retrieved from Freddie Mac: http://www.freddiemac.com/research/indices/house-price-index.page
p. 175

STUDY

Daniel Silverman
Golden Age
pp. 176–179

© Brian Phillips Urban Housing Studio with Alex Tahinos

University of Pennsylvania Weitzman School of Design, 2017

09

ESSAY

© 56 Leonard LLC
Herzog & de Meuron
56 Leonard Street
New York City, 2017
Photography by Alexander Severin Architectural Photography
pp. 180, 182–183, 186–189, 191

U.S. Census Bureau
Current Population Survey/ Housing Vacancy Survey, March 10, 2020
p. 184

Corcoran Sunshine
Manhattan State of the Market Update, May 18, 2020
p. 184

CBRE Research
NCREIF, Q3 2017
p. 185

STUDY

Madison Green
Shifting Hybrids: Adaptive Reuse of the Sunshine Theater, Lower East Side, New York City
pp. 192–199

© Hina Jamelle Urban Housing Studio with Caleb Ehly

University of Pennsylvania Weitzman School of Design, 2019

10

ESSAY

© Bell - Seong
Erasing 70 Years of Progress in Five Years
p. 200

United States Household Debt to GDP, 1947–2019
p. 202

Residential Land, Homes, Structures, Price Index, 1975–2005
Graphic made from research by Morris A. Davis and Jonathan Heathcote
p. 205

Home Value–Structure Cost–Land Value: California, 1975–2016
Graphic made from research by Morris A. Davis
p. 206

Home Value–Structure Cost–Land Value: West Virginia, 1975–2016
Graphic made from research by Morris A. Davis
p. 207

Aggregate Value of Residential Real Estate, Mortgage Debt Outstanding, Consumer Credit
p. 209

Personal Consumption Expenditures, 1959–2019
Silicon Photovoltaic Cell Cost per Watt and Solar Energy Consumption
p. 211

STUDY

Shih-Kai Lin
Hybrid Density
pp. 212–215

© Jonas Coersmeier LoLux Studio with Chao Liu

University of Pennsylvania Weitzman School of Design, 2017

11

ESSAY

© PATTERNS / Marcelo Spina & Georgina Huljich
PATTERNS
1099 Grand
Downtown Los Angeles, 2018–2020
Images by PATTERNS / Marcelo Spina & Georgina Huljich, Daniela Atencio, Justin Tan, Danial Mahfoud, Emily Sun, Aseel Alamoudi, and Maria Sofia Garcia
pp. 218, 228–229

© PATTERNS / Marcelo Spina & Georgina Huljich
PATTERNS in collaboration with SOM
Olympia Towers
Downtown Los Angeles, 2016–2026
Images by PATTERNS / Marcelo Spina & Georgina Huljich, Daniela Atencio, Justin Tan, Danial Mahfoud, Emily Sun, Aseel Alamoudi, and Maria Sofia Garcia
pp. 220–223, 225

© PATTERNS / Marcelo Spina & Georgina Huljich
PATTERNS
Split Block
Arts District, Los Angeles, 2018
Images by PATTERNS / Marcelo Spina & Georgina Huljich, Daniela Atencio, Justin Tan, Danial Mahfoud, Emily Sun, Aseel Alamoudi, and Maria Sofia Garcia
pp. 226–227

STUDY

Jiateng Wang
Trans-Urban Dwelling
pp. 231–235

© Scott Erdy Urban Housing Studio with Ruo Wang

University of Pennsylvania Weitzman School of Design, 2015

12

ESSAY

© Contemporary Architecture Practice NY SH
Contemporary Architecture Practice NY SH
Samsung Haan River Masterplan.
Seoul, South Korea, 2015–2018
pp. 236, 238–247

© Shutterstock
Existing apartment buildings and blocks
Central Seoul, South Korea
Photography by Efired and kyunghyun Min
p. 237

STUDY

Bumjin Park
Shifting Hybrids: New Hotel and Residential Building
TriBeCa, New York City
pp. 248–255

© Hina Jamelle Urban Housing Studio with Fei Chen

University of Pennsylvania Weitzman School of Design, 2013

13

ESSAY

© 2015 Copyright is to MIT, the Mediated Matter Group and to Laia Mogas-Soldevila
Duro-Royo, Daniel Lizardo, and Prof. Oxman
Ocean Pavilion, Media Lab
MIT, Cambridge, Massachusetts, 2015
p. 256

© 2015 Copyright is to MIT, the Mediated Matter Group and to Laia Mogas-Soldevila
Laia Mogas-Soldevila, Jorge Duro-Royo, Daniel Lizardo, and Prof. Oxman
Ocean Pavilion, Media Lab
MIT, Cambridge, Massachusetts, 2015
pp. 258–265, 271

© 2019 Copyright is to the Silklab at Tufts Dept. of Biomedical Engineering and to Laia Mogas-Soldevila
Laia Mogas-Soldevila, Jorge Matzeu, and Prof. Omenetto
Lachesis, Athens Opera House, Nostos Summer Festival 2019
p. 266

© 2018 Copyright is to Laia Mogas-Soldevila
Laia Mogas-Soldevila
Additively manufactured and screen-printed biomaterial blends
MIT and Tufts University, 2015–2019
p. 269

© 2014 The Living
The Living
HyFi, MoMA PS1
NYC, 2014
p. 269

© 2013 ICD, Stuttgart
ICD
Hygro-responsive Wood
p. 269

© 2011 Prof. Jonkers, TuDelft
Prof. Jonkers
Self-healing Concrete
TuDelft, 2011
p. 269

STUDY

Saina Xiang
Material Urbanism
pp. 272–279

© Jonas Coersmeier LoLux Studio with David Forero

University of Pennsylvania Weitzman School of Design 2019

14

ESSAY

© Nader Tehrani, NADAAA
NADAAA
The Macallen Building
Boston, 2007
Photography by John Horner Photography
pp. 280–291

STUDY

Yang Li
Mega-Block Redux-Stuyvesant Town, New York City
pp. 292–297

Kutan Ayata Urban Housing Studio with Alexander Bahr

University of Pennsylvania Weitzman School of Design, 2017

15

ESSAY

© Hufton + Crow
Zaha Hadid Architects
520 West 28th Street
New York, 2018
pp. 298, 304–305, 307

© Zaha Hadid Architects
Zaha Hadid Architects
Concept Design for The Collective
North London, 2016
pp. 300–301

© Hufton + Crow
Zaha Hadid Architects
Argos-Short Term Serviced Apartments
Graz, 2020
pp. 302–303

© Hufton + Crow
Zaha Hadid Architects
One Thousand Museum
Miami, 2019
pp. 308–311

STUDY

Andre Stiles
Shifting Hybrids: New Hotel and Residential Building
North TriBeCa, New York City
pp. 313–319

© Hina Jamelle Urban Housing Studio with Miguel Abaunza

University of Pennsylvania Weitzman School of Design, 2016

D

E

F

G

H

I

J

K

L

M

N

O

P

Q

R

S

T

U

V

W

X

Y

Z

Embossed Series

Edition 7 - 7

For Product Safety Concerns and Information please contact our EU
representative GPSR@taylorandfrancis.com Taylor & Francis Verlag GmbH,
Kaufingerstraße 24, 80331 München, Germany

Batch number: 10722128

Printed by Printforce, the Netherlands